23 First aid, police stations	**28** Centerfield pari-mutuels	**33** Totalizator board	**39** Press box A & B	**46** Derby Day dining room
24 Lane from paddock to track	**29** Presentation stand	**34** Gardens	**40** Main dining room	**47** Section L boxes
25 Parking area	**30** Stewards stand	**35** Room 21	**41** Press box C	**48** Ground level boxes
26 Derby Lounge	**31** Colonel Winn's office	**36** Second floor lounge	**42** Room 20	**49** Clubhouse entrance
27 Stable area	**32** Formal gardens	**37** Third floor lounge	**43** Bus route	**50** Clubhouse parking
		38 Finish pole	**44** Mile chute	
			45 Roof boxes	

JOCKEY CLUB, 1875

Produced By GIBBS-INMAN Co., *Louisville, Ky.*

The
KENTUCKY DERBY
Diamond Jubilee

COMPILED UNDER THE AUSPICES
of
CHURCHILL DOWNS

1875   1949

WRITTEN AND EDITED *BY* BROWNIE LEACH

ART DIRECTION AND DESIGN
BY LOUIS J. FREDERICK

Distributed By DIAL PRESS, *New York*

FOREWORD

To me the Kentucky Derby is, and always has been the outstanding sports event. Perhaps it is because I was born and bred in Kentucky's Bluegrass region where I have spent my entire life. Or perhaps it is because my paternal grandmother was an English Derby; she pronounced her name as we pronounce the great race run at Churchill Downs.

Whatever the reason, the putting together of this book was pleasant work. It was my privilege as a child to romp over the fields at Ashland Stud where three Derby winners were foaled, and to know personally many of the men (a number of them, of course, when they were old men) who are mentioned in this book. Many of the stories recounted in this volume I had the pleasure of hearing from the horsemen they concern, or from men who did have the information first hand.

Had I listened as closely in the school room I might have been able to recall much of the historical data accompanying each Derby story. But then I would have missed the stories—and fun of riding the horses at Ashland Stud, and of leading the broodmares, yearlings, and weanlings to the pastures.

Consequently, to assemble the historical data it was necessary to consult many history books and factual guides as well as newspaper files. I am grateful to the people who wrote or compiled them.

Of course, much of the material regarding the Derby and the horses and people mentioned herein came from sources other than my own memory and notes. I am indebted to the files of The Blood-Horse, The Thoroughbred Record, and a Derby series written a number of years ago by James Hart for many details. The race charts from 1903 forward included here are those copyrighted by Triangle Publications, published in the Daily Racing Form, and repeated here by permission. Miss Frances Kane, of Lexington, was a tremendous help in checking records of the early runnings of the race, as was William S. Evans, also of Lexington.

The layout and art for this volume were done by Louis Frederick, of Louisville. His treatment of these pages and the cover shows why his work is so highly regarded. To the many other persons to whom I have turned for assistance and information while assembling this volume I am grateful.

It is practice in writing of running horses to use the asterisk (*) to denote an imported animal. I have followed that practice. A careful check was made of the racing careers of the Derby winners. Early records were not always complete, especially in the amount of money earned. However, I do not believe the total discrepancy, if any, would buy a ton of hay on the present market.

George B. (Brownie) Leach

February 1, 1949.

N

THIS IS CHURCHILL DOWNS

THE first race over the Churchill Downs track was run May 17, 1875. Only one other present-day American race course existed at that time. That was the Saratoga race track. However, only Churchill Downs has the record of having operated an annual race meeting throughout the past three-quarters of a century. Moreover, no American race other than the Kentucky Derby has been run as continuously or so many times over the same race track.

The 180 acres included in Churchill Downs were outside the city limits of Louisville when the track opened in 1875. Today the corporate limits of Louisville extend far beyond the race course which is only ten minutes from the heart of the city.

Churchill Downs has been fortunate in that two men who have directed its policies have been outstanding men in American racing. The first was Colonel M. Lewis Clark. The second is Colonel Matt J. Winn. In establishing Churchill Downs and founding the Kentucky Derby Colonel Clark perhaps did more than any other man to restore horse racing in the south and west after the War Between the States. He was a brilliant racing judge and many of the rules governing the sport today are the result of his thinking.

Colonel Winn, who as a little boy saw the first Kentucky Derby, took over the management of Churchill Downs in 1902. He built the Derby into America's greatest race, and it is recognized, generally, that no man did more to keep racing alive in one of its most critical periods during World War II.

Prior to the founding of Churchill Downs Colonel Clark visited the great courses of England and France. After his trip there he formulated plans for the Louisville track and drew up its feature races. In addition to the Derby the races were the Kentucky Oaks and Clark Stakes, both run annually since the first year; the St. Leger Stakes, and the Louisville Cup. Changing conditions in racing resulted in changes in these races.

Some were discontinued entirely.

Colonel Clark continued in charge of Churchill Downs until his death in Nashville in 1899. The next three years were troubled ones for the Louisville track. As a result those interested in racing prevailed upon Colonel Winn to forsake other business interests and assume charge of Churchill Downs.

National prominence came to the Kentucky Derby and track from the outset. Racing patrons and horses from throughout the nation were attracted to Louisville by the race from its very beginning. That prestige, however, increased steadily under the guidance of Colonel Winn. Today it is safe to assume that every American Thoroughbred breeder would rather produce a winner of the Kentucky Derby than of any other race. The Derby winner's circle also is the goal of every owner, trainer, and jockey in the sport.

The land on which Churchill Downs is located was purchased from the Churchill family which was interested in a modest way in race horses. When established, the track was known as the Louisville Jockey Club. The name Churchill Downs was given to the course by a writer several years after its founding.

Originally, the grandstand and clubhouse were located on what is now the backside of the property. In 1896 the first unit of the present clubhouse and grandstand was erected. Since that date scarcely a year has passed without the addition of more seats and stands. Today seats extend the entire distance of the front stretch and partially around the first turn, or slightly more than three-eighths of a mile. There are more than 38,000 reserved seats in this area.

The first wagering done at Churchill Downs was through auction pools. Under this system of betting an auctioneer sells each horse in the race, sometimes offering several "outsiders" as one unit. The horse believed to have the best chance of winning naturally sells for the most money. The one thought to have the least chance sells cheapest. As soon as the auctioneer, who retained a commission from the total, sold all horses in one pool, he started another. Often his selling on the next day's racing continued late into the night. It would be resumed the next morning and continued right up to race time.

Bookmaking was started at Churchill Downs in 1882. In this form of betting the bookmaker posts odds against each horse, changing them constantly according to the play on each horse. He attempts to keep his book in balance in order that he will be able to retain something regardless of which horse wins. The present pari-mutuel system of betting was first used in 1878. Since 1908 it has been the only form permitted by law.

A crowd of 10,000 attended the first day of racing ever held at Churchill Downs. It was on that day that the first Kentucky Derby was run. Today more than half that number of persons are required to staff Churchill Downs on Derby Day.

For example, an estimated 1,500 people are needed to take care of the dining rooms, lunch counters, sandwich stands, and other concessions. More than 1,400 employees are required to operate the pari-mutuel department at the track on Derby Day. Another 1,000 members of the state militia aid in maintaining order.

To make a final check of the box and reserved seat areas on Derby morning requires a staff of approximately 200 men. Two complete fire companies are on duty at Churchill Downs throughout Derby Day. The fire-fighting equipment is manned by 110 men.

Sixty program sellers are stationed at the various track entrances. There are four physicians and several nurses on duty throughout the day in first-aid stations. The five bands which provide music in the centerfield gardens include about 250 musicians. There are approximately 200 ticket sellers and takers, and the staff of ushers numbers around 250. The state militia is augmented by approximately 400 policemen, who include those from the City of Louisville, and Jefferson county police departments, state police department, and the track's own guards.

The crew assembled to clean up the plant following Derby Day probably is the largest crew of its kind needed for any sports event. Twenty-four hours after the running of the race practically the entire plant had been cleaned. Those in charge of this work have only one fear—a high wind. For example, take the job in 1948. From daylight until about noon the crew had been sweeping the debris left by more than 100,-000 people into large piles. Trucks carted the trash off as fast as they could. However, at noon a strong wind swept the track, scattering the remaining piles over the entire track area.

Churchill Downs has gone through a number of corporate changes since it was founded. Its corporate name today is Churchill Downs, Incorporated, and its parent company is the American Turf Association. Colonel Winn is president of both corporations. Other officers of the American Turf Association are Samuel H. McMeekin, secretary, and J. Henry Waterman, treasurer. Directors of that corporation are Louie A. Beard, Bruce Campbell, Denver B. Cornett, Charles I. Dawson, C. Benson Dushane, Edward Fleming, Dennis J. Gleeson, Arthur B. Hancock, Louis J. Herrmann, Warner L. Jones, Jr., Frazer LeBus, Donald McDonald, William H. Veeneman, S. Peabody, Jr., Mr. Winn, and Mr. McMeekin.

Mr. McMeekin and Mr. Waterman also serve as secretary and treasurer, respectively, of the Churchill Downs corporation. Louis J. Herrmann is vice president and Russell Sweeney resident manager. The directors, in addition to Mr. Winn and Mr. McMeekin, are J. Graham Brown, Louis J. Herrmann, Charles I. Dawson, Warner L. Jones, Jr., and Mr. Sweeney.

Shown below are the results of the Derby Trials from the year 1938.

YEAR	FIRST	JOCKEY, WT.	SECOND	THIRD	VALUE	TIME
1938	The Chief	G. Woolf, 117	Lawrin	Stagehand	$2,145	1:35 4/5
1939	Viscounty	C. Bierman, 110	Technician	Steel Heels	2,150	1:38 2/5
1940	Bimelech	F. A. Smith, 118	Gallahadion	Sirocco	2,170	1:38
1941	Blue Pair	J. Richard, 115	Whirlaway	Cadmium	2,045	1:36 3/5
1942	Valdina Orphan	C. Bierman, 111	Sun Again	Alsab	2,305	1:36 4/5
1943	Ocean Wave	W. Eads, 112	Slide Rule	No Wrinkles	2,290	1:38 1/5
1944	Broadcloth	F. Zufelt, 110	Broad Grin	Rockwood Boy	4,400	1:37 1/5
1945	Burning Dream	D. Dodson, 111	Best Effort	Foreign Agent	4,570	1:38 1/5
1946	Rippey	F. Zufelt, 110	Spy Song	With Pleasure	9,775	1:40 1/5
1947	Faultless	D. Dodson, 118	Star Reward	Cosmic Bomb	9,075	1:37 3/5
1948	Citation	E. Arcaro, 118	Escadru	Eagle Look	8,525	1:37 2/5

THIS IS THE KENTUCKY DERBY

WHEN asked to describe the Kentucky Derby Irvin S. Cobb replied—

"If I could do that I'd have a larynx of spun silver and the tongue of an annointed angel. But if you can imagine a track that's like a bracelet of molten gold encircling a greensward that's like a patch of emerald velvet . . . all the pretty girls in the state turning the grandstand into a brocaded terrace of beauty and color such as the hanging gardens of Babylon never equaled . . . all the assembled sports of the nation going crazy at once down in the paddock . . . the entire colored population of Louisville and environs with one voice begging some entry to come on and win . . . and just yonder in the yellow dust the gallant kings and noble queens of the kingdom, the princessess royal, and their heirs apparent to the throne, fighting it out . . . each a symphony of satin coat and slim legs and panting nostrils . . . each a vision of courage and heart and speed . . . each topped as though with some bobbing gay blossoms by a silken-clad jockey . . . but what's the use? Until you go to Kentucky and with your own eyes behold the Derby, you ain't never been nowheres and you ain't never seen nothin'."

Another former Kentucky newspaper man, Daniel E. O'Sullivan, who was resident manager at Churchill Downs for many years prior to his death, wrote the following on the occasion of the fiftieth running of the Derby:

"The golden anniversary of Churchill Downs! Sacred and priceless its memories; beyond all price its half century of high ideals and honorable endeavor! What thoughts of departed friends, and old favorites stir the heart and throng the portals of the mind eager for utterance! Aristides, Vagrant, Baden-Baden, Day Star, Lord Murphy, Fonso, Hindoo, Leonatus, Montrose, Proctor Knott, Ben Brush, Old Rosebud, and their fellows, all under the turf which they did so much to ennoble.

"Gone are the countless gay companies where youth and beauty and high estate made the vanished days resplendent. Gone beyond recall are those who lived the historic scenes we now celebrate: M. Lewis Clark, the fearless, peerless Judge; Frank Harper, the quaint owner of Ten Broeck; Gen Abe Buford, who confidently expected to meet his Thoroughbreds on the bluegrass fields of the new Jerusalem; the Churchills, the Clays, the Breckinridges, the Blackburns, the Johnsons, Grinstead, Ten Broeck, Woodford, and the lamented Charles F. Grainger, all gone out into the shadows. But their spirits revisit the Downs, keep green its fields and bright its paths, hover above it in kindly council, inspire its managers and pass judgment on their decisions.

"The month of May, caparisoned in her garments of gladness, violets blooming where she walks, always claims Derby Day as her own. It is a name to conjure with, at once an inspiration and a delight. The bluegrass curtsies a welcome. An infinite, cloudless sky spreads the benison of its silken tent over the scene. The brown ribbon of the course is unfolded as from a golden reel. Thoroughbreds pick their way daintily across the field, or arch their prideful necks in preliminary gallops. Myriads of American flags swim in the sun-kissed air. Glad thousands occupy every coign of vantage, their faces radiant with joy and their hearts free from care. The stands are vibrant with unconcealed emotion. The air is electrical with expectation. A carnival spirit is everywhere. It is Kentucky's annual tribute to the Thoroughbred, in which all America joins.

"Derby Day at Churchill Downs! What happy memories it evokes! What fond hopes have found realization here, and what bright dreams have raveled out into unrealities! At last the bugle sounds—its notes as thrilling as the Marseillaise. Fifty thousand spectators leap to attention at its command. A field of matchless Thoroughbreds file through the paddock gate and pirouette in the parade past the acclaiming stands, the jockeys swaying above the saddles, their colors dancing like painted bubbles in the wind. They face the starter. A brief delay while positions are being taken, a sudden swing into line, and the barrier lifts, the flag falls and 'they're off' in the race of the year. Sweeping past the stand fifty thousand hearts echo the rataplan of the hurrying hoofs and a wild chorus of approval follows the vanishing field. At every point of the swift journey excited partisans speed them on. The quarter is passed, and the half is left behind, and then begins the drive down the backstretch where the cavalcade readjusts itself into divisions, the leaders wearying of the pace, become laggards.

"Now comes the challenge at the crucial turn for home with the goal a full quarter of a mile away. There is a closing of ranks, the vanquished drop back into the ruck and a new pacemaker takes up the fallen gauntlet. At his throatlatch, and saddlegirth, and hard upon his heels crowd the contenders, their jockeys not yet ready to acknowledge defeat. The frenzied thousands, in grandstand, clubhouse and lawn, shriek personal appeals to particular horses and riders to 'Come on! Come on!' Out of the thunder of a hundred

hoofs comes the lightning flash of spurs, the whir of swiftly drawn whips, and the desperate duel is on to the wire where fame and fortune wait. In the very last determinate moment there flashes from the struggling mass a Thoroughbred that will not be denied, and in a whirlwind of speed he sweeps past the post a winner amid the applause of an enraptured multitude.

"And this is Derby day at Churchill Downs."

Athough written a number of years ago, the two foregoing descriptions of the Kentucky Derby are still apropos of America's greatest sports event, except that the thousands viewing each renewal have been more than doubled in the last quarter century and the race has doubled in importance as a yardstick to a Thoroughbred's racing prowess and his ability to beget champions.

No less an authority than John L. Hervey, considered by racing as the most thorough historian of the American Turf, wrote in 1947, "from the beginning the Kentucky Derby, like its historic prototype at Epsom, was a breeders' race. It has remained so to a greater extent than anyone has reason to expect. The surest indication of this is the fact that the winner is almost invariably transferred to the stud, not merely when his usefulness for racing purposes is over, but oftener before then, while the number that have made successful sires is, all things taken into consideration, remarkable."

In connection with that statement it is interesting to note how rapidly the number of Kentucky Derby winners sired by Kentucky Derby winners has mounted in recent years. One in every nine winners of the race has been sired by a horse which ran first, second, or third in the Derby. That is a remarkable record when one considers the number of stallions with sons or daughters racing each year. For example, the get of approximately 2,000 stallions raced in America in 1948.

Not only have Derby horses gone on to great success as stock horses, but a roll call of the winners includes many of the great names of American racing. Three of the winners have become the world's greatest money-winners.

H. F. Sinclair's Zev, winner of the Derby in 1923, was the first. Prior to his retirement at the end of his four-year-old season Zev had won 23 of his 43 races and $313,639. Whirlaway, who established a new time record of 2:01 2/5 in winning the 1941 Kentucky Derby, became the world's leading money-winner when he established a new record of $561,161.

As a four-year-old and not quite fourteen months after he won the Kentucky Derby, Assault displaced Whirlaway as the world's leading money-winner when he won the Brooklyn Handicap on June 21, 1947, and pushed his total earnings up to $576,670. Assault lost top place to Stymie when the latter won the Sussex Handicap at Delaware Park July 5, but regained the lead on July 12 by beating Stymie a head on the Butler Handicap. Before the year was out Assault had again been displaced by Stymie as the world's leading money-winner.

Assault established another record in winning $424,195 as a three-year-old, this being the greatest winnings of any horse in a single year. He also was the seventh horse to which America's Triple Crown, which includes the Kentucky Derby, Preakness Stakes, and Belmont Stakes. Three-year-olds which had previously won this honor were Sir Barton, Gallant Fox, Omaha, War Admiral, Whirlaway, and Count Fleet.

Citation, winner of the seventy-fourth Derby in 1948, may be the greatest horse that ever raced in America. He has been acclaimed as such by many astute horsemen. In only two seasons Citation earned $865,150, placing him near the top as the greatest of all money-winners. Most horsemen believe he will become the largest money-winner if he is raced in 1949, and they are just as confident that he will become the first horse to win $1,000,000.

Citations earnings of $709,470 as a three-year-old was a new record in money-winnings by any horse in a single season. The two previous holders of this record, Gallant Fox and Assault, also had been winners of the Kentucky Derby. Citation also was the eighth horse to win the American Triple Crown.

Since 1936 Churchill Downs has offered the Derby Trial Stakes at one mile, for Derby eligibles only, on the Tuesday preceding the big race. Citation is the only horse which has won both races. He also is the first to win the Futurity and Derby.

Any list of the best three-year-olds of their respective seasons during the last twenty years certainly must include such as these eleven: Reigh Count, Gallant Fox, Twenty Grand, Cavalcade, Omaha, War Admiral, Whirlaway, Shut Out, Count Fleet, Citation, and Assault, all winners of the Kentucky Derby. Head Play, Challedon, Bimelech, and Phalanx, each second in the Kentucky Derby, went on to be acclaimed the best three-year-old of their respective years.

Exterminator, winner of the 1918 Kentucky Derby, is considered to be among the greatest Thoroughbreds seen in America in the present century. Exterminator raced for eight seasons, won fifty races, was seventeen times second, seventeen times third, and earned $252,996. Weight, distance and track condition made little difference to the horse known affectionately as "Old Bones."

Other outstanding horses which raced in the Derby include Mate, Discovery, Cudgel, Star Hawk, Escoba, War Cloud, Billy Kelly, Upset, Display, Donnacona, Cleopatra, Prudery, Tryster, Careful, In Memoriam, Pebbles, Chilhowee, Pompey, Espino, Osmand, Jock, Misstep, Toro, Sun Beau, Gallant Sir, Roman Soldier, He Did, Pompoon, Can't Wait, Fighting Fox, Challedon, Market Wise, Devil Diver, and Blue Swords, to mention only a few.

ARISTIDES, WINNER, FIRST KENTUCKY DERBY

O. LEWIS, JOCKEY ON ARISTIDES

Colonel Matt J. Winn

THIS IS COL. MATT J. WINN

THE State of Kentucky and the City of Louisville each owes Colonel Matt J. Winn a monument, the former for the fame he has added to its fair name, the latter for both the renown and the millions of dollars he has brought to the community.

The Sport of Kings—horse racing—owes him still another monument for contributing its greatest and most spectacular event, and for his untiring efforts down through the years to preserve and enhance the stability and honor of the game.

The sports writing fraternity is in his debt for at least a tablet for affording it a subject of never failing interest to newspaper readers from the time the last leaf falls in autumn until the buds come again in the spring.

And then there is the token that I should personally contribute, perhaps a horseshoe of red, red roses, in memory of some of the greatest thrills I have ever known, and in affectionate tribute to one of the finest characters that sport or any other field has ever produced.

But I suppose we can just let the Kentucky Derby stand as the living symbol of Colonel Winn and his works. No man could want more. At a ripe old age he sits, cheribund and jovial, in his office at picturesque Churchill Downs, gazing out over the landscape that he has brightened into a picture that once seen is never forgotten, and the center of the roar of the crowd that he so dearly loves, and he can well reflect that no one has had a fuller life, that no one has risen higher in the field of his endeavor or enjoyed greater respect of his fellow men.

I give you here a toast.

I give you Colonel Winn, 80 years young this year of Our Lord, 1941, Master of the Downs, Squire of Louisville, First Sportsman of Kentucky, a gentleman bred in the deep purple, and a 22-karat human being.

It is not my purpose to review in detail the history of Colonel Winn, or of the Kentucky Derby, either, though I could do both with scarcely a reference to the record books for data, so often have I, like most writers who have written of sport in bygone years, gone over the stirring story. I come mainly to discuss Colonel Winn as a personality, and what econiums I offer spring from the heart.

I have known a great many men in sport in my time. I have known the champions and the promoters. I have known the magnates and the moguls. I have known those who could take the good and the bad with the same kind of a smile, and I have known the cry babies—the ones who could not stand up when the going got tough. But of them all, I have never known one who has worn as well as Colonel Winn.

I have never known another man in sport to march down the long years with such an elan as Colonel Winn, keeping step with every generation as it came along, with its ideas as well as its spirit, and often moving ahead of the newcomers. If you will examine the record of his racing ventures you will find that Colonel Winn has nearly always been first with innovation, with improvement and with progress. He is one of those men who remain perennially youthful in thought and never permits himself to fall behind the procession.

He is faultless sartorially—one of the best dressed men in the country. He has always taken the deepest draughts of life. He enjoys good company, good food, and, of course, being Kentucky born and raised, he enjoys good juleps. I once asked Colonel Winn his secret for looking so well and keeping so fit physically as he advanced along the years and he said he attributed it to his practice of making regular trips to French Lick, the famous Indiana Spa not far from Louisville and taking the baths and resting.

I am perfectly willing to give French Lick plenty of credit on the physical side, but I am inclined to the belief that it is his faculty for thinking young that keeps the Colonel younger looking than his actual years and young in spirit.

They say this will do it better than anything else. He is fond of the great traditions that he helped establish for the Kentucky Derby and has a marvelous memory that makes him the perfect raconteur on old times and old things, but his life is essentially of the present, and his eye on the future.

It is almost startling to reflect that Colonel Winn saw the first Kentucky Derby in 1875, when he was a boy of 14. He saw it from his father's buggy in the infield. That was the race won by Aristides, the horse that the Turf writers are fond of referring to as "the little red horse." The Colonel has seen every Derby since that day and from 1903 when his friend Charlie Price induced him to reorganize the fading Churchill Downs, they have been under his supervision.

It was not the race thirty-nine years ago that it is today—that is, not in Turf importance or in national interest. It was just a smallish stake that in money value would not compare with some quite ordinary stakes today. It was mainly of local interest, and probably only Colonel Winn himself foresaw that the time would come when it would be the blue ribbon classic of the American Turf, rich in prizes, and with its distinct bearing upon the breeding industry of the nation, and especially of old Kentucky, and that it would draw special trainloads of visitors from all over the land to fairly bend outward the walls of the Louisville hotels. He must have had this vision, because year after year the Colonel was building and expanding it in a manner little short of advertising genius.

And in the meantime he was making a lot of Turf history on the side, fighting big Turf wars, spreading out his racing interests east and west and south, and even went down into Mexico, until he was operating half a dozen tracks at the same time and had become the most powerful figure in the game. But Churchill Downs always remained his greatest pride. Today there is no other sports event in America that comes close to it in color and excitement. Against the competition of higher purses, it is still the one horse race that commands pages of newspaper space for weeks before it takes place, and almost invariably leads the front page of every newspaper in the country the morning after its running.

In his lifetime, Colonel Winn has seen the face of the great globe changed again and again. He has seen great wars and great panics and great disasters. He has had his own ups and downs. But for thirty-seven momentous years he has managed to keep the Kentucky Derby going—and

growing. Whenever it had an economic setback as in the panic years, Colonel Winn redoubled his efforts to regain the lost ground and always add a little more. And through it all he has maintained his good humor, his sense of values, his philosophy and his balance generally.

The greatest horses this country has ever produced have run in the magnificent setting he provides every spring at Churchill Downs. His boxes are filled with the big-wigs of society and of local and national politics. He has entertained there an Earl of Derby, one of whose ancestors gave the name to the English race from which the event is copied, and a Governor of Kentucky would be deemed extremely lax in his official duty were he not present with the Colonel to bid the high and low welcome to Kentucky, in whose diadem of gallant, and kind, and courteous gentlemen, there is none more sparkling than Colonel Matt Winn.

The foregoing tribute to Colonel Matt J. Winn was written in 1941 by Damon Runyan, whose stories of the Kentucky Derby were among the best.

Martin J. Winn was born June 30, 1861, in the Winn home on Fifth Street, between Main Street and the Ohio River, in Louisville, Kentucky. His father was Patrick Winn, who had come to America from Ireland as a thirteen-year-old boy and settled in Louisville. His mother was Julia Flaherty, of Louisville.

After attending grammar school, the boy took a course at Bryant and Stratton Business School in Louisville. His first job after graduation from that school was as a bookkeeper for the Stanger Glass Company. This was followed by a position as traveling salesman for Stege and Reiling, wholesale grocers in Louisville.

In 1887 Winn formed a partnership with Ed Langan and opened a tailoring shop in Louisville. The business prospered and the shop became one of the most popular gathering places in Louisville for businessmen, politicians, and sportsmen.

It was late in 1902 that Colonel Winn was persuaded to give up his tailoring business and take over the management of Churchill Downs. In the same year he was named to the board of public safety for the City of Louisville.

During the next forty-seven years he has been one of the most active men in the racing picture. He was affiliated with tracks throughout the country. In 1947, however, he retired from all race track affiliations except Churchill Downs. Today his entire energy is devoted to Churchill Downs and the Kentucky Derby.

The
KENTUCKY DERBY
Winners

1875
✦
1948

winners pedigrees ★ *tabulated racing records and historic parallels*

General Ulysses S. Grant, lower right, eighteenth president of the United States, occupied the White House on that Monday afternoon, May 17, 1875, when the first Kentucky Derby was run. In that year thirty-seven states with a population of approximately 45,000,000 made up the Union.

The country was beginning its recovery from the great financial panic of 1873, and a topic of conversation was the conviction in 1874 of "Boss" W. M. Tweed on charges of fraud.

In 1875 the name Salvation Army was selected for the organization formed just ten years earlier by General William Booth, and the first catcher's mask was worn in baseball.

At the nation's capital Republicans passed the Resumption Act in an effort to reconcile the inflationist sentiment of the west with the sound-money policies of the east. In protest there was organized in 1875 the National Greenback party.

The clubhouse at Churchill Downs, shown at top, was an attractive building but modest compared to the immense structure of today. The original clubhouse stood on what is now the backside of the track and was later moved from the track property. Today it is used as a residence on the street which runs past the backside of the Downs.

One of Kentucky's outstanding soldiers and politicians, John C. Breckinridge, died at Lexington on the day the first Kentucky Derby was run. It was during 1875 that Congress authorized the coinage of twenty-cent silver pieces. Gold was discovered at Deadwood and Whitewood gulches in South Dakota.

Pedigree

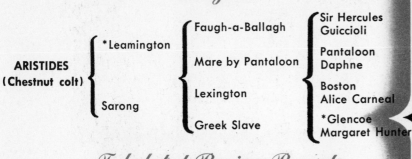

ARISTIDES (Chestnut colt)			
*Leamington	Faugh-a-Ballagh	Sir Hercules	Guiccioli
	Mare by Pantaloon	Pantaloon	Daphne
Sarong	Lexington	Boston	Alice Carneal
	Greek Slave	*Glencoe	Margaret Hunter

Tabulated Racing Record

Year	Age	Sts.	1st	2nd	3rd	Won
1874	2	9	3	3	0	$ 1,525
1875	3	9	4	2	1	15,700
1876	4	2	2	0	0	1,100
1878	6	1	0	0	0	...
		21	9	5	1	$ 18,325

1st Kentucky Derby, May 17, 1875

Aristides

$1,000 added. Net to winner $2,850; second $200. 42 nominations.

	Horse	Wt.	Fin.	Jockey	Owner
	Aristides	100	1	O. Lewis	H. P. McGrath
	Volcano	100	2	—	George H. Rice
	Verdigris	100	3	—	C. A. Lewis
	Ten Broeck	—	—	—	F. P. Harper
	Searcher	—	—	—	J. B. Rode
	Enlister	—	—	—	Springfield and Clay
	Warsaw	—	—	—	Springfield and Clay
	McCreery	—	—	—	Gen. Abe Buford
Also ran	Bill Bruce	—	—	—	S. J. Salyer
	Gold Mine	—	—	—	J. A. Grinstead
	Brown colt by Baywood	—	—	—	Gen. Abe Buford
	Bob Wooley	—	—	—	Robinson, Morgan & Co.
	Vagabond	—	—	—	A. B. Lewis & Co.
	Ascension	—	—	—	W. C. Hull
	Chesapeake	—	—	—	H. P. McGrath

Time: 2:37¾. Track fast.

Winner—Ch.c. by *Leamington—Sarong, by Lexington; trained by A. Anderson; bred by H. P. McGrath.

Aristides   *Stakes Races*

AT 2 YEARS	2ND	Thespian Stakes.
	UNP	Saratoga Stakes.
AT 3 YEARS	WON	Kentucky Derby, Withers Stakes, Jerome Stakes, Breckinridge Stakes.
	2ND	Belmont Stakes, Ocean Hotel Stakes.
	3RD	Travers Stakes.

(Reprinted from Spirit of The Times of May 22, 1875)

The Kentucky Derby, the great racing event of the meeting, and one which has created deep interest throughout the country, in view of the important bearing upon the prospects of future great events, was the second race. It was a sweepstakes of $50 each, p. p., with $1,000 added by the Association, the second horse to have $200; one mile and a half. Of the forty-two entries in the race, fifteen came to the post. This was a magnificent field of three-year-olds, the majority of them having been winners. The betting showed McGrath's entries—Aristides and Chesapeake—to be the favorites in public estimation, for they brought $105 to Ascension's $55, Searcher $65, and the field $270. Chesapeake, from his successful running at Lexington, was generally thought to be the representative of the McGrath stable, especially as Aristides had been cut up badly in the Phoenix Hotel Stakes at that meeting, owing to the fearfully heavy state of the course.

The horses got off at the first attempt, Chesapeake being one of the last to get away. Volcano made the running, closely attended by Verdigris, Aristides, and McCreery, the rest well together, a length or two behind. They ran thus throughout the first half mile, 50½s., but the pace then began to tell on some of the rear division, and Enlister, Vagabond, and Chesapeake fell back. Aristides took second place as they ran along the backstretch, lapped Volcano as they reached the half-mile pole, the starting point (the mile being run in 1:43¼), and showed in front directly afterwards. The tremendous pace had already told a tale upon the field, which was now strung out a hundred yards behind. Chesapeake and Enlister being conspicuously in the rear. Aristides was steadily increasing his lead, Howard having taken a steadying pull on Volcano for a final effort.

At the head of the stretch stood Mr. McGrath, who waved to Lewis, the rider of Aristides, to "go on," and he at once obeyed instructions by loosing his pull on his horse's bridle. Half way home, Volcano came with a determined rush, but Aristides stalled off the challenge in gallant style, and went over to score a winner of the first Kentucky Derby by a length from Volcano, with Verdigris third in 2:37¾, the fastest time ever made by a three-year-old at the distance. Bob Wooley was fourth and Ten Broeck fifth. Searcher, from whom so much was expected, never showed conspicuously in the race. Value of the stakes $3,100; of which $200 goes to the second horse.

Among the 10,000 persons who were present at Churchill Downs on May 17, 1875, for the inaugural running of the Kentucky Derby was Louisville's Mary Anderson, who was preparing for her debut later in the fall. She was destined to become a great American actress. Many of those present wrote "the folks back home" how the "little red horse" won the Derby trophy, a massive punch bowl costing $1,000, and composed of three hundred ounces of sterling silver.

Bred by Price McGrath at McGrathiana Stud outside Lexington, Aristides stood 15.1 hands high. He was one of the smallest horses in the first Derby. As a two-year-old he had won three of nine starts, was three times second. He won his only two starts at four, setting a record of 4:27 1/2 for two and one-half miles at Lexington; did not race at five, and was unplaced in his only start at six. Aristides died June 21, 1893, at the St. Louis Fairgrounds.

McGrath was one of the most colorful of all Kentucky horsemen. Born of poor parents in Woodford County, he had gone west in '49, returned to New York where he opened a gambling house. There he won $105,000 in a single night, closed shop, returned to Kentucky and established McGrathiana Stud. A noted horse breeder, he never drove horses, preferring a team of mules hitched to a Jersey wagon.

"For two and one-half cents I was denied an education," he once told a friend. McGrath related how he gave the first dime he ever earned to a wealthy neighbor, requesting that the latter bring him a blue-back spelling book from the city. The neighbor returned empty-handed, returned the dime with the comment, "The book cost twelve and one-half cents."

By earning $15,700 at three Aristides helped place his sire *Leamington at the top of America's leading sires in 1875. Another great sire, Lexington, died in 1875. Lexington never sired a Derby winner, but his name appears in the pedigree of more Derby winners than the name of any other horse. He led American sires for fourteen straight years, 1861-1874, and again in 1876 and 1878.

1876

While Louisville and Kentucky prepared for the second Kentucky Derby in May, 1876, an expedition in charge of General Alfred H. Terry left Fort Abraham Lincoln in the Northwest. It was directed against the forces of Sitting Bull.

Among the officers was General George Armstrong Custer, who was dispatched with 600 men on June 24 to investigate reports of an Indian village in a bend of Little Big Horn River. Disobeying orders, Custer split his unit and attacked the village on June 25, heedless of the fact that 6,000 Indians faced him. The massacre is known as "Custer's Last Stand." In it Custer and all men in his half of the 600-man unit were killed.

Earlier, on March 10, at Boston the statement, "Mr. Watson, come here; I want you," marked the birth of the tele-

phone. The man speaking was Alexander Graham Bell, lower left, inventor of the telephone. At lower right is an artist's drawing of the scene.

Louisville was a city of great importance. Above appears an artist's drawing of the city, where in 1876 the National Baseball League was organized. The same year saw the admission of Colorado as the thirty-eighth state on August 1. This also was the year of the Centennial Exhibition in Philadelphia and the year when all railroads had converted to the same gauge track.

The Coast Guard Academy was established by law on July 31, 1876. At that time the group was known as the Revenue Cutter Service. In 1915 the Revenue Cutter Service was merged with the Life Saving Service and the name changed to Coast Guard Academy.

Pedigree

VAGRANT (Brown Gelding)			
Virgil	Vandal	*Glencoe	
		Mare by *Tranby	
	Hymenia	*Yorkshire	
		Little Peggy	
Lazy	*Scythian	Orlando	
		Scythia	
	Lindora	Lexington	
		Picayune	

Tabulated Racing Record

Year	Age	Sts.	1st	2nd	3rd	Won
1875	2	6	5	0	1	$ 3,800
1876	3	4	3	1	0	6,450
1877	4	0	0	0	0	...
1878	5	12	0	0	4	...
1879	6	14	3	2	2	1,175
1880	7	23	7	3	3	1,500
1881	8	21	2	5	2	875
1882	9	7	0	1	0	75
1883	10	1	0	0	0	...
		88	20	12	12	$ 13,875

2nd Kentucky Derby, May 15, 1876

Vagrant

$1,500 added. Net to winner $2,950; second $200. 34 nominations.

	Horse	Wt.	Fin.	Jockey	Owner
	Vagrant	97	1	R. Swim	William Astor
	Creedmore	100	2	W. Williams	Williams & Owings
	Harry Hill	100	3	J. Miller	John Funk
Also ran	Parole	97	—	Sparling	P. Lorillard
	Germantown	100	—	Graham	F. B. Harper
	Black colt by Enquirer	97	—	James	F. B. Harper
	Marie Michon	97	—	Stratford	J. A. Grinstead
	Leamingtonian	100	—	Colston	H. F. Vissman
	Bombay	100	—	Walker	D. Swigert
	Red Coat	100	—	Hughes	Green Clay
	Bullion	100	—	Kelso	A. Keene Richards

Time: 2:38¼. Weather clear, track fast.

Winner—Br. g. by Virgil—Lazy, by *Scythian; trained by James Williams; bred by M. H. Sanford.

Auction Pools: Vagrant, $525; Parole, $400; Creedmore, $275; Red Coat, $150; Field $135.

Parole went to front, immediately after the break, but Vagrant came up on the outside, took the lead at the mile, and increased it through the stretch, to win by two lengths.

Vagrant — Stakes Races

AT 2 YEARS	WON	Alexander Stakes, Belle Meade Stakes, Sanford Stakes, Colt Stakes and Colt and Filly Stakes (both at Lexington.)
	3RD	Tennessee Stakes.
AT 3 YEARS	WON	Kentucky Derby, Phoenix Hotel Stakes, Grand Exposition Stakes.
	2ND	Clark Stakes.

Ten Broeck, unplaced to Aristides in the first running of the Kentucky Derby, was one of the real champions of the American Turf during his racing career. He was in the two most-written-of match races run in Kentucky. One was his famous match with Mollie McCarthy at Churchill Downs. The other was against Aristides at Lexington in 1876. Ten Broeck also met Parole and was raced abroad.

The meeting of Aristides and Ten Broeck in 1876 was certainly a colorful affair. Price McGrath selected Bobby Swim to ride Aristides. Frank Harper gave the noted Negro jockey Billy Walker, who was to ride the 1877 Derby winner, the mount on Ten Broeck.

Ten Broeck was the favorite. McGrath, however, had great confidence in Aristides. As race time approached he stood in the track accepting all wagers, regardless of size. A friend noticed McGrath was making no notes of his bets. He approached the owner of Aristides and asked, "Mr. McGrath, don't you think you ought to keep some sort of notes, in case you have to pay off?"

Without looking up, McGrath replied, "Don't worry son, 'the little red horse' will keep the books today." He did, winning by forty lengths.

Two weeks prior to the second running of the Kentucky Derby the winner was purchased by William Astor, of New York, in whose racing silks Vagrant won. Colonel S. D. Bruce, of Lexington, had acted for the New Yorker in paying T. J. Nichols, of Paris, Kentucky, $7,000 in cash for the gelded son of Virgil.

Nichols had purchased the Derby winner for $250 as a yearling. Vagrant was bred by M. H. Sanford, who owned his sire Virgil and the farm which today is Elmendorf Farm. Sanford thought little of Virgil, described as "the blackest horse you ever saw," and gave him away. In fact, the man who received Virgil as a gift made a present of him to still another breeder.

All that happened, however, before Vagrant became the outstanding two-year-old of 1875. When that happened there was a wild scramble on the part of breeders to buy Virgil, and he eventually was sold for $3,500. Virgil, who had been trained as a jumper, is one of three stallions which have sired three Derby winners each. He was leading sire in 1885 and his son, Hindoo, is one of the greatest horses ever to win the Derby. Virgil also sired Ben Ali, Derby winner.

Vagrant had one of the most extensive racing careers of any winner of the Derby. He raced eight seasons, although in his last campaign at ten he started only once, was unplaced. In two other seasons, at five and nine, Vagrant also failed to win. Following his retirement from racing, Vagrant was used to pull a cart about Lexington.

Colonel W. H. Johnson, president of the Nashville Blood Horse Association, who acted as starter for the first Derby, again served in that capacity in 1876. The signal for the start of the race was given by tapping a drum.

Jockey Bobby Swim, who rode the 1876 winner, was "discovered" by a Dr. Weldon, whose attention was attracted to the boy's riding ability when he saw Swim astride a horse, driving cattle through the streets of St. Louis. Swim, rated as one of the best riders of the day, is a legendary character of the Turf.

1877

After the disputed election of the previous year Rutherford B. Hayes, lower left, was inaugurated as nineteenth President of the United States in 1877. His Democratic opponent, Governor Samuel J. Tilden, had won a popular majority, but an electoral commission of eight Republicans and seven Democrats awarded nineteen disputed electoral votes to Hayes.

The Hayes administration was marked by railroad strikes. By the middle of his first year most of the Atlantic seaboard and middlewest railroads were tied up. Pennsylvania's coal fields were terrorized

by mobs. Rioting occurred in Chicago, Baltimore and other cities. More than $10,000,000 worth of railroad property was destroyed in the Pittsburgh area, and eleven Molly Maguires, mining labor agitators, were hanged.

Meanwhile, the young American inventor Thomas A. Edison produced his first phonograph. Edison is shown with the invention in the photograph at the right on this page.

Another inventor, George Baldwin Selden, was hard at work on the princi-

ples of his first automobile, called "1877" and shown in the photograph at upper left. It was two years later that Selden applied for a patent for use of an internal-combustion engine in a "road locomotive."

Local items in Louisville newspapers on Derby Day, 1877, included an announcement, "Miss Mamie Croxton's dancing exhibition will take place at room No. 4 of the Library building tonight," and a story that New Albany, Indiana, was "unusually quiet." Coal was advertised at $2.50 per ton. Brigham Young died in Salt Lake City on August 29. During the year the Missouri, Kansas, and Texas Railroad was involved in a passenger rate war with the Missouri Pacific Railroad. The railroads reached an agreement on Derby Day and ended their differences.

Pedigree

BADEN-BADEN (Chestnut Colt)	*Australian	West Australian	Melbourne / Mowerina
		*Emilia	Young Emilius / Persian
	Lavender	Wagner	Sir Charles / Maria West
		Alice Carneal	*Sarpedon / Rowena

Tabulated Racing Record

Year	Age	Sts.	1st	2nd	3rd	Won
1876	2	4	1	3	0	$ 475
1877	3	6	3	0	1	‡11,950
		10	4	3	1	$ 12,425

‡Including $500 in plate.

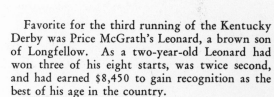

Baden=Baden

3rd Kentucky Derby, May 22, 1877

$1,500 added. Net to winner $3,300; second $200. 41 nominations.

	Horse	Wt.	Fin.	Jockey	Owner
	Baden-Baden	100	1	W. Walker	D. Swigert
	Leonard	100	2	Swim	H. P. McGrath
	Smallwood	100	3	Bailey	Smallwood & Co.
	Vera Cruz	97	—	Murphy	J. T. Williams
	Odd Fellow	100	—	Williams	J. J. Merrill
	McWhirter	100	—	H. Moore	Gen. Abe Buford
Also ran	Malvern	100	—	S. Jones	George H. Rice
	Early Light	97	—	W. James	F. B. Harper
	Dan K.	97	—	McGrath	Johnson & Mills
	Lisbon	100	—	Douglass	D. Swigert
	Headlight	100	—	Shelton	L. B. Fields

Time: 2:38 Weather clear, track fast.

Winner—Ch.c. by *Australian—Lavender, by Wagner; trained by Ed Brown; bred by A. J. Alexander.

Auction Pools: Leonard, $150; Vera Cruz, $100; McWhirter, $50; Swigert, $50; Field, (with Baden-Baden included) $45.

Leonard, the favorite, broke in front. Baden-Baden moved steadily from fifth place, to take second position going into the stretch, with King William, third, and Vera Cruz, fourth. Under slight pressure, Baden-Baden, ridden by Billy Walker, Negro jockey, passed Leonard, and won by two lengths.

Baden=Baden   Stakes Races

AT 2 YEARS	WON	Young America Stakes.
	2ND	Belle Meade Stakes, Sanford Stakes.
AT 3 YEARS	WON	Kentucky Derby, Jersey Derby, Travers Stakes.
	3RD	Belmont Stakes.
	UNP	Clark Stakes, Kenner Stakes.

As a four-year-old in 1876 Ten Broeck had established two track records at Churchill Downs. Both were made racing against time and neither has been broken. They were 7:15 3/4 for four miles, set on September 27; and 5:26 1/2 for three miles, established on September 3. In 1877 Ten Broeck established two more track records. On May 24 he ran one mile in 1:39 3/4. This was an American record for one mile until June 28, 1890, when Racine ran that distance in 1:39 1/2 at Washington Park. On May 27 Ten Broeck ran two miles in 3:27 1/2.

One newspaper account of the 1877 Derby reported, "the best of order prevailed. Not a single person was seen under the influence of liquor during the day." The same writer described as follows the scene which greeted the Derby Churchill Downs visitors: "green fields and woodlands lay to the left, a cottage dotted here and there over the plain. Behind, the Nashville railroad winding its way like a snake through the woodlands. In front, was a cloud of dust that indicated the road over which the vast crowd was approaching."

Favorite for the third running of the Kentucky Derby was Price McGrath's Leonard, a brown son of Longfellow. As a two-year-old Leonard had won three of his eight starts, was twice second, and had earned $8,450 to gain recognition as the best of his age in the country.

In the Derby the McGrath colt was first to show after the start, but he could not withstand the challenge of Baden-Baden despite the superb riding of the top rider Bobby Swim, who had ridden the 1876 winner. Baden-Baden had been brought to Louisville from Lexington where he had done his preliminary training for the Derby, as had the first two winners of the race.

Immediately after the race, J. T. Williams, owner of Vera Cruz, which had finished unplaced, rushed up to Daniel Swigert and offered $2,500 for a match race with Baden-Baden. The owner of the winner declined.

Vera Cruz was ridden by Isaac Murphy, who declared after his retirement that Vera Cruz was one of the greatest horses he ever had ridden. Murphy rode such tops as Leonatus, winner of ten of his eleven races; Emperor of Norfolk, Freeland, Checkmate, Falsetto, Glenmore, Volante, Kingston, Troubadour, and others.

Vera Cruz was troubled by unsoundness. He was left at the post in the Derby, except for which Murphy believed he would have retired from riding with four Kentucky Derby triumphs to his credit. It was on Vera Cruz and at Churchill Downs in 1877 that Jockey Murphy scored his first important stakes triumph as a rider. Astride the Williams colt, Murphy won the St. Leger which was run in the fall at Louisville.

Baden-Baden was a chestnut son of the imported sire *Australian, the latter by West Australian out of *Emilia. The mare *Emilia has the distinction of being the only mare to produce the sire of a Kentucky Derby winner and the dam of a winner. *Emilia's daughter, Ulrica, produced Ben Ali, winner of the Derby in 1886.

Baden-Baden was the first of five winners bred by A. J. A. Alexander.

21

The year 1878 was an extremely important one in the development of artificial light. Man's first electric light was an arc lamp, invented by Sir Humphry Davy in 1801, but it was not until 1878 that C. F. Brush, of Cleveland, perfected an arc-lamp system which proved itself efficient enough to be used commercially.

This was the year that the first electric arc-lamp was put into use in Louisville.

More important, however, than Brush's improved arc-lamp was Thomas A. Edison's successful experiment in 1878 with the incandescent light. The artist's drawing below shows preparation of the first successful incandescent lamp for its life-test at Edison's Menlo Park laboratory. The drawing shows Francis Jehl replenishing the supply of mercury. Francis R. Upton stands behind Edison, and Charles Batchelor looks over his shoulder. At left stands John Kruesi, with Martin Force and Ludwig Boehm in the background.

Between 1878 and 1880 Edison, working with Joseph W. Swan, perfected a practical incandescent lamp. Their principal problem was finding a suitable filament.

In the nation's capital the Bland Silver Bill was passed. This called for the purchase of not less than $2,000,000 worth of silver bullion monthly for coinage of silver dollars at a ratio of 16-to-1. Southern states suffered heavily from an epidemic of yellow fever. More than 20,000 cases were reported, of which 7,000 were fatal.

On December 17, gold sold at par in New York for the first time since January 13, 1862.

Early in the year James Gordon Bennett outfitted the "Jeannette" for a polar expedition. The following year he turned the ship over to the United States Navy and on July 8, 1879, the "Jeannette" sailed from San Francisco to the arctic region. The ship was crushed in arctic ice in 1881, was abandoned and sunk. Only part of the crew was saved.

The coinage of twenty-cent silver pieces which had been authorized in 1875 was discontinued in 1878. It was also in 1878 that the first train ran over New York City's Sixth Avenue elevated line. At Baltimore the American Bar Association was established. In Louisville a Board of Health was established. In New York the former Tammany boss, William M. Tweed, died.

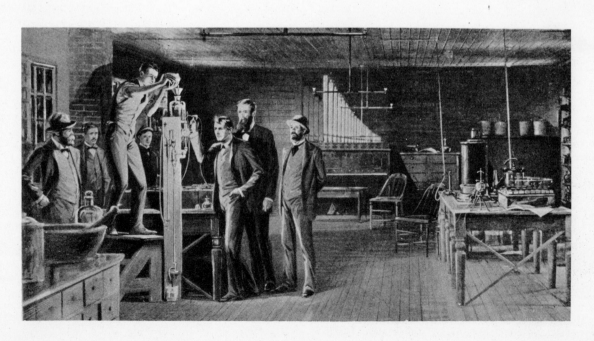

Pedigree

```
                        ┌ *Glencoe ──────┬ Sultan
             ┌ Star Davis                └ Trampoline
             │          └ Margaret Wood ─┬ Priam
DAY STAR ────┤                           └ Maria West
(Chestnut    │          ┌ Lexington ─────┬ Boston
 Colt)       └ Squeeze-'Em               └ Alice Carneal
                        └ Skedaddle ─────┬ *Yorkshire
                                         └ Magnolia
```

Tabulated Racing Record

Year	Age	Sts.	1st	2nd	3rd	Won
1877	2	2	0	1	0	$ 100
1878	3	6	2	1	1	7,050
1879	4	8	0	1	0	125
1880	5	9	3	1	2	1,205
1881	6	10	5	3	1	2,450
1882	7	7	1	0	1	450
		40	11	7	5	$ 11,380

4th Kentucky Derby, May 21, 1878

Day Star

$1,500 added. Net to winner $4,050; second $200. 56 nominations.

Horse	Wt.	Fin.	Jockey	Owner
Day Star	100	1	J. Carter	T. J. Nichols
Himyar	100	2	Robinson	B. G. Thomas
Leveler	100	3	Swim	R. H. Owens
Solicitor	100	—	Edward	L. P. Tarlton
McHenry	100	—	James	Gen. Abe Buford
Respond	100	—	Ramey	Rodes & Carr
Burgundy	100	—	L. Jones	J. M. Wooding
Earl of Beaconfield	100	—	Mahoney	A. Straus & Co.
Charlie Bush	100	—	Miller	Jennings & Hunt

Time 2:37¼ (new Derby record). Weather clear, track good.

Winner—Ch.c. by Star Davis—Squeeze-'Em, by Lexington; trained by Lee Paul; bred by J. M. Clay.

Auction Pools: Himyar, $305; Field, $110. With Himyar out, Day Star, Burgundy and Leveler sold about even.

Mutuel wagering introduced in 1878, with four machines operating, but no prices available.

Day Star led from start to finish, winning by two lengths.

Day Star — Stakes Races

AT 2 YEARS — 2ND Sanford Stakes.

AT 3 YEARS — WON Kentucky Derby, Blue Ribbon Stakes.
2ND Clark Stakes.

AT 4 YEARS — 2ND Merchants' Stakes.

Himyar, second in the Derby, raced until he was six, later proved himself an outstanding sire. His sons include Plaudit, winner of the Derby in 1898, and Domino, from whom descend several Derby winners. Himyar's owner, B. G. Thomas, introduced many Turf inovations, including the practice of putting numbers on saddle cloths.

Leveler, third in the Derby, won the Clark Stakes as Day Star and Solicitor deadheated for second place. Pari-mutuels were used for betting at Churchill Downs for the first time in 1878. This form of betting continued in use until 1889, was then discarded until 1908. Since then it has been the only form of betting used at the track.

It was in 1878 that Ten Broeck and Mollie McCarthy met in their match race at Churchill Downs. The date of the race was July 4 and for weeks prior to the event newspapers were filled with every detail of the event.

Thirty thousand people came from throughout the nation to see the unbeaten heroine from California meet the pride of Kentucky. As the two horses came onto the track the spectators scrambled for any point of vantage. Barn roofs were masses of people. Tree limbs groaned under the weight of younger men.

Mollie McCarthy led at the end of the first of the four miles. She was a neck in front at the end of the second. But after the third mile Ten Broeck was ten lengths in front, and the mare quit entirely in the last mile.

A band entertained the Derby crowd with Southern airs as the field of nine horses paraded out of the Churchill Downs paddock for the fourth running of the Kentucky Derby on May 21, 1878. Watching the parade was the largest crowd in the history of the race. Between six and eight thousand persons took advantage of the free centerfield.

Nineteen cars made up the special train run by the Short Line Railroad which aided in bringing the Derby visitors to Churchill Downs. The weather was bright and clear and the track was good for the race.

Favorite in the field was Barak G. Thomas' Himyar, which had won three of his five starts and $2,200 as a two-year-old. Thomas, one of the outstanding Thoroughbred breeders of Kentucky, spent the night before the Derby sleeping in the stall with his colt.

The rest of the starters were grouped in the field and sold for $110, against $305 for Himyar. With the favorite barred from pools, Day Star, Burgundy, and Leveler sold about even.

T. J. Nichols, owner of the winner, had purchased Day Star for $825 when the colt was a yearling. This marked the second time Nichols, a resident of Bourbon County, Kentucky, had purchased a Kentucky Derby winner as a yearling. In 1874 he had purchased Vagrant, winner in 1876, when that son of Virgil was a yearling, but he later sold him.

Day Star, a son of Star Davis, was bred by John M. Clay, son of Henry Clay, at the Clay estate, Ashland, near Lexington. While the elder Clay had established Ashland Stud, his son took a much keener interest in the breeding of horses. It was also at Ashland that Major Thomas Clay McDowell, great-grandson of Henry Clay, bred the Derby winner Alan-a-Dale.

Day Star did not race at two, but did campaign through his seven-year-old season. He won eleven of his forty races, raced over steeplechase and hurdle courses at six and seven. Day Star won both steeplechase and hurdle races. His race in the Derby was described as the best race ever seen in America.

1879

In 1879 came the birth of what has become one of America's best known store fronts, the five-and ten-center. It was at Lancaster, Pennsylvania, on June 21, 1879, that F. W. Woolworth opened the first store of this kind in the United States. A view of the store is shown above.

Louisville got its first telephone exchange the same year. The photograph at the bottom of the page shows a view of a telephone exchange of that time.

Jacob Ritty, of Dayton, produced the first cash register in 1879. He got the idea for his invention from watching a device that recorded the revolutions of the propeller on a steamboat. His invention was taken over in 1884 by John H. Patterson, who founded the National Cash Register Company.

At Boston in 1879 was organized the First Church of Christ, Scientist. The organizer was Mary Baker Eddy, who has the distinction of being the only woman to establish a great religious faith.

Branches of the church spread throughout the United States and to foreign countries. The original church building, however, was not built until 1894 and was erected in Boston. It was greatly enlarged in 1904.

On November 4, 1879, Thomas A. Edison filed patent for his incandescent electric lamp, which on October 21 of that year had maintained incandescence for more than forty hours.

Frances Elizabeth Willard was elected president of the Chicago Women's Central Temperance Union. She was instrumental in making this organization, established in 1874, worldwide in membership in 1883. She was named national president in 1891.

Pedigree

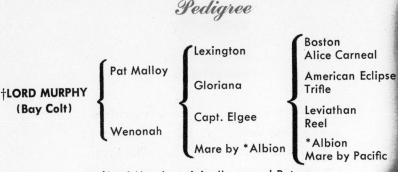

†LORD MURPHY
(Bay Colt)

- Pat Malloy
  - Lexington
    - Boston
    - Alice Carneal
  - Gloriana
    - American Eclipse
    - Trifle
- Wenonah
  - Capt. Elgee
    - Leviathan
    - Reel
  - Mare by *Albion
    - *Albion
    - Mare by Pacific

†Lord Murphy originally named Patmus.

Lord Murphy

Tabulated Racing Record

Year	Age	Sts.	1st	2nd	3rd	Won
1878	2	4	1	2	0	$ 350
1879	3	8	5	3	0	11,050
1880	4	1	0	0	0	...
1881	5	1	0	0	0	...
		14	6	5	0	$ 11,400

5th Kentucky Derby, May 20, 1879

$1,500 added. Net to winner $3,550; second $200. 46 nominations.

Horse		Wt.	Fin.	Jockey	Owner
Lord Murphy		100	1	Shauer	Geo. W. Darden & Co.
Falsetto		100	2	I. Murphy	J. W. H. Reynolds
Strathmore		100	3	Hightower	George Cadwillader
Also ran	Trinidad	100	—	Allen	D. Swigert
	One Dime	100	—	Jones	G. W. Bowen & Co.
	General Pike	100	—	Stoval	Gen. Abe Buford
	Buckner	100	—	Edwards	H. W. Farris
	Wissahicken	97	—	Hawkins	H. P. McGrath
	Ada Glen	97	—	Ramie	G. D. Wilson

Time 2:37 (new Derby record). Weather clear, track fast.

Winner—B.c. by Pat Malloy—Wenonah, by Capt. Elgee; trained by George Rice; bred by J. T. Carter.

Auction Pools: Lord Murphy, $175; Strathmore and Falsetto, $60 each; Trinadad, $45; Ada Glen, $25; Field, $30.

Mutuel tickets sold, but no payoff prices available.

General Pike and Trinidad broke together, and ran head and head to the first turn, with Strathmore, third; Falsetto, fourth; Buckner, fifth. Trying to move up at the turn, Lord Murphy was bumped by a swerving horse, almost knocked to his knees, recovered, and then, from far back, charged at the field, gained the lead on the back stretch, and won by a length, under a hard drive.

Lord Murphy   *Stakes Races*

AT 2 YEARS	2ND	Young America Stakes, Nashville Sweepstakes.
	UNP	Flash Stakes.
AT 3 YEARS	WON	Kentucky Derby, St. Leger Stakes, January Stakes, Bellemeade Stakes.
	2ND	Dixie Stakes, Trial Stakes, Illinois Derby.
AT 4 YEARS	UNP	Chatsworth Plate (England).
AT 5 YEARS	4TH	Newmarket Visitor's Plate (England).

Falsetto, second to Lord Murphy, was the second horse to sire three winners of the Churchill Downs race. His Derby-winning sons were Chant in 1894, His Eminence in 1901, and Sir Huon in 1906. Virgil was the first sire with three winners. *Sir Gallahad III is the only other horse with a similar record.

Bred by J. T. Carter, Lord Murphy was foaled in Summer County, Tennessee. He was purchased by the George Darden & Co., for $400 as a yearling. Sensation was the two-year-old champion of the 1879 racing season.

The well groomed man attending the Kentucky Derby always wore a Derby hat. Even those less well groomed came wearing a Derby if they could obtain one. It was about thirty-five years ago that the Derby began to lose favor as the popular Derby Day headgear.

Not even the Kentucky Derby, which had in a few years taken its place as one of the greatest American racing classics, had offered anything like the race it promised for the 1879 renewal. It was Kentucky against Tennessee: Falsetto against Lord Murphy.

In session at Louisville during Derby time was the Southern Presbyterian convention. It has never been determined how many men bid their families goodbye, saying they were going to Louisville to hear Reverend Henry Ward Beecher, but nodded to their cronies that they would be among those present when Lord Murphy went against Falsetto.

Falsetto, a son of Enquirer, was owned by J. W. Hunt Reynolds, of Frankfort, Kentucky. Lord Murphy, a son of Pat Malloy, was the property of George W. Darden & Co., of Tennessee. The first four winners of the Kentucky Derby had been foaled in Kentucky. Lord Murphy was born in Tennessee, the first of three Derby winners bred in that state, and the first of thirteen winners of America's racing classic born outside Kentucky.

Derby eve found the famous Galt House at Louisville crowded to its capacity. Turfmen from throughout the country were gathered there, participating in the Derby pools which were being sold. Lord Murphy was the favorite. He sold for $175, while Falsetto and Strathmore were equal choices, selling at $60 each.

Lord Murphy's time of 2:37 for the mile and one-half established a new record for that distance at Churchill Downs. It was the second time that Aristides' Derby mark had been broken. In 1878 Day Star had run the Derby distance in 2:37 1/4, which was a full half-second faster than Aristides' time. The latter's record, when made, was the fastest mile and one-half ever run in America by a three-year-old carrying 100 pounds.

At Churchill Downs, Lord Murphy also won the St. Leger Stakes. He was later sold to James R. Keene, one of America's most successful Thoroughbred breeders. For Keene, the Derby winner was second in the Dixie Stakes, Trial Stakes, and Illinois Derby, raced in England at four and five. Lord Murphy made only one start each year he was abroad, finishing unplaced in both races.

1880

Football had been introduced to Eastern colleges earlier, but the first football game west of the Allegheny Mountains was played in 1880 at Lexington, Kentucky. The competing teams were those of Transylvania University, located at Lexington, and Central University (now Centre College), located at Richmond, Kentucky.

The game was played at the City Park, which is now the site of the University of Kentucky stadium. Among the players was John Fox, Jr., the writer. It

A new era in American living was dawning. Fine mansions were going up on New York's Fifth Avenue. Plumbing was becoming general, and the bathtub was no longer an oddity. Transcontinental train service was being completed, and the entertainment field greeted William Frederick Cody's famous "Buffalo Bill Wild West Shows."

The tenth census of the United States was taken in 1880 and gave the population of the country at 50,155,789. This was the year of the birth of Helen Keller, who became famous as a writer and lec-

was in this year that Walter Camp, of Yale, persuaded delegates to a football convention to agree to a rule permitting eleven players on each team.

The Louisville and Nashville Railroad was particularly proud of the engine shown in the photograph on this page. It was the latest thing in locomotives and aided in bringing the Kentucky Derby visitors to Louisville.

This engine did not cost the railroad anything. No. 1, or the "E. D. Standiford," named in honor of the president of the railroad, was a gift to L. & N. in 1879 by the Rogers Locomotive Works in consideration of a large contract placed with them by the road. The locomotive was a 4-4-0 or American-type passenger engine and was constructed from plans furnished by the railroad.

turer. She was credited with raising $1,000,000 for the American Foundation for the Blind. Miss Keller herself was blind.

On December 20 a switch was thrown lighting New York's Broadway with the Brush system which was the latest thing in street lights. In 1880 George Eastman developed the transparent photograph film.

Frank and Jesse James were blamed for the Mammoth Cave stagecoach robbery in Kentucky. The holdup took place near Cave City, Kentucky, and the loot included $836 in cash and one watch.

The desk used by Thomas Jefferson when he wrote the Constitution of the United States was presented as a gift to Congress. It was turned over to the state department.

Pedigree

Fonso

FONSO (Chestnut Colt)	King Alfonso	*Phaeton	King Tom / Merry Sunshine
		Capitola	Vandal / Mare by *Margrave
	*Weatherwitch	Weatherbit	Sheet Anchor / Miss Letty
		Mare by Birdcatcher	Birdcatcher / Colocynth

Tabulated Racing Record

Year	Age	Sts.	1st	2nd	3rd	Won
1879	2	9	3	2	2	$ 2,125
1880	3	3	2	1	0	6,050
		12	5	3	2	$ 8,175

6th Kentucky Derby, May 18, 1880

$1,500 added. Net to winner $3,800; second $200. 47 nominations.

Horse	Wt.	Fin.	Jockey	Owner
Fonso	105	1	G. Lewis	J. S. Shawhan
Kimball	105	2	Lakeland	W. Cottrill
Bancroft	105	3	I. Murphy	M. Young
Also ran { Boulevard	105	—	Allen	W. C. McGavock & Co.
Quito	105	—	McLaughlin	Dwyer Bros.

Time 2:37½. Weather clear, track fast.

Winner—Ch.c. by King Alfonso—*Weatherwitch, by Weatherbit; trained by Tice Hutsell; bred by A. J. Alexander.

Auction Pools: Kimball, $700; Quito, $362; Fonso, $222; Bancroft, $50; Boulevard was not sold because he was not announced as a starter until after the weighing-in bell was rung.

Mutuel tickets sold, but no payoff prices available.

This Derby was run in dust many inches deep, and dust kicked up by leading horse practically obscured the nearest pursuers. Fonso broke in front and stayed there, winning by a length; Kimball was always second, and Bancroft always third. Foul claimed lodged by Kimball's jockey against Fonso, not allowed.

Fonso — Stakes Races

AT 2 YEARS
- WON — Maiden Stakes, Colt Stakes.
- 2ND — Tennessee Stakes.
- 3RD — Bellemeade Stakes, Colt and Filly Stakes.

AT 3 YEARS
- WON — Kentucky Derby, Phoenix Stakes.
- 2ND — Viley Stakes.

In the early days of Woodburn Farm, which produced five winners of the Kentucky Derby, not all the yearlings were sold. R. A. Alexander wanted to keep his best for breeding purposes and sell the rest. However, he found the yearlings brought better prices if none were held out. Consequently, Woodburn started offering all its yearlings.

The sales attracted to Woodburn the country's most successful horsemen, including August Belmont, Pierre and George Lorillard, M. H. Sanford, Colonel David McDaniel, Major Thomas Doswell, William Astor, James R. Keene, Colonel Milton Young, the Dwyer Brothers, and others.

Today yearlings to be offered for sale usually are groomed and kept indoors for weeks prior to sale time. Moreover, the sales companies of today cater to the comfort of the buyers. At Woodburn the yearlings ran out until sales times, collecting burrs in their manes and tails, and the buyers found no comfortable seats awaiting them. They stood under the trees or sat on the grass.

When the great Lexington died at Woodburn Stud in 1875, he was replaced by King Alfonso who entered the stud at the famous nursery in 1876. In the first season King Alfonso was at stud at Woodburn Farm he was mated with *Weatherwitch.

From this breeding came the 1880 Kentucky Derby winner Fonso. It was from the Woodburn yearling sales of 1878 that J. S. Shawhan purchased the chestnut yearling son of King Alfonso and *Weatherwitch for $200. In the same sale George Lorillard had to pay top price of the Woodburn auctions to get Grenada, also by King Alfonso and out of Mattie Gross.

Fonso came out nine times as a two-year-old, winning three races, was second twice, and third in two of his starts. He raced early in the year, winning the Maiden Stakes at Nashville. His only other stakes win at two was the Colt Stakes at Lexington. He was second in the Tennessee Stakes, third in the Bellemeade Stakes at Churchill Downs and the Colt and Filly Stakes at Lexington.

In his three-year-old season Fonso started in and won the Phoenix Stakes at Lexington prior to the Kentucky Derby. His only other start at three, which was the last season he raced, was in the Viley Stakes at Lexington in the fall.

Although he won by a length, Fonso was forced to withstand a strong challenge from the favorite, Kimball, in the stretch. After running the first mile in 1:46 1/4, Fonso turned into the stretch with a length lead. Then Kimball moved up to challenge and raced almost head and head with the winner until the latter pulled away nearing the finish.

With tears streaming down his face, Jockey Billy Lakeland rushed to the judges after the race to claim a foul. "He bumped me at the head of the stretch," declared Lakeland. The claim was not allowed, and the official sign went up.

When Hindoo won the 1881 Derby, it was a daughter of *Weatherwitch, dam of Fonso, which produced the winner.

General James A. Garfield, shown at right, became the twentieth President of the United States in 1881. He had been chosen the Republican Party's nominee the preceding year after an effort to run President Grant for a third term had failed. His election and resulting bitterness led to the resignation of New York's two Senators, Conkling and Platt.

Resignation of the Senators was followed in two weeks by the fatal shooting of President Garfield on

July 2 in Washington's Baltimore and Potomac railroad station. An artist's drawing of the shooting is shown in this column. Charles Guiteau, a fanatic of the other division of the Republican party, shot Garfield.

The President died on September 19, the second man to be killed while holding that office. He was succeeded by Chester A. Arthur, prominent in New York politics, who is shown lower right.

In 1881 the first public electric utilities service was started in Louisville.

There was considerable excitement in the city when an English draft for 1,000 pounds was lost at Eighth and Market streets. The draft was returned to its owner by a small Negro boy who had found it.

Two well known organizations had their founding in this year. On February 2 at Portland, Maine, Reverend Francis E. Clark organized the first Christian Endeavor Society. The other organization was the American Federation of Labor, which was established as the Federation of Organized Trades and Labor Unions of the United States and Canada.

Also founded during 1881 was the American Red Cross. Clara Barton was named president of the organization when it was established at Washington on July 1.

On October 19, 1881, the United States celebrated the one hundredth anniversary of the surrender of Lord Cornwallis in the Revolutionary War. The principal celebration was held at Yorktown, Virginia, which was the scene of the surrender. A bronze statue of Admiral Farragut was unveiled in Washington, D. C. The

American Society of Mechanical Engineers was organized in New York. The total national debt in 1881 was $2,120,-415,370.63.

Pedigree

HINDOO (Bay colt)	Virgil	Vandal	*Glencoe Mare by *Tranby
		Hymenia	*Yorkshire Little Peggy
	Florence	Lexington	Boston Alice Carneal
		*Weatherwitch	Weatherbit Mare by Birdcatcher

Tabulated Racing Record

Year	Age	Sts.	1st	2nd	3rd	Won
1880	2	9	7	1	1	$ 9,800
1881	3	20	18	1	1	$ 49,100
1882	4	6	5	1	0	12,975
		35	30	3	2	$ 71,875

7th Kentucky Derby, May 17, 1881

Hindoo

$1,500 added. Net to winner $4,410; second $200. 62 nominations.

Horse	Wt.	Fin.	Jockey	Owner
Hindoo	105	1	J. McLaughlin	Dwyer Bros
Lelex	105	2	A. Allen	B. G. Thomas
Alfambra	105	3	G. Evans	G. W. Bowen & Co.
Also ran — Sligo	105	—	Donohue	H. P. McGrath
Getaway	105	—	Fisher	M. Young
Calycanthus	105	—	G. Smith	H. P. McGrath

Time 2:40. Weather clear, track fast.

Winner—B.c. by Virgil—Florence, by Lexington; trained by James Rowe, Sr.; bred by Daniel Swigert.

Auction Pools: Hindoo, $600; Lelex, $75; McGrath Entry (Sligo and Calycanthus), $70; Alfambra, $40; Getaway, $25.

Mutuel tickets sold, but no payoff prices availoble.

Hindoo went to the front with the break. At one time or another, every horse came up to challenge him, but Hindoo shook them off, almost without effort, merely galloped through the stretch, and won by four lengths, eased up.

Hindoo — Stakes Races

AT 2 YEARS
- WON: Colt and Filly Stakes, Alexander Stakes, Tennessee Stakes, Juvenile Stakes, Jockey Club Stakes, Criterion Stakes, Tremont Stakes.
- 2ND: Day Boat Line Stakes.
- 3RD: Windsor Hotel Stakes.

AT 3 YEARS
- WON: Blue Ribbon Stakes, Kentucky Derby, Clark Stakes, Tidal Stakes, Coney Stakes, Ocean Stakes, Lorillard Stakes, Monmouth Sweepstakes, Travers Stakes, Sequel Stakes, U. S. Hotel Stakes, Kenner Stakes, Champion Stakes, New Jersey St. Leger Stakes.
- 2ND: Brighton Beach Handicap.
- 3RD: September Handicap.

AT 4 YEARS
- WON: Louisville Cup, Merchants' Stakes, Turf Handicap, Coney Island Handicap, Coney Island Cup.
- 2ND: Dixiana Stakes.

Visitors to Louisville for the Derby received welcome news through handbills which were distributed throughout the city the day prior to the race. They announced that all roads leading to the track would be amply watered on Derby Day to keep the dust down.

It was 1915, or thirty-four years later, before Trainer Rowe saddled his second Derby winner. Since then four men have trained as many as two winners, but none had trained his first in 1915 when Regret won.

Hindoo's time of 2:40 for the 1881 Kentucky Derby is accepted as official, but it was not the colt's actual running time. The man throwing the flag dropped it at the tap of the starting drum instead of when the horses passed the official starting pole. All races are started several feet back of the official starting point to enable horses to be in full stride at the official starting point. Dropping of the flag is a signal for timers to start their watches.

Every type of conveyance, from the cart to the splendid coach and tandem, carried the tremendous crowd to Churchill Downs for the seventh running of the Kentucky Derby on May 17, 1881. All stands, the betting enclosure, and the entire grounds were inconveniently crowded by those who wanted to see the great Hindoo in action.

For $15,000 the son of Virgil had been purchased by the Dwyer Brothers in the fall of his two-year-old season. In 1880 Hindoo had won seven of his nine starts, was second and third in the other two. He had started once prior to the Derby, winning the Blue Ribbon Stakes at Lexington.

Five other three-year-olds faced Hindoo at the start. At one time or another all five attempted to challenge Hindoo, but he held them all off and won easily, giving Trainer James Rowe, Sr., his first of two Derby victories. The Derby was the second of eighteen straight victories for Hindoo as a three-year-old. Hindoo was the first horse to win both the Derby and Clark Stakes.

He was the leading money-winner of the year. Describing him, one Turf writer of the day said, "He lived in an age of Turftitans. He battled with giants and more than held his own." In his other two starts at three Hindoo was once second and once third.

He raced again at four, winning five of his six races, and finishing second in the other. His four-year-old campaign is deserving of more than passing attention. In his first start at that age he was beaten in the Dixiana Stakes at Churchill Downs. Two days later he won the Louisville Cup at two and one-quarter miles; four days later he won the Merchants' Handicap at one and one-eighth miles, and after another four-day rest he won the Turf Stakes at one and one-quarter miles.

In one of his races at three, Hindoo's owners bet $9,000 to win $1,000. No one will question the statement that Hindoo was one of the greatest race horses ever to win the Kentucky Derby and one of the best seen in America. He also was very successful as a sire. After his racing career he was sold to Clay and Woodford.

The first attempt to build the Panama Canal was started in 1882 by a French Company. In charge of the work was Ferdinand de Lesseps, who had completed the Suez Canal in 1869. For seven years the work was continued. Then the company went bankrupt. During the seven years 22,000 men had died of disease. In the photograph below is shown a portion of the tremendous amount of machinery and equipment abandoned at the site of the Canal.

During 1882 a total of 788,992 immigrants entered the United States. This was the largest number until 1903. Chinese immigration presented the gravest problem. It had become a major concern on the Pacific coast.

As a result Congress passed an act in 1882 that excluded Chinese laborers for a period of ten years. This temporary exclusion was extended in 1892 and eventually became the permanent policy of the government.

A Cincinnati banker and grocer, Bernard Henry Kroger, founded the Kroger Grocery and Baking Company in 1882. This company grew into the nationwide chain which today bears his name. It was also in the same year that the first hydroelectric station in the United States was opened, at Appleton, Wisconsin. Louisville celebrated the completion of the steamboat Will S. Hays, one of the finest on the Ohio River The boat was named in honor of the river editor of Louisville's Courier-Journal.

On January 30 of this year at Hyde Park, New York, was born Franklin Delano Roosevelt. Fifty years later he was elected President of the United States after having served as Governor of New York and in other important political posts. The country lost two outstanding men of the literary field. They were Henry Wadsworth Longfellow, who died on March 24, and Ralph Waldo Emerson, who died on April 27.

Pedigree

APOLLO (Chestnut Gelding)	‡Lever	Lexington	Boston / Alice Carneal
		Levity	*Trustee / Mare by *Tranby
	Rebecca T. Price	The Colonel	Albion / Lalla Rookh
		Mare by *Margrave	*Margrave / Rosalie Somers

‡ by *Ashstead or Lever

Tabulated Racing Record

Year	Age	Sts.	1st	2nd	3rd	Won
1881	2	0	0	0	0	$ ...
1882	3	21	10	7	3	14,030
1883	4	30	14	7	6	7,600
1884	5	4	0	1	0	50
		55	24	15	9	$ 21,680

Apollo

8th Kentucky Derby, May 16, 1882

$1,500 added. Net to winner $4,560; second $200. 64 nominations.

Horse		Wt.	Fin.	Jockey	Owner
Apollo		102	1	B. Hurd	Morris & Patton
Runnymede		105	2	J. McLaughlin	Dwyer Bros.
Bengal		105	3	S. Fisher	Bowen & Co.
	Wendover	105	—	Hovey	J. B. Sellers & Co.
	Harry Gilmore	105	—	Gibbs	W. Cottrill
	Ch. c. by Pat Malloy	105	—	Henderson	P. C. Fox
	Robt. Bruce	105	—	L. Jones	A. Jackson
Also	Babcock	102	—	Kelso	W. Lakeland
ran	Newsboy	105	—	Quantrell	T. J. Megibben
	Wallensee	107	—	Parker	Rodes & Carr
	Mistral	105	—	Stoval	L. P. Tarlton
	Lost Cause	102	—	Taylor	M. Young
	Highflyer	105	—	Brown	G. Kuhns & Co.

Time 2:40¼. Weather clear, Track good.

Winner—Ch.g. by *Ashstead or Lever—Rebecca T. Price, by The Colonel; trained by Green B. Morris; bred by Daniel Swigert.

(Three forms of betting in operation, bookmaking odds being quoted for first time.)

Auction Pools: Runnymede, $250; Mistral, $50; Lost Cause, $40; Robert Bruce, $30; Bengal, $75; Field (with Apollo included), $75.

Bookmaking odds: Runnymeade, 4 to 5, favorite; Apollo, 10 to 1.

Mutuels: $5 win tickets on Apollo paid $169. No place tickets sold.

Harry Gilmore broke in front, followed by Babcock, the Pat Malloy colt and Robert Bruce. At the mile, Harry Gilmore was still on top, with Runnymede moving on the outside to take third place. As they were well into the stretch, Runnymede took command, and looked like the winner until Apollo started a cyclonic rush an eighth of a mile from home. Apollo caught Runnymede a few jumps from the wire, and won by half a length.

Apollo   Stakes Races

AT 3 YEARS	WON	Kentucky Derby, Cottrill Stakes, Coal Stakes, St. Leger Stakes, Drummers Stakes, Montgomery Stakes.
	2ND	Kenner Stakes, U. S. Hotel Stakes, Glass Stakes, Pickwick Stakes.
	3RD	Clark Stakes.
AT 4 YEARS	2ND	Cotton Stakes, Howard Cup.
	3RD	Excelsior Stakes, Tennessee Club Post Stakes.
	4TH	Champion Stakes.
AT 5 YEARS	UNP	Wheeler Stakes.

As a four-year-old in 1882 Hindoo, winner of the preceding year's Kentucky Derby, on May 19 ran two and one-quarter miles over the Churchill Downs track in 3:57 3/4.

For the eighth running of the Kentucky Derby the seating capacity of the Churchill Downs was almost doubled. A steeplechase course was laid out in the track's centerfield. Good weather prevailed for the Derby, but the track was decidedly soft and heavy. Bookmaking was used for wagering at Churchill Downs for the first time.

Sixty-four three-year-olds were nominated for the 1882 running of the Kentucky Derby. It was the largest field ever named for the race and the fourteen starters that went to the post on May 16, made the field second in size only to the fifteen which had started in the first running of the race. It is also larger than any field attracted by the race until sixteen started in 1915.

Outstanding favorite was Runnymede, owned by the Dwyer Brothers who had won the preceding year with Hindoo. Runnymede sold in the auction pools for $250, while Mistrial sold for $50, Lost Cause for $40, Robert Bruce for $30, Bengal for $75, and the other nine starters, grouped as the field, sold for $75.

The owner of the 1881 winner was unable to repeat in the eighth running of the race. However, the breeder of Hindoo stretched his record to two straight. Apollo, the winner, was bred by Daniel Swigert, of Fayette County, as had been Hindoo. Morris and Patton, owners of the winner, had purchased Apollo for $800.

The son of *Ashtead or Lever (when a mare is bred to two stallions, the second sire is given credit for the foal) was the second grandson of Lexington to win. Lever was a son of Lexington, as had been Pat Malloy, sire of the 1879 winner Lord Murphy.

Apollo had not started during his two-year-old season, but started racing at three. Prior to shipping to Louisville he had won the Drummers Stakes at Little Rock, Cottrell Stakes at New Orleans, and Montgomery Stakes at Memphis. It is unusual for a horse to win stakes at three different tracks as a three-year-old prior to the Kentucky Derby.

The 1882 winner raced two more seasons. As a four-year-old he won fourteen races, nine of them in succession. He started thirty times during that year. His five-year-old racing was limited to four starts, his best effort being a second.

After being beaten in the Derby, Runnymede won the Clark Stakes in which Apollo was third. The latter won the St. Leger at Churchill Downs.

One of America's truly great landmarks was opened in 1883. This was Brooklyn Bridge. The drawing at the right shows part of the celebration marking the opening of the bridge which connects the two New York City boroughs. At the time of the opening the five boroughs now comprising New York City had not been united.

When New York City and Brooklyn decided to construct the span, John A. Roebling worked hard and was finally able to convince them to make it a suspension bridge and to award the contract to him. Years passed as foundations for the great bridge were poured and cables were spun. The span was completed by his son.

The father had spent his entire life selling the suspension-bridge idea. It had not been easy, especially since some engineers had declared his railroad bridge, completed across the Niagara gorge in 1855, was shaky.

Among Kentucky's more famous Turfmen of this period was Frank Harper, shown at the head of his noted Longfellow in the photograph at lower left. Harper owned Nantura Stud in Woodford County where both Longfellow and Ten Broeck stood as sires and where both are buried.

The world lost an outstanding composer in 1883 with the death of Richard

Wagner. This also was the year that the United States passed the Civil Service Reform Act and passed a new tariff act.

President Arthur was present in Louisville to open the Southern Exposition. The exposition building erected for this event was described as "a masterpiece."

John Joseph Montgomery, professor at California's Santa Clara College, claimed the distinction of making the world's first glider flight. In his first effort the professor covered 100 feet. Santa Fe, New Mexico, celebrated its 333rd anniversary. In Montana Henry Villard drove the final spike in the transcontinental track of the Northern Pacific Railroad.

Karl Marx died March 14 and a few days later a great mass meeting was held in New York City's Cooper Union to honor his memory. At Cincinnati the Ohio River flooded to a height sixty feet above normal level. The year 1883 also was marked by the nation's railroads adopting standard time on November 13 and a strike of the country's telegraph operators.

Pedigree

Leonatus

LEONATUS (Bay colt)			
Longfellow	*Leamington	Faugh-a-Ballagh	Mare by Pantaloon
	Nantura	Brawner's Eclipse	Queen Mary
Semper Felix	*Phaeton	King Tom	Merry Sunshine
	Crucifix	Lexington	Lightsome

Tabulated Racing Record

Year	Age	Sts.	1st	2nd	3rd	Won
1882	2	1	0	1	0	$ 100
1883	3	10	10	0	0	21,335
		11	10	1	0	$ 21,435

9th Kentucky Derby, May 23, 1883

$1,500 added. Net to winner $3,760; second $200. 50 nominations.

Horse	Wt.	Fin.	Jockey	Owner
Leonatus	105	1	W. Donohue	Chinn & Morgan
Drake Carter	102	2	Spellman	Morris & Patton
Lord Ragland	105	3	Quantrell	N. Armstrong
Also ran { Ascender	102	—	Stoval	R. C. Pate
Pike's Pride	102	—	Evans	George Evans
Chatter	105	—	Henderson	W. C. McCurdy
Standiford Keller	105	—	Blaylock	J. R. Watt

Time 2:43.   Weather drizzling, track heavy.

Winner—B.c. by Longfellow—Semper Felix, by *Phaeton; trained by R. Colston; bred by John Henry Miller.

Auction Pools: Leonatus, $800; Ascender, $500; Drake Carter, $450; Field $500.

Bookmaking Odds: Bookmakers operated, but prices not available.

Mutuels: $5 win ticket on Leonatus paid $14.80—odds of 1.96 to 1.

Drake Carter was away first, but Leonatus caught him during the first quarter, and never was headed, winning by three lengths.

Leonatus — Stakes Races

AT 2 YEARS	2ND	Maiden Stakes.
AT 3 YEARS	WON	Kentucky Derby, Blue Ribbon Stakes, Tobacco Stakes, Woodburn Stakes, Hindoo Stakes, Ripple Stakes, Himyar Stakes, Dearborn Stakes, Green Stakes, Illinois Derby.

Vast improvements, directed by Colonel M. Lewis Clark, president of the Louisville Jockey Club, were made at Churchill Downs for the 1883 Derby. They resulted in descriptions of the plant as "the best arranged and most complete course in the country." On March 15, 1883, the great race mare Mollie McCarthy, winner of fifteen of her seventeen races, died at Santa Anita Stud.

Jockey Billy Donohue, who rode the winner, was reported to have bet his life savings on Leonatus to win the Derby. Apollo, winner of the previous Derby, was the winner of the second race on the 1883 Derby Day card, gaining a nose decision after the winner of the first race had paid $233.20 in the pari-mutuels.

Derby Day breakfasts at the track were becoming popular with racing patrons. Following breakfast the morning was spent in inspecting horses that were to start in the Derby that afternoon.

Leonatus was the first of two sons of Longfellow to win the Derby. The other was Riley. Pink Star, Derby winner in 1907, was a grandson of the 1883 winner.

The owners of Leonatus were residents of Harrodsburg, Kentucky, and the only other horse they started in the Kentucky Derby was named Harrodsburg. He ran eighth to Ben Ali in the 1886 Derby.

Leonatus came out at Churchill Downs on September 20, 1882, in the Maiden Stakes for his only start as a two-year-old. He was second, beaten two lengths, racing in the silks of his breeder and then owner, J. H. Miller.

The next appearance of the son of Longfellow was during the spring meeting at Lexington in the spring of 1883. Leonatus in that race, at one and one-half miles, carried the colors of Chinn and Morgan, who had paid $5,000 for the colt. It was an extremely good purchase on the part of his new owners.

The Lexington race was the Blue Ribbon Stakes which the colt won easily under 105 pounds. Six days later he won the Kentucky Derby by three lengths. Five days after the Derby Leonatus went to the post in the Tobacco Stakes, an event of mile heats. He won easily.

The Tobacco Stakes marked the first time Leonatus was ridden by Isaac Murphy, who three days later, on May 31, won the Woodburn Stakes at one and one-eighth miles over the Louisville track. From Louisville, Leonatus was shipped to Latonia where on June 9 Murphy rode him to victory in the Hindoo Stakes (later renamed the Latonia Derby); then on June 13 he won the Ripple Stakes at one and one-quarter miles.

Two days later Leonatus came back to win the Himyar Stakes at one and three-eighths miles. From Latonia the colt went to Chicago where he won the Dearborn Stakes at one and three-quarter miles on July 2, the Green Stakes at one and one-eighth miles on July 4, and the Illinois Derby at one and one-half miles on July 5. From Chicago Leonatus was shipped East where he broke down. He did not start again.

He had won all ten starts at three and had been second in his only start at two. Leonatus was the first of two winners of the Derby sired by Longfellow. The stallion was owned by Frank Harper, of Nantura Stud in Woodford County, Kentucky, and later sired the 1890 winner Riley. At Nantura to mark the graves of Longfellow and Ten Broeck, Harper erected what are said to be the first tombstones ever placed over the graves of horses in this country.

1884

A drop in Wall Street stocks during 1884 caused concern to the nation, and perhaps the sextet of cyclists shown in the photograph below were on their way to the exchange when their picture was taken. They look solemn enough.

Nationally, the year was marked by the Presidential campaign between Grover Cleveland and James G. Blaine. Blaine, a popular man for years and secretary of state under Garfield and Arthur, could not be denied the nomination in the Republican convention of 1884. His selection, however, was denounced by the Mugwumps, who told the Democrats they would support the latter's candidate if he were honest and independent.

For their Presidential candidate the Democrats selected Governor Cleveland of New York, who had formerly been mayor of Buffalo and had established a reputation as an outstanding public official. The campaign was a mud-slinging one from start to finish. Each party attacked the private life of the other party's candidate.

The election was extremely close. Cleveland received 4,874,986 of the popular vote, Blaine 4,851,981. It was New York's vote which decided the election, and Cleveland carried the state by 1,149 votes. It marked the first time in twenty-eight years that a Democrat had occupied the White House.

England was having difficulty with dynamiters, who attempted to blow up both the Times office and London Bridge. An international conference in Washington adopted the Meridian of Greenwich as the universal prime meridian. New Orleans opened its Cotton Exposition.

The Washington Monument in the nation's capital was completed December 6, 1884. In April natural gas had been discovered at Pittsburgh. The American Historical Society was founded in Washington. Iowa adopted statewide prohibition. Standard time was adopted by the entire country. Cyrus Hall McCormick, inventor of the reaper, died during the year.

Mrs. Belva Lockwood, of Washington, D. C., accepted the nomination of the California Women's Rights Convention for the Presidency.

Pedigree

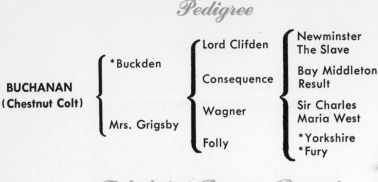

BUCHANAN
(Chestnut Colt)

- *Buckden
  - Lord Clifden
    - Newminster
    - The Slave
  - Consequence
    - Bay Middleton
    - Result
- Mrs. Grigsby
  - Wagner
    - Sir Charles
    - Maria West
  - Folly
    - *Yorkshire
    - *Fury

Tabulated Racing Record

Year	Age	Sts.	1st	2nd	3rd	Won
1883	2	6	0	5	1	$ 500
1884	3	5	3	0	2	9,385
1885	4	13	3	5	2	2,100
1886	5	11	2	4	5	1,125
		35	8	14	10	$ 13,110

Buchanan

10th Kentucky Derby, May 16, 1884

$1,500 added. Net to winner $3,990; second $200. 51 nominations.

Horse	Wt.	Fin.	Jockey	Owner
Buchanan	110	1	I. Murphy	W. Cottrill
Loftin	110	2	Sayres	A. Johnson & Co.
Audrain	110	3	Fishburn	T. J. Megibben
Bob Miles	110	—	McLaughlin	J. T. Williams
Admiral	110	—	C. Taylor	Clay & Woodford
Powhattan III	110	—	D. Williams	R. A. Johnson & Co.
Exploit	110	—	Conkling	Wooding & Puryear
Boreas	110	—	O'Brien	R. M. McClelland
Bob Cook	110	—	Gorham	R. M. McClelland

Time 2:40¼. Weather clear, track good.

Winner—Ch.c. by *Buckden—Mrs. Grigsby, by Wagner; trained by William Bird; bred by Cottrill & Guest.

Auction Pools: Audrain, $700; Bob Miles, $600; Buchanan, $530; Loftin (coupled with Powhattan III as R. A. Johnson & Co.'s entry), $270; Admiral, $125; Field $90.

Bookmaking Odds: Bookmakers did not operate on opening day.

Mutuels: $5 win tickets on Buchanan paid $20.60.

Bob Miles beat the flag, and jumped into a two-length lead, followed by Powhattan III, Audrain, the favorite and Admiral. Buchanan fractious at the post, was away poorly, but Isaac Murphy, his Negro jockey, saved ground for three-quarters of a mile, and then Murphy called upon him for his best effort. Buchanan moved to the front quickly, with gigantic strides, was eased up through the final eighth, and won by two lengths.

Buchanan   Stakes Races

AT 2 YEARS
- 2ND Maiden Stakes, Criterion Stakes, St. James Hotel Stakes, Alexander Stakes, Jackson Stakes.
- 3RD Barrett Stakes.

AT 3 YEARS
- WON Kentucky Derby, Ripple Stakes, Clark Stakes.
- 3RD Hindoo Stakes, Bellemeade Stakes.

AT 4 YEARS
- 2ND Brewers' Stakes.

AT 5 YEARS
- 3RD Granite Mountain Stakes.

Bob Miles, an outstanding two-year-old of the preceding season, was the winter book favorite for the 1884 Kentucky Derby, but was second choice to Audrain on Derby Day. Audrain finished third and Bob Miles was unplaced. The latter was owned by James T. Williams, who had tried to buy Hindoo as a yearling. Bob Miles raced a number of years, including steeplechases at Jerome Park. Bob Miles sired the 1899 Derby winner Manuel. Jockey McLaughlin, who rode Bob Miles, had to take off seventeen pounds to make the Derby weight.

Approximately 5,000 people watched the 1884 Derby from the Churchill Downs centerfield. The field of starters was considered inferior to those which had been seen in the first nine runnings of the race. However, one writer covering the race said, "Each year the interest in the Kentucky Derby increases and the desire to win also increases with breeders and owners. It is a mark of merit for the colt who wins to bear off the Blue Ribbon of the Turf."

One of the five races the great Hindoo lost was at Saratoga when he was a two-year-old. William Bird, Negro trainer, was handling a two-year-old named Crickmore, a delicate horse and an extremely light eater. But when Crickmore would eat, he could really run.

Bird gave a friend $100 and told him to bet on Crickmore that afternoon at Saratoga. "But," counselled the friend, "your horse is running against Hindoo and he ain't been beat." Bird only replied, "When Crickmore eats four quarts of oats, he can beat any horse. He ate four quarts last night. Bet that hundred." Crickmore beat Hindoo in the Windsor Hotel Stakes.

Next year at Sheepshead Bay the same thing happened. Hindoo arrived there the winner of eighteen straight races. Bird went up to bet $100 on Crickmore. His friends advised against it. "But Crickmore ate four quarts of oats last night," was reply. Crickmore won the September Handicap as Hindoo was beaten for the first time in nineteen races.

It was the same Negro trainer, Bill Bird, an outstanding trainer for many years, who saddled Buchanan for the 1884 Kentucky Derby. He had trained horses on both sides of the Atlantic, had gone to England with the horses of Richard Ten Broeck as long ago as the 'fifties.

Buchanan, bred by Cottrill and Guest, had been bought by Captain Billy Cottrill while a yearling. He did not win as a two-year-old. At that age he started only in stakes races and never ran worse than third. All his starts at three also were in stakes events, and again he was never unplaced. He continued racing at four and five. In the latter season he started eleven times, won his first and last races that year.

Buchanan was the first of three Derby winners ridden by Jockey Isaac Murphy, who had to be forced to ride the horse known as a bad actor. Murphy had ridden the horse at Nashville where Buchanan bolted, ran off and proved himself almost completely unmanageable. At Louisville the judges threatened to set the jockey down for the meeting if he did not ride the colt. After winning the Derby Buchanan also won the Clark Stakes.

1885

Grover Cleveland, lower left, was inaugurated as the twenty-second President of the United States in 1885. Thomas A. Hendricks took office as Vice President under Cleveland, but served only until November of that year. His death in that month resulted in the passage of the Presidential Succession Act the following year.

Prior to the passage of this legislation, in the event of the death of a President and vice president the office had gone to the president pro tempore of the Senate, and, after him, to the speaker of the house. At the time Cleveland and Hendricks took office the House was Democratic, but the Senate had a Republican majority. The Senate chose Republican John Sherman as its president pro tem, thus placing him in line for the Presidency if Cleveland died.

To prevent this, the Presidential Succession Act provided that the cabinet members, in the order of the creation of

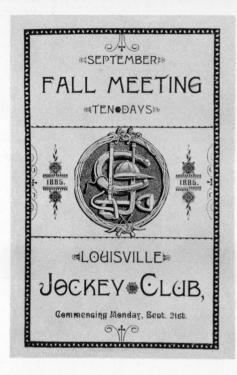

their respective departments, should succeed the vice president. The line of succession established by the act gave the office first to the secretary of state, then to the secretary of treasury, secretary of war, attorney-general, postmaster general, secretary of the navy, and secretary of the interior, provided they were eligible constitutionally.

This order of succession to the Presidency was not changed until July 18, 1947, when President Truman signed a bill placing the speaker of the house next in line to the vice president. Proponents of the 1947 bill argued the office should go to an elected official before going to appointed members of the cabinet. The 1947 act also placed the secretaries of agriculture, commerce, and labor in that order behind the secretary of interior. These cabinet posts had not been created when the 1886 act was passed.

It was in 1885 that Baltimore became the first American city to have an electric railway. In the same year the first chest protector was worn in baseball. The outstanding writers Ring Lardner and Sinclair Lewis were born in 1885.

Pedigree

JOE COTTON (Chestnut colt)	King Alfonso	*Phaeton	King Tom / Merry Sunshine
		Capitola	Vandal / Mare by *Margrave
	*Inverness	Macaroni	Sweetmeat / Jocose
		Elfrida	Faugh-a-Ballagh / Espoir

Joe Cotton

Tabulated Racing Record

Year	Age	Sts.	1st	2nd	3rd	Won
1884	2	12	2	3	1	$ 725
1885	3	11	8	0	1	21,560
1886	4	8	3	0	2	2,455
1887	5	11	3	2	3	3,925
1888	6	10	1	0	0	700
1889	7	2	0	1	0	...
		54	17	6	7	$ 29,365

11th Kentucky Derby, May 14, 1885

$1,500 added. Net to winner $4,630; second $200. 69 nominations.

Horse	Wt.	Fin.	Jockey	Owner
Joe Cotton	110	1	E. Henderson	J. T. Williams
Berson	110	2	West	Morris & Patton
Ten Booker	110	3	Stoval	M. Young
Favor	110	4	Thompkins	Morris & Patton
Irish Pat	110	5	Murphy	E. Corrigan
Keokuk	110	6	Fishbourne	W. P. Hunt
Clay Pete	110	7	Withers	R. C. Pate
Thistle	110	8	Blaylock	P. G. Speth
Playfair	107	9	Conkling	G. W. Darden & Co.
Lord Coleridge	107	10	Hughes	W. Cottrill

Time 2:37¼.   Weather clear, track good.

Winner—Ch.c. by King Alfonso—*Inverness, by Macaroni; trained by Alex Perry; bred by A. J. Alexander.

Auction Pools: Joe Cotton, $500; Bersan and Favor $215 (coupled as Morris & Patton entry); Ten Booker, $75; Irish Pat, $40; Playfair and Thistle, $35 each; Lord Coleridge, $25; Field $30.

Bookmaking Odds: Joe Cotton, even money; Berson, 2 to 1; Ten Booker, 10 to 1.

Mutuels: ($5 win and place betting only): Joe Cotton, $9.30 straight, $8.80 place; Berson, $7.40 place.

Within the first eighth, Favor took the lead, Keokuk, second, the others strung out. They ran that way into the backstretch, where Joe Cotton, in seventh position, started to move. Joe Cotton worked his way to the front, going into the stretch, but had to be ridden to his ultimate effort to stave off the rush of Berson and Ten Booker, who came like whirlwinds in the final eighth.

Joe Cotton   Stakes Races

	2ND	Nursery Stakes, Post Stakes.
AT 2 YEARS	3RD	Hyde Park Stakes.
	UNP	Walnut Hill Stakes, Optional Stakes, Kenwood Stakes.
	WON	Kentucky Derby, Great Western Handicap, Coney Island Derby, Tidal Stakes, Himyar Stakes, Louis and Gus Straus Stakes, Tennessee Derby, Cottrill Stakes.
AT 3 YEARS	3RD	Clark Stakes.
	UNP	Travers Stakes, Oakwood Handicap.
	WON	Farewell Stakes.
AT 4 YEARS	3RD	Fourth of July Handicap.
	UNP	Excelsior Handicap, Suburban Handicap.
AT 5 YEARS	WON	Average Stakes, Twin City Handicap, Welter Stakes.
AT 6 YEARS	UNP	Suburban Handicap.

When Joe Cotton galloped to victory in the 1885 Kentucky Derby he became the third winner of the race to be bred by A. J. Alexander, of Woodford County, Kentucky. Although Alexander bred five winners of the Derby, together with many other brilliant horses, he never owned a starter in the Churchill Downs race.

A commonplace sight at some American race tracks is the hawker of the tip-sheet. Few tracks allow these vendors to sell their "cards" on the track's property. They usually are to be found just outside the premises selling their selections for the day.

It was in 1885 that the first of these cards made their appearance in Kentucky. However, they were not the product of professional clockers as they are today. Instead, they were offered for sale by a group of young boys, who amazed experienced horsemen with their ability to pick winners. When there was a difference in selection of the winner it was usually the youngsters who were right.

Perhaps the practice of Churchill Downs in posting the entries in the various races of the day, together with their respective jockeys, at the entrance gates to the track had something to do with the appearance of the selection cards. In its first ten years, according to one writer of the day, the Kentucky Derby had attracted more ante-race wagering than any other horse race in the country.

Joe Cotton, winner of the eleventh running of the Turf classic, was the first of the Derby winners to race as many as six seasons. He started fifty-four times, including two races at seven. Only Aristides, winner of the first Derby, had raced as many as five seasons, and only Apollo had started more times, running in fifty-five races in his three seasons of campaigning.

Joe Cotton was owned by J. T. Williams, whose Vera Cruz had been left at the post in the 1877 Derby, and whose Bob Miles had been second choice in the 1884 Derby. The 1885 winner had won only two of his twelve starts as a two-year-old, but he was first in his first four races at three, including the Kentucky Derby. However, he was forced to share one of those winning efforts when he ran a deadheat in the Tidal Stakes.

As a five-year-old Joe Cotton started his campaign with a run of three victories in a row. All were in stakes races, but they were the only three races he was able to win during that season. Joe Cotton was the second Derby winner sired by King Alfonso, whose son Fonso had won the 1880 race.

The Statue of Liberty, France's gift to the United States, was unveiled in New York harbor in 1886. Part of the ceremony marking the unveiling is shown in the photograph at the lower left.

The ship in the foreground is the Jamestown, of the United States Navy.

It was in the same year that Kentucky's Trappist Monastery at Gethsemane was consecrated. This is the only Trappist Monastery in the United States and a view of it appears on the left of this page.

The United States lost an outstanding statesman in the death of Charles Francis Adams, who had served as United States Minister to Great Britain during the

War between the States. He was credited with having accomplished a great and very difficult job.

In Australia was born Sister Elizabeth Kenny, who as a nurse became famous for treating infantile paralysis.

This nation's great tragedy of the year came at Chicago in the Haymarket anarchist riots in connection with the strike at the McCormick Reaper Works. Seven policemen were killed by a bomb. Several of the anarchists were executed as a result and another committed suicide while in jail.

At the top of the page is shown the cover of the Churchill Downs condition book of this period.

The young inventor Thomas A. Edison opened a workshop at Schenectady, New York. Joyce Kilmer, the American poet, was born.

Pedigree

BEN ALI
(Brown colt)

- Virgil
  - Vandal
    - *Glencoe
    - Mare by *Tranby
  - Hymenia
    - *Yorkshire
    - Little Peggy
- Ulrica
  - Lexington
    - Boston
    - Alice Carneal
  - *Emilia
    - Young Emilius
    - Persian

Tabulated Racing Record

Year	Age	Sts.	1st	2nd	3rd	Won
1885	2	5	1	0	0	$ 3,340
1886	3	12	7	2	2	18,550
1887	4	17	4	1	0	2,850
1888	5	6	0	0	3	350
		40	12	3	5	$ 25,090

12th Kentucky Derby, May 14, 1886

Ben Ali

$1,500 added. Net to winner $4,890; second $300; third $150. 107 nominations.

Horse	Wt.	Fin.	Jockey	Owner
Ben Ali	118	1	P. Duffy	J. B. Haggin
Blue Wing	118	2	Garrison	Melbourne Stable
Free Knight	118	3	W. Fitzpatrick	P. Corrigan
Lijero	118	4	I. Murphy	E. J. Baldwin
Jim Gray	118	5	Withers	Gray & Co.
Grimaldi	118	6	I. Lewis	J. & J. Swigert
Sir Joseph	118	7	Conkling	R. A. Swigert
Harrodsburg	118	8	J. Riley	Chinn & Morgan
Lafitte	118	9	Stovall	J. G. Greener & Co.
Masterpiece	118	10	West	S. S. Brown

Time 2:36½ (new Derby record). Weather clear, track fast.

Winner—Br.c. by Virgil—Ulrica, by Lexington; trained by Jim Murphy; bred by Daniel Swigert.

Auction Pools: Ben Ali, $500; Free Knight, $385; Blue Wing, $150; Jim Gray, $65; Lijero, $50; Field, $70.

Bookmaking Odds: Bookmakers did not operate because of failure to reach license agreement with management.

Mutuels: $5 win tickets on Ben Ali paid $13.60; $5 place paid $12; $5 place tickets on Blue Wing, $10.

Masterpiece broke in front, and was followed to the first turn by Harrodsburg and Sir Joseph. At the three quarters, Free Knight took command, followed by Blue Wing and Ben Ali. Down through the stretch it was a furious, whipping finish between Ben Ali and Blue Wing, with Ben Ali the winner by half a length.

Ben Ali — Stakes Races

AT 2 YEARS
- WON: Hopeful Stakes.
- UNP: Flatbush Stakes, Autumn Stakes, Champion Stallion Stakes, Goodbye Stakes.

AT 3 YEARS
- WON: Kentucky Derby, Charles Green Stakes, St. Louis Derby, Ocean Stakes, Spirit of the Times Stakes, Winters Stakes.
- 2ND: First Special Sweepstakes, Champion Stakes.
- 3RD: Choice Stakes, Omnius Stakes.
- UNP: American Derby.

AT 4 YEARS
- WON: Free Handicap, Fourth of July Handicap.
- UNP: Woodlawn Handicap, Suburban Handicap.

AT 5 YEARS
- 3RD: Westchester Handicap.
- 4TH: Equality Stakes.

James B. Haggin owned one of the most extensive Thoroughbred nurseries ever operated in Kentucky. It was Elmendorf Farm. The present Elmendorf Farm, owned by P. A. B. Widener III; George D. Widener's Old Kenny Farm, parts of Greentree Farm, and the C. V. Whitney Farm all were included in Elmendorf when it was owned by Haggin.

One of the best fields in the first twelve years of Kentucky Derby history came onto the Churchill Downs track the afternoon of May 14 for the 1886 running of the race. Seven of the ten starters were Kentucky bred.

Favorite in the field was James B. Haggin's Ben Ali, a brown son of Virgil out of Ulrica, by Lexington. Ben Ali was the third son of Virgil to win the Derby, and the last of four winners of the race produced by daughters of Lexington. Other daughters of the same sire had produced the winners Aristides (1875), Day Star (1878), and Hindoo (1881). No other horse has sired the dams of four Derby winners.

As a two-year-old Ben Ali scored only one victory in his five starts. That was in the Hopeful Stakes in New York. He ran unplaced in his other four races. At three, however, the son of Virgil wrote an entirely different story.

His initial start in 1886 was in the Winters Stakes in California on April 10. Under 118 pounds, the entry of Ben Ali and a stablemate had a walkover in that race of one and one-half miles. Two days later, on April 12, Ben Ali beat King of Norfolk in the Ocean Stakes at the same distance.

After another two-day rest Ben Ali shouldered 118 pounds again, and once more beat King of Norfolk, this time in the Spirit of The Times Stakes. The distance of this race was one and three-quarter miles. These were his preparation races prior to the Kentucky Derby.

From Churchill Downs Ben Ali was shipped to St. Louis where on June 5 he won the St. Louis Fair Derby at one and one-half miles. At the same track on June 10 he won the Charles Green Stakes, one and one-quarter miles. Two weeks later Ben Ali lost his only race at three, running unplaced in the American Derby.

All starters in the 1886 Derby carried 118 pounds, marking the first time this weight had been assigned any horse in the race. The weight troubled Ben Ali little as he established a new record of 2:36½ for the mile and one-half.

 **1887** An important factor in the original settlement and development of Louisville was the falls in the Ohio River shown above. Only part of the falls is now visible as the result of a dam in the river. Louisville got its nickname of Falls City from the river falls.

Among the city's favorite gathering places in the late 'eighties was Seelbach's Restaurant, shown at right. The overhead fans were manually operated. They were stressed in all advertising done by the restaurant. The restaurant, however, had no more pride in its fans than did the Pacific Coal Company in its Patent Spring Dumping Cart, shown at lower left. The coal company advertised "50 teams like this busy all the year delivering coal guaranteed to be the best in the market."

In Washington during 1887 the first Interstate Commerce Commission was appointed by the President. The Hatch Act, passed by Congress, gave $15,000 yearly to each state to establish and maintain an agricultural experiment station. Free mail delivery also was extended to include all towns with a population of 10,000, or to any town where the post-office had a gross annual revenue of $10,000.

Women in the first, second, and third class cities of Kansas were given the right

to vote in city elections. An act granting this was passed by the Kansas legislature early in 1887. The Army's hospital corps was established.

The yacht Dauntless won over the Cornet in a trans-Atlantic race from Sandy Hook, New York, to Queenstown, England, and the American sloop Volunteer won over her British rival, Thistle, in the international race off Sandy Hook.

Pedigree

Montrose

MONTROSE (Bay colt)			
Duke of Montrose	Waverly	*Australian	Cicily Jopson
	Kelpie	*Bonnie Scotland	Mare by Sovereign
Patti	*Billet	Voltigeur	Calcutta
	Dora	Pat Malloy	Etta Jr.

Tabulated Racing Record

Year	Age	Sts.	1st	2nd	3rd	Won
1886	2	13	2	2	2	$ 2,690
1887	3	10	3	2	4	10,200
1888	4	12	5	3	0	7,555
1889	5	16	4	4	3	6,876
		51	14	11	9	$ 27,321

13th Kentucky Derby, May 11, 1887

$1,500 added. Net to winner $4,200; second $300; third $150. 119 nominations.

Horse	Wt.	Fin.	Jockey	Owner
Montrose	118	1	I. Lewis	Labold Bros.
Jim Gore	118	2	W. Fitzpatrick	A. G. McCampbell
Jacobin	118	3	J. Stoval	R. Lisle
Banburg	115	4	Blaylock	J. D. Morrisey
Clarion	118	5	Arnold	Fleetwood Stable
Ban Yan	118	6	Godfrey	W. O. Scully
Pendennis	118	7	Murphy	Santa Anita Stable

Time 2:39¼. Track fast.

Winner—B. c. by Duke of Montrose—Patti, by *Billet; trained by John McGinty; bred by Milton Young.

Auction Pools: 8 to 5 against Banburg; 2 to 1, Jim Gore; 4 to 1, Pendennis; 5 to 1, Jacobin; 6 to 1, Ban Yan; 10 to 1 each, Montrose and Clarion.

Bookmaking Odds: Montrose, 10 to 1; Jim Gore, 3 to 1; Jacobin, 6 to 1; Banburg, 7 to 5; Clarion, 10 to 1; Ban Yan, 5 to 1; Pendennis, 4 to 1.

Mutuels: Pay-off figures not available.

Montrose   Stakes Races

AT 2 YEARS	WON	Free Handicap, Cotton Exchange Stakes.
	2ND	Mechanics Stakes.
	3RD	Prospect Stakes, Moet and Chandon Stakes.
	UNP	Autumn Stakes, Optional Stakes, Camden Stakes, Red Bank Stakes, St. Louis Hotel Stakes.
AT 3 YEARS	WON	Kentucky Derby, St. Leger Stakes, Blue Ribbon Stakes.
	2ND	Sheridan Stakes, Phoenix Stakes.
	3RD	Latonia Stakes.
	UNP	American Derby.
AT 4 YEARS	WON	Morrissey Stakes, Kearney Stakes, Great Western Handicap, Distillers and Brewers' Stakes.
	2ND	Grand Prize of Saratoga, Boulevard Stakes, Merchants Stakes.
AT 5 YEARS	WON	Kearney Stakes, Cincinnati Hotel Handicap.
	2ND	Boulevard Stakes, Kentucky Handicap.
	3RD	Excelsior Handicap, Free Handicap, Distillers' and Brewers' Stakes.
	UNP	Merchants' Stakes.

Montrose was the second and one of seven winners of the Derby from the Matchem line. Baden-Baden, in 1877, had been the first. The other winners from same male line have been Exterminator, Clyde Van Dusen, War Admiral, Zev and Flying Ebony.

All our Thoroughbreds today descend from three male lines. In addition to Matchem they are the Eclipse and Herod lines. Fifty-six of the first seventy-four Kentucky Derby winners were descendants of Eclipse. Eleven trace back to Herod.

Among the stallions which stood at Dixiana Farm when that Thoroughbred nursery was owned by its founder, Major Barak G. Thomas, was *King Ban. He sired the top racers Queen Ban, French Park, Ban Fox, King Fox, Jewell Ban, and Banburg. Jewell Ban won the Kentucky Oaks at Churchill Downs two years after Banburg was a beaten favorite in the Kentucky Derby of 1887.

Banburg was one of 119 three-year-olds nominated for the thirteenth running of the Derby on May 11. It was a record field of eligibles. Also in the field was another son of *King Ban. He was Ban Yan, a half-brother to the great Himyar. Of the seven horses that answered the call to the post for the Derby, Banburg was the most highly regarded. He had raced well and the bigger betters backed him down to 8-to-5.

A crowd of 15,000 saw Starter Billy Cheatham get the field away almost at once. Jockey J. Stoval got Jacobin away first, with Ban Yan and Montrose lapped on him. Hustled along by Jockey I. Lewis, Montrose soon moved into the lead, moved out to a two-length lead on the first turn. The favorite made his run at Montrose in the backstretch, failed to overtake him and dropped out of contention after that.

Jim Gore challenged in the stretch under a strong drive, but could not catch Montrose who won easily. The second horse pulled up lame, but a week later had recovered sufficiently to win the Clark Stakes in time that had been bettered only three times in the runnings of that event.

Montrose was bred by Colonel Milton Young, who purchased McGrathiana Stud following the death of Price McGrath. He was sold first to W. S. Barnes, owner of Melbourne Stud at Lexington, who resold the winner to Labold Brothers for $4,100.

The 1887 winner raced a total of four seasons, was a stakes winner in each year. Prior to the Derby he had won the Blue Ribbon Stakes at Lexington.

Fore! It is generally accepted that the introduction of golf in the United States came in 1888 when John Reid and others at Yonkers, New York, laid out a small course on the Reid land, playing with equipment brought over from Scotland.

A major development in the automotive industry took place the same year when Dunlop perfected the pneumatic tire. Important figures in the automotive world at the time were the Stanley Brothers, shown below, the builders of the famous Stanley Steamer.

New York and the eastern part of the United States were hit by a severe blizzard March 11-14, 1888, and among the many who lost their lives as a result of it was Senator Roscoe Conkling.

Henry W. Slocum, Jr., won the United States men's singles championship in tennis, displacing Richard D. Sears, who had held the title for seven straight years.

The Belmont Futurity was run for the first time and was won by Proctor Knott, carrying 112 pounds, including Jockey S. Barnes. The race was worth $40,900 to the winning owner. The distance of the inaugural running was three-quarters of a mile. Race track condition books presented ornate covers as evidenced by the Churchill Downs book, lower right.

In Washington Senator Smith introduced a bill in Congress proposing an amendment to the Constitution whereby Congress could override a Presidential veto with a majority instead of a two-thirds vote.

News highlights on Derby Day included the theft of a sawmill in Pennsylvania.

Pedigree

MACBETH II
(Brown gelding)

- Macduff
  - *Macaroon
    - Macaroni
    - Songstress
  - Jersey Lass
    - *King Ernest
    - Jersey Belle
- Agnes
  - Gilroy
    - Lexington
    - Magnolia
  - Laura Bruce
    - Star Davis
    - Alida

Tabulated Racing Record

Year	Age	Sts.	1st	2nd	3rd	Won
1887	2	8	1	1	0	$ 1,340
1888	3	25	7	5	5	11,745
1889	4	16	3	1	2	1,600
1890	5	35	10	9	5	4,990
1891	6	9	3	3	1	2,195
1892	7	1	0	0	0	...
1893	8	12	1	2	1	300
		106	25	21	14	$ 22,170

Macbeth II

14th Kentucky Derby, May 14, 1888

$2,500 added. Net to winner $4,740; second $500; third $200. 95 nominations.

Horse	Wt.	Fin.	Jockey	Owner
Macbeth II	115	1	G. Covington	Chicago Stable
Gallifet	118	2	A. McCarthy	Melbourne Stable
White	118	3	Withers	W. O. Scully
Alexandria	118	4	Jones	Melbourne Stable
The Chevalier	118	5	Lewis	T. J. Clay
Autocrat	118	6	Hamilton	D. Gibson
Col. Zeb Ward	118	7	Blaylock	G. M. Rye

Time 2:38¼. Weather clear, track fast.

Winner—Br.g. by Macduff—Agnes, by Gilroy; trained by John Campbell; bred by Rufus Lisle.

Auction Pools: Prices not available.

Bookmaking Odds: Gallifet and Alexandria (Melbourne Stable entry), even money; The Chevalier, 3½ to 1; White, 4 to 1; Macbeth II, 6 to 1; Col. Zeb Ward, 12 to 1; Autocrat, 12 to 1.

Mutuels: Pay-off prices not available.

The Chevalier took lead, closely followed by Autocrat and Col. Zeb Ward. Gallifet raced to the front around the first turn, and remained there until an eighth of a mile from the wire, when Macbeth II came with a rush, and won by a length.

Macbeth II — Stakes Races

AT 2 YEARS
- WON — Kimball Stakes.
- UNP — Maiden Stakes, Bellemeade Stakes, Blue Grass Stakes.

AT 3 YEARS
- WON — Kentucky Derby, Kansas City Derby, Gayoso Hotel Stakes, Peabody Hotel Stakes.
- 2ND — Phoenix Stakes, Distillers' Stakes, Merchants' Stakes, Cottrill Stakes.
- UNP — Boulevard Stakes.

AT 4 YEARS
- 3RD — Welter Handicap.

AT 5 YEARS
- WON — Green Stakes, Highweight Handicap.
- UNP — Welter Stakes.

AT 6 YEARS
- WON — Clifton, N. J., New Year's Handicap.

Despite the cold, raw day which prevailed for the 1888 Derby some 10,000 patrons were present in the grandstand. Approximately 4,000 others watched the racing from the centerfield. The track, however, was dry and a strong wind drove the dust into the spectators' eyes. Never had it rained on Derby Day.

The patrons got an extra race when it was necessary to re-run the first race on the program. In that event, the twelve two-year-olds had been started from the four-furlong pole instead of from the five-furlong pole, which was the distance of the race.

Only one winner of the Kentucky Derby has started more times than Macbeth II, winner in 1888. The son of Macduff and Agnes, by Gilroy, started a total of 106 times during the seven seasons he raced. He won twenty-five races, was twenty-one times second, and fourteen times third, earning a total of $22,170.

The son of Macduff was the third gelding to win the race. Prior to him, geldings that had won were Vagrant in 1876 and Apollo in 1882. He was also the last gelding to win the Derby until Old Rosebud established a new track record in winning the 1915 renewal.

Macbeth II won only one of his eight starts as a two-year-old, beating his opposition in Latonia's Kimball Stakes. He also was once second and unplaced in all other starts. Macbeth II began his three-year-old season at New Orleans where he raced with success, was a winner at Nashville where he campaigned prior to the Churchill Downs races.

His pre-Derby victories included the Gayoso Hotel Stakes and Peabody Hotel Stakes. Macbeth II's races, however, had not been particularly impressive and he was held at 6-to-1 in the Derby betting. James Caldwell, known as "Prince of the Starters," got the field away to a good start.

Gillifet, part of the Melbourne Stable's entry, took the lead after something more than a half-mile had been run, held it until the stretch where he tired very badly as the winner moved into the front. Gallifet, managed to outlast White for the place. The 1888 Derby marked the first time that a winner had raced in a stable name, a practice which has since become quite commonplace.

His three-year-old campaign was Macbeth II's most profitable with earnings amounting to $11,745. But his twenty-five starts of that year were second to the thirty-five races in which he started as a five-year-old. It was in 1890 that Macbeth II was sold to W. Angle. He later was sold to the Aetna Stable for which he raced during the last two seasons of his career.

Benjamin Harrison, lower left, took office as the twenty-third President of the United States in 1889. During the same year the Union was further enlarged through the admission of North Dakota and South Dakota (on November 2), Montana (on November 8), and Washington (on November 11).

The mule-and horse-drawn street cars in the City of Louisville, lower right, were definitely on their way out as the first electric street car was placed in service in the city on September 21. On July 8 John L. Sullivan beat Jake Kilrain in seventy-five rounds at Richburg, Mississippi, in the last of bare-knuckle championship fights.

Johnstown, Pennsylvania, was devastated by flood which took a toll of 2,142 lives and which left in its wake many strange sights, one of which is shown in the picture at lower right.

James G. Blaine, secretary of state, presided over the first Pan-American Conference, the tangible result of which was the establishment of the Pan-American Union to facilitate interchange of commercial information. Secretary Blaine also engaged in an exchange of acrimonious notes with Lord Salsbury, of Great Britain, concerning the protection of herds of Alaskan seals in the Bering Sea.

Michigan was the scene of devastating forest fires during the late spring of 1889. In Philadelphia the twenty-eighth international convention of the Young Men's Christian Association was convened.

Kentucky's Governor Buckner missed the Derby, having gone to New York to attend a Grant birthday dinner. Other headlines in the papers on Derby Day of this year highlighted President Harrison's ordering the steamer Dispatch to Washington that he might enjoy a Potomac cruise with members of his cabinet.

Pedigree

Spokane

SPOKANE (Chestnut colt)	Hyder Ali	*Leamington → Faugh-a-Ballagh / Mare by Pantaloon
		Lady Duke → Lexington / Magdalen
	Interpose	*Intruder → Crater / Lady Bountiful
		Lilac → Lightning / Dolly Carter

Tabulated Racing Record

Year	Age	Sts.	1st	2nd	3rd	Won
1888	2	5	2	0	0	$ 1,535
1889	3	8	3	2	1	24,970
1890	4	4	0	2	1	300
		17	5	4	2	$ 26,805

15th Kentucky Derby, May 9, 1889

$2,500 added. Net to winner $4,880; second 300; third $150. 94 nominations.

Horse	Wt.	Fin.	Jockey	Owner
Spokane	118	1	T. Kiley	N. Armstrong
Proctor Knott	115	2	S. Barnes	Scoggan & Bryant
Once Again	118	3	I. Murphy	M. Young
Hindoocraft	118	4	Armstrong	Scoggan Bros.
Cassius	118	5	Taral	Beverwyck Stable
Sportsman	118	6	I. Lewis	J. K. Megibben & Co.
Outbound	118	7	Hollis	Fleetwood Stable
Bootmaker	118	8	Warwick	Wilson & Young

Weather clear, track fast.

Time :24, :48½, 1:14½, 1:41½, 2:09½, 2:34½ (new Derby record).

Winner—Ch.c. by Hyder Ali—Interpose, by *Intruder; trained by John Rodegap; bred by Noah Armstrong.

Auction Pools: Prices not available.

Bookmaking Odds: Proctor Knott, 1 to 2; Spokane, 10 to 1; Once Again and Bootmaker (Young entry), 3 to 1; Hindoocraft, 10 to 1; Cassius, 15 to 1; Outbound, 15 to 1; Sportsman, 15 to 1.

Mutuels: ($2 tickets sold for first time this year.) $2 tickets on Spokane paid $34.80 win, $6.30 place; Proctor Knott, $2.90 place. No show tickets sold.

This was last year when auction pools were sold at track, until the method was revived in 1908 by Colonel Matt J. Winn and associates. The auction pools were ruled out after the 1899 Derby by Colonel Clark, following a protest by bookmakers that their business was being handicapped by the opposition from auction pool sellers.

Proctor Knott, a wild horse at the barrier, broke away twice, to gallop more than an eighth of a mile, and almost unseated his rider, "Pike" Barnes, during several spectacular lunges. But he broke along with his field.

Hindoocraft was the early leader, with Bootmaker, second, Spokane, third. Near the first turn, Proctor Knott was rushed to the front, and led by three lengths entering the backstretch, with Sportsman, second; Hindoocraft, third; and Spokane, fifth, under a careful ride.

All through the backstretch, Proctor Knott was fighting for his head. Leaving the backstretch, Proctor Knott was five lengths in front, with Hindoocraft, second; Spokane had moved into third place, and gradually was increasing speed.

Taking the turn for home, Barnes was unable to control Proctor Knott, and the colt lost many lengths by racing to the outer rail, where Barnes succeeded in getting him straightened. Barnes chose to ride the outer rail, rather than lose ground by steering his horse back toward the inside fence.

Spokane skimmed the inner rail, and ran through the stretch on the inside rail, with Proctor Knott on the outside rail. Proctor Knott had about a half-length advantage an eighth from the wire, but it was obvious that he was a tired horse, while Spokane seemed fresh and strong. As the finish wire was crossed, opinion of spectators was divided as to the outcome of the race. One faction was certain that Spokane, on the inside, had nosed out Proctor Knott on the outer rail; another took the opposite viewpoint. The judges—Colonel Clark, General Robinson and J. K. Megibben—deliberated quite a while then awarded to Spokane by a nose.

Spokane Stakes Races

AT 2 YEARS	WON	Maiden Stakes.
	4TH	Hyde Park Stakes.
AT 3 YEARS	WON	Kentucky Derby, American Derby, Clark Stakes.
	2ND	Sheridan Stakes, Peabody Hotel Handicap.
	3RD	Pelham Bay Handicap.
	UNP	Twin City Handicap (to Tenny), Drexel Stakes.

Spokane often is referred to as the Kentucky Derby winner that was "bred in Illinois, foaled in Montana, and trained in Tennessee."

Hyder Ali, sire of the 1889 winner, was standing at The Meadows in Illinois when Interpose, Spokane's dam, was bred to him in 1885. Interpose was then shipped to the Northwest Territory (for it was not until November 1889 that the states of Montana, North Dakota, South Dakota, and Washington were admitted to the Union) to be born in that part of the territory which was later Montana. Spokane was the second winner of the race which had not been foaled in Kentucky.

As a two-year-old Spokane raced well, winning two of his five starts, including the Maiden Stakes at Latonia. He began his three-year-old racing in Tennessee, his races there including a second to Studaway in the Peabody Hotel Stakes at Memphis.

The largest crowd in the Derby's history, 25,000 persons, was present. They had been drawn there principally by the presence in the field of Proctor Knott, declared by all to be the greatest two-year-old seen in many years. In the crowd were "Diamond Jim" Brady. The day was hot and dusty. Unable to get to the refreshment stand because of the crowd, Colonel John B. Castleman gave a Negro boy $1 to bring him a bucket of water.

Also in the crowd was Frank James, brother to Jesse. He approached a bookmaker with the query, "What's the price on Spokane?" Replied the bookmaker, "10-to-1 and the sky's the limit." The odds-layer counted the money. "There's $5,000 here, and as far as I'm concerned that's the sky," he declared.

Many believed Spokane's victory over Proctor Knott in the Derby was an accident, and it was no less of a surprise to them when the colt owned by N. Armstrong again beat Proctor Knott in the Clark Stakes at Louisville. Once Again, third in the Derby, also was third in the Clark.

Owner Armstrong received a blanket of gold brocade from the citizens of Spokane Falls (later the city of Spokane) in commemoration of the Kentucky Derby victory. Spokane's other win at three was in the American Derby. He was the first horse to win the Kentucky and American Derbys.

1890

The original Polo Grounds, home of the New York baseball team of the National League, took its name from the fact that the site of the field was originally used for polo games introduced in this country in 1876. The Polo Grounds of 1890 is shown below.

Also in 1890 came the Sioux War, last of the wars against the Indians. Two additional states were admitted to the Union. They were Idaho, admitted on July 3, and Wyoming, admitted on July 10.

In the nation's capital, the Republican party's legislation on tariff revision was guided by William McKinley, chairman of the House Committee on Ways and Means. After tariff revisions living costs advanced and Democratic leaders used this fact effectively in winning many of the congressional seats in the elections of 1890.

Sentiment against trusts was vigorous and President Harrison recommended action by Congress. Republican leaders followed his suggestions with the result that the Sherman Anti-Trust Act was passed.

Louisville was struck by a severe tornado which left a path of complete havoc, several city blocks wide, through the heart of the city. Wreckage at the railroad station appears in the photograph at right.

Except for those persons living right on the fringe of the damaged section of the city residents in the western part of Louisville and those in the eastern part at first were unaware that the city had been visited by the tornado. As news of the storm spread those in the western part of the city thought the entire eastern part had been demolished, and those east of the damaged area believed all the city west of them had been wiped out.

Kentucky centered much interest on Lawrenceburg where triplets were born on Derby Day. Many visitors were attracted to the central Kentucky town by the event. Asbury College was established at Wilmore, Kentucky.

In Washington, Kentucky's ex-Congressman Pres Taubee was shot by a Louisville reporter whose nose had been pulled by Taubee as the result of certain articles the newspaper man had written for his publication.

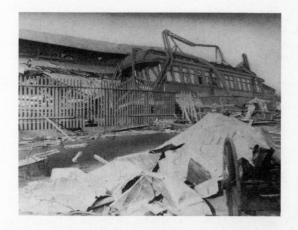

Pedigree

Riley

†RILEY (Bay colt)	Longfellow	*Leamington	Faugh-a-Ballagh Mare by Pantaloon
		Nantura	Brawner's Eclipse Queen Mary
	Geneva	War Dance	Lexington Reel
		La Gitana	Uncle Vic Georgia Wood

†Riley was originally named Shortfellow.

Tabulated Racing Record

Year	Age	Sts.	1st	2nd	3rd	Won
1889	2	12	6	3	0	$ 4,505
1890	3	21	11	6	2	21,065
1891	4	15	8	3	1	14,360
1892	5	3	2	1	0	1,050
1893	6	10	2	4	1	2,150
1894	7	3	1	0	0	300
		64	30	17	4	$ 43,430

16th Kentucky Derby, May 14, 1890

$2,500 added. Net to winner $5,460; second $300; third $150. 115 nominations.

Horse	Wt.	Fin.	Jockey	Owner
Riley	118	1	I. Murphy	E. Corrigan
Bill Letcher	118	2	Allen	W. R. Letcher
Robespierre	118	3	Francis	G. V. Hankins
Palisade	118	4	Britton	S. Willimas
Outlook	118	5	Breckinridge	B. J. Treacy
Prince Fonso	118	6	Overton	J. C. Twymann & Co.

Time 2:45. Track heavy.

Winner—Bay colt by Longfellow—Geneva, by War Dance; trained by Edward Corrigan; bred by C. H. Durkee.

Bookmaking Odds; Robespierre, even money; Riley, 4 to 1; Bill Letcher, 5 to 1; Prince Fonso, 5 to 1; Palisade, 8 to 1; Outlook, 10 to 1.

No auction pools or mutuels sold at track after 1889 until 1908. However, auction pools sold in 1890, 1891 and for years thereafter in downtown Louisville, on night before, and morning of Derby.

Bill Letcher was away first, and Palisade, second. Robespierre, the favorite, took the lead nearing the first turn; Outlook, second. Riley came from last place, going into the backstretch, and took command, winning easily by two lengths.

Riley — Stakes Races

AT 2 YEARS	WON	Railway Stakes, Trial Stakes, Merchants' Stakes.
	2ND	Kimball Stakes, Gaston Hotel Stakes.
	UNP	Westside Stakes.
AT 3 YEARS	WON	Kentucky Derby, Clark Stakes, Speculation Handicap, Fairview Lightweight Handicap, Pelham Bay Handicap.
	2ND	St. Leger Stakes, Latonia Derby, Himyar Stakes.
	3RD	Runnymeade Handicap, Brookwood Handicap.
AT 4 YEARS	WON	Monmouth Cup, Shrewsbury Handicap, Coney Island Cup, Bay Ridge Handicap, Free Handicap, Brooklyn Cup, Montgomery Stakes.
	2ND	Monmouth Champion Stakes, Long Branch Handicap.
	3RD	Distillers' Stakes.
	UNP	Suburban, Metropolitan Handicap, Brooklyn Jockey Club Handicap.
AT 6 YEARS	2ND	Boulevard Stakes.

It was in 1890 that August Belmont I, who established the noted Nursery Stud in Kentucky, died. His death came on November 11. When his horses were offered for sale at Babylon, Long Island, twenty-eight horses sold for $123,600. Forty-one horses were sold in the Dwyer dispersal sale in 1890 for $94,225. In this sale Hanover, son of Hindoo, was sold for $15,500.

Louisville was visited by a heavy rain on Tuesday, May 13, 1890. It rained again the morning of May 14, marking the first time rain had fallen on Derby Day. For the sixteenth running of the race the Churchill Downs track was heavy. Only once prior to 1890 had the track been as bad as heavy for the running of the Derby. That was in 1883 when Leonatus won.

Although the 115 nominations to the race were second in number only to the 119 which had been made eligible for the 1887 running, only six starters filed out of the Churchill Downs paddock. This was the smallest field to date in the history of the race.

Riley was foaled at the Ashland Stud of John M. Clay. It was at the same farm that Day Star, Derby winner in 1878 had been bred and foaled, and where the 1902 winner Alan-a-Dale was to be foaled. Clay, however, was not the breeder of Riley.

It was C. H. Durkee who bred Riley and sold him to Edward Corrigan for $950 when the colt was a yearling. Riley was a son of Frank Harper's Longfellow. Riley was a small horse which probably accounts for the fact that he was originally named Shortfellow. He never raced under that name. The first three horses to finish in the 1890 Kentucky Derby were either by sires standing at Harper's Nantura Stud in Woodford County, or were bred there.

Riley's victory gave both his jockey and his sire a double. Longfellow had sired his first winner of the race in 1883 when Leonatus won over the same kind of a track, in 1884 Isaac Murphy had ridden the first of his three winners of the race.

The son of Longfellow was the third Derby winner to race as many as six seasons. In all, Riley started sixty-four times through his seven-year-old season, won thirty of his races and $43,430. Only Macbeth II had started more times among the horses winning the Churchill Downs race.

1891

"I am as proud of my calling as I am of my record, and I believe my life will be recorded as a success, though the reputation I enjoy was earned in the stable and saddle. It is a great honor to be classed as one of America's greatest jockeys."

Those were the words of the Negro jockey, Isaac Murphy, upper right, who in 1891 became the first jockey to ride three winners of the Kentucky Derby. Nor was Murphy wrong. He is still classed as one of the great riders of America, and will always be as long as there are horse races. The statement by Murphy was made shortly before his death in 1896.

In the winter of 1891 a young instructor in the Y.M.C.A. Training College at Springfield, Massachusetts, invented what has become one of America's greatest college sports. Dr. James Naismith was the instructor and the game he invented was basketball.

During the same year Ignace Paderewski made his first American concert tour. General William Tecumseh Sherman, prominent officer of the Union army, died. Frances Elizabeth Willard was elected president of the world W.C.T.U. organization.

Phineaus Taylor Barnum, founder of the circus which later became known as Barnum and Bailey, died. He was born in 1810. One of Louisville's favorite gathering places of this period was the Seelbach Hotel, lower left.

Kentucky's Democrats assembled in Louisville on the morning of Derby Day in 1891. The opening session was brief as the delegates voted to adjourn in order that they might see the race. The same afternoon at Pineville, Kentucky, a stick of candy was blamed for an argument which resulted in the killing of one person and the stabbing of several others.

Commonplace were advertisements such as the one at lower right, which appeared in race track condition books.

Pedigree

KINGMAN (Bay colt)	*Glengarry	Thormanby	‡Windhound / Alice Hawthorn
		Carbine	Rifleman / Troica
	Patricia	Vauxhall	Lexington / Verona
		Minnie Mc	Planet / Edina

‡Melbourne or Windhound

Tabulated Racing Record

Year	Age	Sts.	1st	2nd	3rd	Won
1890	2	16	4	6	2	$ 3,900
1891	3	12	6	0	4	15,465
		28	10	6	6	$ 19,365

17th Kentucky Derby, May 13, 1891

Kingman

$2,500 added. Net to winner $4,550; second $300; third $150. 83 nominations.

Horse	Wt.	Fin.	Jockey	Owner
Kingman	122	1	I. Murphy	Jacobin Stable
Balgowan	122	2	Overton	T. J. Clay
High Tariff	122	3	R. Williams	Easton & Larabie
Hart Wallace	122	4	Kiley	Bashford Manor

Time 1:05½ (half), 1:35¾ (six furlongs), 2:01 (mile), 2:52¼. Track slow.

Winner—B.c. by *Glengarry—Patricia, by Vauxhall; trained by Dud Allen; bred by A. C. Franklin.

Bookmaking Odds: Kingman, 1 to 2; Balgowan, 3 to 1; High Tariff, 10 to 1; Hart Wallace, 6 to 1.

This was the slowest of all Derbies. Hart Wallace broke on top; High Tariff, second; Balgowan, third; Kingman, fourth. Within a quarter of a mile they all were traveling like a cavalry, side by side, nose and nose, each jockey waiting for the other to set the pace, and none doing it. Each rider had orders to stay back for about a mile and whenever one horse moved a little to the front, his rider restrained him, and the others restrained theirs, too. The mile was covered in 2:01, and the mile and a quarter in 2:26¾. At that point, Murphy started his move with Kingman, and Overton let Balgowan have his head, but Kingman won the race by a length.

Kingman — Stakes Races

AT 2 YEARS

2ND	Edgewater Handicap, Railway Stakes, Hyde Park Stakes.
3RD	Monmouth Free Handicap.

AT 3 YEARS

WON	Kentucky Derby, Phoenix Stakes, Latonia Derby, St. Paul Free Handicap.
3RD	American Derby.
4TH	Sheridan Stakes.

Isaac Murphy, Negro jockey, who rode Kingman in the 1891 Kentucky Derby and thus became the first rider to win this race three times, started his career as a rider in 1874. At the time he was fourteen, weighed scarcely seventy pounds, and went to work for the stable of Williams and Owings, whose Creedmore was second in the 1876 Derby.

During his career as a rider Murphy rode in 1,412 races and won 628, according to records which he kept. His last year in the saddle was in 1895 when he won only two races. Kingman was one of only six winners he was astride in 1891.

Murphy won the first American Derby with Modesty. He also rode three of the next five winners of that race. His most successful day at a track came at Detroit on July 4, 1879, when he rode the entire card of four winners which were Checkmate, Enquiress, and Glenmore. The last named horse won two races. Murphy also won the Clark Stakes four times and the Latonia Derby five times.

Bred in Tennessee by A. C. Franklin, Kingman was the second of three Kentucky Derby winners that were born in that state.

The son of *Glengarry came to the races during the spring meeting in 1890 and finished second to Roseland in his first effort. His second start was during the Latonia meeting later in the year. In that race he again met Roseland. The latter was held at odds of 5-to-4 and led throughout until the stretch where Jockey Fishburn allowed Kingman, at odds of 8-to-1, to pass him and win. As a result Jockey Fishburn was ruled off by the stewards and all bets on the race were declared off.

Kingman started fourteen more times during his two-year-old season, won three other races. He also was six times second, and twice third. He was unable to win a stakes race at that age, but did place in several.

As a three-year-old Kingman again started racing at Lexington where he won the Phoenix Stakes. From Lexington Kingman was shipped to Louisville to win the Derby, thence to Kentucky's other track, Latonia, where he won the Latonia Derby. Thus he had won the most important spring race at each of the three Kentucky race courses. His other stakes win as a three-year-old was the St. Paul Free Handicap. In the American Derby Kingman carried top weight of 129 pounds and finished third to Strathmeath. The Tennessee-bred colt was retired after his 1891 racing.

One newspaperman reporting on the 1891 Derby wrote, "The crowd was so great that locomotion was almost impossible. The inner field presented one mass of humanity from the head of the stretch nearly to the quarter pole. Grandstand and lawn have been improved, a new betting shed and paddock have been built."

The crowd was large enough that it was necessary to provide Starter Jim Ferguson with a police escort in order that he could reach the starting point.

A number of persons prominently connected with the Turf died during 1891. They included B. G. Bruce, Leonard W. Jerome, and Ben Ali Haggin, for whom the Derby winner of 1886 had been named.

1892

The lowest temperature ever recorded and verified was minus 90 degrees Fahrenheit at Verkhoyansk, Siberia, February 5 and 7, 1892.

On the warmer days that year Coney Island was an extremely popular place. The bathers, shown below, were dressed in the latest fashion. Across the Atlantic the Diesel engine was invented in this year.

In the political field, Cleveland was again chosen as the Democratic Presidential candidate despite opposition from the machine politicians, and he swamped his Republican opponent, carrying into office with him a Democratic majority in both the House of Representatives and the Senate. A new political party was born in the preceding year as the Grangers expanded into the Farmers' Alliance and united with the Knights of Labor in a convention at Cincinnati.

1892 also was marked by the Homestead strike riots near Pittsburgh, in which many were killed. Richard D. Sears won the first national championship in court tennis, and baseball talk centered around plans to increase the distance between the pitcher's mound and the plate.

Society leaders at Lexington, Kentucky, who remained away from the Derby to attend a wedding were agog when they arrived at the church to find tacked on the door a sign which read, "Wedding Postponed." Neither the bride nor groom would issue a statement.

Louisville merchants were advertising "Spring suits at $10.00 and $12.50." A women's ready-to-wear store advertised, "Don't matter what others say, we carry the largest line of corsets in the city. Seven styles at 50 cents each. Did you ever try one of our dollar corsets?"

From London Mrs. Antonia Navarro (Mary Anderson) wrote the Associated Press to deny a story dispatched by that press service stating that she was planning to quit the stage.

Pedigree

Azra

AZRA (Bay colt)	Reform	*Leamington	Faugh-a-Ballagh Mare by Pantaloon
		*Stolen Kisses	The Knight of Kars Defamation
	Albia	Alarm	*Eclipse *Maud
		Elastic	Kentucky Blue Ribbon

Tabulated Racing Record

Year	Age	Sts.	1st	2nd	3rd	Won
1891	2	13	2	2	3	$ 5,690
1892	3	10	3	1	4	15,020
		23	5	3	7	$ 20,710

18th Kentucky Derby, May 11, 1892

$2,500 added. Net to winner $4,230; second $300; third $150. 68 nominations.

Horse	Wt.	Fin.	Jockey	Owner
Azra	122	1	A. Clayton	Bashford Manor
Huron	122	2	Britton	Ed Corrigan
Phil Dwyer	122	3	Overton	Ed Corrigan

Time 2:41½. Track heavy.

Winner—B.c. by Reform—Albia, by Alarm; trained by John H. Morris; bred by George J. Long.
Bookmaking Odds: Azra, 3 to 2; Huron and Phil Dwyer (coupled as Corrigan entry), 11 to 20.
Huron broke in front and had a six-length lead well along the backstretch. Then Clayton, aboard Azra, made his move, caught Huron near the wire, and won by a nose.

Azra — Stakes Races

AT 2 YEARS	WON	Champagne Stakes.
	2ND	Essex Stakes.
	3RD	Nursery Stakes, Dunmow Stakes, Partridge S.
	UNP	Select Stakes, Carteret Handicap, White Plains Handicap, Sapphire Stakes.
AT 3 YEARS	WON	Kentucky Derby, Travers Stakes.
	2ND	Choice Stakes.
	3RD	Jerome Stakes, Bridge Handicap, Lorillard Stakes, Garfield Park Derby.
	4TH	American Derby.

Most of the Kentucky farms producing Thoroughbreds have been doing so for generations; at least, most of the people breeding race horses grew up in families which had been Thoroughbred breeders for generations. That George J. Long's family did not continue the successful nursery he founded makes the history of Bashford Manor Farm as unusual as it was successful.

Long, a successful Louisville industrialist operating the Dennis J. Long Foundry, decided it would be more pleasant to live in the country than in the city. Accordingly, in 1877 he purchased the farm owned by J. B. Wilder.

As far as he knew, none of Long's ancestors had shown any interest in breeding or racing horses. He had no interest in any other type of livestock and Long decided to purchase a few Thoroughbreds. He made a trip to Erdenheim, the famous stockyards of Commodore Kittson, which produced Iroquois, Sensation, and other noted horses. There he purchased Alarm, Pardee, Luminous, and Albia, the latter dam of Azra.

Long formally launched his career as breeder and owner in 1888. Within four years he was known throughout the racing world. In his fifth racing season he won the Kentucky Derby for the first time. He also won it in 1906, and bred the winner of the 1899 running. He became a dominant figure in the country's racing, was a director at Churchill Downs where one of the stakes carries the name of his Bashford Manor Stud.

In 1881 the American-bred and owned Iroquois won the English Derby at Epsom. Thirty-six years later, in 1917, *Omar Khayyam, bred in England, won the Kentucky Derby.

Favorite in the 1882 Kentucky Derby was Huron, a son of Iroquois. He was coupled with his stablemate Phil Dwyer as the Edward Corrigan entry, which was held at odds of 11-to-20. Azra, a son of Reform, was held at odds of 3-to-2.

These three horses made up the smallest field that ever had started in the Kentucky Derby. Only once since that date, in 1905, have as few as three horses gone to the post in this race. Originally, Azra's owner had planned to have a stablemate run in the Derby with him as the George J. Long entry.

However, when rain left the course heavy for the running of the race Owner Long and Trainer John H. Morris decided to scratch Bashford. Azra, Bashford, and Ignite all had raced brilliantly in the silks of Long during the 1891 season. They were rated among the best two-year-olds of that season.

Azra had won the Champagne Stakes and had run second or third in four other added money races. Bashford had won the Friendly Stakes and Quickstep Stakes at Chicago, while Ignite had won the Clipsetta Stakes at Chicago. Following the Derby triumph, Azra won the Clark Stakes before leaving Churchill Downs for the East where he won the Travers Stakes, placed in other features.

The 1892 Derby winner's death was unexpected. Trainer Morris had invited a number of friends to the track for breakfast and to inspect the racing stable. Shortly after Azra had been led out before the guests, a groom rushed to Trainer Morris with word that the Derby winner was down in his stall. He never got up.

Bashford also was very successful at three, his victories including one over the great racer Yo Tambien, against whom the Long colt broke the Latonia mark for one and one-eighth miles. But like Azra, Bashford died suddenly after he had been shipped East. Ignite proved herself just as good a filly at three years as she had been in 1891. Among her victories at three was the Alabama Stakes.

1893 Grover Cleveland had scarcely taken office as President of the United States for the second time before the country was in the grip of a financial panic comparable to that of 1873.

By mid-summer nineteen national banks, many state banking houses in southern and western states had suspended their operations, and by October of 1893 more than 8,000 business houses had failed. A total of 156 railroad companies went into the hands of receivers.

Meanwhile, the great World's Fair (Columbian Exposition) was in progress at Chicago, a feature of which was the Ferris wheel, shown below.

Two great industries were being born. Charles E. Duryea, upper right, tested the first gasoline automobile at Springfield, Massachusetts, on April 19. Thomas A. Edison introduced the first motion picture camera.

In Louisville the postoffice building at Fourth and Chestnut Streets was completed and opened. In the Hawaiian Islands a revolt was staged against Queen

Liliualani by the big planters, who were financed by foreign capital.

Sharing the front pages of Louisville's newspapers with the big race on May 10 were such events as: Thomas Nelson Page, the Southern novelist, announcing his engagement; assembling of the National Republican League in convention at Louisville's Macauley's Theater; escape of two prisoners from New York's Sing Sing prison; dynamiting in Iowa of the homes of three persons who had campaigned vigorously against saloons; a bomb being tossed at the night watchman at Maysville, Kentucky, marking the second time an attempt had been made on his life, and the almost complete destruction of Warsaw, Indiana, by fire.

Pedigree

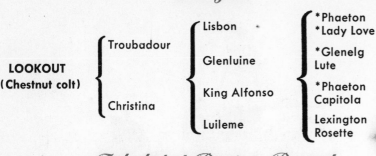

LOOKOUT
(Chestnut colt)

- Troubadour
  - Lisbon
    - *Phaeton
    - *Lady Love
  - Glenluine
    - *Glenelg
    - Lute
- Christina
  - King Alfonso
    - *Phaeton
    - Capitola
  - Luileme
    - Lexington
    - Rosette

Tabulated Racing Record

Year	Age	Sts.	1st	2nd	3rd	Won
1892	2	20	9	4	2	$ 5,585
1893	3	8	3	0	0	8,730
1894	4	18	2	2	0	1,000
1895	5	18	3	5	3	1,910
1896	6	2	0	1	0	125
		66	17	12	5	$ 17,350

Lookout

19th Kentucky Derby, May 10, 1893

$3,000 added. Net to winner $3,840; second $400; third $150; fourth $100. 60 nominations.

Horse		Wt.	Fin.	Jockey	Owner
Lookout		122	1	E. Kunze	Cushing & Orth
Plutus		122	2	A. Clayton	Bashford Manor
Boundless		122	3	R. Williams	Cushing & Orth
Also ran	Buck McCann	122	—	Thorpe	Scoggan Bros.
	Mirage	122	—	I. Murphy	James E. Pepper
	Linger	122	—	Flynn	C. E. Railey

Time 2:39¼. Weather clear.

Winner—Ch.c. by Troubadour—Christina, by King Alfonso; trained by William McDaniel; bred by Scoggan Brothers.

Bookmaking Odds: 7 to 10 (Cushing & Orth's entry), Lookout, Boundless; 3 to 1, Plutus.

Within the first eighth, Lookout, coupled with Boundless, took the lead, held it throughout, and won by five lengths.

Lookout   Stakes Races

AT 2 YEARS	WON	Minneapolis Stakes.
	2ND	Turf Exchange Stakes.
	3RD	Merchants' Hotel Handicap.
AT 3 YEARS	WON	Kentucky Derby, Gibson Stakes, Annual Stakes.
	UNP	American Derby.
AT 5 YEARS	WON	Coney Island Highweight Handicap.
	3RD	Toronto Cup.
	UNP	Royal Canadian Hurdle Handicap.

During the Nashville race meeting, which preceded the Churchill Downs spring program, Colonel M. Lewis Clark made a ruling which is recognized by all race tracks in America today. He ruled that horses of different ownership but trained by the same man must run as an entry. There was great indignation over this ruling at the time, but the fact that this rule is now universal in this country is evidence of its soundness.

Domino was the champion two-year-old of 1893. He was trained by William Lakeland. His winning races at two included the Great American Stakes, Great Eclipse Stakes, Great Trial Stakes, Hyde Park Stakes, Futurity Stakes, and Matron Stakes. He was unbeaten in nine races but ran a deadheat with Dobbins in a match at six furlongs. The Derby winners Shut Out, Brokers Tip and Black Gold trace to Domino.

In 1892 the Derby attendance had been held down by cool weather and a heavy track. For the nineteenth running on May 10, 1893, however, the weather was clear and warm. The race drew its biggest crowd since Spokane had beaten Proctor Knott in 1889.

The crowd was estimated at 25,000, many of the spectators being in the centerfield. The Churchill Downs management had provided free admission to the centerfield on the days of the running of the Derby and the Clark Stakes.

Two of the six starters had been bred by the Scoggan Brothers. They were Lookout and Buck McCann. The former was foaled at the McClellan Farm at West Point, Kentucky, and had been sold as a yearling for $1,100. The Scoggan Brothers kept Buck McCann and he started in their name in the 1893 Derby.

Coupled with Lookout as the Cushing and Orth entry was Boundless, a bay or brown son of Harry O'Fallon out of Endless, by Enquirer. The entry was favorite in the field at 7-to-10, and it marked the first time that Cushing and Orth ever had started a horse in the Derby. Nor did they ever have another entry.

Lookout's two-year-old form had not been impressive. He had won nine of his eighteen starts. One had been in stakes races. The Derby was one of his first three starts in 1893, all of which he won.

The winner was much the best of his field, moved out to a long lead in the early stages of the race and maintained it throughout while his stablemate and Plutus battled it out for second money. Later in the year Boundless established a new track record to win the American Derby, in which Lookout was unplaced.

Lookout continued to race through his six-year-old season. At four he was sold to J. E. Seagram, who raced him in Canada over the hurdles, steeplechase courses, and on the flat.

1894

Unemployment was widespread in the nation by 1894 and bands of men and boys roamed the countryside, some organized as armies, seeking help from the national and state governments. Most famous of these was that organized by "General" Jacob Coxey, of Ohio.

"Coxey's Army" converged on Washington, lower left, before the dome on the capitol building was completed. While most of Coxey's group marched afoot, the "General" himself rode in a carriage, lower right.

In this period Louisville's Galt House, upper right, was a favorite gathering place of residents and visitors to the city, as it had been for a long time and as it was to continue to be for years. Pools were sold there the night before each running of the Kentucky Derby, and it was the scene of great social activity at Derby time.

1894 was the year of the Pullman Palace Car Company strike, President Cleveland sending federal troops to keep the trains moving. When miners went on strike, coal advanced to the outlandish price of $4.00 per ton.

In New York, the Barnum and Bailey circus had to destroy "Tip," its lead elephant, after he had killed seven keepers. The Wells-Fargo Express Company was the victim of a $35,000 holdup.

Among the news stories which "broke" on the afternoon of the twentieth Derby included one from Fulton, Illinois, where the residents made up a purse of $500 to be used in an effort to get Kentucky's silver-tongued orator, Colonel W. C. P. Breckinridge, to deliver the July 4 address in that city. The same day it was announced by the Louisville and Nashville and Chesapeake and Ohio Railroads that "an elegant Pullman car was being added to the train between Louisville and Ashland, Kentucky.

Papers also carried stories that 20,000 sheep perished in the foothills of California's Sierra Nevada mountains as the result of snow, rain, and wind storms. The price of wheat dropped to 59½ cents, bringing realization to an earlier prediction that the price would go as low as sixty cents.

Pedigree

Chant

CHANT (Bay colt)			
Falsetto	Enquirer	*Leamington	Lida
	Farfaletta	*Australian	Elkhorna
Addie C.	Voltigeur	Vandal	Duet
	Aerolite	Lexington	Florine

Tabulated Racing Record

Year	Age	Sts.	1st	2nd	3rd	Won
1893	2	25	8	5	3	$ 3,900
1894	3	33	13	7	3	13,835
1895	4	4	1	3	0	545
1896	5	1	0	0	0	. . .
		63	22	15	6	$ 18,280

20th Kentucky Derby, May 15, 1894

$2,500 added. Net to winner $4,020; second $300; third $150; fourth $100. 55 nominations.

Horse	Wt.	Fin.	Jockey	Owner
Chant	122	1	F. Goodale	Leigh & Rose
Pearl Song	122	2	R. Williams	C. H. Smith
Sigurd	122	3	Overton	Bashford Manor
Al Boyer	122	4	Ray	Anderson & Gooding
Tom Elmore	122	5	Irving	S. K. Hughes & Co.

Time 2:41. Weather clear.

Winner—B.c. by Falsetto—Addie C., by Voltigeur; trained by Eugene Leigh; bred by A. J. Alexander.

Bookmaking Odds: Chant, 1 to 2; Pearl Song, 3 to 1; Sigurd, 12 to 1.

Sigurd broke first, followed by Chant, which took the lead at the half and won by two lengths.

Chant — Stakes Races

AT 2 YEARS	UNP	Sensation Stakes, Harold Stakes.
AT 3 YEARS	WON	Kentucky Derby, Clark Stakes, Phoenix Stakes.
AT 4 YEARS	2ND	Country Club Stakes.

Trainer Hughes, to whom Owner Leigh attempted to sell the 1894 Derby winner, trained a number of horses for Leigh, including Chant after he had won the race at Churchill Downs. For C. Head Smith, owner of Pearl Song, he also trained the 1900 Derby winner.

Hughes rated Clifford the greatest horse he ever handled. Clifford was a brown colt foaled in 1890. He started sixty-two times, won forty-two races, was ten times second, eight times third. He raced unplaced in two of his starts, and as a three-year-old won thirteen of his seventeen starts. Owner Leigh described Clifford as "the best horse I ever saw until twenty years later in France when I saw Sardanapale."

Among the outstanding horses trained by Eugene Leigh in France was Epinard. The great son of Badajoz and Epine Blanche was unbeaten in his six races at two. As a three-year-old he won five of his six races, was beaten a neck in the other.

Leigh brought him to the United States for a series of three special races in 1924. The four-year-old invader ran in all three of the International Specials with one hoof in such bad condition that it had to be taped. Nevertheless, his owner refused to withdraw him from any of the three. Epinard was second in each of the races, and in each he was beaten by an American horse outstanding at the distance. Wise Counsellor, a horse of brilliant speed, beat him at six furlongs at Belmont Park; Ladkin, third in the first race, beat him at one mile, as Wise Counsellor was third. The mighty Sarazen barely beat him in the richest and longest of the three, a mile and one-quarter at Latonia. Epinard carried 130 pounds against Wise Counsellor's 125, 126 against Ladkin's 119, and 126 against Sarazen's 120.

Eugene Leigh, an outstanding trainer on both sides of the Atlantic, took his colt Chant south for his preparation for the Kentucky Derby of 1894. He raced at both Little Rock and Memphis and later at Lexington before shipping to Churchill Downs.

It was while Chant was training at Memphis that Charles H. Hughes went to the Tennessee city for the running of the Derby there. Among the friends he called on was Owner-Trainer Leigh who offered to sell him Chant and Lazzarone. Leigh was anxious to get back east and train Clifford.

He insisted to Trainer Hughes that Chant was good enough to win the Kentucky Derby. "However, I was pretty cocky about Pearl Song," Trainer Hughes liked to recall after he had retired from training, "so I told him I had the Kentucky Derby winner right in my own stable." Instead of taking advantage of Leigh's offer, Hughes bet him $500 that Pearl Song would beat Chant in the Derby.

The two were favorites when the field came out for the twentieth running of the Derby on May 15. Chant was held at odds of 1-to-2, and Pearl Song at 3-to-1. The winner's careful preparation in the south was much in evidence in the running of the race.

Getting off in second place, Chant went to the front after a half mile and won as his rider pleased. Pearl Song was best of the other starters, but Trainer Leigh's $500 bet was never in doubt.

Only one among the horses that have won the first seventy-four runnings of the Kentucky Derby ever started more times as a two-year-old than Chant. His twenty-five starts at two are second only to the forty-one races in which Donau ran during 1909. But Chant's thirty-three starts in his three-year-old season are second to no other winner of the Derby at the same age.

Chant was the first of three winners of the race sired by Falsetto and the fourth winner bred by A. J. Alexander. He also was the sixth Derby winner to finish first in the Clark Stakes.

Jockey Frank Goodale, who rode the winner, was killed several days later when the horse he was riding, Judge Payne, stumbled and fell in a race.

1895

The year 1895 marked an important milestone for medical science. It was in that year that Roentgen, at right, discovered the X-ray.

It also was in 1895 that President Cleveland was bitterly denounced after he had negotiated with John P. Morgan for the government to obtain from a financial syndicate a loan of 3,500,000 ounces of gold coin to protect the Treasury against the withdrawal of gold. In return the President offered the syndicate government bonds at a figure lower than public offerings.

The Monroe Doctrine was invoked in a dispute between Venezuela and British Guinea, which were involved in a boundary dispute dating back to 1876. Great Britain was attempting to use the boundary disagreement as a means for acquisition of additional territory.

Cuba was the scene of a bloody insurrection against Spain. The revolt was due largely to the declining prices of sugar and tobacco, but was not supported by the majority of the conservatives who had large financial interests at stake.

The United States Supreme Court reversed its 1880 decision which declared income tax unconstitutional.

Many of the race riders of the day were Negro boys, and the saddle stars included J. "Soup" Perkins (with the cane, lower right) who rode the 1895 Kentucky Derby winner.

The first "Little Colonel Book" was produced in 1895 by the Kentucky writer Anne Fellows Johnston. In Cincinnati on Derby Day a man died as the result

of having cut his tongue while moistening the flap of an envelope he was attempting to seal. At left is reproduced an advertisement which appeared in the Churchill Downs condition book.

Louisville music lovers were being treated to the best concerts available in this era. Lilli Lehmann, of the Metropolitan, visited the city. Walter Damrosch brought to Louisville his new York orchestra for a series of concerts. Mme. Adelina Patti appeared in the Louisville amphitheater.

Pedigree

Halma

HALMA
(Black colt)

- Hanover
  - Hindoo
    - Virgil
    - Florence
  - Bourbon Belle
    - *Bonnie Scotland
    - Ella D.
- Julia L.
  - Longfellow
    - *Leamington
    - Nantura
  - Christine
    - *Australian
    - La Grande Duchesse

Tabulated Racing Record

Year	Age	Sts.	1st	2nd	3rd	Won
1894	2	9	2	1	2	$ 1,785
1895	3	5	4	1	0	13,635
1896	4	0	0	0	0	. . .
1897	5	2	1	0	1	465
		16	7	2	3	$ 15,885

21st Kentucky Derby, May 6, 1895

$2,500 added. Net to winner $2,970; second $300; third $150; fourth $100. 57 nominations.

Horse	Wt.	Fin.	Jockey	Owner
Halma	122	1	J. Perkins	B. McClelland
Basso	122	2	W. Martin	C. H. Smith
Laureate	122	3	A. Clayton	Pastime Stable
Curator	122	4	Overton	Bashford Manor

Time 2:37½. Weather clear.

Winner—Blk.c. by Hanover—Julia L., by Longfellow; trained by B. McClelland; bred by Eastin & Larrabie.

Bookmaking Odds: Halma, 1 to 3; Basso, 9 to 2; Laureate, 5 to 1; Curator, 20 to 1.

Halma led from start to finish, only galloping through the stretch, to win by three lengths.

Halma   Stakes Races

AT 2 YEARS
- 2ND Nursery Stakes.
- 3RD Dunmow Stakes.
- UNP White Plains Handicap, Matron Stakes, Seashore Stakes, Autumn Stakes.

AT 3 YEARS
- WON Kentucky Derby, Latonia Derby, Clark Stakes, Phoenix Stakes.
- 2ND Himyar Stakes.

Had Phil Dwyer's Hanover been ready to start in the Kentucky Derby of 1887, think what the record today might have been. It is safe to assume that Hanover, a truly great horse at three, outclassed the Derby winner of that year. Had he started in the Derby the record would read Hindoo, winner in 1881, sired Hanover, winner in 1887, who sired Halma, winner in 1895, who sired Alan-a-Dale, winner in 1902.

During his four seasons of racing Hanover started fifty times, won thirty-two races, was fourteen times second, and twice thrid. He earned $118,887.50. Hanover was bred by Clay and Woodford in Bourbon County, Kentucky, and sold to Dwyer for $1,350 as a yearling. Following his racing career he was sold to Colonel Milton Young and stood at that breeder's McGrathiana Stud (now Coldstream Stud) until his death, March 23, 1899.

Although Hanover sired only one Derby winner, he was sire of the dams of the winners Worth, Donerail, and Sir Barton. Halma was the first of two Derby winners out of mares by Longfellow.

The first winner of the Kentucky Derby that sired a winner of the race was Halma, which was first past the wire in the 1895 running of the classic at Churchill Downs. It was Halma's son Alan-a-Dale that won the 1902 running of the race.

This was not duplicated until 1932 when Burgoo King, son of the 1926 winner Bubbling Over, defeated his Derby field. Since then Derby winners that have sired other winners have been: Gallant Fox (1930, sire of Omaha (1935); Reigh Count (1928), sire of Count Fleet (1943), and Bold Venture (1936), sire of Assault (1946).

Halma was a son of Hanover, who was the best son of the 1881 Derby winner Hindoo. Hanover was the country's leading sire in the year of Halma's victory, again in 1896, 1897, and 1898. Only one other stallion ever led the American list of sires in four successive years since 1860. That was Lexington.

Not only did Halma's sire top all American stallions in 1895. The jockey who rode him in the Derby, J. "Soup" Perkins, was America's leading rider that season. Will Perkins, brother of the noted Negro rider, had preceded "Soup" to racing and became an outstanding trainer.

As a two-year-old Halma had won two of his nine starts, was once second, and twice third. He started his three-year-old racing at Lexington where he won a purse race and the Phoenix Stakes on May 2. In the latter race the son of Hanover, ridden by Perkins, established a track record of 1:52 1/2 for one and one-eighth miles. That record remained on the Lexington track's books until May 10, 1911, when Governor Gray, named for Alabama's chief executive, ran the distance in 1:51 1/5.

Like Halma, when he set the record, Governor Gray was prepping for the Kentucky Derby when he established the mark. But Meridian, second to Governor Gray in his record-breaking performance at Lexington, beat him in the Derby.

Following the Derby victory Halma won the Clark Stakes at Louisville, went to Latonia where he won the Latonia Derby. He retired following his three-year-old racing.

1896

Boating has always been one of the major sports at Louisville since the first settlers stopped at the Falls of the Ohio, and the 1896 headquarters of the Louisville Boat Club, one of the city's oldest social and sport organizations, is shown in the photograph at the top. The picture of New York's Coney Island at the bottom was taken on a busier afternoon.

Utah became the forty-fifth state to gain admission to the Union when it was admitted on January 4. The state took its name from an Indian tribe.

Two persons who today play an important posthumous part in America's academic picture were prominent in the news of 1896. It was in this year that Alfred Nobel, inventor of dynamite, died and left an estate of $9,000,000 to establish the famous Nobel prizes. The first prizes were awarded on December 10, 1901, five years after the death of the Swedish chemist and inventor. Cecil Rhodes, who founded the Rhodes Scholarships, resigned as premier of the Cape Colony.

The modern Olympic Games had their start in Athens in this year. Princeton University celebrated its sesquicentennial. S. A. Andree and his companion attempted to cross the North Pole in a balloon. Their bodies were recovered in 1930.

The United States Supreme Court rendered a decision in favor of the Leland Stanford estate, which had been sued by the federal government for $15,000,000. An earthquake and tidal wave took the lives of between 10,000 and 30,000 in Japan.

New York City, Baltimore, Boston, Chicago were among the American cities in which occurred strikes in the tailor-

ing business. Both tailors and cutters walked off their jobs in these cities. Boston also was plagued by a street car strike.

Lieutenant Robert E. Peary left this country on another of his arctic expeditions. In Florida the tracks of the Florida East Coast Railroad were completed as far as Miami.

Ballington Booth and his wife were recalled to England. They had headed the Salvation Army in America for nine years. Their recall was protested by many civic leaders in this country.

The Cave of the Winds at Niagara Falls was practically dry. It was the first time in fifty years that this had happened.

Pedigree

Ben Brush

```
                              ┌ *Bonnie Scotland ┌ Iago
                   ┌ Bramble ┤                   └ Queen Mary
                   │          │
                   │          │ Ivy Leaf         ┌ *Australian
BEN BRUSH          │          └                  └ Bay Flower
(Bay colt)        ┤
                   │          ┌ Reform           ┌ *Leamington
                   └ Roseville┤                  └ *Stolen Kisses
                              │
                              └ Albia            ┌ Alarm
                                                 └ Elastic
```

Tabulated Racing Record

Year	Age	Sts.	1st	2nd	3rd	Won
1895	2	16	13	1	1	$ 22,517
1896	3	8	4	1	1	27,340
1897	4	16	8	3	3	17,045
		40	25	5	5	$ 66,902

22nd Kentucky Derby, May 6, 1896

Value $6,000. Net to winner $4,850; second $700; third $300. 171 nominations.

Horse	Wt.	Fin.	Jockey	Owner
Ben Brush	117	1	W. Simms	M. F. Dwyer
Ben Eder	117	2	Tabor	Hot Springs Stable
Semper Ego	117	3	Perkins	L. B. Ringgold
First Mate	117	4	Thorpe	Eastin & Larabie
The Dragon	117	5	Overton	James E. Pepper
Parson	117	6	Britton	Himyar Stable
The Winner	117	7	Walker	William Wallace
Ulysses	117	8	R. Williams	Ed Brown

Time 2:07¾. Weather clear, track good.

Winner—B.c. by Bramble—Roseville, by Reform; trained by Hardy Campbell; bred by Clay & Woodford.

Bookmaking Odds: Ben Brush, 1 to 2; Ben Eder, 2 to 1; Semper Ego, 9 to 1.

At post, 20 minutes, Semper Ego took an immediate lead, followed by The Winner and First Mate. On the first turn, First Mate was in command, and led to the three-quarter pole. Ben Brush, who had stumbled at the start, nearly unseated his rider, and seemed hopelessly out of it, began to move on the backstretch, together with Ben Eder. This pair caught the tired pacemakers going into the stretch, fought it out for almost a quarter of a mile, and Ben Brush won by a nose.

Ben Brush   Stakes Races

AT 2 YEARS	WON	Champagne Stakes, Albany Stakes, Nursery Stakes, Heavy Handicap (all ages), Prospect Handicap, Holly Handicap, Diamond Stakes, Emerald Stakes, Harold Stakes, Cadet Stakes.
	2ND	Flatbush Stakes.
	UNP	Great Eastern Handicap.
AT 3 YEARS	WON	Kentucky Derby, Latonia Derby, Buckeye Stakes, Schulte Stakes.
	2ND	National Derby.
	3RD	Oakley Derby.
	UNP	Fall Handicap.
AT 4 YEARS	WON	Second Special, First Special, Omnium Handicap, The Citizens Handicap, Brighton Handicap, Suburban Handicap.
	2ND	Oriental Handicap.
	3RD	Brighton Cup, Midsummer Handicap.
	UNP	Long Island Handicap, Sheepshead Bay Handicap.

The Dill starting machine, the invention of a Louisville resident, was used in all the races at Churchill Downs in 1896 with the exception of the Derby. Colonel Jack Chinn, of Harrodsburg, Kentucky, used "the old flag, flat-footed and unaided" for starting the Derby which was run at one and one-quarter miles for the first time.

Ben Brush was the leading sire of 1909 when his sons and daughters won $75,143. Among his top money winners was Sweep, champion among the two-year-olds of that year. Sweep did not start in the Derby but his daughters produced Bubbling Over, War Admiral, and Whirlaway, all winners.

Ben Brush, winner of the 1896 Kentucky Derby, is not only prominent in the pedigrees of several other winners of that race. His name also has been prominent in the pedigrees of many noted race horses since he was retired as a sire. One of his sons, Broomstick, sired two winners of the Derby and was a foundation sire of the noted nursery now owned by C. V. Whitney.

The son of Bramble and Roseville started his racing as a two-year-old in Kentucky as the property of Ed Brown. He won his first five starts before he went East to finish third in his first race there. The colt completed his first season of racing in brilliant fashion, winning his last seven races.

As a two-year-old he was sold to Mike Dwyer for $15,000. The Dwyer Brothers had paid the same price for the great Hindoo in the fall of his two-year-old season. Hindoo had started once prior to the Derby he won, but for Ben Brush the Churchill Downs event was the first race at three.

Earlier, William "Umbrella" McGuigan's Lady Inez and Ben Eder had run one-two in the Arkansas Derby. It was Ben Eder who was conceded to be the Dwyer colt's only real rival at Louisville. One of the smallest horses to win the Derby, Ben Brush was given a masterful ride by Jockey Simms.

Several days after the Derby the son of Bramble met Ben Eder's stablemate, Lady Inez. They ran a deadheat and when McGuigan refused to split the purse the race was re-run with Ben Brush winning in time which was a full second faster than the first running. The Derby winner did not start in the Clark Stakes, which was won by Ben Eder with Semper Ego third.

Fearing that Ben Brush had injured himself during his racing at Louisville, Owner Dwyer purchased Ben Eder from McGuigan, who got his name "Umbrella" from the fact that he always carried one. "He never carried it like anyone else would," recalled John H. Morris, prominent trainer of that day. "He always held an umbrella as if he was going to hit you with it."

Ben Brush started seven more times at three, his other wins including the Latonia Derby.

1897

The United States inaugurated its twenty-fifth President in 1897. William B. McKinley, at right, had defeated his Democratic opponent, William Jennings Bryan, for this office.

This also was the year of the great Klondike gold rush in Alaska. During 1897 approximately 200,000 persons from all walks of life went to the interior of Alaska, or at least attempted to make their way there.

Most of them went by way of the White Pass or the Chilkoot Pass, the latter thirty-five miles long and at one point there were a thousand steps cut in the ice. Those seeking the gold had to carry a pack ranging from seventy-five to two hundred pounds, and the ordeal was too much for many who tried.

At one time, it is stated, 3,700 horses lay dead on White Pass trail. During an eight-year period starting in 1896 it is estimated that one hundred million dollars in gold was taken from the Klondike, but only a few of those who set out in quest of a fortune were able to make expenses.

In the photograph below is shown Front Street in Dawson during the great gold rush. The prospectors included many professional men.

In Washington the new Library of Congress was opened in 1897. At Chicago the Yerkes Observatory, built and equipped for the University of Chicago by Charles T. Yerkes, also was opened and dedicated.

Delaware passed a law in 1897 which provided that after 1900 no citizen who could not read or write would be allowed to vote. During the year 5,000 postmasters went on strike for an increase in salary.

Pedigree

Typhoon II

TYPHOON II (Chestnut colt)	*Top Gallant	Sterling	Oxford Whisper
		Sea Mark	Adventurer Sea Gull
	Dolly Varden	*Glenelg	Citadel *Babta
		Nannie Black	Virgil Nannie Butler

Tabulated Racing Record

Year	Age	Sts.	1st	2nd	3rd	Won
1896	2	18	8	6	1	$ 7,565
1897	3	11	8	2	1	12,420
1898	4	10	3	1	1	2,340
		39	19	9	3	$ 22,325

23rd Kentucky Derby, May 12, 1897

Value $6,000. Net to winner $4,850; second $700; third $300. 159 nominations.

Horse	Wt.	Fin.	Jockey	Owner
Typhoon II	117	1	F. Garner	J. C. Cahn
Ornament	117	2	A. Clayton	C. T. Patterson & Co.
Dr. Catlett	117	3	R. Williams	Turney Bros.
Dr. Shepard	117	4	J. Hill	Foster Bros.
Goshen	117	5	Willhite	J. Rodegap
Ben Brown	117	6	Ballard	C. Fleischmann

Time 2:12½. Track heavy.

Winner—Ch.c. by *Top Gallant—Dolly Varden, by *Glenelg; trained by J. C. Cahn· bred by John B. Ewing.

Bookmaking Odds: Typhoon II, 3 to 1; Ornament, even; Dr. Catlett, 4 to 1.

Typhoon II led from the start to finish, to win by a head. Ornament, the favorite, was off poorly, and in deep going all the way.

Typhoon II   Stakes Races

AT 2 YEARS	WON	Westchester Highweight Handicap, Golden Rod Stakes, Brewers' Stakes.
	2ND	Nursery Stakes, Great Eastern Stakes, Two-Year-Old Champion Stakes.
	3RD	Kindergarten Stakes.
	UNP	White Plains Handicap, Rancocas Stakes, Champagne Stakes.
AT 3 YEARS	WON	Kentucky Derby, St. Louis Club Members Handicap, Memorial Handicap, Peabody Hotel Handicap, Luehrmann Hotel Stakes, Chickasaw Club Handicap.
	2ND	Tennessee Derby.
	3RD	St. Louis Derby.
AT 4 YEARS	WON	Highweight Handicap.
	3RD	Coney Island Handicap.
	UNP	Fall Handicap, Toboggan Handicap, Metropolitan Handicap.

Long-shot players enjoyed the May 25, 1897, program at Churchill Downs immensely. In the second race on that date a double disqualification resulted in the winner's paying 40-to-1. Locust Blossom, first past the wire at odds of 6-to-5, was disqualified for fouling Flora Louise, 4-to-5 favorite, and the latter was disqualified for fouling Nada in the five-horse race. Penitence, 40-to-1, was placed first; Nada, 30-to-1, second; and Incidental, 100-to-1, third.

In the last race on the program, Fillibuster won at odds of 100-to-1. Gallante, 7-to-5 favorite, finished out of the money.

Jockey F. Garner, who was astride the 1897 Derby winner, rode a total of 116 winning races during the year. He also had seventy-four seconds and fifty-eight thirds from his 401 races during the year. Two American time records were made during the 1897 season.

Typhoon II had been quite impressive in his two-year-old season. Ten of his eighteen starts in 1896 had been in stakes races. He had won three, finished second in three others, and was third in one.

As a three-year-old Typhoon II began his campaign in Tennessee, where he was foaled. He was the third winner of the Kentucky Derby to be foaled in that state. At Memphis he had won the Peabody Hotel Handicap before shipping to Louisville.

The big winter book favorite, however, was Ornament, a chestnut son of *Order and Victorine, by Onondaga. He continued the choice right up to post-time on May 12, closing at even money. Typhoon II was second choice in the field of six starters.

Riding Typhoon II was Jockey F. "Buttons" Garner, one of the top riders of the country. Astride Ornament was the good Negro rider A. Clayton, who had won with Azra in 1892. Garner displayed all his saddle mastery that afternoon in outriding Clayton. He took Typhoon II to the front immediately after the break, as Clayton got away next to last.

In the first half mile Garner, with his mount showing a lot of early speed, pulled away to a lead of three lengths. The rider kept Typhoon II out from the rail to escape the worst part of the heavy track. Clayton, however, drove Ornament into second place by moving up on the rail.

As the field turned in the stretch for the run to the wire Garner took Typhoon II even farther out into the track where there was better footing. Clayton stayed on the rail, hoping to save ground. Both riders displayed great riding ability in the last stages of the race. Garner was afraid to hit Typhoon II with his whip, he said, fearing the colt would go to pieces under the punishment.

While Garner hand-rode the winner to wire, Clayton drew his whip on Ornament and rained blows on him throughout the last quarter. Ornament responded gamely, slowly cut down the margin of the leader, but was a head back at the finish.

The year 1898 was an eventful one in the history of the United States.

On February 15, the battleship Maine was blown up in the harbor at Havana with the loss of 260 men. This was followed with a declaration by Congress on April 19 that Cuba was independent, and a declaration of war against Spain on April 21.

Admiral Dewey's destruction of the Spanish Fleet at Manila Bay on April 30 is depicted by an artist in the painting reproduced below, which shows the Naval hero on the bridge of his flagship. The battles of San Juan Hill and El Caney were fought July 1-3, and Admiral Cervera's fleet was destroyed in the battle of Santiago de Cuba on July 3. On August 12 preliminaries for peace with Spain were signed.

It was in 1898 that the world's greatest city was born. Andrew Green, upper right, was the father of the plan which incorporated the five boroughs of the Bronx, Queens, Brooklyn, Manhattan, and Richmond into New York City.

Meanwhile, in France the first record

test for one mile in an automobile was being made. Chasseloup Laubat drove a Jentlaud car in the test, establishing an average of 39.23 miles per hour.

On June 27 Captain Joshua Slocum arrived at Newport, Rhode Island, in his sloop Spray. His arrival marked the end of a voyage alone around the world. Captain Slocum had started his venture from Boston on April 24, 1895.

Earlier in June at the conference of the Social Democracy in Chicago, Eugene V. Debs and thirty others representing a membership of about 2,000 withdrew and formed the new Social Democratic Party of America. On June 13 the new party adopted a platform which favored public ownership of all utilities, mines, gas wells, etc., in the United States.

It was also in 1898 that Hawaii, the Philippines, Puerto Rico, and Guam were acquired by the United States. Principal strikes of the country were those involving the New England cotton mills and shoemakers.

Pedigree

Plaudit

PLAUDIT (Brown colt)

- Himyar
  - Alarm
    - *Eclipse
    - *Maud
  - Hira
    - Lexington
    - Hegira
- *Cinderella
  - ‡Tomahawk
    - Blue Mantle
    - Raffle
  - Manna
    - Brown Bread
    - Tartlet

‡by Blue Ruin or Tomahawk.

Tabulated Racing Record

Year	Age	Sts.	1st	2nd	3rd	Won
1897	2	12	4	1	0	$ 8,345
1898	3	8	4	4	0	23,720
		20	8	5	0	$ 32,065

24th Kentucky Derby, May 4, 1898

Value $6,000. Net to winner $4,850; second $700; third $300. 179 nominations.

Horse	Wt.	Fin.	Jockey	Owner
Plaudit	117	1	W. Simms	J. E. Madden
Lieber Karl	122	2	T. Burns	J. W. Schorr
Isabey	117	3	Conley	Stanton & Tucker
Han d'Or	117	4	Connelly	G. A. Singerly

Time 2:09. Weather clear.

Winner—Br.c. by Himyar—*Cinderella, by Tomahawk or Blue Ruin; trained by John E. Madden; bred by Dr. J. D. Neet.

Bookmaking Odds: Plaudit, 3 to 1; Lieber Karl, 1 to 3; Isabey, 12 to 1; Han d'Or, 25 to 1.

Lieber Karl, the favorite, broke in front and made a runaway race of it until nearing the turn for home, when Plaudit came with a terrific rush, and won by a neck.

Plaudit — Stakes Races

AT 2 YEARS
- WON: Champagne Stakes, Nursery Stakes, Emerald Stakes.
- 2ND: Dash Stakes.
- UNP: Great Plains Handicap, Futurity, Diamond Stakes.

AT 3 YEARS
- WON: Kentucky Derby, Buckeye Stakes, Oakley Derby, Clark Stakes.
- 2ND: Realization, St. Louis Derby, Latonia Derby.

Plaudit was a son of Himyar, who had been second to Day Star in the 1878 Derby. Himyar also was sire of the great Domino and was owned by Major Barak G. Thomas, who purchased the present Dixiana Farm in 1877 and named it for his mare Dixie. After selling Dixiana to J. S. Coxey, of Ohio, Major Thomas established another breeding nursery which he called Hira Villa after Himyar's dam, Hira.

The story is told that Himyar got his name as the result of Major Thomas' asking a Negro groom which of the colts he considered best. "Him yar," the Negro replied.

Himyar was a horse of great speed. W. O. Scully, whose White was third in the 1888 Derby, was taken to the track one morning before daybreak by Major Thomas who wanted him to see Himyar work. It was impossible to see the starting point of the workout. In order to time the horse, Thomas instructed a groom to strike the rail with a plank as the colt passed the starting point, saying that he would start his watch when he heard the sound. From out of the early morning fog raced a horse past the finish wire. It was Himyar. From down the track came the sound of a plank hitting the rail. "That is a fast horse!" exclaimed Scully.

The name of John E. Madden has a place of distinction in the annals of American Thoroughbred breeding and racing. He was prominent as a breeder, owner, and trainer, and he is credited with developing numerous improvements in caring for Thoroughbreds. Almost every Thoroughbred nursery of any size has what is known as the "Madden barn."

He was America's leading breeder, in the number of races won, from 1918 until 1927, inclusive. From a monetary standpoint he was the country's leading breeder in 1922, 1923, and 1925. He bred eight winners of more than $100,000 each. They were Zev, Princess Doreen, Grey Lag, Spinach, Boniface, Sir Barton, King James, and Joy Smoke.

Madden's Hamburg Place, outside Lexington, was as well known for its production of Standardbreds as it was for its Thoroughbreds. Each year the farm also produced an outstanding harvest of bluegrass seed. He was the first breeder to produce a winner of America's Triple Crown, and prior to his death in 1929 he bred five winners of the Kentucky Derby.

None of the five carried Madden's colors in the Churchill Downs race. The master of Hamburg Place started three horses in the Derby. His first and only winner was Plaudit, who won in 1898. Plaudit was bred by Dr. J. D. Neet, of Versailles, Kentucky.

As a two-year-old Plaudit had started twelve times. One of his wins was over the 1896 Derby winner Ben Brush, then four, in an event for all ages. In winning the Champagne Stakes at two Plaudit carried top weight of 125 pounds.

Plaudit did his pre-Derby training at Louisville and the Churchill Downs race was his first start at three. While the owner also is listed in the official summary of the Derby as trainer, Albert Simmons actually prepped the horse with Madden commuting from his Lexington farm on work days. The owner was reported at the time to have bet heavily on Plaudit, getting as good as 4-to-1 against the colt. The winner was second choice to Lieber Karl in the books.

He was ridden by Jockey Simms who had been astride Ben Brush in the Derby.

It was in 1899 that Andrew Carnegie consolidated the immense steel works centering around Pittsburgh into the great Carnegie Steel Company. This preceded by two years Carnegie's withdrawal from the industrial world. He transferred his steel interests to the United States Steel Corporation.

Carnegie's wealth at the time he retired as an industrialist was estimated at $500,000,000. His fortune was the largest ever acquired by a foreign-born American citizen.

Marie Curie, upper right, discovered radium in 1899. She and her brilliant husband did much through their research to revolutionize theories regarding the nature of matter and the universe.

Another brilliant scientist of this era was Guglielmo Marconi, lower left, who was the first to master wireless. The first practical application of wireless took place in the preceding year. Aboard a tug Marconi had followed the Kingston Regatta races and had flashed results of the races to a newspaper. Queen Vic-

toria had a wireless set aboard the Prince of Wales' yacht to keep her informed on the Prince's illness.

The Spanish-American War came to an official close with the signing of the Treaty of Paris, which was ratified by the United States Senate on February 6. On February 4, however, the Philippine insurrection started.

On Derby Day of 1899 the Ute Indian Reservation in Colorado was opened to white settlers. The year also was marked by the completion of the Dismal Swamp Canal in Virginia. The original survey for this work had been done by George Washington.

Dr. Charles A. Briggs, who had been suspended by the Presbyterian church in 1893 on charges of heresy, was ordained a priest by the Protestant Episcopal church. A fire which caused $1,000,000 property damage swept the Brooklyn Navy Yard.

At Natick, Massachusetts, on July 18 the writer Horatio Alger died. Robert Green Ingersoll, attorney and agnostic, died at Dobbs Ferry, New York.

Pedigree

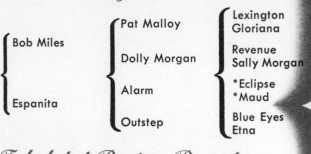

MANUEL (Bay colt)			
Bob Miles	Pat Malloy	Lexington	
		Gloriana	
	Dolly Morgan	Revenue	
		Sally Morgan	
Espanita	Alarm	*Eclipse	
		*Maud	
	Outstep	Blue Eyes	
		Etna	

Tabulated Racing Record

Year	Age	Sts.	1st	2nd	3rd	Won
1898	2	17	3	4	4	$ 4,540
1899	3	4	1	1	0	5,200
		21	4	5	4	$ 9,740

25th Kentucky Derby, May 4, 1899

Manuel

Value $6,000. Net to winner $4,850; second $700; third $300. 151 nominations.

Horse	Wt.	Fin.	Jockey	Owner
Manuel	117	1	F. Taral	A. H. & D. H. Morris
Corsini	122	2	T. Burns	E. Corrigan
Mazo	117	3	Connelly	J. E. Madden
His Lordship	110	4	Turner	J. D. Smith
Fontainebleu	117	5	Overton	J. M. Forsythe

Time 2:12. Weather clear.

Winner—B.c. by Bob Miles—Espanita, by Alarm; trained by Robert J. Walden; bred by George J. Long.

Bookmaking Odds: Manuel, 11 to 20; Corsini, 3 to 1; Mazo, 8 to 1.

Manuel broke in front, was taken back, and His Lordship led to the half-mile. Then the wraps were taken off Manuel, he was permitted to open, won by two lengths, and never was extended.

Manuel — Stakes Races

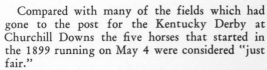

AT 2 YEARS
- WON — Prospect Stakes.
- 2ND — White Plains Handicap, Surf Stakes.
- 3RD — Champagne Stakes, Algeria Stakes, Wenonah Stakes.
- UNP — Nursery Stakes, Great Eastern Stakes, Autumn Maiden Stakes, Flatbush Stakes.

AT 3 YEARS
- WON — Kentucky Derby.
- 2ND — Montgomery Handicap.
- UNP — Twin City Handicap.

The spirit of the twenty-fifth running of the Kentucky Derby was dulled by the death about two weeks earlier of Colonel M. Lewis Clark, founder of Churchill Downs and the Kentucky Derby. Colonel Clark died Saturday, April 22, at the Gaston Hotel in Memphis, Tennessee, as the result of a self-inflicted wound. His act was attributed to bad health and financial difficulties.

Not only was Colonel Clark the first president of the Louisville Jockey Club, but he was the first presiding judge. He also founded the American Turf Congress and established the first uniform scale of weights used in America, as well as introducing many other rules of racing which are followed throughout the country today.

In addition to patterning the Kentucky Derby, the Clark Stakes, and the Kentucky Oaks, each of which has been run for seventy-four years without interruption, he also wrote the conditions for the Louisville St. Leger, the Louisville Cup, and many of the other most popular stakes races prior to the turn of the century.

His body was returned to Louisville and buried in the Cave Hill Cemetery.

For the second season in a row there were no track marks established at Churchill Downs during 1899. Ten of the fifteen track records for distances up to the Derby's mile and one-quarter had been established during the 'nineties.

Compared with many of the fields which had gone to the post for the Kentucky Derby at Churchill Downs the five horses that started in the 1899 running on May 4 were considered "just fair."

However, this was the twenty-fifth running of the classic. The Kentucky Derby alone was enough to attract a big attendance, but the added fact that this was the twenty-fifth anniversary swelled the crowd to between 25,000 and 30,000.

One of the better two-year-olds that had raced during the 1898 season was Manuel, a bay son of Bob Miles, who had raced unplaced in the 1884 Derby. Manuel was out of Espanita, by Alarm, the latter one of the first stallions purchased by George J. Long, who bred Manuel. In 1898 Manuel had raced in the silks of Owner Long, starting seventeen times and winning three races. He was four times second and four times third.

He won only one stakes race at two, but he was in the money in five others, including the Champagne Stakes. Among those impressed with the racing quality of the son of Bob Miles were A. H. and D. H. Morris, Eastern sportsmen. They offered Long $15,000 for the colt, which was accepted.

Manuel started his 1899 season in Tennessee. He was second in the Montgomery Handicap and fell in one other race. For the Kentucky Derby the owners engaged Fred Taral to ride Manuel. Taral was recognized as a brilliant jockey. He also was recognized as a great whip rider. He could literally cut a horse to pieces with his whip.

Taral had ridden the great Domino in many of his races. That champion of the Turf was scared to death of the jockey. Trainers who remembered Domino's racing days tell of seeing him standing peacefully until Jockey Taral would approach him and prepare to mount. Then Domino would begin to lunge and rear and act, generally, like a mad horse. "The only way you could get Domino quiet long enough for Taral to get into the saddle was to hold a rubbing cloth over the horse's eyes," declared one trainer.

Manuel was so much the best in the 1899 Derby, however, that he never felt his rider's whip.

Dr. Walter Reed, of the United States Army, and his associates in 1900 were completing their research proving that yellow fever was passed from man to man by the mosquito. This research played an important part in the success of the United States in building the Panama Canal, and the Walter Reed Hospital in Washington was named in honor of this man.

Dr. William Crawford Gorgas was in actual charge of the health work in the Canal zone, but Dr. Reed, who is shown at right, was associated with him there.

On September 8, 1901, a West Indian hurricane of 120 miles per hour struck Galveston, Texas, and practically destroyed the city. Tremendous waves took the lives of some 5,000 residents.

America's automobile industry was coming into its own. The first automobile show was held in old Madison Square Garden, lower left. Two of the more prominent men affiliated with the industry at the time were Henry Ford and Barney Oldfield, shown at right. Oldfield is the driver of the car.

Kentucky suffered one of her greatest

political tragedies in January, 1900, when Governor William Goebel was fatally wounded on the sidewalk in front of the old Capitol building, the spot marked by a bronze plaque embedded in the walk.

Goebel died five days after the shooting.

Twenty-nine persons, including Kentuckians Henry Clay and Abraham Lincoln, were voted into the Hall of Fame, which was established in 1900 on the campus of New York University. Another Kentuckian gained undying fame on April 30, 1900, when Casey Jones "died with his hand on the throttle" of No. 382. On the day the Derby was run 300 men died in a mine disaster in Utah, and the Nicaraguan Canal Bill was passed by the House by a vote of 225 to 35.

Pedigree

Lieut. Gibson

LIEUT. GIBSON
(Bay colt)

- G. W. Johnson
  - Iroquois
    - *Leamington
    - Maggie B. B.
  - Brunette
    - *Bonnie Scotland
    - Variella
- Sophia Hardy
  - *Glengarry
    - Thormanby
    - Carbine
  - Unaka
    - Enquirer
    - Wampee

Tabulated Racing Record

Year	Age	Sts.	1st	2nd	3rd	Won
1899	2	18	7	4	2	$ 8,475
1900	3	6	3	1	1	13,015
		24	10	5	3	$ 21,490

26th Kentucky Derby, May 3, 1900

Value $6,000. Net value to winner $4,850; second $700; third $300. 131 nominations.

Horse	Wt.	Fin.	Jockey	Owner
Lieut. Gibson	117	1	J. Boland	Charles H. Smith
Florizar	122	2	C. Van Dusen	H. J. Scoggan
Thrive	122	3	J. Winkfield	J. C. Cahn
Highland Lad	—	4	—	H. J. Scoggan
His Excellency	—	5	—	T. C. McDowell
Kentucky Farmer	—	6	—	Woodford & Buckner
Hindus	—	7	—	George J. Long

Time 2:06¼ (new Derby record). Weather clear.

Winner—B.c. by G. W. Johnson—Sophia Hardy, by *Glengarry; trained by Charles H. Hughes; bred by Baker & Gentry.

Bookmaking Odds: Lieut. Gibson, 7 to 10; Florizar, 5 to 1; Thrive, 7 to 1.

Hindus broke first; Kentuck Farmer, second; Lieut. Gibson third. Going around the first turn, Lieut. Gibson moved into leadership and merely breezed the rest of the way, to win by four lengths, never extended.

Lieut. Gibson · Stakes Races

AT 2 YEARS
- WON Kentucky Central Stakes, Kimball Stakes, Flatbush Stakes, Sensation Stakes.
- 2ND Westchester Highweight Handicap.
- 3RD Harold Stakes.

AT 3 YEARS
- WON Kentucky Derby, Clark Stakes, Latonia Derby.
- 3RD American Derby.
- UNP Great Western Handicap.

There was an unusual parallel in the two colts that Trainer Charles H. Hughes purchased for C. Head Smith, of Chicago. First, he paid $10,000 for each colt in their respective two-year-old seasons. Lieut. Gibson won the Derby; Garry Herrmann was winter book favorite, but did not start.

However, the strangest part of the parallel concerned the dams of the respective colts. Colonel Bob Baker, of Lexington, who was the breeder of Lieut. Gibson, decided that Sophia Hardy wasn't much of a broodmare. So he shipped her south to sell as a work mare in the cotton fields. Somewhere along the journey Colonel Baker changed his mind, took the mare off the train, returned her to Kentucky where she was bred to G. W. Johnson. The next spring she foaled Lieut. Gibson.

The dam of Garry Herrmann was sold through the St. Louis stockyards when that colt was a yearling. After Garry Herrmann developed into a sensational colt at two, horsemen searched through five or six states in an effort to find the mare. However, the search availed them nothing.

Only two previous winners of the Kentucky Derby started in more races as two-year-olds than did Lieut. Gibson, winner of the Churchill Downs race in 1900. Chant, winner in 1894, had raced twenty-five times at two; Lookout, winner in 1893, started twenty times in his first season.

Lieut. Gibson went to the post eighteen times at two in 1899. He won seven, was second four times, twice third, and earned $8,475. The son of G. W. Johnson and Sophia Hardy won four stakes events in his first season, was second in another, and third in one added-money race. He was ranked among the better colts of his age in 1899.

Among those horsemen whose attention was drawn to Lieut. Gibson was Trainer Charles H. Hughes, who was handling the horses of C. Head Smith, of Chicago. Hughes approached the owners of Lieut. Gibson with an offer of $10,000 for the colt during his two-year-old season. The offer was accepted. During Lieut. Gibson's three-year-old season Trainer Hughes purchased for Owner Smith the good colt Garry Herrmann for $10,000. Garry Herrmann was the winter book favorite for the 1901 Derby, but did not get to the post.

Lieut. Gibson did not start at three prior to the Kentucky Derby. His trainer, however, had him dead ready for the mile and one-quarter classic. The result was that Lieut. Gibson won the Derby in new record time of 2:06 1/4. After taking the lead at the first turn, the winner merely breezed along in front of his field and was actually under a pull at the finish.

Closest to him at the finish was H. J. Scoggan's Florizar. The second horse was ridden by Clyde Van Dusen, who turned trainer after his retirement as a jockey and won the Derby with his namesake in 1929.

Following the Kentucky Derby, Lieut. Gibson started in five other races at three. He won the Clark Stakes at Churchill Downs, went to Latonia where he had a walkover in the Latonia Derby. These were all his stakes wins in the 1901 racing season.

It was at the Pan-American Exposition held at Buffalo in 1901, a view of which is shown above, that President William B. McKinley was assassinated. The artist's drawing below shows him being shot by Leon F. Czolgosz while attending a reception at the Exposition on September 6.

McKinley died on September 14, the third President of the United States to be assassinated while in office. The others were James A. Garfield and Abraham Lincoln. Two others, William Henry Harrison and Zachary Taylor, had died in office.

Theodore Roosevelt, lower right, succeeded McKinley as President. Roosevelt had been an outstanding figure in the Spanish-American War, Governor of New York, Assistant Secretary of the Navy, and Commissioner of Police in New York City.

William Howard Taft was named the first civil governor of the Philippine Islands, and the United States Supreme Court decided that the Constitution does not follow the flag to possessed territory.

In Louisville the last of the horse-drawn street cars, introduced to the city in 1864, was withdrawn from service. From England Marconi signalled the letter "S" to Newfoundland. Henry Ford perfected a gasoline engine and predicted automobiles for everyone. Tolstoi was exiled.

In Pittsburgh a doctor announced on Derby Day that his bill against a former patient had been increased from $190,-000 to $784,000.

Pedigree

HIS EMINENCE (Bay colt)	Falsetto	Enquirer	*Leamington
			Lida
		Farfaletta	*Australian
			Elkhorna
	Patroness	Pat Malloy	Lexington
			Gloriana
		*Inverness	Macaroni
			Elfrida

Tabulated Racing Record

Year	Age	Sts.	1st	2nd	3rd	Won
1900	2	17	6	1	2	$ 1,925
1901	3	7	2	1	1	8,370
1902	4	12	2	2	0	2,740
1903	5	12	1	1	3	3,110
1904	6	5	0	2	2	150
		53	11	7	8	$ 16,295

27th Kentucky Derby, Apr. 29, 1901

His Eminence

Value $6,000.   Net to winner $4,850; second $700; third $300. 113 nominations.

Horse	Wt.	Fin.	Jockey	Owner
His Eminence	117	1	J. Winkfield	F. B. Van Meter
Sannazarro	117	2	O'Connor	William Hayes
Driscoll	110	3	J. Boland	Woodford Clay
Amur	110	4	Dupree	George J. Long
Alard Scheck	117	5	J. Woods	J. W. Schorr

Time 2:07¾. Weather clear.

Winner—B.c. by Falsetto—Patroness, by Pat Malloy; trained by F. B. VanMeter; bred by A. J. Alexander.

Bookmaking Odds: His Eminence, 3 to 1; Sannazarro, 4 to 1; Driscoll, 20 to 1; Amur, 25 to 1; Alard Scheck, 7 to 10.

His Eminence broke in front and stayed there, winning easily by two lengths.

His Eminence   Stakes Races

AT 2 YEARS	3RD	Wenonah Stakes.
AT 3 YEARS	WON	Kentucky Derby, Clark Stakes.
	UNP	American Derby, Sheridan Stakes.
AT 4 YEARS	2ND	Russet Handicap.
AT 5 YEARS	2ND	Russet Handicap.
	3RD	Twin City Handicap.
	UNP	Turf Handicap, Advance Handicap, Sheepshead Bay Handicap, Suburban Handicap.

His Eminence was the last Kentucky Derby winner also to win the Clark Stakes in his three-year-old season. After the 1901 season the Clark was changed to a handicap race and has remained a handicap event ever since. Only two horses that won the Derby have won the Clark Handicap. Old Rosebud won it as a six-year-old and Exterminator won it as a seven-year-old.

At Chicago's Harlem race track on October 2, 1901, the two-year-old McChesney, carrying 105 pounds, established a new American record for six and one-half furlongs. McChesney ran the distance in 1:18 4/5. At Sheepshead Bay the same year Brigadier set a new American record for one mile. The country's lightweight jockey was L. A. Jackson, who weighed only eighty pounds.

The Kentucky Derby is traditionally a May race. Only twice has it been run in any other month. In 1945 the ban on racing during the early part of the year prevented the race's being run prior to June 9. In 1901 the race was run on April 29.

F. B. Van Meter's His Eminence was the winner. The Derby was the colt's first start at three. Nonetheless, he broke in front, set all the pace to win by two lengths.

His Eminence was the second son of Falsetto to win the race, and the fifth winner to be bred by A. J. Alexander at Woodburn in Woodford County. Only one other breeder ever produced five winners of the Derby. He was John E. Madden, who shared with Vivian Gooch the honor of breeding one of his five.

Falsetto was one of the many outstanding sires that stood at Woodburn. Others included Lexington, *Australian, Planet, Asteroid, *Glen Athol, King Alfonso, Lisbon, and Pat Malloy. Of these *Australian, Pat Malloy, and King Alfonso, in addition to Falsetto, sired winners of the Kentucky Derby. Lexington, who died in the first year of the Kentucky Derby, sired the dams of four winners; mares by Pat Malloy produced two, as did daughters of King Alfonso.

Woodburn was established by Robert Aitchison Alexander. At the outset it was principally devoted to Alderney, Ayrshire, Durham, and Shorthorn cattle, Southdown sheep, Shetland ponies, and Standardbreds. At Woodburn were bred the great trotters Maud S., and Jay-Eye-See, and at Woodburn stood Alexander's Abdallah, sire of Goldsmith Maid.

After the death of R. A. Alexander in 1867, the farm was continued by his younger brother, A. J. Alexander. During the last half of the nineteenth century the number of Turf champions that came from the Woodburn pastures was amazing. A few of them, in addition to the Derby winners, were Norfolk, Asteroid, Maiden, Pat Malloy, Bayonet, Preakness, Kingfisher, Kildare, Harry Bassett, Salina, Springbok, Fellowcraft, Spendthrift, Tom Ochiltree, Duke of Magenta, Grenada, Foxhall, and many others.

1902

Although the per capita debt in the United States was $16.56 the men in charge of the nation's purse strings at Washington went right ahead and added the executive offices to the White House.

Another highlight of the year in Washington was a story in the Washington Evening Star of March 21, which read in part:

"That wireless telephony is possible was demonstrated yesterday beyond question by Nathaniel Stubblefield, of Murray, Kentucky, in a series of public tests on the Potomac River and on the Virginia shore."

The inventor refused offers of as high as $500,000 for his invention, arguing that it was worth $1,000,000. Stubblefield wound up with nothing for his effort, returned to his Kentucky home where he claimed shortly before his death in 1928 that he was about to perfect "lights which would be as far ahead of electric lights as the electric light was ahead of the candle."

On May 8, 1902, at Martinique in the West Indies, Mt. Pelee erupted and wiped out the city of St. Pierre. More than 40,-000 lost their lives in the destruction of the city, a view of which is shown above.

It was in this year that the first Rose Bowl game was played. The Michigan team defeated Stanford by a 49-to-0 score. Not until 1916 was the Rose Bowl game revived.

The first Pacific cable was put down in 1902 from Vancouver to Australia. The cable was more than 8,000 miles long, and included one span of 3,600 miles. In this country approximately 145,000 coal miners went on strike in Pennsylvania.

Louisville was proud of its new fire-fighting equipment, one unit of which is shown below.

Pedigree

ALAN-A-DALE
(Chestnut colt)

- Halma
  - Hanover
    - Hindoo
    - Bourbon Belle
  - Julia L.
    - Longfellow
    - Christine
- Sudie McNairy
  - Enquirer
    - *Leamington
    - Lida
  - Nannie McNairy
    - Jeff Davis
    - Elizabeth McNairy

Tabulated Racing Record

Year	Age	Sts.	1st	2nd	3rd	Won
1901	2	4	3	0	0	$ 8,570
1902	3	1	1	0	0	4,850
1903	4	9	5	3	0	3,940
1904	5	10	5	3	0	5,170
1905	6	13	3	1	1	2,665
		37	17	7	1	$ 25,195

28th Kentucky Derby, May 3, 1902

Alan=a=Dale

Value $6,000.   Net to winner $4,850; second $700; third $300.   112 nominations.

Horse	Wt.	Fin.	Jockey	Owner
Alan-a-Dale	117	1	J. Winkfield	T. C. McDowell
Inventor	117	2	R. Williams	T. W. Moore
The Rival	117	3	N. Turner	T. C. McDowell
Abe Frank	122	4	Coburn	G. C. Bennett & Co.

Time 2:08¾.   Weather clear.

Winner—Ch.c. by Halma—Sudie McNairy, by Enquirer; trained by T. C. McDowell; bred by T. C. McDowell.

Bookmaking Odds: Alan-a-Dale (Coupled with The Rival), 3 to 2; Inventor, 11 to 1; Abe Frank, 3 to 5.

The Rival was first to show, but Alan-a-Dale caught him in the first eighth, opened a four-length lead going into homestretch, went lame in the final eighth, carried on with flawless courage, and won by a nose.

Alan-a-Dale   Stakes Races

AT 2 YEARS	WON	Brighton Junior Stakes.
	UNP	Foxland Stakes.
AT 3 YEARS	WON	Kentucky Derby.
AT 4 YEARS	WON	Oakwood Handicap.
	UNP	Harlem National Handicap.
AT 5 YEARS	2ND	Fall Handicap, The Ocean Handicap, The Flight Handicap.
AT 6 YEARS	UNP	Omnium Handicap, Ocean Handicap, Saratoga Handicap, Test Handicap.

Sudie McNairy, dam of Alan-a-dale, was one of the first broodmares owned by Major Thomas C. McDowell. Another of his first mares was Bracegirdle, dam of The Rival, who ran coupled with Alan-a-Dale as the McDowell entry.

Sire of Sudie McNairy was Enquirer, a son of *Leamington, who sired the first Derby winner. Enquirer, Longfellow, and Littleton were three of the best foals got by *Leamington the only year he stood in Kentucky. Enquirer stood at General Abe Buford's Bosque Bonita Farm, later owned by John H. Morris.

Morris told many interesting stories about Buford, whose family had owned Woodburn before it was acquired by the Alexanders. The trainer of Azra on one occasion recalled, "Abe Buford disliked the Alexanders immensely and the thing he liked to do best was beat an Alexander horse. One day at Louisville A. J. Alexander's Lisbon beat Buford's McWhirter in the Alexander Stakes. Buford yelled so loud you could hear him downtown. A few days later McWhirter beat Lisbon. Buford lay right down in the middle of the track, wallered like a dog, and hollered, 'I beat Alexander! I beat Alexander!'"

Derby Day in 1902 was a half-holiday in Louisville by virture of resolution passed by the City Council. Every stable at Churchill Downs was filled with horses there for the spring meeting. A great many more were stabled at nearby Douglas Park. Admission to Churchill Downs on Derby Day cost the patrons $1.50 each.

Alan-a-Dale was the third winner of the Derby foaled at Ashland which had been the home of Henry Clay and which is still owned by his heirs. It was John M. Clay, son of Henry Clay, who bred Day Star, first of the Derby winners produced there. Riley, bred by C. H. Durkee, was foaled at Ashland in 1887.

Major Thomas Clay Mcdowell, great-grandson of Henry Clay, was the breeder, owner, and trainer of Alan-a-Dale. Only one other man ever bred, owned, and trained a winner. He was Thomas P. Hayes, whose Donerail won the race in 1913. At the time that Alan-a-Dale was foaled, Standardbreds as well as Thoroughbreds were being raised at Ashland. Major Henry Clay McDowell, father of the owner of the Derby winner, was more interested in trotters of which he owned more than sixty head, including the outstanding sire Dictator. Following his racing career Alan-a-Dale was retired to the stud at Ashland and upon his death was buried alongside the grave of Dictator.

The 1902 Derby winner has the distinction of being the only winner of the race who made his only start at three in the Churchill Downs classic. Regret, winner in 1915, started only twice at three, while several winners started only three times during the years in which they won the Derby.

As a two-year-old Alan-a-Dale won three of his four races, including the $10,000 Brighton Junior Stakes. He was unplaced in his fourth start. The 1902 winner raced again at four, five, and six before retiring. He came out of the Derby lame which accounted for his retirement from racing for the remainder of the year.

In winning with Alan-a-Dale the top Negro rider Jimmy Winkfield became the second jockey to win two successive runnings of the race. The other was also a Negro, Isaac Murphy.

1903

Man's first flight in a motor-driven, heavier-than-air machine came at Kitty Hawk, North Carolina, on December 17, 1903. In the picture below, Orville Wright is lying prone in the plane as he piloted it in the first effort.

His brother and co-worker, Wilbur Wright, is shown running alongside the machine. The inaugural flight lasted twelve seconds and covered 120 feet. Later on the same date Wilbur made a flight which lasted fifty-nine seconds and covered 852 feet.

It was in 1903 that the first World Series was played. Boston of the American League and Pittsburgh of the National League met in an eight-game series. Boston, managed by J. J. Collins, was the winner. F. C. Clarke managed the Pittsburgh team.

The Ford Motor Company was organized in this year, and a cable was laid from San Francisco to Manila.

The same year saw the United States recognize the Republic of Panama after a mild revolution, which President Roosevelt was accused of instigating. On November 18, the Hay-Bunau-Varilla Treaty was adopted and provided for the outright purchase by the United States of a ten-mile strip across the isthmus.

John Hay, co-author of the Treaty, was father of Mrs. Payne Whitney, whose horses won two runnings of the Kentucky Derby. In 1903 Churchill Downs offered the view at top.

"The Little Shepherd of Kingdom Come," whose author was John Fox, Jr., was published in 1903. Fox had attended school at Transylvania University. Georgetown, Kentucky, was troubled with two factions claiming the city offices and Cleveland's Kohl Torpedo Factory was wrecked by an explosion. Wine was ruled out as a drink at future dinners given by the Knight Templars. This action was taken at the fraternal organization's convention in California.

Pedigree

JUDGE HIMES (Bay colt)	*Esher	Claremont	Blair Athol / Coimbra
		Una	‡Dusk / Conjecture
	Lullaby	Longfellow	*Leamington / Nanura
		Lady Richards	War Dance / Lucretia

‡by Ellington or Dusk.

Tabulated Racing Record

Year	Age	Sts.	1st	2nd	3rd	Won
1902	2	10	1	1	2	$ 400
1903	3	28	7	1	9	19,865
1904	4	32	5	5	3	3,500
1905	5	31	5	6	7	4,155
1906	6	3	0	1	1	75
		104	18	14	22	$ 27,995

29th Kentucky Derby, May 2, 1903

Judge Himes

Value $6,000.   Net to winner $4,850; second $700; third $300. 140 Nominatioss.

Horse	Eqt	Wt	PP	St	½	¾	1	Str	Fin	Jockey	Owner	Odds $1 Str't
Judge Himes	w	117	4	3	$3\frac{1}{2}$	$3\frac{1}{2}$	4^3	2^2	$1\frac{3}{4}$	Booker	Ellison	10.00
Early	w	117	2	4	4^6	4^6	$1\frac{1}{2}$	$1\frac{1}{2}$	2^6	Winkf'd	Tich'r & Co	.60
Bourbon	w	110	5	5	5^2	$5\frac{1}{2}$	$5\frac{1}{2}$	4^3	$3\frac{1}{2}$	Cowh'st	McDowell	4.00
Bad News	w	114	1	2	$2\frac{1}{2}$	2^{nk}	3^1	$3\frac{1}{2}$	4^3	Davis	Wo'd-Buc'r	5.00
Woodlake	wb	117	3	1	1^1	1^1	2^{nk}	5^1	5^5	Helg'sen	McDowell	4.00
Treacy	w	110	6	6	6	6	6	6	6	Landry	Stevens	15.00

†Coupled in betting as T. C. McDowell entry.

Time, :25½, :51, 1:16½, 1:42, 2:09.   Track fast.

Winner—Ch.c. by *Esher—Lullaby, by Longfellow; trained by J. P. Mayberry; bred by Johnson N. Camden.

Start poor. Won driving; second easily. Jockey Booker waited with Judge Himes until well in the last quarter before making a move, came through on the inside at the turn into the homestretch, caught Early tiring and, after a sharp struggle, was going away at the finish. Winkfield made his run too soon with Early, made up a lot of ground while rounding the far turn, but had nothing left when Judge Himes challenged. Bourbon finished well and outgamed Bad News. Woodlake quit badly after going a good half-mile. Treacy was never a contender.

Scratched—Dan McKenna, 117; The Picket, 110.

Judge Himes — Stakes Races

AT 3 YEARS	WON	Kentucky Derby, Hawthorne Handicap, Excelsior Handicap, Endurance Handicap, Oak Park Handicap.
	3RD	Latonia Club Membership Handicap, Flyaway Handicap, Maywood Handicap, Blue Grass Stakes.
	UNP	Tennessee Derby, Hotel Gayoso Stakes, Latonia Derby, American Derby.
AT 4 YEARS	3RD	Elmridge Handicap, Superior Handicap, August Stakes.
AT 5 YEARS	WON	Whirlpool Stakes.
	2ND	Speculation Stakes, Park Hotel Stakes.
	3RD	Eastman Hotel Stakes.
	UNP	Country Club Handicap.

The 1903 Kentucky Derby was the first started with the web barrier. This was an elastic tape, about four inches wide, which was stretched across the track at the starting point and fastened at either end to an iron arm. The starter controlled the barrier. When the horses were in line he pressed a button releasing the two iron arms which threw the barrier slightly forward and upward, out of the horses' way. It was not unusual for horses to break the barrier several times before a start was made. An assistant starter would repair the damage by merely tying the loose ends together. This form of starting was used for the Derby until 1930 when the first type of mechanical starting gate was used.

The new clubhouse at Churchill Downs was ready for the twenty-ninth running of the Kentucky Derby on May 2, 1903. It was in this Derby that Jockey James Winkfield got the mount on the favorite Early and made a brilliant effort to equal the record of Jockey Isaac Murphy by winning the race three times.

Early went to the post at the short price of 3-to-5. He might have won had not his rider been so eager to get to the wire first and used up the favorite in the early part of the race. As a result Early had nothing left to withstand the stretch run of the winner, and Winkfield saw his third Derby slip away by three-quarters of a length.

Judge Himes, a son of *Esher, had been a forward factor throughout the entire mile and one-quarter, but Jockey H. Brooker saved his mount for the final drive to the wire. The winner was held at odds of 10-to-1, only one starter going to the post at longer odds.

C. R. Ellison's colt had been unimpressive as a two-year-old. He had won only one of his ten starts at that age, was once second, twice third, and unplaced in his other six races. His record at three prior to the Derby also had been unimpressive, and Judge Himes was troubled by sore heels. All this combined to result in horsemen giving him little chance to win at Churchill Downs.

Johnson N. Camden, owner of Hartland Farm, was the breeder of Judge Himes. He was sold by his breeder as a yearling for $1,700. The colt was full brother to Garry Herrmann, who had been the winter book favorite for the Derby two years earlier. Camden himself attempted to win the Derby on five different occasions, but his horses were never able to finish better than second.

The Derby was one of seven races won by Judge Himes during his three-year-old season during which he started twenty-eight times. He raced for three more seasons, starting thirty-two times at four, thirty-one times at five, and three times at six. In all, the 1903 winner started 104 times before he quit racing.

Only two Derby winners started more times.

1904 was election year in the United States and a group of influential senators carefully made their plans to take the Republican nomination away from Theodore Roosevelt. Senator Mark Hanna, of Ohio, was selected as the man they would back for the candidacy. Hanna had been campaign manager for McKinley the first time the latter was elected. However, Hanna died in February before the convention.

Opposition to Roosevelt faded and he was nominated unanimously. To oppose him the Democrats nominated Judge Alton B. Parker, of the New York Court of Appeals. Roosevelt was returned to the White House by an electoral vote of 336 to 140.

Russia and Japan were at war over Chinese ports in Manchuria and Korea. Roosevelt invited them to meet at Portsmouth, New Hampshire, in August to arrive at a peace. In the photograph above are shown the Russian and Japanese delegates assembled at Portsmouth. For this effort the President received the Nobel Peace Prize in 1906.

This was the year that the United States started plans for building the Panama Canal. In the photograph at lower right the President is shown operating a steam shovel in the early stages of construction. It was also in 1904 that the Olympic Games were held for the first time in this country. The site was St. Louis.

The Wright brothers, who in 1903 had made the first successful flight, scored two more firsts in aviation during 1904. On September 15 Orville Wright became the first man to negotiate a turn in a plane. Five days later Brother Wilbur flew the plane in a complete circle.

Sunday baseball was declared legal in Brooklyn. In California railroad section hands refused to work near the wreck of a circus train from which all wild animals and snakes escaped.

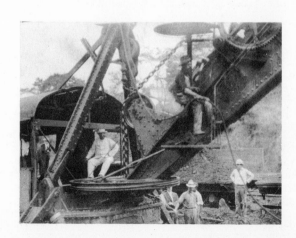

Pedigree

			*Phaeton Fanny Holton
	Ten Broeck		
Free Knight		Belle Knight	Knighthood Kentucky Belle
ELWOOD (Bay colt)			
	Alarm		*Eclipse *Maud
Petticoat			
	Lady Scarborough		*Leamington *Lady Lumley

Elwood

Tabulated Racing Record

Year	Age	Sts.	1st	2nd	3rd	Won
1903	2	17	1	2	1	$ 950
1904	3	23	6	4	3	13,580
1905	4	12	1	1	1	1,060
1906	5	3	0	0	0	...
1907	6	3	0	0	0	...
		58	8	7	5	$ 15,590

30th Kentucky Derby, May 2, 1904

Value $6,000. Net to winner $4,850; second $700; third $300. 140 Nominations.

Horse	Eqt	Wt	PP	St	½	¾	1	Str	Fin	Jockey	Owner	Odds $1 Str't
Elwood	wb	117	3	4	4¹	4ʰ	4½	5½	1½	Prior	Mrs Dur'l	15.00
Ed Tierney	w	117	5	3	3¹	3¹½	3¹	3²	2³	Domin'k	Fay & We'f	1.10
Brancas	w	117	4	5	5	5	5	2½	3²½	Lyne	Gerst	2.50
P Silverw'gs	w	117	1	2	2²	1¹	1¹	1ʰ	4¹	D Austin	Talb't Bros	7.00
Proceeds	wb	122	2	1	1¹½	2½	2ʰ	4½	5	Helges'n	Brown	1.00

Time, :13, :25, :49½, 1:51¼, 1:28½, 1:42, 1:54, 2:08½. Track fast.

Winner—B.c. by Free Knight—Petticoat, by Alarm, trained by C. E. Durnell; bred by Mrs. J. B. Prather.

Went to Post—4:15. Off at 4:19.

Start good. Won driving; second easily. Elwood was well ridden. Prior rated him along for the first seven furlongs and never made a move until rounding the turn into the homestretch, where he moved up on the outside and fought it out in turn with Brancas, Prince Silverwings and Ed Tierney in the last quarter, and outstayed the latter in the final drive. Dominick nursed Ed Tierney along for the first half and made a determined effort in the stretch run, tiring in the last fifty yards. Brancas stumbled at the start and Lyne kept taking him back in the first half-mile, moved him up fast at the home turn and was in front for a few strides, but tired. Prince Silverwings showed much early speed, but tired after a mile. Proceeds stumbled at the start but this cut no figure in the result.

Scratched—Batts, 117.

Elwood   *Stakes Races*

AT 2 YEARS	2ND	Youngster Stakes, Competition Stakes.
AT 3 YEARS	WON	Kentucky Derby, Latonia Derby.
	2ND	California Derby.
	3RD	St. Louis Derby.
	UNP	American Derby, M. Lewis Clark Stakes.

Elwood was the third winner of the Kentucky Derby produced by a daughter of Alarm, whose daughters Albia and Espanita had produced Azra (1892) and Manuel (1899), respectively. Not only was Albia the dam of a Derby winner, but she was the dam of a mare who produced one. Ben Brush, winner in 1896, was out of a daughter of Albia.

*Inverness, by Macaroni, also was the dam of a Derby winner, Joe Cotton (1885), and granddam of another, His Eminence (1901). The only other mare who was the dam and grandam of winners was *Weatherwitch. She produced Fonso (1880) and one of her daughters produced Hindoo (1881).

Delhi, later a successful sire, was the country's leading money-winner in 1904. His earnings were $75,225. Delhi was one of the first foals of Ben Brush. The two-year-old champion of the year was the great filly Artful.

Not only was Elwood the first winner of the Kentucky Derby owned by a woman. He also was the first starter ever owned by a woman and the first winner bred by a woman. Mrs. C. E. Durnell was the owner and Mrs. J. B. Prather bred Elwood who was foaled in Missouri. He is the only winner of the race to come from that state.

Elwood had raced in California prior to coming to Churchill Downs for the Derby. On the west coast the son of Free Knight, himself second in the Derby, had won three races. One of his winning efforts had been at one and one-half miles in 2:37. He had also been second in the California Derby. After arriving at Louisville Elwood had been given a severe training schedule and came up to the race as hard as nails.

However, the 1903 Derby field was considered rather ordinary. Fresh in the memory of the fans was the recent Tennessee Derby triumph of S. S. Brown's Proceeds. That winning effort had considerable to do with the public's sending Proceeds to the post as favorite at odds of 1-to-1.

Starter Jake Holtman lost little time in getting the field of five on its way. Proceeds was first to show, holding the lead throughout the first half-mile. Then it was Prince Silverwings who took command of the field. As Jockey D. Austin sent the Talbot Brothers' colt the first six furlongs in 1:15 3/4 horsemen declared, "He can't keep that up."

However, the pacemaker did hold his length lead until the field reached the stretch where the winner, Ed Tierney, and Brancas passed him. At the end of the first mile Elwood was dead last.

As a yearling Elwood was sold for $700. In his two-year-old season he won only one of his seventeen races, and as a four-year-old he won only one out of twelve starts. It was in his four-year-old season that Elwood ran at Brighton Beach in a race exclusively for jockeys who had never ridden a winner.

Elwood was the longest-priced winner in the Derby history to that date.

On April 27, 1905, Andrew Carnegie, who is shown in the photograph below, announced another of the many outstanding gifts from the tremendous fortune he had acquired in the United States. He gave $10,000,000 to establish a pension fund for college professors in the United States, Canada, and Newfoundland. Other gifts by Carnegie included $43,000,000 for free public libraries, $15,000,000 to colleges, universities and schools, $15,000,000 to the Carnegie Foundation for the Advancement of Teaching, and $10,000,000 to the Carnegie Hero Fund.

There were 2,186 strikes and lockouts during the year, affecting 302,000 persons. On July 1, the government indicted five corporations and seventeen individuals engaged in the meat packing business for alleged violations of the Sherman Anti-Trust law.

In Washington a protocol was signed with Santo Domingo. It was designed to guarantee the integrity of the Dominican territory, undertake the adjustment of foreign claims, administer the finances, and assist in maintaining order. Also in Washington, the engineering commission of the Panama Canal Commission unanimously recommended a sea-level canal to be constructed in not more than twelve years at a cost of $230,500,000.

A six-year search for the grave of John Paul Jones, who had been buried in France on July 20, 1792, was brought to a successful end in 1905 when General Horace Potter discovered the grave in Paris. Immediately plans were made for returning the remains to the United States.

On May 7, three days prior to the running of the Kentucky Derby, 12,039 immigrants reached New York ports. The immigrants were chiefly Italians and the number broke all immigration records for one day.

To oppose the American Federation of Labor there was organized in 1905 the Industrial Workers of the World. On January 1 it was announced there were 3,779,519 telephones in the United States.

Pedigree

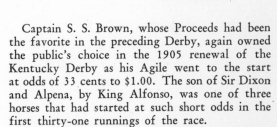

AGILE (Bay colt)			
	Sir Dixon	*Billet	Voltigeur / Calcutta
		Jaconet	*Leamington / Maggie B. B.
	Alpena	King Alfonso	*Phaeton / Capitola
		Penumbra	Pat Malloy / Penelope

Tabulated Racing Record

Year	Age	Sts.	1st	2nd	3rd	Won
1904	2	21	5	4	2	$ 4,530
1905	3	10	5	5	0	32,835
1906	4	21	2	2	2	1,485
1907	5	14	2	1	5	950
		66	14	12	9	$ 39,800

Agile

31st Kentucky Derby, May 10, 1905

Value $6,000.   Net to winner $4,850; second $700; third $300. 145 nominations.

Horse	Eqt	Wt	PP	St	½	¾	1	Str	Fin	Jockey	Owner	Odds $1 Str't
Agile	w	122	1	1	1¹½	1¹½	1¹½	1²	1³	Martin	Brown	.33
Ram's Horn	ws	117	2	2	2⁵	2¹⁰	2¹⁵	2²⁰	2²⁰	Lyne	Will'ms Co	2.50
Layson	w	117	3	3	3	3	3	3	3	Austin	Hayes	16.00

Time, :25½, :50, 1:16, 1:42¾, 2:10¾. Track heavy.

Winner—B.c. by Sir Dixon—Alpena, by King Alfonso; trained by R. Tucker; bred by E. F. Clay.

Went to Post—4:20. Off at 4:21.

Won easily; second the same. Agile was full of speed all the way and Martin never let him down at any part of the trip. He drew away under restraint in the last furlong, and was only galloping at the end. Lyne made his move with Ram's Horn while rounding the turn into the homestretch, but could not get to the winner.

Scratched—Dr. Leggo, 122; McClellan, 110.

Agile   Stakes Races

AT 2 YEARS	WON	Waldorf Stakes.
	2ND	Southhold Handicap.
	UNP	Nursery Handicap, Matron Stakes, Hopeful Stakes, Great Trial Stakes, The Daisy Stakes.

AT 3 YEARS	WON	Kentucky De by, Advance Stakes, Phoenix Stakes, Tennessee Derby.
	2ND	Brighton Derby, Tidal Stakes, Broadway Stakes.

| AT 4 YEARS | UNP | Suburban Handicap, Edgemere Handicap, Election Day Handicap. |

| AT 5 YEARS | UNP | Thanksgiving Handicap, Special. |

The owner of the 1905 Derby winner owned a steel mill in Pittsburgh. He also owned a fleet of river boats, which hauled coal and ore to his mills. It was from the operation of those boats that he gained the title of "Captain." He also owned the Senorita Stud in Kentucky at which were produced a number of outstanding race horses. At one time he owned the race track at Lexington.

The original dates for the spring meeting at Churchill Downs in 1905 were extended for five days when the American Turf Association met at the track on Derby Day. Presiding at the meeting was President Matt J. Winn.

The great Sysonby was never beaten at three, although he ran in one deadheat. He was the leading money winner with earnings of $144,380 and J. R. Keene led money-winning owners. Sysonby was beaten only once at two, losing to the champion Artful in the futurity.

Captain S. S. Brown, whose Proceeds had been the favorite in the preceding Derby, again owned the public's choice in the 1905 renewal of the Kentucky Derby as his Agile went to the start at odds of 33 cents to $1.00. The son of Sir Dixon and Alpena, by King Alfonso, was one of three horses that had started at such short odds in the first thirty-one runnings of the race.

For the first time a bugle summoned the Derby field from the paddock. The call echoed and died among the greatest crowd that had ever witnessed any running of the race. Among those present was Lillian Russell, who also attended the opening of the new Seelbach Hotel on Derby Eve.

No winter book odds had been quoted on the race. Consequently, all those who wanted to wager on the race, which had been referred to as "Brown's Agile against Williams' $250 horse," did so at the track. The choice had to be between Agile and Ram's Horn for the only other starter was not conceded any chance against those two. It was the second and last time the Derby drew only three starters.

Agile, who won his first four races as a three-year-old including the Tennessee Derby and Phoenix Stakes, was a good mud runner and the heavy track suited him perfectly. He was first away when the start came and never relinquished his lead, despite a determined bid on the part of Ram's Horn in the late stages of the race. Layson was five lengths out of the race in the first half mile, gradually falling farther behind to finish twenty lengths back of the second horse.

Lucien Lyne, who was a leading jockey in this country before going to Europe to ride, was astride Ram's Horn in the Derby. Lyne proved an equal sensation as a jockey in both Spain and France. Following his retirement as a rider he became trainer for the stable owned by the king of Spain, also trained for other European stables.

From Churchill Downs Agile was shipped East where he was beaten twice by the great Sysonby, owned by James R. Keene and considered one of the all-time great horses of the American Turf.

1906

On April 18, 1906, scarcely two weeks prior to the running of the Kentucky Derby, San Francisco, California, was struck by earthquake and fire which razed more than four square miles of the city. A view of the devastated area is shown above.

Between 500 and 1,000 persons lost their lives during the 'quake and fire. Property damage was estimated at between $250,000,000 and $300,000,000.

In the nation's Capital, Congress passed the Hepburn Rate Bill. This greatly strengthened the Interstate Commerce Act giving the commission greater powers to regulate rates. President Roosevelt also brought about an investigation of packing houses. In the same year Congress passed the Pure Food and Drugs Act.

At Los Angeles, California, on February 23, Tommy Burns beat Marvin Hart, of Louisville, in a twenty-round heavyweight fight, with James J. Jeffries refereeing. Burns claimed the championship of the heavyweight division as a result of the match.

George J. Long, lower right, had become one of the most prominent Turfmen of the country. A Louisville industrialist, he had established the noted Bashford Manor Stud, and had gained national recognition as a breeder, owner, and race track director.

On Derby Day, 1906, educators from throughout the nation assembled in Kentucky for the Convention for Education in the South. President of the convention was Robert C. Ogden, of New York, who brought to Kentucky a special train of eight cars. Governors of several states also were in attendance.

The same day the President of the United States received a cablegram from Athens, Greece, telling of the victories scored by the United States representatives in the Olympic Games.

On February 17 Alice Roosevelt, eldest daughter of the President, and Nicholas Longworth, representative from Ohio, were married in the White House.

Pedigree

SIR HUON (Bay colt)	Falsetto	Enquirer
		{ *Leamington / Lida
		Farfaletta
		{ *Australian / Elkhorna
	Ignite	*Woodlands
		{ Nutbourne / Whiteface
		Luminous
		{ Alarm / *Lady Lumley

Tabulated Racing Record

Year	Age	Sts.	1st	2nd	3rd	Won
1905	2	9	4	2	0	$ 3,775
1906	3	7	5	1	0	34,655
1907	4	1	0	0	0	. . .
1908	5	1	1	0	0	550
		18	10	3	0	$ 38,980

Sir Huon

32nd Kentucky Derby, May 2, 1906

Value $6,000. Net to winner $4,850; second $700; third $300. 110 nominations.

Horse	Eqt	Wt	PP	St	½	¾	1	Str	Fin	Jockey	Owner	Odds $1 Str't
Sir Huon	w	117	4	2	2^2	2^2	1^{nk}	1^2	1^2	Troxler	Long	1.10
Lady Nav'rre	w	117	3	4	4^h	3^{nk}	4^6	2^{nk}	2^3	Burns	Ellison	1.80
J's Redd'k	wsb	117	5	5	5^2	4^3	3^h	3^1	3^5	Domin'k	Ellison	1.80
Hyper'n II	wsb	114	2	1	1^3	1^2	$2^{1\frac{1}{2}}$	4^h	4^{10}	Austin	Hawk's Co	8.00
De Bar	w	117	1	6	6	$5^{1\frac{1}{2}}$	5^6	5^{10}	5^3	Nicol	Shann'n Co	3.50
Velours	wsb	117	6	3	3^{nk}	6	6	6	6	Walsh	Franklin	40.00

†Coupled in betting as C. R. Ellison entry.

Time, :24-3/5, :49-4/5, 1:15, 1:41-2/5, 2:08-4/5. Track fast.

Winner—B.c. by Falsetto—Ignite, by *Woodlands; trained by P. Coyne; bred by George J. Long.

Went to Post—4:00. Off at 4:02.

Start good; won driving; second same. Jockey Troxler rode a well judged race on Sir Huon, saved him from the pace set by Hyperion II, and never made a move until well around the far turn, where the colt came fast, and taking command entering the homestretch, held the race safe all through the last quarter. Lady Navarre was interfered with while rounding the turn into the backstretch and made a determined effort on the turn for home, but could never get to the winner. James Reddick was sore in his warm-up, but ran to his best race. Hyperion II. forced a fast pace, but could not stay the route. De Bar was always outrun. Velours cut no figure.

Scratched—Creel, 117.

Sir Huon   *Stakes Races*

AT 2 YEARS	WON	Harold Stakes.
	2ND	Cincinnati Trophy.
	UNP	Golden Rod Stakes.
AT 3 YEARS	WON	Kentucky Derby, Latonia Derby, Queen City Handicap, Commonwealth Stakes, Seagate Stakes.
	2ND	Saratoga Cup.
	UNP	The Advance Stakes.

Sir Huon was the third Kentucky Derby winner sired by Falsetto. The other two were Chant and His Eminence in 1894 and 1901, respectively. Falsetto, who had previously stood at Woodburn Farm, died at Bashford Manor on July 23, 1904.

Falsetto was bred by J. W. Hunt Reynolds, in whose silks he was second in the 1879 Kentucky Derby. He had been raced as a two-year-old. However, no less an authority than James R. Keene attempted to purchase Falsetto for $10,000 prior to the Derby, fearing what he might do when he came east to meet Keene's Spendthrift. The offer carried the condition that Falsetto must win the Derby. Keene's fears were well founded for Falsetto did go east to beat Spendthrift in the Travers Stakes and Kenner Stakes.

When George J. Long decided to enter Thoroughbred breeding and racing in 1887, one of the first mares he purchased was Luminous. In 1888 Owner Long bred that daughter of Alarm to the eighteen-year-old stallion *Woodlands. The following year Luminous foaled a bay filly, which Long named Ignite. As a two-year-old Ignite was an outstanding filly. She also was a good stakes winner in her three-year-old season.

Following her racing career Ignite was retired to Owner Long's Bashford Manor Farm at Louisville. In 1902 she was bred to Falsetto, then twenty-six years old. The result of that mating was Sir Huon, winner of the 1906 running of the Kentucky Derby. In 1896 Ignite had been bred to Volante. From that mating she produced Hindus, who ran unplaced in the 1900 Kentucky Derby.

The 1906 Derby winner was named for one of the knights of Charlemagne's court, and a filly foaled at Bashford Manor the same spring was given the name Regia, wife of Sir Huon. The Derby winner was described as a horse of beautiful conformation. He was compared to Sysonby.

Trained by Pete Coyne, who had succeeded John H. Morris as the Bashford Manor trainer in 1905, Sir Huon won four of his nine races as a two-year-old. His winning efforts in that season included the Harold Stakes at Latonia.

The Kentucky Derby was his first race as a three-year-old and the first of three straight stakes triumphs. Following the Kentucky Derby, Sir Huon won the Latonia Derby and Queen City Handicap. He was then unplaced in the Advance Stakes, won the Commonwealth Stakes and Seagate Stakes in order. His final race of 1906 was the Saratoga Cup in which he was second to the five-year-old Go Between. Sir Huon made one start each in his four- and five-year-old seasons. He was then retired to Bashford Manor as a sire.

1907

Kentucky's new state capitol building, above, at Frankfort was completed and dedicated in 1907, as the number of states of the Union was increased to forty-six with the admission of Oklahoma (from the Choctaw Indian word meaning red people) on November 16.

The Lusitania, British-owned and destined to be sunk shortly after the outbreak of World War I, established a new record for a trans-Atlantic crossing. The famous ship is shown at lower right.

In 1907 Carrie Nation, lower left, was prominent on the national scene. With her hatchet she crusaded against saloons. She was a native of Lancaster, Kentucky.

In 1904, President Theodore Roosevelt had suggested a second Hague Peace Conference. However, this had to be postponed until 1907 because of the Russo-Japanese War. For its second meet-

ing the conference gathered in the new palace which had been built for such use by Andrew Carnegie, the American steel capitalist.

A young federal jurist named Kenesaw Mountain Landis handed down a decision imposing a fine of $29,240,000 on the Standard Oil Company of Indiana on charges of taking rebates from railroads.

The Southern Pacific, Pere Marquette, and New York Central Railroads all experienced bad wrecks during 1907. Mrs. Russell Sage created the Sage Foundation.

Around the country news highlights on Derby Day included a collision between a street sweeper and a train in Kalamazoo, Michigan; a severe cyclone in Texas where two cities were almost completely destroyed, and a telephone and street car strike in San Francisco. The price on Kentucky oil reached a new high.

Pedigree

PINK STAR (Bay colt)	Pink Coat	Leonatus	Longfellow Semper Felix
		Alice Brand	Hindoo Lady of the Lake
	Mary Malloy	Pat Malloy	Lexington Gloriana
		Favorite	*King Ernest Jersey Belle

Tabulated Racing Record

Year	Age	Sts.	1st	2nd	3rd	Won
1906	2	8	2	1	0	$ 825
1907	3	8	1	0	2	4,925
		16	3	1	2	$ 5,750

33rd Kentucky Derby, May 6, 1907

Pink Star

Value $6,000. Net to winner $4,850; second $700; third, $300. 128 nominations.

Horse	Eqt	Wt	PP	St	½	¾	1	Str	Fin	Jockey	Owner	Odds $1 Str't
Pink Star	wb	117	6	6	6	6	4^h	3^4	1^2	Minder	Woodford	15.00
Zal	w	117	3	1	$1^{\frac{1}{2}}$	1^h	$1^{1\frac{1}{2}}$	$1^{1\frac{1}{2}}$	$2^{1\frac{1}{2}}$	Boland	Gerst	8.00
Ovelando	w	117	1	2	3^h	2^3	2^1	2^h	3^2	Nicol	Doyle	3.00
Red Gauntlet	w	117	5	5	5^5	4^1	5^4	4^1	4^5	Austin	Hayes	1.50
Wool Sandals	w	117	4	4	$2^{1\frac{1}{2}}$	3^h	3^1	5^5	5^6	Koerner	Applegate	3.00
Orlandwick	w	110	2	3	$4^{1\frac{1}{2}}$	5^2	6	6	6	Lee	Steele	10.00

Time, :24, :36-3/5, :50, 1:17, 1:45, 2:12-3/5. Track heavy.

Winner—B.c. by Pink Coat—Mary Malloy, by Pat Malloy; trained by W. H. Fizer; bred by J. Hal Woodford.

Went to Post—4:08. Off at 4:09.

Start good. Won easily, second driving, third same. Pink Star, restrained in the early stages, trailed far back for the first three-quarters, moved up gradually until straightened out for the stretch run, where he came with a rush, wore the leaders down and won going away. Zal showed the most early speed and hung on well for the first mile. Ovelando was a forward and game contender for a mile. Red gauntlet was under a hard drive, but was not good enough. Wool Sandals retired after a mile. Orlandwick had no mishap.

Scratched——Arcite, 117; Boxara, 117.

Pink Star Stakes Races

AT 3 YEARS	WON	Kentucky Derby.
	UNP	Latonia Derby, Crescent City Derby, City Park Derby.

On the afternoon of June 6, 1907, exactly one month after the Kentucky Derby had been run, Jockey James Lee rode the entire card of six winners at Churchill Downs. This feat was never duplicated until 1948 and again the track was Churchill Downs. On Saturday, May 15, 1948, Jockey Steve Brooks rode the first six winners on the eight-race program.

Eight horses either equaled race records or established new ones at Churchill Downs in 1907. On May 18, a three-year-old Wing Ting, carrying 93 pounds, ran a mile in 1:39 3/5 to equal the record established by Ten Broeck, racing against time in 1877. John Marrs set a new record of :54 for four and one-half furlongs; Haughty and R. C. Penn each ran five furlongs in 1:00 on May 8; on successive days Zal and Dainty Dame ran six furlongs in 1:13; Pasadena ran seven furlongs in 1:25 4/5, and Light Wool ran one and one-eighth miles in 1:53.

The leading money-winner of the year was the two-year-old Colin, unbeaten champion of his division. His earnings at two amounted to $131,007.

J. Hal Woodford, prominent farmer and horse breeder of Bourbon County, Kentucky, bred and raced many good Thoroughbreds during his lifetime. Pink Star, however, was the only horse ever to carry his silks in the Kentucky Derby.

Pink Star, bred by his owner at his farm just outside Paris, Kentucky, was a son of Pink Coat, who had been a prominent contender in stakes races for a number of years. The 1907 winner also was a grandson of the 1883 Kentucky Derby winner Leonatus, and the tenth winner of the American racing classic that traced in tail male line to *Leamington, sire of the first winner Aristides.

Twenty thousand persons were present at Churchill Downs that Monday afternoon, May 6, 1907. Included in the gay crowd were Nicholas and Alice Roosevelt Longsworth, of Cincinnati. With them were Mr. and Mrs. Julius Fleischmann, of Cincinnati, and other guests from Louisville and Lexington.

Also in Louisville for the race were Col. Jack Chinn, noted Kentucky horseman; Congressman McAndrews, Silas F. Leachman, Aldermen Brennan and Powers, all of Chicago, and all the guests of Edward Corrigan.

For the thirty-third running of the Derby the track was heavy, the day warm. Tom Hayes' colt Red Gauntlet was the favorite. He opened at 7-to-5 and went to the post at 3-to-2. Second choice was Ovelando who opened at 2½-to-1 and closed at 3-to-1, even with Wool Sandals, who had opened at 6-to-1. The fact that he was Louisville-owned, by Col. W. E. Applegate, had much to do with the heavy backing for Wool Sandals.

Pink Star opened at odds of 10-to-1, closed at 15-to-1—the longest odds in the race. The starter was Jake Holtman, and there was practically no delay in getting the field away.

A sixteenth of a mile from the finish Jockey Minder gave Pink Star his head and the whip. Pink Star responded with a rush and was easily the best of his field.

This was an eventful year in aviation development. Among the prominent figures in this development was Glenn Curtiss, who is shown above in one of his early planes.

On March 12 he made a successful trial trip of the Curtiss plane over Lake Kenka, New York. His plane in that trial was called the "Red Wing." On July 4 at Hammondsport, New York, Curtiss flew his "June Bug" 5,090 feet to win the Scientific American Cup. On December 17 over a measured mile course Curtiss flew at the rate of forty miles an hour.

He made two flights the following day. In the first he made a continuous flight of ninety-five miles in one hour and fifty-four minutes. The second time he went aloft on December 18 Curtiss' plane rose to a height of 360 feet, breaking all previous records.

Orville and Wilbur Wright also were prominent in aviation developments of the year. The former established a new record by remaining in the air one hour, fourteen and one-third minutes at Fort Meyer, near Washington. Wilbur Wright was in Europe where he made his first flight over that continent on August 4. Later he flew 56 miles in one hour, thirty-one minutes and twenty-five seconds at Le Mans, France. On December 31 he set a new endurance record by remaining aloft two hours, twenty minutes,

twenty-three and one-half seconds.

New York opened its tunnel between the Battery and Brooklyn on January 12. In February the first of the tunnels under the Hudson, connecting New York and New Jersey, was opened. During April Dr. Frederick Cook claimed to have reached the North Pole, but his claim was never proved. Three months later Robert E. Peary sailed from New York on a polar expedition.

The steamship Lusitania made a record crossing from Queentown to New York in June, and in August lowered her record to four days, five hours. New York's governor signed the anti-racetrack gambling law in June. This act stopped horse racing in that state. New York City passed the Sullivan Ordinance which made smoking by women in public illegal.

In Kentucky Caleb Powers and James Howard, sentenced in 1900 in connection with the murder of Governor Goebel, were pardoned. The Louisville library shown below was opened.

Pedigree

STONE STREET
(Bay colt)

- Longstreet
  - Longfellow
    - *Leamington
    - Nantura
  - Semper Idem
    - *Glen Athol
    - Semper Vive
- Stone Nellie
  - *Stonehenge
    - Blair Athol
    - Coimbra
  - Nell
    - *King Ernest
    - Miss Nellie

Tabulated Racing Record

Year	Age	Sts.	1st	2nd	3rd	Won
1907	2	17	3	3	1	$ 1,450
1908	3	25	3	1	5	5,828
1909	4	20	3	7	1	1,250
1910	5	10	1	4	0	617
1911	6	20	8	2	2	3,667
		92	18	17	9	$ 12,812

34th Kentucky Derby, May 5, 1908

Stone Street

Value $6,000.   Net to winner $4,850; second $700; third $300.   114 nominations.

Horse	Eqt	Wt	PP	St	½	¾	1	Str	Fin	Jockey	Owner	Odds $1 Str't
Stone Street	wb	117	4	6	2¹½	2ʰ	1ⁿᵏ	1¹	1³	Pickens	Hamilton	23.72
Sir Cleges	w	117	2	7	4¹	3¹½	2½	3½	2ʰ	Koerner	Long	1.74
Dunvegan	wb	114	1	5	3ʰ	4²	4⁴	2¹	3ʰ	Warren	Camden Jr	†7.37
Synchr'zed	wsb	112	8	2	5²	5³	5⁵	4¹	4ʰ	Burton	Armstrong	68.92
Banbridge	wsb	110	5	3	1¹½	1²	3¹	5⁵	5⁶	Powers	Schreiber	3.24
Milford	wb	117	3	1	6¹	6⁴	6⁶	6¹	6ʰ	Minder	Fizer	3.64
Bill Heron	wb	114	6	4	7¹⁰	7²⁰	7¹⁵	7²⁰	7²⁰	Lee	Young	†7.37
Frank Bird	wb	110	7	8	8	8	8	8	8	Williams	Hughes	22.43

†Dunvegan and Bill Herron coupled as Camden, Jr., and Young entry.

Time, :25, :50-1/5, 1:17-2/5, 1:46, 2:15-1/5.   Track heavy.

$5 Mutuels Paid—Stone Street, $123.60 straight, $37.90 place, $14.50 show; Sir Cleges, $11.10 place, $8.50 show; Dunvegan, $11.10 show.

Winner—B.c. by Longstreet—Stone Nellie, by *Stonehenge; trained by J. W. Hall; bred by J. B. Haggin.

Went to Post—4:20.   Off at 4:21.

Start good.   Won easily; second and third driving.   Stone Street, favored by the going and in prime condition, ran the best race of his career.   He followed Banbridge close up to the three-quarters post, where he went into the lead and easily held the others safe for the rest of the trip.   Sir Cleges disliked the going and sprawled repeatedly, but made a game effort.   Dunvegan ran fairly well.   Synchronized closed a big gap in the last half-mile.   Banbridge showed the most early speed, but tired after three-quarters.   Milford was never a factor.   The others were always badly outpaced.

Scratched—Balbus, 117; Gilvedear, 117; Dr. Mathews, 117.

Synchronized and Frank Bird, added starters.

Stone Street   Stakes Races

AT 2 YEARS	UNP	Juvenile Stakes.
AT 3 YEARS	WON	Kentucky Derby.

One week after the Derby was over, on Tuesday, May 12, horses racing at the Louisville track launched an assault on the time records which brought a new record each day for the rest of the week, with the exception of one day.   On May 12 the filly Hasty Agnes (3) set a new six-furlongs mark of 1:12 3/5.   The following afternoon Water Cooler lowered the mark for one and three-sixteenth miles to 2:00 1/5; on May 14 Goldproof (5) ran five and one-half furlongs in 1:05 4/5 for a new mark.   There were no marks set on May 15, but the following day Acquia (2) ran four and one-half furlongs in :53 2/5 for a new mark, and Altuda (4) equaled Hasty Agnes' record of four days earlier.   During the same meeting King's Daughter set a record of 1:38 4/5 for a mile; Cymbal set a mark of 1:45 4/5 for one and one-sixteenth and four days later it was equaled by another horse.   Tennessee Boy also equaled the five-furlong record, while mutuel players got a big thrill when Percy Green won at 138-to-1 on May 13.

Of the eight owners who had starters in the thirty-fourth Kentucky Derby on Tuesday, May 5, 1908, only one ever had started a horse in any previous renewal of the Turf classic.   That one owner was George J. Long, owner of Bashford Manor at Louisville, who had won with Azra in 1892, with Sir Huon in 1906; had been second with Plutus in 1893; third with Sigurd in 1894; and unplaced with his horses in 1891, 1895, 1900, and 1901.

Dunvegan, carrying the silks of Johnson N. Camden, Jr., was the first of several Derby starters owned by this sportsman who was to have a prominent role in Kentucky Thoroughbred breeding and racing for more than a half-century.   The other owners—C. E. Hamilton, D. Armstrong, Barney Schrieber, W. H. Fizer, W. J. Young, and W. A. Hughes—were seeing their first Kentucky Derby starters go to the post in the thirty-fourth renewal.   None of them ever owned another Derby horse.

Stone Street was a product of James B. Haggin's Elmendorf Farm, just outside Lexington.   Although Mr. Haggin maintained extensive Thoroughbred breeding operations both in Kentucky and California and many prominent stallions stood at Elmendorf Farm, Stone Street was the only Derby winner he was able to breed.   Mr. Haggin's own winner of the Kentucky Derby, Ben Ali in 1886, had been bred by Daniel E. Swigert, who established Elmendorf Farm.

Stone Street was the eleventh and last tail male descendant of *Leamington, sire of the 1875 Derby winner Aristides, to win the race.   In addition to Aristides other male line descendants of *Leamington that had previously won the Derby were Leonatus (1883), Spokane (1889), Riley (1890), Azra (1892), Chant (1894), Lieut. Gibson (1900), His Eminence (1901), Sir Huon (1906), and Pink Star (1907).

1909

William Howard Taft, right, was inaugurated as the twenty-sixth President of the United States in 1909. He had served as secretary of war under Theodore Roosevelt, who had strongly urged his selection as the Republican candidate. Taft won over William Jennings Bryan, who was beaten for the Presidency for the third time.

Taft's first test came in his efforts to revise the tariffs, and he proved successful in a special session of Congress with the passage of the Payne-Aldrich Act.

Admiral Robert Edwin Peary, lower left, on September 6, 1909, flashed the message "Stars and Stripes nailed to the North Pole." That message brought to a successful conclusion three centuries of effort on man's part to reach the North Pole. Peary actually found the pole on

April 6, 1909. His message was sent after he had returned to his base five months later.

With Harry Payne Whitney playing the No. 3 position, the United States polo team defeated Great Britain at Hurlingham, 9-5, 8-2. The victory was the first for the United States, which had been defeated in two previous matches, in 1886 and 1902.

While the Derby was being run at Churchill Downs on May 3, 1909, a reunion of two brothers and their sister was being held in another part of Louisville. It was the first time the three had been together in fifteen years. They had been cared for as children in an orphan asylum and became separated when adopted by different families.

It also was on Derby Day of this year that Paducah, Kentucky, was named the country's "Peanut Capital." From Africa came word that "Teddy" Roosevelt had killed his fourth lion.

Major L'Enfant, who planned Washington, D. C., was reburied with distinguished honors in Arlington Cemetery, Virginia. The United States battleship "North Dakota" was given her first trial trip November 4. The boat was declared the fastest of the dreadnaught type afloat.

Pedigree

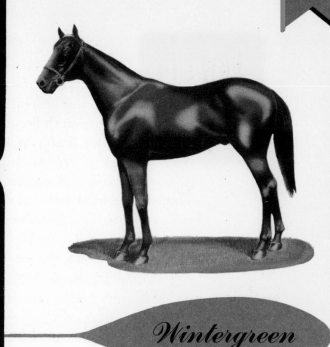

Wintergreen

WINTERGREEN (Bay colt)	Dick Welles	King Eric	*King Ernest / *Cyclone
		Tea's Over	Hanover / Tea Rose
	Winter	Exile	*Mortemer / *Second Hand
		Wildflower	*Mr. Pickwick / Woodflower

Tabulated Racing Record

Year	Age	Sts.	1st	2nd	3rd	Won
1908	2	10	5	1	3	$ 1,660
1909	3	8	1	4	0	5,550
1910	4	5	1	3	1	795
1911	5	5	3	0	1	1,490
1912	6	22	6	4	0	2,940
1913	7	11	0	2	3	385
		61	16	14	8	$ 12,820

35th Kentucky Derby, May 3, 1909

Value $6,000. Net to winner $4,850; second $700; third $300. 117 nominations.

Horse	Eqt	Wt	PP	St	½	¾	1	Str	Fin	Jockey	Owner	Odds $1 Str't
Wintergreen	wb	117	6	1	1¹½	1²	1¹½	1¹	1⁴	Powers	Respess	1.96
Miami	w	117	1	8	2¹½	2²	2½	2ʰ	2³	Shilling	Camden	2.90
Dr Barkley	w	117	3	2	4²	4½	5³	5²	3ʰ	Page	Smitha	41.34
Sir Catesby	w	110	9	9	6¹½	5²	4²	3½	4⁴	Heidel	Hayes	33.58
Fr'nd Harry	wb	117	7	7	3ʰ	3ʰ	3ʰ	4²	5³	Musgrove	Alvey	5.61
Direct	wsb	117	5	3	7²	7⁶	7³	6²	6³	Walsh	Mack'e	†10.01
Mich'l Angelo	w	117	8	4	9³	8³	8¹⁰	7²	7³	Taplin	Hendrie	6.97
Warfield	w	117	10	6	5½	6½	7⁴	8²	8⁸	Austin	Lesh	†10.01
Campeon	w	110	2	5	8²	9¹½	9ʰ	9¹	9²	McGee	Long	51.25
Match Me	wsb	107	4	10	10	10	10	10	10	Lee	Gorey	56.11

†Direct and Warfield coupled as Mackenzie and Lesh entry.

Time, :25, :49-3/5, 1:15-4/5, 2:08-1/5. Track slow.

$5 Mutuels Paid—Wintergreen, $14.80 straight, $8.75 place, $8.60 show; Miami, $9.15 place, $9.25 show; Dr. Barkley, $20.70 show.

Winner—B.c. by Dick Welles—Winter, by Exile; trained by C. Mack; bred by J. B. Respess.

Went to Post—4:41. Off at 4:44.

Start good. Won easily; second and third driving. Wintergreen was bumped into soon after the start by Dr. Barkley, but recovered quickly and, taking a good lead, held sway throughout and won in a canter. Miami, free of interference, followed Wintergreen in closest pursuit and finished fast, but was not good enough. Dr. Barkley ran a cracking good race and outgamed Sir Catesby in the last few strides. Sir Catesby closed a gap and finished resolutely. Friend Harry tired badly after three-quarters. Direct dropped out after three-quarters. Michael Angelo began slowly; closed a good gap in the last quarter. The others were never close contenders.

Scratched—T. M. Green, 114; Ada Meade, 112; Woolwinder, 117.

Wintergreen — Stakes Races

AT 2 YEARS	3RD	Hurricane Stakes.
AT 3 YEARS	WON	Kentucky Derby.
	2ND	Saranac Handicap, Saratoga Cup.
AT 4 YEARS	3RD	Brewers Exchange Stakes.
AT 5 YEARS	3RD	Merchants' Stakes.
	UNP	Frank Fehr Stakes.

The owner of the 1909 Derby winner was one of the best loved of Kentucky's horsemen. He gave financial backing to many race tracks, including those in Kentucky. The farm on which he was born he later purchased and there developed a successful Thoroughbred breeding farm.

Eight new track records were established at Churchill Downs in 1909. The track mark of 1:05 3/5 for five furlongs was twice equaled, in the spring by Enfield and in the fall by Gypsy King.

J. B. "Rome" Respess was like most of the other owners of American racing stables. He wanted to win the Kentucky Derby more than he wanted to win any other race.

Respess, however, probably did one thing which no other owner of a Derby winner ever accomplished. When Wintergreen was but a few weeks old his breeder and owner singled him out as "the winner of the Kentucky Derby in 1909." Raised at the Oakley race track near Cincinnati, Wintergreen raced with moderate success as a two-year-old. He won five of his ten starts that year. His only stakes placing that season was a third in the Hurricane Stakes.

Alex Gordon, lifetime friend of Respess, recalled that the owner never wavered once from the time Wintergreen was a weanling until the Derby was over that the colt would be the winner of the Churchill Downs race.

"Rome never took a horse to Memphis for winter training prior to the winter of 1908-1909, and he never went back there again," recalled Gordon. "But he took Wintergreen to Memphis at the end of his two-year-old season. He wanted to give the colt every chance to win the Derby and what he spent getting him ready cost him a whole lot more than the race was then worth. Rome would have gone five miles farther to get a better price on a bag of beans, but winning the Derby meant so much to him that he didn't count the expense."

The ten horses which filed out of the Churchill Downs paddock for the Derby on May 3, 1909, was the largest field which had started in this event since 1886 when Ben Ali beat nine other starters. Like Ben Ali, Wintergreen was the favorite. The former's odds were just slightly greater than the price against Wintergreen.

Second choice was Johnson N. Camden's Miami. It was practically a two-horse race between Wintergreen and Miami from flag fall to finish. No other horse ever got close to this pair and Wintergreen held a comfortable lead over the Camden colt throughout.

Vince Powers, later a trainer, who rode the winner was the leading rider of 1909. He also led the jockeys in 1908.

The earth passed through the tail of Halley's Comet in 1910 and there was great interest in it.

The United States also was conscious of the fact that it had lost two very prominent figures of the literary world in this year. Both writers were much better known, and still are, by their pen names than by their real ones. They were Samuel Longhorne Clemens, alias Mark Twain, and William Sydney Porter, alias O. Henry.

Theodore Roosevelt was given a tumultuous reception in New York on June 18, 1910, when he returned from his European tour. His trip through Italy, Austria, France, Germany, England and Holland had been one great welcome. Monarchs of the continent welcomed him and he was showered with honors.

Air flights took an important forward step on November 14 when Eugene Ely took a Curtiss plane off from the deck of the cruiser Birmingham, anchored at Hampton Roads, Virginia, and flew to Norfolk. Democrats carried the House of Representatives in the Congressional by-elections, after Republicans early in the year had staged a revolt against "Uncle Joe" Cannon's dictatorial tactics.

Admission to the Churchill Downs infield was free this year, and the rail inside the track, above, was lined with people.

A view of the stretch appears below.

Western Kentucky vied with Churchill Downs in excitement on the day the 1910 race was run. At Glasgow, Kentucky, a balloon carrying the New York astronomer J. C. Yates and a companion crashed, injuring seriously both men. The two had gone aloft in Illinois the preceding day, hoping to sail to New York.

In New York James B. Hammond, typewriter inventor, made news the same day by filing suit in an effort to recover $1,000,000 which he previously had given to his employees. At Detroit Herbert Booth, son of the founder, withdrew from the Salvation Army. Owingsville, Kentucky, lost its oldest resident, a ninety-eight-year-old veteran of the War Between the States. He had been wed four times and was father of thirty children.

Chattanooga's court house was destroyed by fire. Residents of northern Illinois and Minnesota were concerned with forest fires on Derby Day.

Bloomington, Indiana, was designated as the center of population in the United States after completion of the tenth census in 1910. The census showed the population of the nation to be 92,757,702. It was estimated that 28,153,420 immigrants had come to the United States since 1821.

Pedigree

DONAU
(Bay colt)

- *Woolsthorpe
  - Tibthorpe
    - Voltigeur
    - Little Agnes
  - Light of Other Days
    - Balfe
    - Meteor
- Al Lone
  - *Albert
    - Albert Victor
    - Hawthorn Bloom
  - Fronie Louise
    - *Glengarry
    - Rosa Clark

Donau

Tabulated Racing Record

Year	Age	Sts.	1st	2nd	3rd	Won
1909	2	41	15	6	14	$ 6,980
1910	3	10	4	0	1	7,186
1911	4	30	6	3	8	2,701
1912	5	30	5	9	7	3,289
		111	30	18	30	$ 20,156

36th Kentucky Derby, May 10, 1910

Value $6,000. Net to winner $4,850; second $700; third $300. 117 nominations.

Horse	Eqt	Wt	PP	St	½	¾	1	Str	Fin	Jockey	Owner	Odds $1 Str't
Donau	w	117	7	2	$1^{1\frac{1}{2}}$	1^3	1^3	$1^{1\frac{1}{2}}$	$1^{\frac{1}{2}}$	Herbert	Gerst	1.65
Joe Morris	wb	117	1	1	2^h	2^2	$2^{1\frac{1}{2}}$	2^h	2^h	Powers	Ander'n	2.77
Fight'g Bob	wb	117	4	5	7	5^1	$3^{1\frac{1}{2}}$	3^4	3^n	Page	Reif	3.49
Boola Boola	w	117	3	3	6^h	6^{nk}	5^2	4^6	4^{15}	Rice	Camden	17.90
Topland	w	114	5	7	3^h	4^2	4^h	5^1	5^2	Austin	V'n Meter	25.17
John Furlong	w	107	2	6	$5\frac{1}{2}$	3^h	6^4	6^4	6^8	Scoville	Rogers	14.09
Gal't Pirate	wb	117	6	4	4^1	7	7	7	7	Kennedy	W'wright	37.55

Time, :24, :48-4/5, 1:14, 1:39-4/5, 2:06-2/5. Track fast.

$5 Mutuels Paid—Donau, $13.25 straight, $7.50 place, $7.50 show; Joe Morris, $7.50 place, $7.50 show; Fighting Bob, $8.50 show.

Winner—B.c. by Woolsthorpe—Al Lone, by *Albert; trained by G. Ham; bred by Milton Young.

Went to Post—4:50. Off at 4:51.

Start good. Won driving; second and third same. Donau went into the lead soon after the start, was restrained in front for a mile and when called on, drew away but tired, and just lasted. Joe Morris tried to run out on the first turn, moved up with a rush on the stretch turn, tired, only to come again near the end. Fighting Bob stood the final drive gamely. Boola Boola closed a big gap and was going fastest at the end. The others never were serious contenders.

Scratched—Eye White, 114.

Donau   Stakes Races

AT 2 YEARS	WON	Wakefield Stakes.
	2ND	San Gabriel Stakes.
	3RD	Essex Handicap, Cincinnati Trophy, Bashford Manor Stakes.
	UNP	Bell Stakes.
AT 3 YEARS	WON	Kentucky Derby, Camden Handicap.
	3RD	Latonia Derby.
	UNP	Clark Stakes, Brewers' Exchange Stakes, Independence Handicap.
AT 4 YEARS	3RD	Brewers Selling Stakes.

William Gerst, owner of the 1910 Kentucky Derby winner, came to the United States as a child from Germany, which explains the name of his colt. Donau is German for Danube. A resident of Nashville, Tennessee, at the time Donau won, Owner Gerst had previously been a resident of Cincinnati where he was in the brewery business.

One of the shortest prices ever paid in a horse race was offered in 1910. On July 4, Sweep, two-year-old-champion of the preceding season, and Suffragist were coupled as an entry for the Lawrence Realization. The price against the entry was 1-to-100. Hindoo Star was the only other starter.

Once more a two-year-old led the money-winners in 1910. Novelty earned $72,630 during the year in which 4,180 horses raced for a total of $2,942,333. Two deadheats marked the season's racing.

In his four seasons of racing Donau started more times than any other Derby winner. His total races were 111, of which he won thirty. Not only did Donau start more times than any other Kentucky Derby winner, but he also started more times at two than any other winner of the race. His two-year-old career included forty-one starts, which is one of the most strenuous campaigns ever asked of a horse of that age.

However, the 1910 Derby winner came by his extensive racing career naturally. His dam, Al Lone, started an even greater number of times. She faced the barrier 128 times, won sixteen races, was thirteen times second, and twenty-five times third.

As a yearling Donau was offered for sale in the auctions at Sheepshead Bay. Bred by Col. Milton Young, owner of McGrathania Stud, near Lexington, the colt was sold by him for $350. Donau was the second Derby winner bred by Colonel Young, whose first was Montrose.

The grandstand was packed; there was scarcely room to move in the clubhouse enclosure, and the infield was jammed as ideal weather prevailed for the thirty-sixth running of the Derby. Mingling with the spectators were a number of Eastern fashion editors, busy with their notes of Derby Day fashions.

Horsemen present for the Derby had more than one reason to expect exceptionally fast time when the Derby was run. The track was in its best condition of several years. In one of the earlier races on the program Round the World, a two-year-old carrying 103 pounds had equaled the track record of :47 for one-half mile. In 1900 Lieut. Gibson had run the fastest of all renewals of the Kentucky Derby since it had been reduced to one and one-quarter miles. His time was 2:06 1/4.

It was in 1906 that the race was first timed in fifths of seconds, instead of quarters of seconds. When Donau's time of 2:06 2/5 was posted by the timers it was only three-twentieths of a second slower than the time of Lieut. Gibson, and the fastest Derby since that of the latter.

1911

Roald Amundsen, shown in the photograph above, reached the South Pole on December 14, 1911. The trip from his base to the pole and back again required ninety-nine days. Not only was Amundsen the first man to reach the South Pole, but he also was the first to sail around the world within the arctic circle, and the first to fly over the North Pole in a dirigible. The last named feat was accomplished in 1926.

Indianapolis was host to its first 500-mile speedway race in 1911. Winner of the inaugural race was Harroun, at right, who drove a Marmon car. His average speed for the first race was 74.59 miles per hour.

Two pitching records in major league baseball, both still unbroken, were established during the 1911 season. Cy Young, who started his major league career in 1890, brought his play to a close in this year. He had pitched 472 games in the National League, 402 in the American League, giving him a total of 874 games pitched. Also he won a record 511

games while hurling for the Cleveland, St. Louis, and Boston teams in the National League and for Boston and Cleveland in the American League.

Between September 10 and November 4 took place the first trans-continental air flight in the United States. Charles P. Rogers took off from Pasadena, California, on the earlier date. After eighty-four hours of flying time he set his plane down in New York City.

The political picture centered around Senator La Follette, of Wisconsin, who organized the progressive movement. On January 21, 1911, a meeting was held in the Washington home of Senator La Follette at which definite plans were made for capturing the Republican convention the following year. Organized at this meeting was the National Progressive Republican League for the promotion of a more popular government.

In 1911 the Supreme Court ordered the dissolution of The Standard Oil Company of New Jersey and the American Tobacco Company after ruling them ille-

gal combinations in the restraint of trade.

Andrew Carnegie on January 20, 1911, gave an additional $10,000,000 to the Carnegie Institution in Washington, thereby increasing the endowment to $25,000,000.

President Taft made the principal speech at the dedication of a memorial to Abraham Lincoln at his birthplace in Kentucky.

Pedigree

MERIDIAN
(Bay colt)

- Broomstick
  - Ben Brush
    - Bramble
    - Roseville
  - *Elf
    - Galliard
    - *Sylvabelle
- Sue Smith
  - *Masetto
    - St. Simon
    - Lady Abbess
  - Ethel Lee
    - *Whistle Jacket
    - Marmora

Tabulated Racing Record

Year	Age	Sts.	1st	2nd	3rd	Won
1910	2	12	3	3	1	$ 2,395
1911	3	17	6	6	1	11,655
1912	4	23	8	4	2	7,186
1913	5	8	2	0	4	3,780
1914	6	6	1	2	2	1,475
		66	20	15	10	$ 26,491

37th Kentucky Derby, May 13, 1911

Meridian

Value $6,000.   Net to winner $4,850; second $700; third $300.   117 nominations.

Horse	Eqt	Wt	PP	St	½	¾	1	Str	Fin	Jockey	Owner	Odds $1 Str't
Meridian	w	117	5	1	1⁴	1³	1²	1²	1¾	Archib'ld	R F Carmen	2.90
Gov'n'r Gray	w	119	7	3	6¹	4¹	3¹	2ʰ	2¹⁵	Troxler	R N Smith	1.00
Colston	w	110	1	7	3⁴	3½	4²	4⁴	3²	Conley	R Colston	19.00
Mud Sill	w	107	2	6	4½	6	6	6	4ʰ	Koerner	Woodf'd-Buckn'r	17.00
Jack Denm'n	w	117	3	5	5¹	5²	5¹	5¹	5¹	Wilson	F J Pons	21.00
R-the-World	w	117	6	2	2²	2³	2ʰ	3²	6¹⁵	McGee	W G Yanke	6.50
Col Hogan	w	110	4	4	7	7	7	7	7	McIntyre	Henderson-Hogan	6.00

$2.00 mutuels sold for first time this year.

Time, :23-3/5, :47-4/5, 1:39-1/5, 2:05 (equals track record).   Track fast.

$2.00 mutuels paid—Meridian, $7.80 straight, $2.70 place, $2.70 show; Governor Gray, $2.70 place, $2.60 show; Colston, $3.80 show.

Winner—B.c. by Broomstick—Sue Smith, by *Masetto; trained by A. Euring; bred by C. L. Harrison.

Went to Post—5:00.   Off at 5:02.

Start good. Won driving; second and third same. Meridian was rushed into a long lead from the start, and after having disposed of Round-the-World and other serious contenders in the first three-quarters, had enough speed in reserve at the end to outstay the fast coming Governor Gray. The latter was allowed to drop too far back in the first half, and, coming with a great rush in the last quarter, was going fastest at the end. Colston outstayed Mud Sill for third place. Round-the-World tired in the last quarter. Mud Sill finished fast.

Scratched—Ramazan, 110; Jabot, 117; Captain Carmody, 117.

Meridian was foaled on the Darnaby farm near Lexington, Kentucky, which was also the birthplace of the 1895 Kentucky Derby winner. Halma was bred by Eastin and Larrabie, but Meridian was bred by C. L. Harrison.

The son of Broomstick and Sue Smith came to the races as a two-year-old in the silks of his breeder, and it was after his race in the Saratoga Special that Harrison sold the colt to Richard F. Carmen, of New York, for $5,100. He proved an excellent bargain for the latter, winning more than twice that amount in his three-year-old season alone.

The Kentucky Derby was Meridian's third start at three. Twice he had gone to the post at Lexington's Kentucky Association race track. Both times he had finished second, and in each race a track record had been set. One of the races was the Blue Grass Stakes.

Meridian — Stakes Races

AT 2 YEARS
2ND Double Event.
3RD Foam Stakes.

AT 3 YEARS
WON Kentucky Derby, National Handicap, Frontier Stakes.
2ND Blue Grass Stakes, Hamilton Derby, Fourth of July Stakes, Kentucky Stakes.
3RD Canadian Sportsmen's Handicap.

AT 4 YEARS
WON Washington Breeders Handicap, Argyle Hotel Handicap, Kentucky Stakes.
2ND Charleston Hotel Handicap, Latonia Inaugural.
3RD Criterion Stakes, Juarez Handicap.

AT 5 YEARS
WON Excelsior Handicap.
3RD Paumonok Handicap, Kings County Handicap.

AT 6 YEARS
2ND Queens County Handicap.
3RD Brookdale Handicap, Yonkers Handicap.

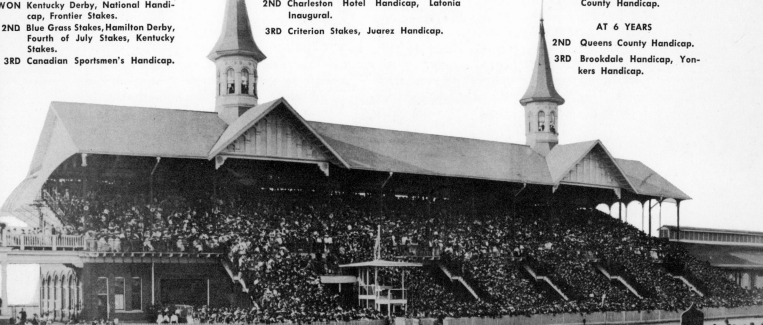

1912

The forty-seventh and forty-eighth stars were added to the flag of the United States in 1912. On January 6 New Mexico gained her statehood, and on February 14 Arizona became the forty-eighth state. For the latter ceremony movie cameras were set up for the first time in the White House.

The Titanic, largest ship afloat, was sunk on her maiden voyage when she struck an iceberg off the coast of Newfoundland. A total of 1,513 persons lost their lives in the disaster. At lower right is shown the giant ship, and lower left is shown a view in front of a New York newspaper office, as bulletins concerning the sinking were printed by hand.

The bulletins on the board announced: Justice Davidson, of Montreal, Received Private Message: "All Montreal People

at Louisville, upper right, moved on November 27, 1912.

National politics of the year were marked by Theodore Roosevelt's bolt from the Republican party and creation of the Progressive Party which convened at Chicago on August 5. Governor Hiram Johnson, of California, was named Roosevelt's running mate. With Republicans divided, the Democrats at Baltimore nominated Woodrow Wilson after Bryan had attempted to deadlock the convention and ultimately gain the nomination.

On Derby Day in 1912 Kentucky newspapers headlined stories which reported Ed Callahan, "last of the noted Breathitt County feud leaders," as being near death. It was reported that he had been ambushed. In eastern Kentucky triplets were born to a Lawrence County family.

Safe"—Among Prominent Persons Rescued are Mrs. J. J. Astor, Countess of Rothes, Cosmo Duff Gordon.

First traffic over the K & I bridge

Pedigree

Worth

WORTH (Brown colt)			
	*Knight of The Thistle	Rosebery	Speculum / Ladylike
		The Empress Maud	Beauclerc / Stella
	Miss Hanover	Hanover	Hindoo / Bourbon Belle
		Miss Dawn	Strathmore / Dawn of Day

Tabulated Racing Record

Year	Age	Sts.	1st	2nd	3rd	Won
1911	2	13	10	1	0	$ 16,645
1912	3	18	5	6	3	8,945
		31	15	7	3	$ 25,590

38th Kentucky Derby, May 11, 1912

Value $6,000. Net to winner $4,850; second $700; third $300. 131 nominations.

Horse	Eqt	Wt	PP	St	½	¾	1	Str	Fin	Jockey	Owner	Odds $1 Str't
Worth	w	117	5	1	$1^{1\frac{1}{2}}$	$1^{1\frac{1}{2}}$	1^1	1^1	1^{nk}	Shilling	H C Hallenbeck	.80
Duval	wb	117	7	4	4^3	$4\frac{1}{2}$	2^1	2^2	2^5	Fain	Gallaher Bros	20.00
Flamma	wb	112	1	7	7	5^1	$3^{1\frac{1}{2}}$	3^1	3^4	Loftus	G F Condran	17.00
Free Lance	wb	117	4	6	$2\frac{1}{2}$	$2\frac{1}{2}$	$5\frac{1}{2}$	$4^{1\frac{1}{2}}$	4^1	Peak	G J Long	7.00
Guaranola	wb	117	3	3	6^2	3^n	4^2	5^4	5^6	Molesw'h	Henderson & Hogan	80.00
Sonada	wb	117	6	5	3^h	7	6^8	6^{10}	6^{20}	Koerner	C Woolford	12.50
Wheelwright	w	117	2	2	$5\frac{1}{2}$	$6\frac{1}{2}$	7	7	7	Byrne	J N Camden	4.20

Time, :24-3/5, :49-2/5, 1:16-1/5, 1:42-3/5, 2:09-2/5. Track muddy.

$2 Mutuels Paid—Worth, $3.60 straight, $3.90 place, $3.30 show; Duval, $14.00 place, $5.70 show; Flamma, $4.50 show.

Winner—B.c. by *Knight of the Thistle—Miss Hanover, by Hanover! trained by F. M. Taylor; bred by R. H. Mac. Potter.

Went to Post—4:39. Off at 4:41.

Start bad and slow. Won driving; second and third same. Worth was hustled into the lead and, maintaining an easy advantage under restraint, appeared to be an easy winner to the stretch turn, but tired and had to be hand ridden near the end to shake off Duval. The latter was going gamest at the end. Flamma acted badly at the post and was away poorly, but closed a big gap into a good third. Free Lance tired in the stretch. Wheelwright and Sonada ran disappointingly.

Scratched—The Manager, 117; Patrouche, 110.

Worth — Stakes Races

AT 2 YEARS	WON	Raceland Stakes, Bashford Manor Stakes, Private Sweepstakes of $10,000.
AT 3 YEARS	WON	Kentucky Derby, Chesapeake Stakes.
	2ND	Washington Handicap.
	3RD	Latonia Derby.

Havre de Grace, one of the country's major race tracks today, was among the six new courses opened during the year of the thirty-eighth Kentucky Derby. Other tracks which opened the same year included Palmetto Park at Charleston, S. C.; Piping Rock Racing Association of Long Island; Universal Exposition Company at the St. Louis Fair; Hillcrest Park at Toronto, and the Mineral Springs Jockey Club at Porter, Ind. Louisville's Douglas Park reopened after having been closed in 1908.

Sotemia, a five-year-old, was among the best of the older horses of the 1912 season, and among her best races was her record-breaking 7:10 4/5 for four miles at Churchill Downs on October 7. Three other new track marks were established and two equaled during the season. On May 20, Round the World ran five and one-half furlongs in 1:05, a record equaled October 7 by Grover Hughes; May 20 Yankee Notions ran five furlongs in :59; on May 27 Free Lance ran one mile and seventy yeards in 1:42 1/5.

Five dead heats were a feature of the racing season during which 3,553 horses raced for a distribution of $2,391,625. The leading money winner was Star Charter, winner of $14,655, and the two-year-old champion was Helios.

Although his breeder was R. H. McCarter Potter, owner of Request Stud at Andover, New Jersey, Worth was foaled March 15 at Bosque Bonita Farm in Woodford County, Kentucky, which at one time had been owned by the famous Turfman General Abe Buford and later by John H. Morris, trainer of the 1892 Derby winner Azra.

At Lexington the colt by *Knight of the Thistle was sold as a yearling to C. T. Worthington. The price was $425. He was turned over to the Gallaher Brothers for breaking. So impressed were his trainers with the colt following his trials that during the winter before Worth became a two-year-old they offered and purchased for $3,500 the colt from Owner Worthington.

Worth made his first start at two at Jacksonville. He was unplaced. His next two races were won by Worth. Then he was second in an allowance race. Then followed his streak of seven winning races, including the Raceland Stakes and Bashford Manor Stakes.

By Kentucky's spring race season Worth attracted the attention of many horsemen, including Frank Taylor, trainer for H. C. Hallenbeck. For the latter Taylor paid $10,000 for the colt.

Following his seven straight wins, Worth ran unplaced, then closed his two-year-old campaign by winning a $10,000 private sweepstakes. He was acclaimed the two-year-old champion with earnings of $16,645.

The Derby was his second start as a three-year-old. Worth died as a three-year-old, and racing will never know just how good a horse died.

Worth was given a masterful ride by Carroll Shilling, one of the best of American jockeys, in gaining his neck decision over Duval. The second horse was owned by Gallaher Brothers, who first trained Worth.

Hallenbeck, wealthy New Yorker, was third on the list of leading owners in 1912, his second year in racing. Trainer Taylor was seventh on the list of leading trainers, and Jockey Shilling had the highest winning percentage of all jockeys.

" The Congress shall have the power to lay and collect taxes on incomes, from whatever source derived, without apportionment among the several States, and without regard to any census or enumeration."

The above is the sixteenth amendment to the Constitution of the United States which had been proposed to the States by the Sixty-First Congress on July 12, 1909. In a proclamation dated February 25, 1913, the secretary of state declared the amendment had been ratified by forty-two of the forty-eight States. It became part of the Constitution on May 13, 1913, and made March 15 of each year an extremely important date in the life of practically every wage earner in the United States. Those states which rejected the amendment were Connecticut, Rhode Island, and Utah.

The proclamation came shortly before Woodrow Wilson, upper right, took office as the twenty-seventh President of the United States. In the first year of Wil-

and so often heard in the Democratic convention of the preceding year.

Also passed during the first year of the Wilson administration was the Federal Reserve Act, which divided the country into twelve federal banking districts, each containing a federal reserve bank. The

INDIVIDUAL INCOME TAXES *(as a percent of gross national income)*

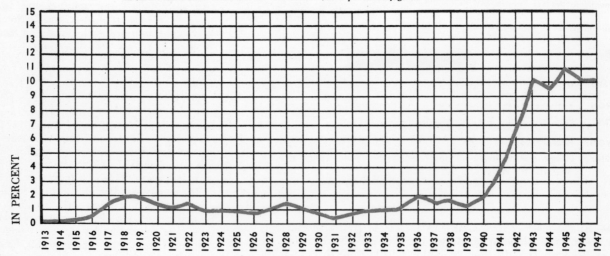

son's administration the Underwood Tariff Bill was enacted. Author of this legislation was Oscar Underwood, chairman of the House Ways and Means Committee, whose name had been so prominent

bill, known as the Glass-Owen Bill, was introduced by Congressman Carter Glass, of Virginia, and Senator Owen, of Oklahoma. Also passed by this Congress was the Clayton Anti-Trust Act.

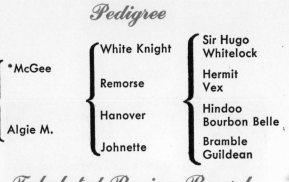

Pedigree

DONERAIL (Bay colt)	*McGee	White Knight	Sir Hugo / Whitelock
		Remorse	Hermit / Vex
	Algie M.	Hanover	Hindoo / Bourbon Belle
		Johnette	Bramble / Guildean

Tabulated Racing Record

Year	Age	Sts.	1st	2nd	3rd	Won
1912	2	10	2	0	3	$ 1,025
1913	3	15	3	3	2	8,588
1914	4	28	5	5	5	5,180
1916	6	8	0	3	0	363
1918	8	1	0	0	0	...
		61	10	11	10	$ 15,166

39th Kentucky Derby, May 10, 1913

Donerail

5,000 added. Net value to winner $5,475; second $700; third $300. 32 nominations.

orse	Eqt	Wt	PP	St	½	¾	1	Str	Fin	Jockey	Owner	Odds $1 Str't
onerail	w	117	5	6	6¹	6¹½	5¹	5²	1½	Goose	T P Hayes	91.45
n Point	w	117	4	1	1²	1³	1²	1½	2¹½	Buxton	A L'Aste	1.20
owell	w	112	3	5	5²	4ʰ	4¹½	4¹	3ʰ	McCabe	J T Weaver	87.00
undation	w	117	8	2	2¹	2½	2ʰ	3ʰ	4ⁿᵏ	Loftus	C W McKenna	2.30
Notions	wb	117	6	3	3½	3ʰ	3½	2½	5⁵	Glass	H K Knapp	4.90
d Marsh'll	wb	117	1	7	7¹	7¹	6²	6¹	6⁸	Steele	J O & G H Keene	183.00
mmie Gill	wb	110	2	8	8	8	8	7¹⁰	7¹⁵	Borel	Doerhoefer & West	36.00
ochares	w	114	7	4	4ʰ	5½	7ʰ	8	8	Peake	J W Schorr	14.00

me, :23-4/5, :47-4/5, 1:12-3/5, 1:39-3/5, 2:04-4/5 (new track record). Track fast.

$2 Mutuels Paid—Donerail, $184.90 straight, $41.20 place, $13.20 show; Ten Point, $3.50 lace, $3.30 show; Gowell, $14.10 show.

inner—B.c. by *McGee—Algie M., by Hanover; trained by T. P. Hayes; bred by T. P. Hayes.
ent to Post—4:51. Off at 4:52.

Start good and slow. Won driving; second and third same. Donerail, showing startling im-rovement over his Lexington form, was restrained to the stretch turn, where he moved up with rush, and, under punishment, drew away in the last sixteenth. Ten Point showed superior speed r the first mile, tired in the last eighth and was distressed at the finish. Gowell made a fast d game stretch effort. Foundation raced with Ten Point to the stretch, then tired. Yankee otions ran prominently to the homestretch and tired in the final drive. Leochares was hope-ssly beaten.

Scratched—Prince Hermis, 117; Sam Hirsch, 114; Floral Park, 112; Flying Tom, 114.

Donerail ⸱ Stakes Races

2 YEARS	3RD	Golden Rod Stakes, Rosedale Stakes.
3 YEARS	WON	Kentucky Derby, Canadian Sportsmen's Handicap.
	2ND	Windsor Special, Dominion Handicap.
4 YEARS	WON	Hamilton Cup.
	2ND	Latonia Autumn Inaugural, Independence Handicap, George Hendrie Memorial Handicap.

One of the most controversial time records in American racing is that credited to Whisk Broom II for one and one-quarter miles. It was at Belmont Park on June 28, 1913, a little more than a month after the Derby, that Whisk Broom II was timed that distance in two minutes flat. At the time Whisk Broom II was six years old and he carried 139 pounds. Whisk Broom II was later to sire the 1927 Kentucky Derby winner Whiskery, also owned by H. P. Whitney.

Highlights of the 1913 racing season included the resumption of racing in New York, opening of Connaught Park at Ottawa and Dorval Park at Montreal; a distribution of $2,920,963; 3,541 horses racing in North America, of which 2,717 earned money; four deadheats, and 1,026 registered trainers. H. P. Whitney lead the owners for the first time.

Thomas P. Hayes shares one record equaled by only one other man during the seventy-four runnings of the Kentucky Derby. He was the second person to breed, own, and train a winner.

Donerail, known to practically everyone who ever read two paragraphs about the Derby as the longest-priced winner of the event, established another record that May 10 afternoon. The lightly regarded son of *McGee broke the track record when he ran the ten furlongs in 2:04 4/5. His track record did not last long, being lowered the following year to a mark which was to stand for seventeen years.

Donerail's record for the mile and one-quarter was one of four track records established that year, two during the spring meeting and two during the fall. Three days after the Derby was run, Froglegs, a four-year-old, ran a mile and twenty yards in 1:39. During the autumn the two-year-old Bringhurst set a record of 1:04 3/5 for five and one-half furlongs, and eight days later ran six furlongs in track record time of 1:11.

The Hayes colt was the first of two Derby winners for his imported sire, who did not gain honors as America's leading sire until 1922. Donerail also was the second straight Kentucky Derby winner out of a daughter of the top race horse and sire Hanover. Worth, winner the preceding year, was a son of Miss Hanover, by Hanover.

Roscoe Goose, rider of the 1913 winner, never gained top honors among the country's jockeys. As a matter of fact 1913, during which he won 85 races, was one of his best seasons. Following his retirement from the saddle, however, he developed a number of outstanding jockeys. Among the top riders he tutored was Charley Kurtsinger, another Louisville native, who won the Kentucky Derby in 1931 with Twenty Grand and again in 1937 with War Admiral.

It was Kentucky's Governor James McCreary who presented the bouquet of flowers to Jockey Goose in the winner's circle. Among the prominent racing patrons watching the ceremony from the clubhouse were Mr. and Mrs. August Belmont, she the former stage star Eleanor Robson.

1914

In 1914, thirty-three years after construction was undertaken unsuccessfully by a French company, the Panama Canal finally was ready in August for the passage of the first boat through the isthmus, shown above. The canal shortened the trip from New York to San Francisco by 7,700 miles.

The canal had cost $375,000,000 and its construction had been under the direction of Colonel George W. Goethals. The United States had started work on the project in June, 1906, after outright purchase which followed the French company's abandonment of the project.

Almost simultaneously with the opening of the canal came the start of World War I, which was touched off July 28 as Austria declared war on Serbia. Other European nations were drawn into conflict rapidly. The Austrian declaration was precipitated by the assassination of the Archduke of Austria on June 28. The Archduke is shown, in the photograph at right, preparing to enter his automobile shortly before he was killed.

History moved rapidly in our nation's

capital after the outbreak of hostilities. President Wilson asserted our neutrality on August 4. American Marines seized Haiti, and from the national bank took $500,000 of gold, which the bank had refused to turn over to the American government.

Churchill Downs had torn down the betting shed and stable which stood between the original grandstand and the stretch turn. The paddock, which appears at left in the picture below, stood just in the rear of the present stadium.

On Derby Day in 1914 woman suffragists strongly protested the appointment of Representative Harvey Meyers as the Kentucky Commissioner to the Panama Exposition. They alleged he was opposed

to woman suffrage. At the University of Kentucky the same day the Kentucky Academy of Science was organized. The Ford Motor Car Company announced it was producing a new car every twenty-four seconds.

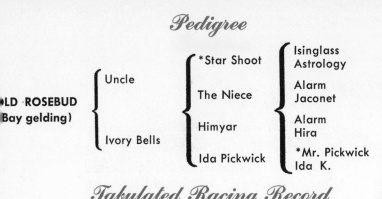

Pedigree

OLD ROSEBUD
(Bay gelding)

- Uncle
  - *Star Shoot
    - Isinglass
    - Astrology
  - The Niece
    - Alarm
    - Jaconet
- Ivory Bells
  - Himyar
    - Alarm
    - Hira
  - Ida Pickwick
    - *Mr. Pickwick
    - Ida K.

Tabulated Racing Record

Year	Age	Sts.	1st	2nd	3rd	Won
1913	2	14	12	2	0	$ 19,057
1914	3	3	2	0	0	9,575
1917	6	21	15	1	3	31,720
1919	8	30	9	7	5	12,182
1920	9	8	1	2	0	1,295
1921	10	2	1	0	0	700
1922	11	2	0	1	0	200
		80	40	13	8	$ 74,729

Old Rosebud

40th Kentucky Derby, May 9, 1914

$10,000 added. Net value to winner $9,125; second $2,000; third $1,000. 47 nominations.

Horse	Eqt	Wt	PP	St	½	¾	1	Str	Fin	Jockey	Owner	Odds $1 Str't
Old Rosebud	w	114	6	1	1²	1¹½	1²	1⁶	1⁸	McCabe	H C Applegate	.85
Hodge	w	114	7	2	2²	2½	2⁴	2⁴	2¹½	Taylor	K Spence	5.40
Bronzew'ng	wb	117	4	7	7	7	6½	3²	3⁴	Hanover	A P Humphrey Jr	13.50
John Gund	wb	117	3	6	3½	3½	3½	4²	4⁶	Byrne	A Baker	10.00
Old Ben	wb	114	1	3	6⁵	6³	5¹½	5¹	5²	Turner	W G Yanke	12.50
Surprising	w	117	5	4	5¹	4¹	4ʰ	6⁵	6³	Peak	R F Carman	14.00
Watermelon	wb	112	2	5	4¹½	5¹	7	7	7	French	J E Madden	15.00

Time, :23-3/5, :47-4/5, 1:13, 1:38-4/5, 2:03-2/5 (new track record). Track fast.

$2 Mutuels Paid—Old Rosebud, $3.70 straight, $3.00 place, $2.80 show; Hodge, $3.60 place, $3.60 show; Bronzewing, $4.00 show.

Winner—B.g. by Uncle—Ivory Bells, by Himyar; trained by F. D. Weir; bred by J. E. Madden.

Went to Post—5:03. Off at 5:05.

Start good and slow. Won easily; second and third driving. Old Rosebud set the pace under restraint, although going fast to the stretch turn, where, when called upon, he moved away from the others to win hard held as his rider pleased. Hodge raced in closest pursuit until the last eighth, where he tired, but stood the drive gamely. Bronzewing closed and came with a rush through the last quarter. John Gund tired racing well up to the stretch. Old Ben and Surprising ran fairly well. Watermelon quit after three-quarters.

Scratched—Ivan Gardner, 114; Buckley, 110; Belloc, 117; Constant, 117.

Old Rosebud — Stakes Races

AT 2 YEARS	WON	Yucatan Stakes, Spring Trial Stakes, Harold Stakes, Flash Stakes, U. S. Hotel Stakes, Cincinnati Trophy.
	2ND	Idle Hour Stakes, Bashford Manor Stakes.
AT 3 YEARS	WON	Kentucky Derby.
	UNP	Withers Stakes.
AT 6 YEARS	WON	Clark Handicap, Queen City Handicap, Carter Handicap, Frontier Handicap, Bayview Handicap, Latonia Inaugural Handicap, Delaware Handicap.
	3RD	Brooklyn Handicap.
	UNP	Kentucky Handicap, Saratoga Handicap.
AT 8 YEARS	2ND	Paumonok Handicap, Mt. Vernon Handicap.
	3RD	Thanksgiving Handicap.
	UNP	Yonkers Handicap, Arverne Handicap, Kingsbridge Handicap.
AT 9 YEARS	UNP	Harford Handicap, Paumonok Handicap, Toboggan Handicap.

Only one Kentucky Derby winner raced more seasons than did Old Rosebud. That was Exterminator. And to a man, horsemen who saw this pair race will tell you no two more honest Thoroughbreds ever walked on a race track. Old Rosebud raced seven seasons, Exterminator eight. Old Rosebud may have been the gamer of the two. He was never too sound, a fact which forced him to the sidelines for two years, but he came back to campaign until it was necessary to destroy him at Jamaica in 1922 after he had injured a leg.

As a yearling Old Rosebud was purchased for $500 by Frank D. Weir, who trained him. Bred by John E. Madden at Hamburg Place, outside Lexington, Old Rosebud raced for the first time in H. C. (Ham) Applegate's colors as a two-year-old in the Idle Hour Stakes at Lexington. In that race he was second.

Old Rosebud also was second in the Bashford Manor Stakes at Churchill Downs. He won his other twelve starts as a two-year-old and earned $19,057. He was acclaimed champion of that division for 1913. In his early three-year-old training he displayed the same ability that had marked his first season of racing.

Consequently it was not surprising that Jefferson Livingston offered $30,000 for him on April 4, 1914. Nor was it surprising that Owner Applegate turned the offer down. Twenty-one days later the son of Uncle and Ivory Bells, by Himyar, won over the Lexington track by six lengths.

Old Rosebud came up to the Kentucky Derby in grand condition and the money that flooded the mutuel machines backed the gelding down to odds-on favoritism. Only one of the other six horses was held at less than 10-to-1.

He was bred to break on top and stay there. That's just what he did, increasing his lead at almost every step of the way to win by eight lengths. He ran the first quarter in 23 3/5 seconds, the last in 24 3/5 seconds to establish a track record of 2:03 2/5, which stood until 1931 when Twenty Grand came roaring down the stretch like a runaway train.

Only one other track record was broken that year. Gowell, who had run third to Donerail in the preceding Derby, set a record of 1:51 2/5 for one and one-eight miles ten days after the 1914 Derby.

Old Rosebud went sore at the end of his three-year-old campaign. For two years he was turned out in Texas while racing wondered what had become of him. He reappeared on the scene as a six-year-old in 1917 to win fifteen of his twenty-one races.

1915

With war raging in Europe, President Wilson exerted every effort to maintain this country's neutrality, but suffered a great blow to hope on May 7, 1915, when the English Cunard Liner Lusitania was sunk with the loss of 1,198 lives, of which 114 were Americans.

Earlier, on February 10, following Germany's announcement of her war zone around the British Isle, the President had notified Germany that the United States would hold Germany's government accountable for any American lives lost.

Henry Ford, the automobile manufacturer, in an effort to end the war, chartered the "Ford Peace Ship" and headed a party which went to Norway. Ford and his party, shown leaving aboard the peace ship in the photograph below, failed in their efforts.

It was in this year that Germany's first air raids upon England were made, on January 19. In World War II Ford's River Rouge plant was to play an important part, through production of aircraft, in the aerial warfare against Germany.

This also was the last year that the Churchill Downs clubhouse appeared as shown in the photograph at top. It was in 1916 that the original unit of the pres-

ent structure was built. Part of the structure shown above was left as part of the new unit.

Daniel Boone, who opened Kentucky to the white man, was elected to the Hall of Fame in 1915. At Bowling Green, Kentucky, early in the morning of Derby day a man, during a terrific rain storm, was dreaming his mother and sister were drowning. Still asleep he jumped from his bed and through his bedroom window, falling two stories to the ground. Fifteen stitches were required to close the wounds he received.

R. J. Reynolds, of the tobacco company, declared the most effective advertising medium in reaching the public was the newspaper.

In New York a woman willed her brother $1,000 providing he "went on the wagon for five years." George L. Pratt died in Chicago on May 21. He was known as the "greatest hog buyer in the United States." During his life he purchased twice as many hogs as any other two men. He was associated with P. D. Armour and his buying affected the rise and fall of the hog market more than any other factor. Armour said Pratt made more money for him than any other person.

Pedigree

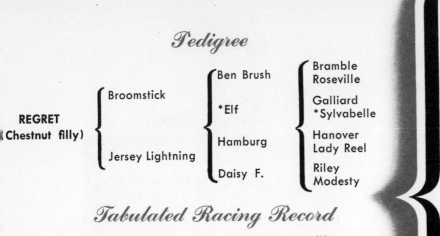

REGRET (Chestnut filly)	Broomstick	Ben Brush	Bramble Roseville
		*Elf	Galliard *Sylvabelle
	Jersey Lightning	Hamburg	Hanover Lady Reel
		Daisy F.	Riley Modesty

Tabulated Racing Record

Year	Age	Sts.	1st	2nd	3rd	Won
1914	2	3	3	0	0	$ 17,390
1915	3	2	2	0	0	12,500
1916	4	2	1	0	0	560
1917	5	4	3	1	0	4,643
		11	9	1	0	$ 35,093

41st Kentucky Derby, May 8, 1915

Regret

$10,000 added. Net value to winner $11,450; second $2,000; third $1,000; fourth $225. 68 nominations.

Horse	Eqt	Wt	PP	St	½	¾	1	Str	Fin	Jockey	Owner	Odds $1 Str't
Regret	w	112	2	1	$1^{1\frac{1}{2}}$	$1^{\frac{1}{2}}$	$1^{\frac{1}{2}}$	$1^{1\frac{1}{2}}$	1^{2}	Notter	H P Whitney	2.65
Peebles	wb	117	3	3	2^{1}	$2^{1\frac{1}{2}}$	$2^{1\frac{1}{2}}$	2^{2}	2^{2}	Borel	J Butler	6.35
Sharpsh'ter	wb	114	8	7	$3^{\frac{1}{2}}$	$3^{\frac{1}{2}}$	3^{h}	3^{1}	3^{1}	Butwell	S L Parsons	9.60
Royal II	wb	117	10	16	12^{2}	9^{1}	6^{nk}	5^{h}	4^{3}	Neylon	J Livingston	15.10
E'n Cochran	w	117	5	2	$6^{\frac{1}{2}}$	4^{1}	$7^{\frac{1}{2}}$	$4^{\frac{1}{2}}$	$5^{\frac{1}{2}}$	Taylor	R L Baker	16.15
Leo Ray	w	117	11	13	10^{h}	$8^{1\frac{1}{2}}$	8^{h}	7^{h}	$6^{1\frac{1}{2}}$	T McTag't	J T Looney	17.90
D'ble Eagle	wsb	117	13	12	9^{h}	$7^{1\frac{1}{2}}$	$9^{\frac{1}{2}}$	6^{2}	7^{4}	Burl'game	J F Johnson	17.20
Dortch	w	110	1	11	7^{1}	$6^{\frac{1}{2}}$	$5^{1\frac{1}{2}}$	$8^{\frac{1}{2}}$	8^{5}	Mott	W W Darden	†5.40
For Fair	wb	117	4	15	16	15	$10^{\frac{1}{2}}$	$9^{\frac{1}{2}}$	$9^{\frac{1}{2}}$	Warton	G M Miller	†5.40
Ed Crump	wb	117	7	4	$4^{1\frac{1}{2}}$	$5^{\frac{1}{2}}$	$4^{\frac{1}{2}}$	$10^{\frac{1}{2}}$	10^{h}	Goose	J W Schorr	‡5.90
L'tle Strings	w	117	12	10	$11^{1\frac{1}{2}}$	12^{2}	11^{1}	11^{1}	$11^{1\frac{1}{2}}$	Pool	M B Gruber	†5.40
Golder't Boy	w	114	6	8	$8^{\frac{1}{2}}$	$10^{\frac{1}{2}}$	13^{1}	12^{1}	12^{2}	Kederis	J W Schorr	‡5.90
Uncle Bryn	wsb	117	16	14	14^{1}	14^{1}	$12^{\frac{1}{2}}$	13^{1}	13^{2}	J McTag't	R W Walden	†5.40
Tetan	w	117	15	6	13^{2}	13^{2}	14^{6}	14^{6}	14^{2}	Smyth	Johnson & Crosthwaite	x†5.40
Norse King	wb	117	9	9	$5^{\frac{1}{2}}$	11^{1}	15^{1}	15	15^{4}	O'Brien	F B Le Maire	36.90
Booker Bill	wb	117	14	5	15^{1}	16	16	16	16	Andress	M C Moore	x†5.40

Time, :23-3/5, :48-3/5, 1:13-3/5, 1:39-2/5, 2:05-2/5. Track fast.

Ed Crump and Goldcrest Boy coupled in betting as J. W. Schorr entry; Tetan and Booker Bill coupled as Johnson and Crosthwaite-McMoore entry; Dortch, For Fair, Little Strings, Uncle Bryn, Tetan and Booker Bill coupled in betting as field horses.

$2 Mutuels Paid—Regret, $7.30 straight, $4.00 place; $3.60 show; Pebbles, $7.60 place, $4.80 show; Sharpshooter, $7.10 show.

Winner—Ch.f. by Broomstick—Jersey Lightning, by Hamburg; trained by James Rowe; bred by H. P. Whitney.

Went to Post—5:18. Off at 5:22.

Start good and slow. Won easily; second and third driving. Regret, from a fast start and well ridden, took the lead at once and was rated in front until the last eighth, where she drew away, to win easing up. Pebbles raced in nearest pursuit and held on gamely in the final drive. Sharpshooter also ran a good race and stood a hard drive resolutely. Royal II. closed a big gap. Emerson Cochran and Leo Ray ran good races. Ed Crump showed speed, but failed to stay.

Scratched—Kilkenny Boy, 117; Phosphor, 117; Commonada, 117.

Regret *Stakes Races*

AT 2 YEARS	WON	Saratoga Special, Sanford Memorial Handicap, Hopeful Stakes.
AT 3 YEARS	WON	Kentucky Derby, Saranac Handicap.
AT 4 YEARS	UNP	Saratoga Handicap.
AT 5 YEARS	WON	Gazelle Handicap.
	2ND	Brooklyn Handicap.

"I do not care if she never wins another race or if she never starts in another race. She has won the greatest race in America and I am satisfied." Those were the words of an excited Harry Payne Whitney after watching his great filly Regret win the 1915 running of the Kentucky Derby. However, Regret did race again; in fact in two more seasons, and although she did not have an extensive racing career she was a brilliant race mare.

Regret, only filly ever to win the Kentucky Derby, was the star of a racing stable that included Borrow, leading money-winner and at seven the oldest horse ever to attain that honor; the two-year-old champion Dominant. Regret herself had been the 1914 two-year-old champion.

This was the stable that made its owner the leading money-winning owner of the year; its trainer, James Rowe, Sr., the leading trainer in money won. Jockey Joe Notter ended the season with a high percentage of .38.

Regret started only three times at two, winning all her races which were the Sanford Stakes, Saratoga Special, and Hopeful Stakes. Her earnings placed her fourth to Roamer, Luke McLuke, and David Craig on the list of leading money-winners.

The Kentucky Derby was her first start as a three-year-old and the field she faced was the largest that had started in the Churchill Downs event to that time. The great-grandaughter of Modesty, winner of the first American Derby in 1884, never left the outcome in doubt. She led all the way to win by two lengths and please the biggest part of the crowd of 40,000 which had made her the favorite.

Regret was the first of nineteen horses Mr. Whitney was to start in different renewals of the Kentucky Derby. No other owner has ever started so many horses in the racing classic. Mr. Whitney won one other Derby, in 1927 with Whiskery.

At Mr. Whitney's Brookdale Farm at Red Bank, New Jersey, on September 10, 1915, died Hamburg, sire of Jersey Lightning who was the dam of Regret. Foaled in 1895 and bred by C. J. Enright, Hamburg had been leading sire in 1905. Regret died in 1934 without having produced a foal of any great prominence.

Among those who came from New York to witness the Whitney family's first Derby triumph were Foxhall P. Keene, E. F. Albee, Henry Ziegler, Charles B. Whitney, Schuyler Parsons, and Phil Dwyer. From Cleveland came James Corrigan and Price McKinney, and from other parts of the country came men and women of national prominence.

1916

The national election of 1916 provided one of the great surprises in the history of Presidential races. Charles Evans Hughes, former governor of New York and Supreme Court justice, was the Republican candidate. Woodrow Wilson sought re-election as the Democratic candidate. Theodore Roosevelt was nominated by the Progressive Party, but refused to run when Hughes was nominated.

Candidate Hughes retired on election night, having received congratulatory messages from throughout the nation, and the voters retired believing Hughes had defeated Wilson, which was reported in practically all newspapers. The following day, however, the country learned that California had gone Democratic and that it was Wilson who had won.

On March 9, Pancho Villa had raided Columbus, New Mexico, and with the permission of President Carranza, of Mexico, the United States sent a punitive expedition into Mexico, April 12 to November 24. The expedition was in charge of General John J. Pershing, upper right. It did not capture Villa, and was withdrawn as America's entry into the World War loomed.

When the unarmed French Channel steamer Sussex was sunk on March 24, with the loss of many American lives, President Wilson sent an ultimatum to Germany to which the latter replied that it would confine its fighting to belligerents. The Germans promised merchant

ships would not be sunk without warning and that efforts would be made to save the lives of all aboard any merchant ships which might be sunk.

American Marines seized Santo Domingo, and also intervened in Nicaragua.

The starting gate had not yet been invented and Derby starts were being made from the web barrier, as shown in the photograph below.

Passage of the Federal Farm Loan Act in 1916 made it possible for farmers to obtain long-term mortgage credit at six per cent through the Federal Loan Bank System instead of paying ten per cent for three - to five-year credit. During the same year coal miners in western Kentucky went out on strike seeking a pay increase. It was the first time in eighteen years that there had been a walkout in this coal field.

Pedigree

GEORGE SMITH
(Black colt)

- *Out of Reach
  - Persimmon
    - St. Simon
    - Perdita II
  - *Sandfly
    - Isonomy
    - Sandiway
- *Consuelo II
  - Bradwardine
    - Barcaldine
    - Monte Rosa
  - *Miss Pepper II
    - Pepper and Salt
    - Great Dame

George Smith

Tabulated Racing Record

Year	Age	Sts.	1st	2nd	3rd	Won
1915	2	12	9	0	0	$ 10,140
1916	3	4	1	2	0	11,600
1917	4	7	3	1	1	2,594
1918	5	8	4	2	2	18,550
		31	17	5	3	$ 42,884

42nd Kentucky Derby, May 13, 1916

$10,000 added. Net value to winner $9,750; second $2,000; third $1,000; fourth $225. 56 nominations.

Horse	Eqt	Wt	PP	St	½	¾	1	Str	Fin	Jockey	Owner	Odds $1 Str't
George Smith	w	117	8	6	3²	3ʰ	1¹	1²	1ⁿᵏ	Loftus	J Sanford	4.15
Star Hawk	w	117	3	9	9	7½	5⁴	3²	2³	Lilley	A K Macomber	†4.45
Franklin	wb	117	1	2	2²	2¹½	2¹	2ʰ	3½	Rice	Weber & Ward	‡6.45
Dodge	w	117	4	1	5¹	4¹½	4½	4²	4⁶	Murphy	Weber & Ward	‡6.45
Thunderer	w	117	5	7	7¹	5½	6¹	6¹	5¹	T McTag't	H P Whitney	§1.05
The Cock	wb	110	7	8	8³	6ʰ	7²	7²	6⁵	Garner	A K Macomber	†4.45
Dominant	w	117	2	3	1³	1½	3½	5¹	7⁵	Notter	H P Whitney	§1.05
Kinney	wb	117	9	5	6½	8⁶	8⁶	8¹⁰	8¹²	Gentry	T P Hayes	32.55
Lena Misha	w	117	6	4	4ʰ	9	9	9	9	Dugan	Beverwyck Stable	35.30

Time, :22-2/5, :46-2/5, 1:12-1/5, 1:38-4/5, 2:04. Track fast.

Star Hawk and The Cock coupled in betting as Macomber entry; Franklin and Dodge coupled in betting as Weber and Ward entry; Thunderer and Dominant coupled in betting at H. P. Whitney entry.

$2 Mutuels Paid—George Smith, $10.30 straight, $4.80 place, $2.90 show; Star Hawk, $6.00 place, $4.40 show; Franklin, $3.50 show.

Winner—B.c. by *Out of Reach—*Consuelo II, by Bradwardine; trained by H. Hughes; bred by Chinn & Forsythe.

Went to Post—5:15. Off at 5:16.

Start good and slow. Won driving; second and third same. George Smith was well ridden and, after being saved for the first three-quarters, rushed into the lead, but had to be urged at the end to outstay Star Hawk. The latter, away slowly and trailing for a half-mile, came with a rush through the stretch and almost got up to win. Franklin showed good speed, but tired after racing in close pursuit. Dodge raced well up throughout. Thunderer had no mishap. Dominant set a fast early pace, but quit badly. Lena Misha pulled up lame.

Scratched—St. Isidore, 114; Bulse, 117; Huffaker, 117.

George Smith — Stakes Races

AT 2 YEARS
- WON: Aberdeen Stakes, Juvenile Stakes, Victoria Stakes, Spring Brewery Stakes, Annapolis Stakes.
- UNP: Sanford Memorial Handicap, Eastern Shore Handicap, Erdenheim Handicap.

AT 3 YEARS
- WON: Kentucky Derby.
- 2ND: Latonia Derby.
- UNP: Carter Handicap.

AT 4 YEARS
- WON: Warwick Handicap.
- 2ND: Long Beach Handicap.
- 3RD: Belmont Autumn Handicap.
- UNP: Saratoga Handicap.

AT 5 YEARS
- WON: Excelsior Handicap, Edgemere Handicap, Yorktown Handicap, Bowie Handicap.
- 2ND: Bay View Handicap, October Handicap.
- 3RD: Brooklyn Handicap, Continental Handicap.

During the 1916 racing season several hundred Thoroughbreds were imported to this country from England because of wartime conditions there. Among those which were brought over were *Sun Briar, *North Star III, and *Omar Khayyam.

An even dozen three-year-olds were entered for the forty-second running of the Kentucky Derby on May 13, 1916, but the scratching of St. Isidore, Bulse, and Huffaker reduced the field to nine at post time.

Included in the field was the two-year-old champion of 1915, Dominant, who was coupled with Thunderer as the entry of H. P. Whitney, who had won the preceding year. Astride Dominant was Jockey Joe Notter, who had won with Regret. Thunderer was unbeaten. Little wonder then that the Whitney pair was the favorite in the mutuels, where $99,468 was bet on the Derby.

Churchill Downs was a veritable flower garden that afternoon. Everywhere shrubs bloomed. No less than 8,000 red geraniums added to the colorful spectacle.

There was but a minute delay at the post and the field was away. The Weber and Ward entry of Dodge and Franklin was first to show, closely pursued by Dominant, while Star Hawk was practically left at the post. In the first quarter Dominant went to the front, by a length, by two, and after a half-mile he was three in front. The favorite players knew they had picked right.

Star Hawk was still trailing the field, three lengths back of the eighth horse. His backers wondered if he hadn't left his Derby race on the track when he worked the Derby distance in 2:06 three days earlier.

After six furlongs Dominant weakened under the challenge from George Smith and Franklin who moved into the front at the mile, the former a good length in front. As they straightened out for the stretch run George Smith was pulling away, but back there in the ruck the colors of A. K. Macomber were moving. Was it Star Hawk or The Cock?

Those with binoculars said it was Star Hawk. He was really running. He was fifth; now fourth; now third; now second, and charging down on the leading George Smith. The crowd screamed itself hoarse as Jockey Marshall Lilley drove Star Hawk through that last hundred yards.

By the beginning of 1917 practically the whole of the United States expected this country to join the European conflict. The likelihood increased on February 1 when Germany resumed its unrestricted submarine warfare.

President Wilson took office for his second term on March 4, and on April 2 called Congress into special session, declaring that war already existed as a result of acts by Germany. The actual declaration came in April, with few dissenting votes being recorded.

On May 18 came a call under the Selective Service Act for the registration of all men between the ages of twenty-one and thirty-one. A total of 10,679,-814 registered.

Meanwhile, recruits poured into camps throughout the nation and many of them went through their preliminary training in civilian clothes, as can be seen in the photograph at upper right. The first

American soldiers reached France on June 26, and on July 4 marched through Paris where General Pershing placed a wreath on Lafayette's tomb, and where he is reported to have declared, "Lafayette, we are here." The first American division to enter actual combat fired its initial shot on October 23, 1917.

In the United States women seeking the right to vote staged demonstrations in practically all major cities. In the two photographs at the bottom of this page are shown scenes from two of these demonstrations.

It was also in 1917 that the Eighteenth Amendment to the Constitution was submitted to the states for ratification.

Tornadoes swept through Kansas, Illinois, Indiana, Kentucky, Tennessee, Arkansas, and Alabama during May. On October 13 fire on New York's East River destroyed 70,000 bushels of wheat. Three days later 200,000 bushels were lost in a Brooklyn fire. The same day thousands of head of cattle and hogs were lost in a fire at the Kansas City stockyards.

Pedigree

*OMAR KHAYYAM (Chestnut colt)	Marco	Barcaldine	Solon Ballyroe
		Novitiate	Hermit Retty
	Lisma	Persimmon	St. Simon Perdita II
		Luscious	‡Royal Hampton Alveole

‡*Harpenden or Royal Hampton.

Tabulated Racing Record

Year	Age	Sts.	1st	2nd	3rd	Won
1916	2	5	1	2	0	$ 3,465
1917	3	13	9	2	0	49,070
1918	4	10	2	1	4	4,475
1919	5	4	1	1	1	1,426
		32	13	6	5	$ 58,436

Omar Khayyam

43rd Kentucky Derby, May 12, 1917

$15,000 added. Net value to winner $16,600; second $2,500; third $1,000; fourth $275. 76 nominations.

Horse	Eqt	Wt	PP	St	½	¾	1	Str	Fin	Jockey	Owner	Odds $1 Str't
Omar Kh'm	wb	117	8	11	10ʰ	10¹	6½	2¹	1²	Borel	Billings & Johnson	12.80
Ticket	wb	117	3	1	3ʰ	3½	4½	1½	2½	J M'Tag't	A Miller	1.45
Midway	wb	117	1	12	12¹	9¹	8½	3ʰ	3⁴	Hunt	J W Parrish	14.65
Rickety	w	117	11	5	7½	5¹	1ʰ	4½	4¹	Robins'n	H P Whitney	4.55
War Star	wb	110	9	6	5½	6¹	5½	5ʰ	5ʰ	Buxton	A K Macomber	†8.65
Manis'r Toi	wb	117	14	15	13½	11½	10¹	6¹	6ʰ	Keogh	E Hertz	15.45
Skeptic	w	117	4	14	6¹	4ʰ	9¹	7¹	7½	Martin	H H Hewitt	‡16.45
Guy F'tune	wb	117	2	2	14¹	12¹	12¹	11¹	8½	Connelly	Pastime Stable	‡16.45
Star Mast'r	wb	117	12	9	4½	2ʰ	2ʰ	8¹¹	9ʰ	Loftus	A K Macomber	†8.65
Star Gazer	wb	110	13	10	1½	1½	3ʰ	9½	10²	Crump	A K Macomber	†8.65
Cudgel	wb	117	5	13	11¹	7¹	13¹	12½	11⁵	Murphy	J W Schorr	23.00
Green Jones	w	117	7	3	9ʰ	13¹	11½	13¹	12⁸	Goose	W H Baker	‡16.45
T O'T Wave	wb	117	10	4	15	14²	14¹	14¹	13⁴	Morys	Beverwyck Stable	‡16.45
Berlin	wb	117	6	7	2½	8ʰ	8½	10¹	14¹²	Andress	J S Ward	16.20
Acabado	wb	114	15	8	15	15	15	15	15	Schutt'r	Wickliffe Stable	75.45

Time, :23-3/5, :47-3/5, 1:12-4/5, 1:38, 2:04-3/5. Track fast.

War Star, Star Master and Star Gazer coupled in betting as A. K. Macomber entry; Skeptic, Guy Fortune, Green Jones and Top o' the Wave coupled in the field.

$2 Mutuels Paid—Omar Khayyam, $27.60 straight, $10.90 place, $6.20 show; Ticket, $3.70 place, $2.80 show; Midway, $5.10 show.

Winner—Ch.c. by Marco—Lisma, by Persimmon; trained by C. T. Patterson; bred in England by Sir John Robinson.

Went to Post—4:53. Off at 4:57 New York Time.

Start good and slow. Won easily; second and third driving. Omar Khayyam began slowly, gained steadily and, saving much ground when turning into the stretch, outstayed Ticket. The latter, well up from the start, raced into the lead in the stretch, but tired. Midway began slowly, was far back for the first half, but closed an immense gap into a game third. Rickety tired after taking the lead while rounding into the stretch. War Star raced fairly well. Star Gazer tired badly in the last quarter. Berlin quit in the stretch. Manister Toi ran a good race. Star Master failed to stay.

Scratched—Penrod, 114; Sol Gilsey, 117; Diamond, 112.

*Omar Khayyam — Stakes Races

AT 2 YEARS	2ND	Piping Rock Invitation Handicap, Hopeful Stakes.
	UNP	Grand Union Hotel Stakes.
AT 3 YEARS	WON	Kentucky Derby, Prospect Handicap, Brooklyn Derby, Kenner Stakes, Travers Stakes, Saratoga Cup, Lawrence Realization, Havre de Grace Handicap, Pimlico Autumn Handicap.
	2ND	American Champion Stakes, Bowie Handicap.
	UNP	Derby Trial, Brooklyn Handicap.
AT 4 YEARS	WON	Marines Liberty Bond Handicap.
	2ND	Bowie Handicap.
	3RD	Pimlico Spring Handicap, Dixie Handicap, Arlington Handicap, Monumental Handicap.
	UNP	Metropolitan Handicap, Baltimore Handicap, Washington Handicap.
AT 5 YEARS	WON	Rennert Handicap.
	2ND	Merchants Handicap.
	3RD	Pimlico Special Handicap.
	UNP	Elmont Handicap.

Purchased at England's Newmarket sales for $1,500 by C. K. G. Billings and Fred Johnson in 1915, *Omar Khayyam was imported as a yearling. He won only one race at two, was unplaced in his only race at three prior to the Derby.

No wonder then that he went to the post at better than 12-to-1. Winner of the Derby by two lengths, *Omar Khayyam won seven more races in succession. Shortly after the Derby the Billings-Johnson partnership was dissolved and the colt sold to Wilfred Viau, of Montreal, for $28,000.

*Omar Khayyam's wins included two over *Hourless, which didn't suit the latter's trainer, Sam Hildreth. Hildreth challenged for a match race, which Colonel Winn arranged at Laurel at one and one-quarter miles. *Hourless won by a length in 2:02, and there were many to claim *Omar Khayyam had gone stale after his rigorous campaign.

*Omar Khayyam raced through his five-year-old season, was then retired to the stud. He gained recognition as one of the country's top sires.

The son of Marco and Lisma was the champion and leading money-winning three-year-old of 1917, with $49,070 in earnings. Another Kentucky Derby winner, Old Rosebud, winner of the third race on the 1917 Derby Day card, was the leading money-winner among the older horses.

The imported horse, *North Star III, broke down while training for the Derby and thus did not get to start in America. Churchill Downs went through the entire season without a time record's being equaled or broken, but the great mare Embroidery won the Louisville Cup at two miles and the St. Leger Handicap at two and one-quarter miles.

Horses from England, imported in large numbers in 1916 because of the war, pretty much dominated the 1917 racing picture. *Sun Briar was the leading money-winning two-year-old with $59,505. Thus, both the two- and three-year-old champions were born across the Atlantic.

1918

The United States and the world celebrated the end of World War I in 1918 with scenes such as the one shown below in the photograph taken in Louisville at the intersection of Fourth and Jefferson streets on Armistice Day.

It was a "hot time in the old town tonight" across the continent when the sun went down that day of November 11, 1918.

Earlier in the year, however, it had been an entirely different story During January and February almost the entire nation suffered from bitter cold, unusual in many of the places it struck. Southern states were swept by their worst blizzard in history; many factories throughout the country were forced to close in order to conserve fuel; schools were dismissed; all theaters in New York City were closed for the first time in history, and that city was whipped by a severe hurricane.

On March 31 daylight-saving time was put into effect in various parts of the country, marking the first time this was ever done in the United States. Regular air-mail service in the country also was opened and on May 15 army fliers carried mail from New York City to Washington in three hours and twenty-two minutes.

In Louisville, Colonel Henry Watterson retired from active newspaper work on August 6. He was one of the most famous newspaper editors of his generation, covered the inauguration of Abraham Lincoln, edited the "Rebel" for the Confederacy, started the chant, "To Hell With the Hohenzollerns and Hapsburgs."

It was also in 1918 that Canadian soldiers refused to listen to William Jennings Bryan speak on prohibition; that the federal government took control of the Philadelphia police to protect the soldiers and sailors from vice; that Lenin was seriously wounded in Moscow, and that a new star was discovered in the constellation of Aquila.

Throughout Kentucky on Derby Day in 1918 school children started a "swat-the-fly" campaign.

Pedigree

(XTERMINATOR Chestnut gelding)	*McGee	White Knight	Sir Hugo / Whitelock
		Remorse	Hermit / Vex
	Fair Empress	Jim Gore	Hindoo / Katie
		Merry Thought	*Pirate of Penzance / Raybelle

Tabulated Racing Record

Year	Age	Sts.	1st	2nd	3rd	Won
1917	2	4	2	0	0	$ 1,350
1918	3	15	7	4	3	36,147
1919	4	21	9	6	3	26,402
1920	5	17	10	3	2	52,805
1921	6	16	8	2	5	56,827
1922	7	17	10	1	1	71,075
1923	8	3	1	1	1	4,250
1924	9	7	3	0	2	4,140
		100	50	17	17	$252,996

44th Kentucky Derby, May 11, 1918

Exterminator

$15,000 added. Net value to winner $14,700; second $2,500; third $1,000; fourth $275. 70 nominations.

Horse	Eqt	Wt	PP	St	½	¾	1	Str	Fin	Jockey	Owner	Odds $1 Str't
Exterminator	w	114	5	5	5^1	$4\frac{1}{2}$	1^h	2^4	1^1	Knapp	W S Kilmer	29.60
Escoba	wb	117	1	2	$3^{1}\frac{1}{2}$	2^h	2^1	1^n	2^8	Notter	K D Alexander	4.25
Viva America	w	113	2	1	$1^{1}\frac{1}{2}$	$1^{1}\frac{1}{2}$	3^4	3^2	3^4	War'on	C T Worthington	29.00
War Cloud	w	117	4	7	4^h	5^2	4^4	4^3	4^2	Loftus	A K Macomber	1.45
Lucky B	w	117	6	4	6^h	7^8	$5^{1}\frac{1}{2}$	5^6	5^6	McCabe	O A Bianchi	6.15
J T Clark	wb	117	8	8	7^3	6^3	7^6	7^3	6^{12}	Morys	J W Schorr	8.90
Sew'l Combs	wb	117	3	3	2^{nk}	3^1	6^2	$6^{1}\frac{1}{2}$	7^1	Gentry	Gallaher Bros	8.75
Am'n Eagle	wsb	117	6	6	8	8	8	8	8	Sande	T C McDowell	19.25

Time, :24-1/5, :49-1/5, 1:16-1/5, 1:43-3/5, 2:10-4/5. Track muddy.

$2 Mutuels Paid—Exterminator, $61.20 straight, $23.10 place, $12.40 show; Escoba, $4.90 place, $4.60 show; Viva America, $13.20 show.

Winner—Ch.g. by McGee—Fair Empress, trained by H. McDaniel; bred by F. D. Knight.

Went to Post—5:19. Off at 5:21.

Start good and slow. Won handily; second and third driving. Exterminator moved up fast after going three-quarters and, slipping through on the inner rail, raced into the lead and outstayed Escoba. The latter faced forwardly from the start, made a resolute effort in the last eighth, but tired in the last sixteenth. Viva America showed the most early speed, but found the distance a trifle too far. War Cloud met with much interference on the first two turns, but remained close up to the last quarter, where he tired. Sewell Combs raced well for three-quarters. James T. Clark was sharply cut off when he moved up fast at the half-mile ground.

Scratched—Aurum, 117; Jim Heffering, 117.

Overweight—Viva America, 1 pound.

Exterminator — Stakes Races

AT 3 YEARS	WON	Kentucky Derby, Carrollton Handicap, Ellicott City Handicap, Pimlico Autumn Handicap, Latonia Cup, Thanksgiving Handicap.
	2ND	Latonia Derby, Kenner Stakes, National Handicap.
	3RD	Cohoes Handicap, Washington Handicap, Bowie Handicap.
	UNP	Travers Stakes.
AT 4 YEARS	WON	Ben Ali Handicap, Camden Handicap, Galt House Handicap, Saratoga Cup, Pimlico Cup Handicap.
	2ND	Champlain Handicap, Harford County Handicap, Havre de Grace Handicap, Annapolis Handicap, Latonia Cup.
	3RD	Kentucky Handicap, Delaware Handicap, Merchants' and Citizens' Handicap.
	UNP	Suburban Handicap, Excelsior Handicap, Bowie Handicap.
AT 5 YEARS	WON	Long Beach Handicap, Brookdale Handicap, Windsor Jockey Club Handicap, George Hendrie Memorial Handicap, Saratoga Cup, Autumn Gold Cup, Toronto Autumn Cup, Ontario Jockey Club Cup, Pimlico Cup.
	2ND	Saratoga Handicap, Champlain Handicap.
	3RD	Suburban Handicap, Frontier Handicap.
	UNP	Brooklyn Handicap, Bowie Handicap.

There was no doubt about it. Willis Sharpe Kilmer, the Binghamton, New York, publisher and Thoroughbred breeder, was conceded to have the outstanding candidate for the forty-fourth running of the Kentucky Derby in 1918. The horse was *Sun Briar, champion two-year-old of the previous year, who had cost his owner $6000 as a yearling.

In the same year that Kilmer had bought *Sun Briar, the Lexington, Kentucky, horseman Cal Milam had bought a yearling by *McGee at Saratoga Springs for $1,500, merely as a speculation. At two, the Milam colt, which had been named Exterminator, had started four times, won two unimportant races.

But in the spring of 1918 Trainer Henry McDaniel saw him work at Lexington, decided he needed just such a horse to get *Sun Briar really sharp for the Derby. For $10,000, of which $9,000 was cash and the rest represented by two fillies, McDaniel bought Exterminator.

The rest, of course, has been written many times. *Sun Briar didn't get to the post in the Derby. Exterminator made his first start at three when he won the Derby.

Exterminator was bred by F. D. Knight on the farm which is now known as Almahurst. Here also was bred Greyhound, the great trotter.

In the Bowie Handicap, one and one-half miles, in the fall of 1918, Kentucky Derby winners ran one-two-three. They were George Smith (1916) first; *Omar Khayyam (1917), second; Exterminator (1918), third. George Smith carried 130 pounds, set a new track record of 2:31 1/5. He was one of the best in the older division.

In his six-, seven-, eight-, and nine-year-old seasons Exterminator won the Long Beach, Independence, Merchants' and Citizens,' Harford, Pimlico Spring, Clark, Kentucky, Bayside, Garden City, Brooklyn, Philadelphia Handicaps, Laurel Stakes, Saratoga Cup (twice), Autumn Gold Cup, Toronto Autumn Cup (twice), Pimlico Cup, and Saratoga Cup. He was second in Kings County, Excelsior, Philadelphia, Old Dominion, Handicaps, third in Brooklyn, Daniel Boone, Frontier, Annapolis, Pimlico Cup, Harford, Merchants,' Queen's Hotel Handicaps. He also was unplaced in Suburban, Independence, Saratoga, Arundel, Washington, Cofforth, and Philadelphia Handicaps.

World War I officially ended on June 28, 1919, with the signing of the Versailles Peace Treaty. Twenty-seven nations were represented by sixty delegates at the peace conference which was held at Paris.

Cincinnati, of the National League, defeated Chicago, of the American League, in the World Series, five games to three. It was principally because a scandal resulting from this series that baseball later named a high commissioner for the sport.

Louisville's Fourth and Broadway street intersection was a comparatively quiet scene. Traffic police directed the flow of automobiles by means of a "fishing pole" attached to an overhead semaphore. The confectionery building in photograph at upper right was replaced a few years later by the Brown Hotel.

To provide facilities for automobiles at Churchill Downs was rapidly becoming a problem, as shown in the photograph below. To accommodate the ever increasing attendance, the clubhouse was beginning to be enlarged toward the first turn of the track.

In the nation's capital there was grave concern over foreign affairs. Also confronting the country was strife between labor and capital, marked by strikes in the coal and steel industries. The "Red

Scare," as it was called, developed. Many persons openly embraced Communism with the result that several states passed laws to suppress Communism.

It was announced in Washington on the afternoon that the Kentucky Derby was run that the demobilization of our wartime Army had passed the 2,000,000 mark. At the same time the employment office set up to obtain jobs for the veterans declared that the old jobs did not appeal to the returning soldiers. It was especially difficult to get any to return to farming, the report said. Another announcement from Washington stated the fifth and final war loan had been oversubscribed by a big margin.

Pedigree

SIR BARTON
(Chestnut colt)

- *Star Shoot
  - Isinglass
    - Isonomy
    - Deadlock
  - Astrology
    - Hermit
    - Stella
- Lady Sterling
  - Hanover
    - Hindoo
    - Bourbon Belle
  - *Aquila
    - Sterling
    - Eagle

Sir Barton

Tabulated Racing Record

Year	Age	Sts.	1st	2nd	3rd	Won
1918	2	6	0	1	0	$ 4,113
1919	3	13	8	3	2	88,250
1920	4	12	5	2	3	24,494
		31	13	6	5	$116,857

45th Kentucky Derby, May 10, 1919

$20,000 added. Net value to winner $20,825; second $2,500; third $1,000; fourth $275. 75 nominations.

Horse	Eqt	Wt	PP	St	½	¾	1	Str	Fin	Jockey	Owner	Odds $1 Str't
Sir Barton	wb	112½	1	1	1²	1½	1²	1½	1⁵	Loftus	J K L Ross	‡2.60
Billy Kelly	w	119	11	8	3½	3⁴	2³	2⁴	2¹	Sande	J K L Ross	‡2.60
Under Fire	w	122	7	11	9½	9½	6½	3¹	3¹	Garner	P Dunne	19.15
Vulcanite	w	110	6	10	10½	5ʰ	4½	4¹	4⁶	Howard	W F Polson	70.00
Senn's Park	wb	122	8	9	6²	4½	5½	5¹	5¹	Lunsf'rd	O A Bianchi	†14.10
Be Frank	w	119	2	6	7ʰ	7½	7½	6½	6½	Butwell	C M Garrison	27.45
Sailor	wb	119	10	12	12	10²	10½	8½	7⁸	McIntyre	J W McClellan	§2.10
St Bernard	w	119	4	2	5ʰ	6¹	9¹	7²	8²	Pool	B J Brannon	†14.10
Regalo	w	117	9	7	8²	8½	8¹	9²	9⁴	Murphy	Gallaher Bros	6.05
Eternal	w	122	5	3	2½	2½	3½	10⁵	10¹⁰	Schutt'r	J W McClelland	§2.10
Frogtown	w	119	12	4	11²	11½	11²	11¹⁰	11²⁰	Morys	W S Kilmer	22.45
Vindex	w	122	3	5	4ⁿᵏ	12	12	12	12	Knapp	H P Whitney	8.15

Time. :24-1/5, :48-2/5, 1:14, 1:41-4/5, 2:09-4/5. Track heavy.

Sir Barton and Billy Kelly coupled in betting as J. K. L. Ross entry; Sailor and Eternal coupled as J. W. McClelland entry; Sennings Park and St. Bernard coupled in betting as field horses.

$2 Mutuels Paid—J. K. L. Ross Entry (Sir Barton and Billy Kelly), $7.20 straight, $6.70 place, $6.00 show; Under Fire, $10.80 show.

Winner—Ch.c. by *Star Shoot—Lady Sterling, by Hanover, trained by H. G. Bedwell; bred by Madden and Gooch.

Went to Post—5:10. Off at 5:14.

Start good and slow. Won easily; second and third driving. Sir Barton raced into the lead at once and, well ridden, led under restraint until reaching the stretch, where he was shaken up and easily held Billy Kelly safe in the last eighth. Billy Kelly held to his task well, was under restraint in the early running and finished gamely. Under Fire gained steadily from a slow beginning and finished fast and gamely. Vulcanite ran well and finished close up. Eternal was done after going three-quarters. Regalo ran disappointingly. Sennings Park tired in the stretch.

Scratched—Corson, 122; Clermont, 122. Overweight—Sir Barton, 2½ pounds.

Sir Barton   Stakes Races

AT 2 YEARS
- **2ND** Belmont Futurity.
- **UNP** Tremont Stakes, Flash Stakes, United States Hotel Stakes, Sanford Memorial, Hopeful Stakes.

AT 3 YEARS
- **WON** Kentucky Derby, Preakness Stakes, Withers Stakes, Belmont Stakes, Potomac Handicap, Maryland Handicap, Pimlico Fall Serial No. 2, Pimlico Fall Serial No. 3.
- **2ND** Dwyer Stakes.
- **3RD** Havre de Grace Handicap, Pimlico Autumn Handicap.

AT 4 YEARS
- **WON** Climax Handicap, Rennert Handicap, Saratoga Handicap, Dominion Handicap, Merchants' and Citizens' Handicap.
- **2ND** Kenilworth Park Gold Cup (match race with Man o' War), Pimlico Fall Serial No. 3.
- **3RD** Marathon Handicap, Laurel Stakes, Pimlico Fall Serial No. 2.
- **UNP** Belair Handicap, Philadelphia Handicap.

Vivian Gooch, an oldtime English trainer, was visiting John E. Madden, during the 1915-1916 winter when the host gave his guest a half-interest in Lady Sterling's unborn foal. The foal was Sir Barton, born April 26. Madden bought his partner's interest while the colt was still a weanling.

Sir Barton came to the races as a two-year-old in the silks of John E. Madden. It was after the Sanford Memorial Stakes when the colt was unplaced for the fourth straight time that Commander J. K. L. Ross bought him for $10,000. Earlier the Canadian sportsman had purchased Billy Kelly from W. F. Polson.

This was the pair that carried the silks of Commander Ross in the 1919 Kentucky Derby on the afternoon of May 10. The only horse among the other ten starters that afternoon able to challenge the pair was Eternal, champion of the two-year-olds the preceding year.

Sir Barton broke on top of his field, and for the first three-quarters of a mile the son of *Star Shoot led Eternal, by a half-length, with Billy Kelly the same distance back of the second horse. After six furlongs, however, Sir Barton drew out by two, and Billy Kelly by three. Eternal was through after the mile.

Given a brilliant ride by Johnny Loftus, who had ridden George Smith in 1916, Sir Barton was five lengths in front at the wire. Astride Billy Kelly was Earle Sande. Loftus was acclaimed the best rider of the year. His weight prevented his getting more mounts, but he was the leading money-winner. H. G. Bedwell, who trained the winner, was second in the number of winners, first in monies won.

Sir Barton went on to win the Preakness Stakes and Belmont Stakes, thus becoming the first of America's Triple Crown winners. His owner led money-winning owners for the second straight year, and Sir Barton was the first three-year-old since Roamer to be the leading money-winner.

The 1919 Derby winner continued to race at four. His races at that age included a match with Man o' War, champion of the two-year-olds in 1919. For the match Sir Barton turned up lame and was not at his best.

Two other former Derby winners were among the leading money-winners for the year, Exterminator topping the four-year-olds and Old Rosebud winning more than any other eight-year-old.

1920

Two amendments to the Constitution of the United States became effective in 1920. The first was the Prohibition Amendment, whose author was Andrew J. Volstead, lower left. The amendment became effective January 16.

Seven months later, on August 26, the nineteenth amendment giving suffrage to women went into effect. Tennessee was the thirty-sixth state to ratify the amendment.

It was also in 1920 that organized baseball named its first commissioner, selecting Kenesaw Mountain Landis, shown in the photograph above, who was a well known federal jurist. Another baseball

highlight of the same year was the longest major league game on record.

At Boston, the Brooklyn and Boston teams of the National League played a 1-to-1 deadlock which was called on account of darkness after twenty-six innings. Both starting pitchers went the route.

Wall Street was rocked by an explosion, a view of which is shown below. Coal miners and operators settled their strike which had been called the preceding November. The miners were granted a twenty-seven per cent raise in March.

On October 27 radio station KDKA obtained a license to broadcast and on November 2 the station's broadcast of election returns did much to popularize the radio and make it a common article in the home.

In Hoboken, New Jersey, on the afternoon of the 1920 Kentucky Derby, a bull ran amuck in the streets, charged onto the Hoboken ferry where he sent passengers scurrying, and finally jumped into the river. The last seen of the bull he was swimming in the direction of Europe. The same day it was announced in New York that a giant chess board would be built in the Manhattan Opera House on which people would be used as the "pieces" in a game to be played May 22.

Pedigree

Paul Jones

PAUL JONES
(Brown gelding)

*Sea King	Persimmon	St. Simon / Perdita II
	Sea Air	Isonomy / Re-echo
May Florence	Hamburg	Hanover / Lady Reel
	Fiesole	*Goldfinch / Firenze

Tabulated Racing Record

Year	Age	Sts.	1st	2nd	3rd	Won
1919	2	12	5	2	2	$ 6,404
1920	3	13	4	2	2	44,636
1921	4	12	1	1	3	2,708
1922	5	13	2	2	2	5,432
1923	6	15	2	5	4	4,991
		65	14	12	13	$ 64,171

46th Kentucky Derby, May 8, 1920

$30,000 added. 3-year-olds. Weight for age. Net value to winner $30,375; second $4,000; third $2,000; fourth $275. 107 nominations.

Horse	Eqt	Wt	PP	St	½	¾	1	Str	Fin	Jockey	Owner	Odds $1 Str't
Paul Jones	w	126	2	1	$1^1\frac{1}{2}$	$1^\frac{1}{2}$	1^2	1^h	1^h	Rice	R Parr	‡16.20
Upset	w	126	5	4	3^h	3^h	$2^\frac{1}{2}$	2^h	2^4	Rodrig'z	H P Whitney	††1.65
On Watch	wb	126	13	16	$13^\frac{1}{2}$	7^1	$3^\frac{1}{2}$	3^1	3^4	Barrett	G W Loft	§4.30
Damask	b	126	8	9	$7h$	4^h	4^1	4^1	4^2	Ambrose	H P Whitney	††1.65
Donnacona	w	126	7	10	6^h	$6^\frac{1}{2}$	$5^\frac{1}{2}$	5^2	5^4	O'Brien	G W Loft	§4.30
Blazes	w	126	15	7	$8^\frac{1}{2}$	5^1	$6^\frac{1}{2}$	6^1	$6^\frac{1}{2}$	Kummer	R Parr	‡16.20
By Golly	w	126	4	5	2^h	8^1	$8^1\frac{1}{2}$	8^1	7^h	Lyke	E R Bradley	†13.20
Wildair	w	126	14	8	$4^\frac{1}{2}$	2^h	7^1	$7^\frac{1}{2}$	8^h	Fator	H P Whitney	††1.65
Bersagliere	wb	126	9	3	$10^\frac{1}{2}$	$11^\frac{1}{2}$	9^1	9^1	$9^\frac{1}{2}$	Murray	C A Cochran	22.75
Patches	wb	126	6	12	14^1	10^h	10^2	10^h	10^4	Hanover	F C Bain	†13.20
Herron	w	126	1	6	9^h	13^2	$11^\frac{1}{2}$	11^2	$11^\frac{1}{2}$	Butwell	E Alvarez	†13.20
Sandy Beal	w	126	10	14	15^2	14^2	12^1	12^1	$12^\frac{1}{2}$	Williams	W S Murray	12.50
Prince Pal	w	126	3	2	5^1	12^h	13^2	13^2	13^2	Schut'r	Simms & Oliver	18.90
David Har'm	wb	126	11	11	$11^\frac{1}{2}$	$9^\frac{1}{2}$	14^2	14^2	$14^1\frac{1}{2}$	Fairb'er	W R Coe	‡‡35.20
Cleopatra	wb	121	12	13	12^{nk}	15^4	15^5	15^1	15^5	McAtee	W R Coe	‡‡35.20
Peace Pen'nt	wb	126	17	15	16^{10}	16^{20}	16^{20}	16^{20}	16^{20}	Garner	W F Polson	6.35
Sterling	wb	126	16	17	17	17	17	17	17	Callahan	C C Van Meter	33.00

†Mutuel field. ‡Coupled in betting as R. Parr entry. ††Coupled in betting as H. P. Whitney entry. §Coupled in betting as G. W. Loft entry. ‡‡Coupled in betting as W. R. Coe entry.

Time, :23-4/5, :48-1/5, 1:14-4/5, 1:42, 2:09. Track slow.

$2 Mutuels Paid—Ral Parr entry (Paul Jones and Blazes), $34.40 straight, $12.30 place, $6.60 show; H. P. Whitney entry (Upset and Damask), $3.20 place, $3.00 show; G. W. Loft entry (On Watch and Donnacona), $4.00 show.

Winner—Br.g. by *Sea King—May Florence, by Hamburg, trained by William Garth; bred by J. E. Madden.

Went to Post—5:08. Off at 5:12.

Start good and slow. Won driving; second and third same. Paul Jones was away fast, raced into the lead at once and, holding on in game style, outstayed Upset in the final drive. The latter moved up menacingly after going a half-mile and, saving ground when coming into the stretch, appeared a winner a sixteenth out, but tired right at the end. On Watch came from far back in the last half-mile and finished well. Damask raced forwardly, but tired in the stretch. By Golly quit. Donnacona had no mishap. Peace Pennant was always far back. Sandy Beal retired after going a half-mile and so did Bersagliere.

Scratched—Golden Broom, 126; Kinnoul, 126; Simpleton, 126; Ethel Gray, 121; Westwood, 126.

Paul Jones   Stakes Races

AT 2 YEARS	WON	Aberdeen Stakes, Boquet Selling Stakes, Endurance.
	3RD	Albany Handicap.
	UNP	Flash Stakes, Belmont Futurity, Eastern Shore Stakes.
AT 3 YEARS	WON	Kentucky Derby, Newark Handicap, Suburban Handicap.
	2ND	Chesapeake Stakes, Oxford Handicap.
	3RD	Whitehall Handicap, Pimlico Cup.
	UNP	Potomac Handicap, Annapolis Handicap, Maryland Handicap, Pimlico Autumn Handicap, Bowie Handicap.
AT 4 YEARS	WON	Susquehanna Handicap.
	2ND	Pimlico Special Handicap.
	3RD	Olambala Handicap, Lake George Handicap, Champlain Handicap.
	UNP	Harford Handicap, Delaware Handicap, Philadelphia Handicap, Suburban Handicap, Brooklyn Handicap, Merchants' and Citizens' Handicap, Manhattan Handicap.
AT 5 YEARS	2ND	Calvert Handicap, Pimlico Cup Handicap.
	3RD	Stafford Handicap.
	UNP	Joppa Handicap, Washington Handicap, Forest Park Handicap, Bowie Handicap, Prince George Handicap, Thanksgiving Handicap.
AT 6 YEARS	2ND	Philadelphia Handicap, Stafford Handicap.
	3RD	Old Diminion Handicap. American Independence Handicap.

Paul Jones was the last of the Derby winners to race as many as five full seasons, and only one winner since 1920 approaches the Derby champion of that year in number of starts. Paul Jones ended his campaigning after his six-year-old season with a total of sixty-five starts.

Whirlaway, who started only twice at five, is closest to him in number of starts. Whirlaway started in a total of sixty races.

As a two-year-old Paul Jones had won five of his twelve starts, and prior to the forty-sixth Derby he had won the Newark Handicap, was second in the Chesapeake Stakes. His Derby marked the first $1,000,000 Derby Day.

An estimated 45,000 persons wagered $1,055,191 on Derby Day, $375,249 of it on the Derby itself. The year also was marked by a new high in the added value of the race. In 1920 the added money was increased from $20,000 to $30,000.

Three owners not only took down all the gross $36,650 which the Derby was worth, but also their horses were the first six past the wire. The three owners were Ral Parr, H. P. Whitney, and G. W. Loft, each with a two-horse entry.

Derby Day in 1920 was marred by the late arrival of programs. It was almost time for the first race before the programs reached the track and when they did vendors were practically mobbed by eager purchasers.

Upset, only horse ever to beat Man o' War, made a brilliant run through the stretch, but was unable to overhaul Paul Jones, who had been first away from the barrier and had set the pace throughout. Paul Jones was the first gelding to win the Derby at level weights with colts.

The $5,000 prize for Jockey Rice, who rode the winner, was the largest ever paid, and Rice split the prize with Clarence Kummer, who rode the other horse owned by Parr.

On May 24, 1920, the three-year-old filly Distinction, under 110 pounds, and the five-year-old horse The Porter, under 122 pounds, each ran seven furlongs in 1:25 to establish a new mark at Churchill Downs. The following year, however, Distinction, under 110 pounds, ran the distance in 1:23 1/5 to set a record which still stands.

1921

The twenty-eighth President of the United States took office in 1921. He was Senator Warren G. Harding, at right. His running mate on the successful Republican ticket was Governor Calvin Coolidge, of Massachusetts.

This Republican ticket had been picked after a convention deadlock developed between General Leonard A. Wood and Governor Frank O. Lowden, of Illinois. The Democratic ticket, defeated in the election, was headed by Governor James A. Cox, of Ohio, and Franklin D. Roosevelt.

In the first year of Harding's administration the Fordney-McCumber Tariff Act was passed, returning the nation to high rates; a national budget system was enacted, and the Agricultural Credits Act was passed to furnish some relief for farmers. Also passed by the Congress was an act limiting immigration for the next thirteen months to three per cent of the nationals living here by the 1910 census.

After refusing to join the League of Nations, the United States in this year signed a separate peace treaty with Germany and Austria, and in Washington was held the Conference against War with nine major nations participating. It was here a naval treaty was adopted.

In the field of sports the Dempsey-Carpentier fight at Boyle's Thirty Acres, below, drew the first $1,000,000 gate, and little Centre College's "Prayin' Colonels" from Danville, Kentucky, defeated Harvard's mighty eleven.

Louisville housewives who entertained guests for the forty-seventh running of the Kentucky Derby found the following prices at the corner grocery: sausage, 20 cents per pound; bacon, 30 cents per pound; eggs, 24 cents per dozen.

Pedigree

Behave Yourself

BEHAVE YOURSELF (Bay colt)	Marathon	Martagon — Bend Or / Tiger Lily
		*Ondulee — St. Simon / Ornis
	Miss Ringlets	Handball — Hanover / Keepsake
		Bessie — *The Ill-Used / Belle of Nantura

Tabulated Racing Record

Year	Age	Sts.	1st	2nd	3rd	Won
1920	2	7	3	0	1	$ 17,972
1921	3	11	1	2	0	40,800
		18	4	2	1	$ 58,772

47th Kentucky Derby, May 7, 1921

50,000 added. 3-year-olds. Weight for age. Net value to winner $38,450 and $5,000 gold cup; second $10,000; third $5,000; fourth $2,000. 109 nominations.

Horse	Eqt	Wt	PP	St	½	¾	1	Str	Fin	Jockey	Owner	Odds $1 Str't
Behave Y'self	w	126	1	9	8½	8¹	6½	1½	1ʰ	Thomp'n	E R Bradley	†8.65
B'k Servant	w	126	7	2	1¹	1ʰ	1½	2½	2⁶	Lyke	E R Bradley	†8.65
Prudery	w	121	2	4	5¹½	4¹½	3ʰ	3ʰ	3½	Kummer	H P Whitney	‡1.10
Tryster	w	126	10	8	6ʰ	5¹½	5ʰ	4¹	4⁴	Coltiletti	H P Whitney	‡1.10
Careful	w	121	3	7	4ʰ	3ʰ	4ʰ	5²	5⁴	Keogh	W J Salmon	13.60
Coyne	w	126	5	3	7²	6ʰ	7²	7¹	6¹	Garner	Harned Bros	11.20
Leonardo II	w	126	4	5	3½	2³	2½	6½	7½	Schut'r	Xalapa Farm Stable	§4.30
Uncle Velo	ws	126	12	1	11¹	10²	9¹½	8²	8²	Pool	G F Baker	65.30
Bon Homme	wb	126	11	6	10¹	11⁶	11²	10¹	9⁶	Rob'son	Xalapa Farm Stable	§4.30
Planet	wb	126	6	12	12	12	12	11¹½	10⁵	King	H P Headley	81.30
Star-Voter	w	126	8	11	9¹	7¹	8ʰ	9²	11¹	Ensor	J K L Ross	8.55
Muskall'nge	wb	126	9	10	2¹	9¹	10¹	12	12	Carroll	H C Fisher	96.25

†Coupled in betting as E. R. Bradley entry. ‡Coupled in betting as H. P. Whitney entry. §Coupled in betting as Xalapa Farm Stable entry.

Time, :23-1/5, :46-4/5, 1:11-3/5, 1:38-3/5, 2:04-1/5. Track fast.

$2 Mutuels Paid—E. R. Bradley entry (Behave Yourself and Black Servant), $19.30 straight, 13.00 place, $5.60 show; H. P. Whitney entry (Prudery and Tryster), $3.30 show.

Winner—Br.c. by Marathon—Miss Ringlets, by Handball, trained by H. J. Thompson; bred by E. R. Bradley.

Went to Post—4:50. Off at 4:56.

Start good and slow. Won driving; second and third same. Behave Yourself began slowly, but saved much ground on the last two turns and, gaining steadily in the stretch, outstayed Black Servant in a game finish. The latter showed fine speed in pacemaking and disposed of Leonardo II. before going three-quarters, then held on well in the final drive, but tired near the end. Prudery made a wide turn into the stretch and finished gamely. Tryster was far back in the early running, but finished fast and gaining. Leonardo II. tired after going well for the first mile. Careful was done after going three-quarters. Coyne ran fairly well.

Scratched—Grey Lag, 126; Billy Barton, 126; Firebrand, 126.

Behave Yourself — Stakes Races

AT 2 YEARS	WON	Queen City Handicap.
	3RD	Kentucky Jockey Club Stakes.
AT 3 YEARS	WON	Kentucky Derby.
	2ND	Blue Grass Stakes, Latonia Derby.
	UNP	Ben Ali Handicap, Kentucky Handicap, Proctor Knott Handicap, Saranac Handicap, Greenwich Handicap, Latonia Handicap, Latonia Championship Stakes, Twin City Handicap.

The 1921 racing season brought many outstanding horses to Churchill Downs. As a result the track records took a sound drubbing. Three two-year-olds ran four furlongs in :46 3/5. They were Fair Phantom on May 7, Casey on May 9, and Miss Joy on May 18. Three days later Miss Joy set a new mark of :52 3/5 for four and one-half furlongs. Distinction set a six and one-half furlongs mark of 1:17 3/5, after establishing her record for seven furlongs. Broomspun and the eight-year-old Sands of Pleasure each ran one mile in 1:36 1/5, a new track record. Dr. Clark set a record of 1:49 4/5 for one and one-eight miles and Woodtrap ran the mile and one-quarter in 2:03 1/5 for a new mark.

When Behave Yourself swept past his stable-mate, Black Servant, in the last quarter, withstood the latter's determined drive in the final stages to win the 1921 Kentucky Derby by a neck, one of the most often written stories on the Derby was born. It has been recorded countless times since that May afternoon that it was Black Servant —not Behave Yourself—that Colonel E. R. Bradley, owner of both horses, wanted to win.

The stories read that Colonel Bradley had wagered heavily on Black Servant at the winter odds, but had wagered nothing on Behave Yourself. Colonel Bradley had no comment about this for reporters trying to interview him.

During the 1920 season Colonel Bradley had enjoyed his best racing success up to that time with Jockey L. Lyke, who rode Black Servant in the Derby, contributing much to the stable's winnings. Behave Yourself was considered one of the better two-year-olds in the middlewest, having run a mile in 1:38 4/5, the fastest eight furlongs for a two-year-old in Kentucky until Tryster ran the distance in 1:38 2/5 at Churchill Downs a few weeks later.

Behave Yourself had been unplaced in the Ben Ali Handicap and second to Black Servant in the Bluegrass Stakes in his two races prior to the Kentucky Derby at three.

Added money for the Derby was raised to $50,000 in 1921 and his one-two finish was worth $48,450 to Colonel Bradley, who not only owned but bred both horses, marking the first time any owner had done this. During the season the Bradley horses won more than $100,000, a new high for the owner.

Behave Yourself was the first of four Derby winners to be owned by Colonel Bradley. Both Behave Yourself and Black Servant retired as stallions at Idle Hour Farm. Behave Yourself died in 1938.

When Colonel E. R. Bradley was asked which of all the top horses he owned was his favorite, his reply was Bit of White. He described her "like a bit of Dresden china." In winning the two-mile Louisville Cup in 1921, Bit of White set a new track mark of 3:22 3/5.

The names of many men who had been important in national and world affairs, or were to become extremely important, were prominent in the headlines of 1922. Among them were Samuel Gompers, Will Hays, and Mahatma Ghandi, whose pictures appear on this page.

Gompers, shown below, was elected to his forty-first term as president of the American Federation of Labor. Gompers, a native of London, had helped organize the federation and served as its president, with the exception of one year, until he died in 1924. Hays, who had been named postmaster general by President Harding in 1921, resigned to serve as president of

the Motion Picture Producers and Distributors of America at a salary of $150,-000 a year. Hays is shown lower right.

The arrest of Ghandi, leader of the passive revolt in India, was ordered. Ghandi is shown upper right.

Death came to Alexander Graham Bell, inventor of the telephone, on August 2, 1922. During his funeral service every telephone in North America was silenced.

It was late in the fall of this year that Benito Mussolini began negotiations to procure certain portfolios in the Italian government. On October 28 the king of Italy summoned him to form a new government, and Mussolini himself took the interior and foreign affairs portfolios.

The soldiers' bonus bill, destined to haunt capitol hill in Washington for many years, was vetoed by President Harding. It failed to get the necessary majority in the Senate to over-ride the Presidential veto. In Washington the President and Secretary of Agriculture Wallace held a National Agricultural Congress to effect a program of farm relief.

This also was the year that the tomb of King Tut was discovered near Luxor, Egypt. Contained in the tomb were treasures of priceless historical and intrinsical worth. On October 15, 1922, Billy Mitchell established a new airplane record, flying 224.5 miles per hour.

Pedigree

Morvich

MORVICH (Black Colt)			
Runnymede	*Voter	Friar's Balsam	
		*Mavourneen	
	Running Stream	Domino	
		Dancing Water	
Hymir	Dr. Leggo	Puryear D.	
		Sevens	
	Georgia Girl	*Solitaire II	
		Georgia VI	

Tabulated Racing Record

Year	Age	Sts.	1st	2nd	3rd	Won
1921	2	11	11	0	0	$115,234
1922	3	5	1	2	1	57,675
		16	12	2	1	$172,909

48th Kentucky Derby, May 13, 1922

50,000 added, also $5,000 gold cup and $2,000 other gold trophies. 3-year-olds. Weight or age. Net value to winner $46,775; second $6,000; third $3,000; fourth $1,000. 92 nominations.

orse	Eqt	Wt	PP	St	½	¾	1	Str	Fin	Jockey	Owner	Odds $1 Str't
orvich	w	126	4	2	$1^{1\frac{1}{2}}$	$1^{1\frac{1}{2}}$	$1^{1\frac{1}{2}}$	$1^{1\frac{1}{2}}$	$1^{1\frac{1}{2}}$	Johnson	B Block	1.20
et Mosie	w	126	7	8	$8^{\frac{1}{2}}$	6^3	$5^{\frac{1}{2}}$	4^1	2^h	Burke	Idle Hour Stock Farm	†2.90
hn Finn	ws	126	1	4	5^1	5^1	6^2	2^h	3^1	Pool	G F Baker	22.60
eadlock	w	126	6	6	4^1	$4^{\frac{1}{2}}$	$4^{1\frac{1}{2}}$	3^h	4^4	Mooney	R H Shannon	6.90
y Play	w	126	3	1	2^h	2^h	3^1	5^2	5^4	Rob'son	Lexington Stable	19.05
etterman	w	126	9	9	$7^{\frac{1}{2}}$	$7^{\frac{1}{2}}$	7^1	7^1	6^1	Rice	Greentree Stable	24.80
urf Rider	wb	126	8	7	6^1	8^1	$8^{1\frac{1}{2}}$	8^1	$7^{\frac{1}{2}}$	Scobie	Montfort Jones	35.75
artle	w	121	2	3	3^2	3^1	2^h	$6^{\frac{1}{2}}$	8^{nk}	Connelly	H H Hewitt	13.90
y Gosh	w	126	10	10	9	9	9	9	9	Barnes	Idle Hour Stock Farm	†2.90
usy Amer'n	wb	126	5	5	Broke down					Barrett	Idle Hour Stock Farm	†2.90

†Coupled in betting as Idle Hour Stock Farm Stable entry.

me, :23-4/5, :47-3/5, 1:13, 1:39-1/5, 2:04-3/5. Track fast.

$2 Mutuels Paid—Morvich, $4.40 straight, $4.30 place, $3.50 show; E. R. Bradley's Idle our Stock Farm entry (Bet Mosie, By Gosh and Busy American), $2.90 place, $2.70 how; John Finn, $6.60 show.

inner—Br.c. by Runnymede—Hymir, by Dr. Leggo, trained by F. Burlew; bred by A. B. reckels.

ent to Post—4:50. Off at 4:53.

Start good and slow. Won easily; second and third driving. Morvich ran as if he outclassed e others, was kept in the lead under hard restraint for the first mile and drew away in the retch to win under a pull. Bet Mosie was ridden wide on the turns and lost much ground, but osed a big gap and finished gamely. John Finn raced prominently all the way and finished solutely. Deadlock raced well, but tired in the last quarter. My Play ran well, but finished uite lame. Startle was done after going three-quarters. Busy American broke down in the rst quarter.

Scratched—Banker Brown, 126.

Morvich — Stakes Races

T 2 YEARS	WON	Suffolk Selling Stakes, Greenfield Selling Stakes, U. S. Hotel Stakes, Saratoga Special, Hopeful Stakes, Eastern Shore Handicap, Pimlico Futurity.
T 3 YEARS	WON	Kentucky Derby.
	2ND	Carlton Stakes.
	3RD	Kentucky Special.
	UNP	Latonia Fall Highweight Handicap.

Distinction, who had previously set Churchill Downs records for six and one-half and seven furlongs, came back at five in 1922 to equal the track mark of 1:11 for six furlongs. High Cloud set a seven and one-half furlong record of 1:30 and Lady Madcap ran one and one-sixteenth miles in 1:44, a new record. On May 18 De Bonero won at odds of 164-to-1.

For the fourth straight year Exterminator was leading money-winner among the older horses, and in this year won the most money ever earned by a seven-year-old. Pillory was best of the money-winners, and Sally's Alley was the best two-year-old. Rancocas Stable got a bigger share of the $9,096,215 distribution than any other owner.

"I just sprinted Morvich, and on Derby Day I found he had won. That's something you can do once, but not twice." Such was the way Trainer Fred Burlew described the Kentucky Derby victory of Benjamin Block's Morvich in 1922. Prior to the Derby strong opinions had been expressed on both sides regarding Morvich's ability to go the Derby distance.

The son of Runnymede had been unbeaten as a two-year-old, winning eleven races. The Derby was his first start as a three-year-old. It also was the last time he visited the winner's circle, although he was second in the Carlton Stakes, Greenwich Handicap, and third in the Kentucky Special at three. The $115,234 which Morvich won as a two-year-old placed him at the top of all money-winners in 1921.

Although some questioned Morvich's ability to go the mile and one-quarter, the public took little stock in the arguments and made the colt favorite at $1.20 to $1.00. Colonel E. R. Bradley's three-horse entry of Bet Mosie, By Gosh, and Busy American was second choice, with most of the entry's supporters believing Busy American would be a match for Morvich's speed, and that Bradley might even run one-two again.

Busy American, however, broke down on the clubhouse turn. Bet Mosie did come from far back to finish second to the winner. Third place went to John Finn, who like Bet Mosie had moved strongly through the final quarter, but was beaten a head at the wire.

H. H. Hewitt's grand filly Startle, only one of her sex in the forty-eighth Derby, had been a prominent contender in the early stages, but had faded after the first mile. Finishing in sixth place was Letterman, first of a long list of horses racing for Greentree Stable in the Kentucky Derby.

Morvich, bred by A. B. Spreckels in California, was brought east early in 1921 by William Carroll. Trainer Max Hirsch purchased the colt for $4,000 at Jamaica and later resold him to Wall Street's Benjamin Block.

1923

At his boyhood home in Vermont just after midnight of August 2, 1923, Calvin Coolidge, lower right, received news of the death of President Warren G. Harding in San Francisco. By the light of a kerosene lamp, Coolidge's father administered the oath of office to his son.

Coolidge, who had served Massachusetts as an assemblyman, state senator, lieutenant governor, and finally governor retained the Harding cabinet and announced he intended to carry out the policies of his predecessor.

The new President, however, was not too effective in dealing with Congress, which paid little heed to his recommendations and at times overrode his vetoes. Among the bills passed over his veto was a modified bonus bill. The Congress would not listen to his support of a bill to reduce surtaxes on large incomes, or his favoring entry of the United States into the World Court at The Hague. The Congress turned a deaf ear to many of his other proposals.

It was in 1923 that Sarah Bernhardt, the great French actress, died. She made her debut in 1862 and continued her stage career almost until her death. Among her favorite roles were L'Aiglon, La Tosca, Camille, and Cleopatra.

At Churchill Downs plans were being drawn up for the extension of the two-story clubhouse. Contracts were let for the improvements, badly needed to care for the ever-increasing Kentucky Derby attendance, and 1923 was the last year the clubhouse appeared as it does in the photograph at the top of the page.

In Louisville to conduct a revival during early May the great evangelist Billy Sunday declared the signs of the times point to an imminent second coming of Christ. At Baltimore on Derby Day doctors in the Franklin Square hospital declared a baby which had been dead for fifteen minutes was revived through the use of adrenalin.

Residents of Williamsburg, Kentucky, discovered a large number of fish dead in Stevens Creek, hundreds of others in a stupefied condition. The pouring of slop from moonshiners' stills into the creek was blamed. Jonas Mulford, a Negro of Paris, Kentucky, had a dream that Zev won the Kentucky Derby, bet his $200 life-savings on the colt, won $3,800. He announced he would buy a home, go on an excursion to Cincinnati.

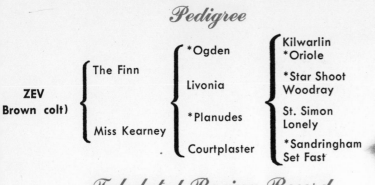

Pedigree

ZEV Brown colt)	The Finn	*Ogden	Kilwarlin *Oriole
		Livonia	*Star Shoot Woodray
	Miss Kearney	*Planudes	St. Simon Lonely
		Courtplaster	*Sandringham Set Fast

49th

Zev

Tabulated Racing Record

Year	Age	Sts.	1st	2nd	3rd	Won
1922	2	12	5	4	2	$ 24,665
1923	3	14	12	1	0	272,008
1924	4	17	6	3	3	16,966
		43	23	8	5	$313,639

49th Kentucky Derby, May 19, 1923

$50,000 added. 3-year-olds. Weight for age. Net value to winner $53,600 and $5,000 gold cup; second $6,000; third $3,000; fourth $1,000. 145 nominations.

Horse	Eqt	Wt	PP	St	½	¾	1	Str	Fin	Jockey	Owner	Odds $1 Str't
Zev	wb	126	10	5	1^2	1^2	$1\frac{1}{2}$	1^2	$1^{1\frac{1}{2}}$	Sande	Rancocas Stable	19.20
Martingale	w	126	19	12	2^2	$2\frac{1}{2}$	2^h	2^1	2^1	Kummer	J S Cosden	‡19.75
Vigil	wb	126	5	14	$10\frac{1}{2}$	8^1	$6\frac{1}{2}$	5^1	3^1	Marinelli	W J Salmon	15.25
Nassau	w	126	8	4	3^1	3^h	$3^{1\frac{1}{2}}$	3^1	4^n	Garner	F Johnson	3.25
Chittagong	wb	126	1	2	9^2	7^1	4^1	6^1	$5^{1\frac{1}{2}}$	Heupel	J Hertz	†5.85
Enchantm't	wb	126	11	11	6^h	4^1	$5\frac{1}{2}$	$4\frac{1}{2}$	6^2	McAtee	H P Whitney	§2.30
Rialto	w	126	17	15	$12\frac{1}{2}$	10^1	8^h	$7\frac{1}{2}$	7^2	Coltiletti	Greentree Stable	§2.30
Aspiration	wb	126	9	7	7^1	$5\frac{1}{2}$	7^{nk}	9^1	$8^{1\frac{1}{2}}$	Kennedy	B Block	††29.20
Prince K	w	126	4	1	4^1	$9\frac{1}{2}$	9^h	$11\frac{1}{2}$	$9\frac{1}{2}$	Kelsay	Marshall Bros	†5.85
Br't Tom'w	wb	126	7	3	14^h	11^2	10^{nk}	8^1	$10\frac{1}{2}$	Ponce	Idle Hour Stock Farm	28.05
In Memoriam	w	126	21	10	11^h	$12\frac{1}{2}$	$11\frac{1}{2}$	16^1	$11\frac{1}{2}$	Mooney	C Weidemann	†5.85
Bo McMillan	w	126	20	8	5^1	6^3	12^1	15^h	12^1	Connelly	T J Pendergast	11.95
Better Luck	w	126	6	18	8^1	15^1	14^h	$17\frac{1}{2}$	13^1	Johnson	B Block	††29.20
Wida	w	126	12	9	15^1	$13\frac{1}{2}$	13^h	14^h	14^8	Yerrat	T E Mueller	†5.85
Picketer	w	126	18	16	13^1	14^2	15^1	$10\frac{1}{2}$	15^2	Corcoran	H P Whitney	§2.30
Gen Thatch'r	w	126	16	17	16^1	16^2	17^1	13^1	16^2	Rob'son	Nevada Stock Farm	12.80
Calcutta	wb	126	14	13	18^1	17^1	$16\frac{1}{2}$	$19\frac{1}{2}$	17^1	Yeargin	G R Allen	†5.85
The Clown	w	126	2	21	$17\frac{1}{2}$	19^2	19^1	$18\frac{1}{2}$	18^4	Lunsf'rd	Audley Farm	†5.85
Golden Rule	w	126	15	6	19^1	$18\frac{1}{2}$	18^h	$12\frac{1}{2}$	19^{10}	Lang	J S Cosden	‡19.75
Cherry Pie	w	126	3	20	21	21	20^1	20^4	20^2	Penman	Greentree Stable	§2.30
Pravus	wb	126	13	19	20^1	$20\frac{1}{2}$	21	21	21	Owens	F Wieland	†5.85

†Mutuel field. ‡Coupled in betting as J. S. Cosden entry. §Coupled in betting as Greentree Stable and H. P. Whitney entry. ††Coupled in betting as B. Block entry.

Time, :23-2/5, :47-2/5, 1:12-2/5, 1:39, 2:05-2/5. Track fast.

$2 Mutuels Paid—Zev, $40.40 straight, $30.60 place, $18.40 show; J. S. Cosden entry (Martingale and Golden Rule), $25.80 place, $16.60 show; Vigil, $12.30 show.

Winner—Br.c. by The Finn—Miss Kearney, by *Planudes, trained by D. J. Leary; bred by J. E. Madden.

Went to Post—4:47. Off at 4:53.

Start good and slow. Won easily; second and third driving. Zev broke forwardly and, showing high speed, raced into a good lead at once and, withstanding a drive through the stretch, gamely held Martingale safe at the end. Martingale was in closest pursuit nearly throughout and held his position well in the stretch drive. Vigil began slowly and had to race wide, but closed a big gap and may have been best. Nassau raced well and saved much ground on the last turn. Chittagong ran a fine race. Enchantment tired. Rialto closed a big gap. Prince K. quit. Beau McMillan was away poorly. Cherry Pie had little chance from the start.

Scratched—Anna M. Humphrey, 121; Chickvale, 126; Everhart, 126.

Zev — Stakes Races

AT 2 YEARS	WON	Grand Union Hotel Stakes, Albany Handicap.
	2ND	Belmont Futurity.
	3RD	Hopeful Stakes.
	UNP	Hudson Stakes.
AT 3 YEARS	WON	Kentucky Derby, Paumonok Handicap, Rainbow Handicap, Withers Stakes, Belmont Stakes, Queens County Handicap, Lawrence Realization, International Special No. 3, Autumn Championship Stakes, Pimlico Fall Serial No. 3, Match Races with In Memoriam ($75,000).
	2ND	Latonia Championship Stakes.
	UNP	Preakness Stakes.
AT 4 YEARS	WON	Kings County Handicap, Havlin Hotel Handicap, Pimlico Serial No. 1.
	2ND	Paumonok Handicap, Arverne Handicap, Interborough Handicap.
	3RD	Excelsior Handicap, Continental Handicap, Pimlico Fall Serial No. 2.
	UNP	Brooklyn Handicap, International Special No. 1, Southampton Handicap, International Special No. 2.

Although Zev had won the Paumonok Handicap and Rainbow Handicap in two of his first three starts as a three-year-old, it was the urging of Jockey Earl Sande that persuaded Owner H. F. Sinclair and Trainer Sam Hildreth to start the son of The Finn in the Kentucky Derby on May 19, 1923. Zev had run unplaced to Vigil in the Preakness, and owner and trainer were discouraged with the colt.

Sande, however, argued long. Finally, Zev went to the post to face the second largest field that ever started in the Derby. The 75,000 persons present considered him a sprinter and a mudder, thus letting him go to the post at odds of $19.20 to $1. Sande also considered sprinting Zev's best ability. So he took the colt out on top at once, kept him there throughout the mile and one-quarter.

The Derby was the second of nine straight races Zev was to win as a three-year-old before he was second to In Memoriam in the Latonia Championship Stakes. Zev returned east from Latonia to win the Pimlico Special No. 3, but there were cries for a match race between the Rancocas colt and his Latonia conqueror.

Accordingly, Colonel Winn arranged a $25,000 match race between the two at Churchill Downs. Zev was the winner by inches and horsemen who witnessed the spectacle will be talking about the race until they die. In the International at Belmont earlier, Zev had run away from the French challenger Papyrus.

The $272,008 won by Zev as a three-year-old not only made him the leader for the year, but it was the largest amount of money that had been won by a Thoroughbred in one year. He raced again at four, and his total earnings made him the world's greatest money-winner.

As Zev moved into the lead as the world's greatest money-winner, another Derby winner, Exterminator, was third on the list. The grand old campaigner had gone lame in 1923 when he was eight. Zev's winnings placed Rancocas Stable at the top of the money-winning owners with a total of $438,849. This was the third successive year Rancocas had led the list.

113

The Kentucky Derby was fifty years old in 1924. The addition to the clubhouse had been completed and now reached almost to the first turn to accommodate the largest crowd in the history of the race. A view of the Derby crowd appears below.

On October 12, the dirigible Los Angeles, formerly the German Z R 3, made a non-stop flight from Friedrickshafen, Germany, to Lakehurst, New Jersey, a distance of 5,060 miles, in eighty-one hours, seventeen minutes. The dirigible is shown upper right.

The same year brought the first round-the-world airplane flight. On April 6 four Douglas cruiser bi-planes of the Army Air Corps took off from Seattle, and in 175 days two of the planes returned, completing the first globe circling trip by air.

Politics was enlivened by the Democratic national convention which required 103 ballots before John W. Davis, of West Virginia, was selected as the Presidential candidate. For two weeks during the convention the powerful voice of Alabama's Governor William Brandon roared "Twenty-four votes for Underwood" as each new roll call was started.

President Coolidge was re-elected, receiving 293 electoral votes against 151 for Davis.

Two other important items in the nation's capital were the Teapot Dome scandal, and the Dawes plan whereby the German reparations were materially reduced and German industries were extended long-term credits.

During its 1924 session the Kentucky Legislature enacted a law which required daily readings from the Bible in all public schools. On June 19 a gas bomb exploded in the Rhode Island Senate chamber ending a filibuster. As a result twenty Republican members of the senate went across the state line into Massachusetts where they remained until January 1, 1925, to prevent a quorum of the senate.

Air mail between New York City and San Francisco was established, reducing the delivery time from one city to the other to twenty-four hours. General John J. Pershing was retired from active service on September 24.

Pedigree

Black Gold

```
                    ┌ Peter Pan      ┌ Commando
       ┌ Black Toney┤                │ *Cinderella
       │            │
       │            └ Belgravia      ┌ Ben Brush
BLACK GOLD                           │ *Bonnie Gal
(Black colt)┤
       │            ┌ Bonnie Joe     ┌ Faustus
       └ Useeit     ┤                │ Bonnie Rose
                    │
                    └ Effie M.       ┌ Bowling Green
                                     │ Alma Glyn
```

Tabulated Racing Record

Year	Age	Sts.	1st	2nd	3rd	Won
1923	2	18	9	5	2	$ 19,163
1924	3	13	9	0	2	91,340
1927	6	3	0	0	0	50
1928	7	1	0	0	0	...
		35	18	5	4	$111,553

50th Kentucky Derby, May 17, 1924

50,000 added and $5,000 Gold Cup. 3-year-olds. Weight-for-age. Net value to winner 52,775; second, $6,000; third, $3,000; fourth, $1,000. 152 nominations.

Horse	Eqt	Wt	PP	St	½	¾	1	Str	Fin	Jockey	Owner	Odds $1 Str't
Black Gold	w	126	1	3	5^h	6^h	$3\frac{1}{2}$	3^2	$1\frac{1}{2}$	Mooney	Mrs R M Hoots	1.75
Chilhowee	w	126	13	6	4^1	3^h	$4^{1}\frac{1}{2}$	1^h	2^n	Johnson	Gallaher Bros	15.25
Beau Butler	wb	126	10	8	15^h	11^{nk}	10^1	10^h	3^h	Lyke	Idle Hour Stock Farm	‡10.25
Altawood	w	126	7	19	19	14^1	7^4	5^2	4^h	McDer'tt	C B Head	19.10
Bracadale	wb	126	12	4	$1\frac{1}{2}$	1^3	1^2	$2\frac{1}{2}$	5^8	Sande	Rancocas Stable	§3.40
Transmute	w	126	2	1	6^1	4^h	2^2	4^3	6^h	McAtee	H P Whitney	¶10.25
Revenue Ag't	w	126	5	9	$10\frac{1}{2}$	8^1	8^h	7^1	7^h	Hurn	G A Cochran	26.75
Thorndale	wb	126	6	11	7^1	$7^{1}\frac{1}{2}$	5^3	$6\frac{1}{2}$	8^2	Marinelli	B Block	†10.70
Klondyke	w	126	3	13	8^{h-}	10^h	9^1	9^4	9^4	Parke	H P Whitney	¶10.25
Mad Play	wb	126	9	14	11^h	$9\frac{1}{2}$	$6\frac{1}{2}$	8^h	$10\frac{1}{2}$	Fator	Rancocas Stable	§3.40
Big Gorin II	w	126	4	12	12^2	17^2	12^1	13^1	11^2	Garner	P Coyne	36.60
Cann'n Shot	wb	126	8	18	$18^{1}\frac{1}{2}$	19	$11\frac{1}{2}$	12^1	$12^{1}\frac{1}{2}$	Ellis	C A Hartwell	†10.70
Modest	ws	126	16	15	13^1	18^2	14^h	$11\frac{1}{2}$	13^1	Wallace	E B McLean	†10.70
Diogenes	w	126	15	10	16^h	15^1	13^1	14^1	14^2	Ponce	Mrs W M Jefford	†10.70
Nautical	w	126	19	7	9^h	16^h	15^1	15^h	$15\frac{1}{2}$	Lang	J S Cosden	†10.70
Mr Mutt	w	126	17	17	17^1	$13\frac{1}{2}$	17^1	16^1	16^2	Merimee	H C Fisher	35.00
Baffling	wb	126	18	2	$2\frac{1}{2}$	$2\frac{1}{2}$	$16\frac{1}{2}$	17^h	17^1	Carroll	Idle Hour Stock Farm	‡10.25
Wild Aster	w	126	11	5	3^1	5^1	18^1	18^2	18^4	Coltiletti	Greentree Stable	†10.70
Bob Tail	w	126	14	16	14^1	$12\frac{1}{2}$	19	19	19	Blind	Idle Hour Stock Farm	‡10.25

†Mutuel field. ‡Coupled in betting as Idle Hour Stock Farm Stable entry. §Coupled in betting as Rancocas Stable entry. ¶Coupled in betting as H. P. Whitney entry.

Time, :23-2/5, :47-3/5, 1:13, 1:39-1/5, 2:05-1/5. Track fast.

$2 Mutuels Paid—Black Gold, $5.50 straight, $5.40 place, $4.40 show; Chilhowee, $12.30 place, $7.30 show; E. R. Bradley's Idle Hour Stock Farm Stable entry (Beau Butler, Baffling and Bob Tail), $4.70 show.

Winner—Blk.c. by Black Toney—Useeit, by Bonnie Joe, trained by H. Webb, bred by Mrs. R. M. Hoots.

Went to Post—4:43. Off at 4:45.

Start good and slow. Won driving; second and third same. Black Gold, well ridden and prominent in the early racing, moved up resolutely after reaching the stretch and disposed of the others in the last seventy yards. Chilowee ran a good race and headed Bracadale in the last eighth, but tired slightly near the end. Beau Butler closed a great gap and ran an excellent race. Altawood closed an immense gap after making a slow beginning. Bracadale tired after leading to the stretch. Transmute was done after going the first three-quarters. Mad Play was always outrun. Baffling ran a good three-quarters. The others were never prominent.

Scratched—Glide, 121.

Black Gold Stakes Races

AT 2 YEARS	WON	Bashford Manor Stakes.
	2ND	Cincinnati Trophy, Tobacco Stakes.
	3RD	Breeders' Futurity.
	UNP	Harold Stakes, Queen City Handicap.
AT 3 YEARS	WON	Kentucky Derby, Louisiana Derby, Derby Trial, Ohio State Derby, Chicago Derby.
	3RD	Latonia Derby, Raceland Derby.
AT 6 YEARS	UNP	Christmas Handicap.

As nineteen three-year-olds paraded down the Churchill Downs track toward the start of the Golden Jubilee Kentucky Derby, Mrs. Rosa M. Hoots watched her Black Gold, the favorite, with Indian stoicism; wealthy Harry F. Sinclair, owner of the powerful second-choice entry of Bracadale and Mad Play, nervously chewed at his cigar.

Astride Black Gold was little Joe Mooney, a moderately successful jockey. Holding the reins on Bracadale was the peerless Earl Sande, while another top rider, Laverne Fator, rode Mad Play. The crowd anticipated the Sinclair stable's strategy would be for Sande to kill off all speed in the field in order that Mad Play could come on in the latter stages of the race and win.

Most of these details have been forgot in the quarter-century which has lapsed. The story of Black Gold's victory will never be forgot as long as there is horse racing in America. Each year at Derby time it is one of the favorite stories of writers.

Useeit, dam of Black Gold, had been raced by Mrs. Hoots' husband who did not live to see the Derby victory. Useeit had been started in a claiming race, but when her owner refused to give up the mare to the person who had claimed her he was told he would not be permitted to race horses again. If that was the way it had to be, Owner Hoots would take the penalty rather than part with his mare.

In 1920 Useeit was bred to Colonel E. R. Bradley's stallion Black Toney. The colt she foaled in 1921 was coal black and was the Golden Jubilee Derby winner.

Colonel Winn recalls that no owner ever came to the Derby presentation stand with more calmness than did Mrs. Hoots, despite the thrilling finish her colt made to win. In recalling that day he also remembers her acceptance of the trophy as one of the most gracious speeches ever made by any winning owner.

Black Gold is buried in the centerfield at the Fairgrounds race track in New Orleans. It was at that track that he had to be destroyed after breaking his leg in his only race in 1928.

The last performance in Macauley's Theatre, Louisville landmark for more than a half-century, came August 29, 1925. Since even before the running of the first Kentucky Derby most of the outstanding artists who toured this country had appeared on its stage. A view of the theatre appears in the photograph above.

Calvin Coolidge, twenty-ninth President of the United States, was inaugurated the same year for a full four-year term, with Brigadier General Charles G. Dawes as his Vice President. A major newspaper story of the year was the Scopes trial at Dayton, Tennessee, with William Jennings Bryan and Clarence Darrow participating.

At Caldwell, Ohio, the giant U. S. dirigible Shenandoah broke apart while in flight, killing the crew. The same year saw the withdrawal of the Marines from Nicaragua. Louisville abandoned the last of its horse-drawn fire equipment.

On January 5 the first woman governor in the United States went into office as Mrs. Nellie T. Ross became Wyoming's chief executive. Less than a month later, Mrs. Miriam A. Ferguson became the governor of Texas.

The eastern states of the nation were treated to a view of a total eclipse of the sun on January 21.

Lower right is shown the plaque of the foaling barn at Hamburg Place, one of Kentucky's more famous Thoroughbred nurseries.

Two new cables from the United States to European countries went into use during 1925. The first connected this country with Spain. The other was the first direct cable to Italy. The American Telephone and Telegraph Company sent pictures of the Coolidge inauguration over its wires to newspapers in New York and Chicago.

Henry Ford inaugurated commercial aviation on a schedule with a flight between Detroit and Chicago. Gertrude Ederle swam twenty-one miles from New York City's Battery to Sandy Hook in seven hours, eleven minutes, and thirty seconds. Standard Oil of New Jersey established the eight-hour working day.

Federal income tax records opened to the public showed John D. Rockefeller paid the largest individual tax. The opening of Louisville's newest hotel, the Kentucky Hotel, took place on September 1.

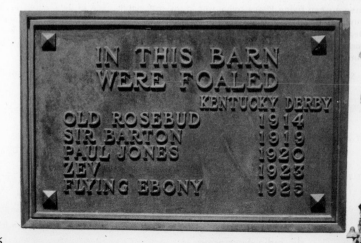

Pedigree

FLYING EBONY (Black colt)	The Finn	*Ogden	Kilwarlin *Oriole
		Livonia	*Star Shoot Woodray
	Princess Mary	Hessian	*Watercress *Colonial
		Royal Gun	Royal Hampton *Spring Gun

Tabulated Racing Record

Year	Age	Sts.	1st	2nd	3rd	Won
1924	2	8	4	1	1	$ 5,320
1925	3	5	2	0	1	57,100
		13	6	1	2	$ 62,420

51st Kentucky Derby, May 16, 1925

Flying Ebony

$50,000 added and $5,000 Gold Cup. 3-year-olds. Weight-for-age. Net value to winner $52,775; second $6,000; third $3,000; fourth $1,000. 139 nominations.

Horse	Eqt	Wt	PP	St	½	¾	1	Str	Fin	Jockey	Owner	Odds $1 Str't
Fly'g Ebony	wb	126	6	4	1½	2½	2³	1ʰ	1¹½	Sande	G A Cochran	†3.15
Captain Hal	w	126	11	5	2¹½	1¹½	1ʰ	2½	2ⁿ	Heupel	A A Kaiser	5.60
Son of John	w	126	12	8	3ʰ	3²	3²	3²	3⁴	Turner	D W Scott	‡16.40
Single Foot	w	126	3	1	5¹	5¹½	4½	4½	4¹	Johnson	J E Griffith	30.15
Step Along	wsb	126	9	7	6½	6ʰ	6ʰ	5¹	5²	Pool	F M Grabner	‡16.40
Swope	w	126	4	9	8ʰ	7²	7¹	6¹	6ⁿ	Legere	H C Fisher	†3.15
P of B'rbon	wb	126	14	15	9²	10½	8¹	7¹	7½	Schut'ger	Lexington Stable	§3.15
Needle Gun	wb	126	2	3	4ʰ	4½	9½	9¹	8⁵	Ponce	W Zeigler Jr	†3.15
Ky. Cardinal	w	126	13	10	10¹	11¹	10¹	8ʰ	9ʰ	Garner	G F Croissant	7.50
B. Compan'n	w	126	19	16	11¹	14²	11¹	10¹	10ʰ	Ambrose	S A Cowan	†3.15
B'way Jones	w	126	8	11	12½	13¹	12¹	12ʰ	11ⁿᵏ	Meyer	Idle Hour Stock Farm	50.85
Quatrain	wb	126	17	13	14¹	12¹	14²	13¹	12½	Bruening	F Johnson	1.95
Almadel	wb	126	20	17	19¹	9¹	13¹	14²	13⁴	McD'm't	H P Headley	26.45
Backbone	w	126	18	18	18¹	19¹	16²	15²	14²	McAtee	H P Whitney	¶16.20
Sw'p'g Away	w	126	10	19	13²	18¹	15¹	17¹	15¹½	Robinson	Xalapa Farm Stable	§3.15
Elector	wb	126	7	20	20	20	20	19¹½	16²	Mooney	La Brae Stable	†3.15
The Bat	wb	126	1	6	15¹	15ʰ	17¹	16¹	17¹½	Parke	H P Whitney	¶16.20
Lee O Cot'r	wb	126	15	12	7¹	8½	5½	11⁴	18⁶	Fronk	R W Collins	†3.15
Voltaic	w	126	16	14	16½	16¹	18¹	18²	19²⁰	Coltiletti	R L Gerry	160.75
Chief Uncas	w	126	5	2	17¹	17¹	19¹	20	20	McCleary	A A Busch	†3.15

†Mutuel field. ‡D. W. Scott and F. M. Grabner entry; §Lexington Stable and Xalapa Farm Stable entry; ¶H. P. Whitney entry.

Time, :23-2/5, :47-3/5, 1:12-3/5, 1:39-3/5, 2:07-3/5. Track sloppy.

$2 Mutuels Paid—Flying Ebony (Field), $8.30 straight, $3.80 place, $2.80 show; Captain Hal, $5.50 place, $4.40 show; Son of John (coupled with Stepalong as D. W. Scott and F. M. Grabner entry), $5.50 show.

Winner—Blk.c. by The Finn—Princess Mary, by Hessian, trained by W. B. Duke; bred by J. E. Madden.

Went to Post—4:32. Off at 4:36.

Start good and slow. Won easily; second and third driving. Flying Ebony, well ridden and away forwardly, set the early pace, then followed Captain Hal closely and, after a sharp drive through the stretch outstayed the latter and won going away. Captain Hal showed fine speed and raced into a good lead, but tired slightly and appeared to have suffered from some interference when Flying Ebony came over in the last eighth. Son of John raced prominently all the way and was in close quarters through the last eighth. Single Foot raced well all the way. Step Along closed a considerable gap. Swope raced well. Quatrain began slowly and was far back all the way. Almadel was always outrun. Kentucky Cardinal was always beaten. Needle Gun ran fairly well.

Scratched—Reminder, 126; Chantey, 126; Reputation, 126; King Nadi, 126; Elsass, 126.

Flying Ebony   Stakes Races

AT 2 YEARS
- 3RD : Saratoga Sales Stakes.
- UNP : Cincinnati Trophy, United States Hotel Stakes.

AT 3 YEARS
- WON : Kentucky Derby.

The 1925 Kentucky Derby was the first to be broadcast by radio on a nationwide hook-up. It was estimated more than 6,000,000 heard the radio description.

The Kentucky Derby of 1925 resembled that of 1923 in several ways. Outsiders had to prevail on the owners of the winners in those two years to start their respective horses in the Kentucky Derby. In 1923 it had been Jockey Earl Sande who persuaded Harry F. Sinclair to start Zev.

In 1925 Sande was without a mount for the fifty-first Derby. Every owner he approached already had contracted with some other rider. Turf writers intervened to ask Gifford A. Cochran to start his Flying Ebony in order that Sande might have a horse to ride.

Moreover, Flying Ebony, like the winner of two years earlier, was a son of The Finn and had been bred by John E. Madden at Hamburg Place, near Lexington. With Zev, Sande had gone to the front at the start and had set the entire pace to win by one and one-half lengths. He took Flying Ebony to the front at the start, and was in front at every call except two when Captain Hal held a slight lead.

Except for the fact that he was included, along with nine other horses, in the pari-mutuel field, Flying Ebony no doubt would have been held at much longer odds than the $3.15-to-$1 at which the field was held. The favorite was Frederick Johnson's Quatrain at $1.95 -to-$1, who was never a contender in the sloppy going.

At two Flying Ebony had won four straight races, and was first in his only race at three prior to the Derby. He was retired to his owner's farm at Lexington following his three-year-old season, was sold in the dispersal sale of the Cochran estate, and moved to California where he died in 1943. Flying Ebony's best son was Flying Heels, an outstanding sire of two-year-olds. His other sons and daughters included Dark Secret, Microphone, Ebony Lady, Black Hand, Vicar, Vicaress, and others.

The Finn, sire of two Derby winners, died September 4 at the age of thirteen. He had been bought by W. R. Coe in 1923 from J. E. Madden at a reported price of $110,000. Coe's Pompey was the leading two-year-old winner with $121,-630, as 6,438 horses raced for $12,577,270 in prize money.

1926

In the Sesquicentennial Stadium at Philadelphia on September 23, 1926, came the first of the two great Jack Dempsey-Gene Tunney prizefights. At Philadelphia, Tunney won the world's championship. This was the first fight to draw more than 100,000 admissions.

On September 22 of the following year the fighters were rematched at Soldiers Field, Chicago, in what has become famous as the fight of "the long count." A view of that fight is shown above. At Chicago the match drew 104,943 persons who paid $2,658,660. Both figures are records for the prize ring.

The Philadelphia fight was part of that city's celebration in 1926 of the 220th anniversary of the birth of Benjamin Franklin. The exposition was visited by 4,622,221 persons.

In January Dr. Edwin Hubble announced his discovery of a new universe, located some 700,000 light years from the earth. Two months later communications on this globe were improved when a wireless telephone conversation between New York and London was sustained for a four-hour period.

On May 9 Commander Richard F. Byrd and Pilot Floyd Bennett circled the North Pole in fifteen and one-half hours from their base in Spitzbergen. By midsummer Henry Ford had his "flivver" monoplane on display.

Two views of the Churchill Downs clubhouse grounds in 1926 are shown below.

In Los Angeles on Derby Day the world's record for one hundred yards was lowered to nine and five-tenths seconds by Charley Paddock. The runner ran against the wind in setting the new mark. A Chicago opera singer started for New York with her pet pig Patrick. The baggage car attendant refused to let Patrick in his car, and the pig rode in his owner's drawing room. A murder trial was postponed in Louisville because there were no overnight rooms available for the jurors.

Pedigree

Bubbling Over

UBBLING OVER (Chestnut colt)	*North Star III	Sunstar	Sundridge / Doris
		Angelic	St. Angelo / Fota
	Beaming Beauty	Sweep	Ben Brush / Pink Domino
		Bellisario	Hippodrome / Biturica

Tabulated Racing Record

Year	Age	Sts.	1st	2nd	3rd	Won
1925	2	10	7	2	1	$ 24,737
1926	3	3	3	0	0	53,815
		13	10	2	1	$ 78,552

52nd Kentucky Derby, May 15, 1926

50,000 added and $5,000 Gold Cup. 3-year-olds. Weight for age. Net value to winner 50,075; second $6,000; third $3,000; fourth $1,000. 164 nominations.

Horse	Eqt	Wt	PP	St	½	¾	1	Str	Fin	Jockey	Owner	Odds $1 Str't
Bub'g Over	wb	126	11	1	1¹	1¹	1¹	1²	1⁵	Johnson	Idle Hour Stock Farm	‡1.90
B'g'nbag'ge	wb	126	3	3	7ʰ	6²	5⁵	2¹	2³	Blind	Idle Hour Stock Farm	‡1.90
Rock Man	w	126	2	2	3ʰ	3³	2ʰ	3⁴	3ⁿ	Coltiletti	Sagamore Stable	42.10
Rhinock	w	126	12	8	8ʰ	10ʰ	9¹	5⁵	4⁴	Garner	Parkview Stable	14.60
Pompey	w	126	9	5	2½	2ʰ	3ʰ	4½	5²	Fator	W R Coe	2.10
Espino	wb	126	6	6	9¹	5ʰ	7²	7⁴	6⁶	Smith	W Ziegler Jr	39.70
Light C'bine	wb	126	1	4	6ʰ	11¹	10ʰ	8¹	7⁵	Griffin	I B Humphreys	61.00
Canter	w	126	8	11	4ʰ	4ʰ	4ʰ	6²	8²	Turner	J E Griffith	24.10
Blondin	wsb	126	4	9	10¹	7½	11¹	9¹	9ʰ	McAtee	H P Whitney	9.30
Display	wb	126	10	13	12⁵	12⁸	8²	11¹	10ʰ	Maiben	W J Salmon	16.20
Recollection	wb	126	7	12	13	13	13	12¹	11ʰ	Callahan	Kohn & Theisen	†11.40
Ch'p de Mars	w	126	5	7	5ʰ	8¹	6½	10½	12¹	Pool	Keeneland Stud Farm	†11.40
Roycrofter	w	126	13	10	11¹	9¹	12⁴	13	13	Scobie	G F Croissant	†11.40

†Mutuel field. ‡Coupled in betting as Idle Hour Stock Farm Stable entry.
Time, :23, :47, 1:12-1/5, 1:38-1/5, 2:03-4/5. Track fast.

$2 Mutuels Paid—E. R. Bradley's Idle Hour Stock Farm Stable entry (Bubbling Over and Bagenbaggage), $5.80 straight, $5.80 place, $4.60 show; Rock Man, $30.00 show.

Winner—Ch.c. by *North Star III.—Beaming Beauty, by Sweep, trained by H. J. Thompson; bred by Idle Hour Stock Farm.

Went to Post—5:05. Off at 5:09 New York Time.

Start good and slow. Won easily; second and third driving. Bubbling Over raced into the lead at once and setting a great pace under restraint, showed the way until the stretch, where his rider permitted him to sprint away from the others and win away off by himself. Bagenbaggage, began slowly but, making up ground gamely, passed the others and finished a fast-going second. Rock Man raced prominently from the start, but was tiring and just lasted to save third place. Rhinock came with a surprisingly rush near the end. Pompey was done after racing well for three-quarters and had no mishap. Espino raced well. Canter was close up for most of the way, but quit in the stretch.

Scratched—Boot to Boot, 126; Take a Chance, 126; Bolton, 126; Rasuli, 126.

Bubbling Over   Stakes Races

AT 2 YEARS	WON	Champagne Stakes, Nursery Handicap.
	2ND	Breeders' Futurity, Pimlico Futurity.
	3RD	Grab Bag Handicap.
AT 3 YEARS	WON	Kentucky Derby, Blue Grass Stakes.

Zev and Exterminator, both Derby winners, ranked one-two in 1926 on the list of the world's greatest money-winners. Tenth was the 1922 winner Morvich, with Sir Barton (1919) twenty-third, and Black Gold (1924) thirty-sixth on the list.

Lincoln Fields opened in 1926. Crusader was the leading money-winner. Fair Star was the best of the two-year-olds. Seven deadheats were recorded, the greatest number since 1910.

Like his sire *Sun Briar, who had failed to start in the 1918 Derby, Pompey had been the two-year-old champion of his year. A great debate was waged during early 1926 whether Pompey or Bubbling Over was the better horse. Arguments continued right up to Derby post-time when Bubbling Over and his stablemate, Bagenbaggage, were favorites at $1.90-to-$1.00, with Pompey second choice at $2.10-to-$1.00.

Bubbling Over and Pompey went to the front when the barrier was sprung, with the former leading by a length until the stretch where Bubbling Over began to pull away and Pompey faded from the picture. Bubbling Over won by five lengths, with his stablemate second, in 2:03 4/5, and everyone was saying after the time had been posted that the winner might easily have broken Old Rosebud's record had he been pushed.

For Albert Johnson, who had ridden Morvich in 1922, it was his second Derby winning. He was the fifth jockey to win two renewals of the Derby, and the third white jockey to win two runnings of the classic. Having ridden Exterminator many times, Johnson was asked which of the two Derby winners was the better horse, but he would not compare Bubbling Over to Exterminator.

The Derby was the Bradley colt's final start. He entered the stud at his owner's Idle Hour Farm where he sired the Derby winner Burgoo King from his second crop of foals. His other foals included Boys Howdy, Chouette, Bien Fait, and others. Bubbling Over died in 1938. He was the second Derby winner to sire a winner of the event. Halma, winner in 1895, was the first, siring Alan-a-Dale.

The $56,075 earned by Colonel Bradley by his second one-two Derby finish helped place his Idle Hour Farm second on the list of leading money-winning owners, which was led by H. P. Whitney for the fourth time. The Whitney stable earned $407,139, Idle Hour Farm $273,825.

The year 1927 was one of big headlines. Biggest story of the year was Charles A. Lindbergh's solo, trans-Atlantic flight in the "Spirit of St. Louis," the first non-stop flight from New York to Paris.

Leaving Roosevelt Field at 7:15 A. M. on the morning of May 20, the flyer reached Le Bourget Field at Paris at 5:21 P.M. on May 21, having flown 3,610 miles in thirty-three hours and thirty-nine minutes. The flyer and his plane are shown above.

It was on August 2 at his summer camp at Rapid City, South Dakota, that President Coolidge issued his famous statement, " I do not choose to run."

The same year the Supreme Court voided the Doheny oil leases, and Secretary of the Treasury Mellon authorized reduction in size of paper money by about one-third. The size of the new bills was set at six and one-eighth by two and five-eighth inches.

New York City barbers staged a successful strike as 1,300 walked out to obtain a wage of $35 per week, and one-half of all receipts over $50 per week. At Daytona Beach, Florida, Major H. O. D. Seagrave drove his racing car at an average of 203.79 miles per hour.

The first successful demonstration of television was made in the office of Secretary Herbert Hoover in Washington. Disastrous floods struck the Mississippi Valley when 138,573 square miles were inundated. It was the country's worst flood.

Babe Ruth, of the New York Yankees, hit sixty home runs during the 1927 baseball season. He is shown below with Mike Barrow, left, and Jacob Ruppert.

Pedigree

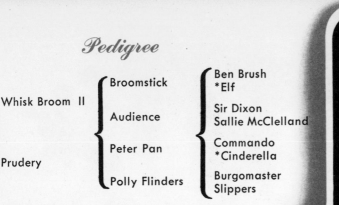

WHISKERY
(Bay colt)

Whisk Broom II	Broomstick	Ben Brush *Elf
	Audience	Sir Dixon Sallie McClelland
Prudery	Peter Pan	Commando *Cinderella
	Polly Flinders	Burgomaster Slippers

Whiskery

Tabulated Racing Record

Year	Age	Sts.	1st	2nd	3rd	Won
1926	2	18	6	3	7	$ 13,115
1927	3	18	6	4	5	94,950
1928	4	1	0	0	0	500
1929	5	16	0	5	10	1,196
1930	6	15	2	3	9	3,250
1931	7	2	0	1	1	200
		70	14	16	8	$122,211

53rd Kentucky Derby, May 14, 1927

$50,000 added and $5,000 Gold Cup. 3-year-olds. Weight for age. Net value to winner $51,000; second $6,000; third $3,000; fourth $1,000. 162 nominations.

Horse	Eqt	Wt	PP	St	½	¾	1	Str	Fin	Jockey	Owner	Odds $1 Str't
Whiskery	wb	126	7	6	5^h	3^h	$3\frac{1}{2}$	3^2	1^h	McAtee	H P Whitney	‡2.40
Osmand	w	126	10	4	2^1	2^3	$2\frac{1}{2}$	1^h	$2^1\frac{1}{2}$	Sande	J E Widener	§6.90
Jock	w	126	1	3	1^5	1^5	$1\frac{1}{2}$	$2\frac{1}{2}$	3^1	Lang	E B McLean	¶37.80
Hydromel	wsb	126	5	8	6^h	7^1	4^{nk}	$4\frac{1}{2}$	4^h	W Garner	J N Camden	16.00
Bostonian	w	126	12	11	9^2	$8\frac{1}{2}$	$7\frac{1}{2}$	6^4	5^4	Abel	H P Whitney	‡2.40
B'dy Bauer	w	126	4	10	10^{nk}	$9\frac{1}{2}$	5^3	$5^1\frac{1}{2}$	6^2	G Johns'n	Idle Hour Stock Farm	‖15.40
Royal Julian	w	126	2	1	$7^1\frac{1}{2}$	5^h	$6\frac{1}{2}$	7^{nk}	7^4	Lilley	W H Whitehouse	†14.70
Fred Jr	wb	126	13	15	15	14^2	9^1	9^3	8^6	Burger	S W Grant	18.30
Scapa Flow	wb	126	15	7	3^h	$4\frac{1}{2}$	8^2	$8\frac{1}{2}$	9^2	Coltiletti	W M Jeffords	7.00
Bl. Panther	wb	126	6	5	8^h	10^1	10^1	10^1	10^8	Schaefer	W J Salmon	†14.70
Kiev	wb	126	8	14	11^h	11^2	12^2	12^2	11^2	M Garner	J E Widener	§6.90
R. Stocking	wb	126	3	2	$4^1\frac{1}{2}$	6^h	$11\frac{1}{2}$	11^2	12^3	Pool	J W Parrish	4.70
Rip Rap	wb	126	11	13	12^1	12^1	13^4	14^4	13^4	O'Donnell	Sage Stable	11.60
Bewithus	wb	126	9	9	$13\frac{1}{2}$	15	14^2	13^1	14^5	A Johnson	Idle Hour Stock Farm	‖15.40
War Eagle	wb	126	14	12	$14^1\frac{1}{2}$	13^2	15	15	15	Ambrose	E B McLean	¶37.80

†Mutuel field. ‡H. P. Whitney entry, §J. E. Widener entry, ¶E. B. McLean entry; ‖Idle Hour Stock Farm entry.

Time, :23-1/5, :47-1/5, 1:12-2/5, 1:38-4/5, 2:06. Track slow.

$2 Mutuels Paid—Whiskery (coupled with Bostonian as H. P. Whitney entry), $6.80 straight, $3.80 place, $3.40 show; Osmand (coupled with Kiev as J. E. Widener entry), $6.40 place, $5.80 show; Jock (coupled with War Eagle as E. B. McLean entry), $14.20 show.

Winner—Br.c. by Whisk Broom II.—Prudery, by Peter Pan, trained by F. Hopkins; bred by H. P. Whitney.

Went to Post—5:09. Off at 5:11.

Start good and slow. Won driving; second and third same. Whiskery moved up steadily, though racing a trifle wide and, holding on gamely, wore down Osmand in the last sixteenth. The latter, always well up for the entire distance, held on much gamer than expected in the final drive. Jock began fast, showed high speed but tired in the last eighth. Hydromel showed a fine performance and continued gamely in the stretch. Bostonian was far out of it for a half-mile and closed a big gap. Buddy Bauer also closed a big gap from a slow beginning.

Scratched—Saxon, 126; My Son, 126; Mr. Kirkwood, 126.

Whiskery   Stakes Races

	WON	Ardsley Handicap.
AT 2 YEARS	2ND	Endurance Handicap.
	3RD	Pimlico Futurity.
	UNP	Juvenile Stakes, Youthful Stakes, Colorado Stakes.
	WON	Kentucky Derby, Twin City Handicap, Stanley Produce Stakes, Chesapeake Stakes, Huron Handicap.
AT 3 YEARS	2ND	Fairmount Derby, Maryland Handicap, Potomac Handicap.
	3RD	Preakness Stakes, Prince Georges Handicap.
	UNP	American Derby, Gasden D. Bryan Memorial Handicap, Latonia Championship Stakes, Toronto Autumn Cup Handicap, Manhattan Handicap.
AT 4 YEARS	3RD	Whitney Stakes.
AT 5 YEARS	UNP	Covington Handicap.
AT 6 YEARS	UNP	Covington Handicap, Francis S. Peabody Memorial Handicap, Grainger Memorial Handicap.

A lot of Kentucky Derby history was wrapped up in the victory of Whiskery in 1927. Ben Brush, great-grandsire of the winner, won the Derby in 1896, also was grandsire of the winners Meridian and Regret, both by Broomstick, grandsire of Whiskery. Prudery, dam of Whiskery, had been third in the 1921 Derby. Her sire, Peter Pan, also was grandsire of the 1924 winner Black Gold and the 1933 winner Brokers Tip, and great-grandsire of Shut Out, winner in 1942. Peter Pan's granddaughter also produced the 1946 winner Assault.

There was no doubt about it. The field of fifteen three-year-olds that went to the post for the 1927 Derby included brilliant speedsters. Despite the slow condition of the track the 80,000 persons present anticipated an extremely fast pace.

They were not disappointed. Jockey "Chick" Lang brought Jock away from the barrier literally flying. At the quarter Jock was three lengths in front; at the half he was in front by five. He ran the first quarter in 23 1/5 seconds, the half in 47 1/5. Both times were faster than Old Rosebud's when the latter set the record in 1914. Twenty Grand did not match those times when he set a new record in 1931, and Whirlaway ran an even slower first quarter when he lowered the mark in 1941.

Second to Jock throughout the first mile was Osmand, ridden by Earl Sande. Third was Whiskery, coupled with Bostonian and favorite in the pari-mutuels. Sande took Osmand to the front as the field reached the stretch, but could not withstand Whiskery, ridden by Linus "Pony" McAtee, in the stretch drive.

H. P. Whitney, owner of the winner, was the year's leading money-winning owner, and the leading breeder in monies won. The Derby winner was the top winner in his stable. Whiskery proved impotent when retired to the stud, was returned to racing. After retirement from racing he was used as a saddle horse until his death.

Yearling prices brought a new high average of $2,758.78 in 1927. W. R. Coe paid a record $70,000 for a son of Hurry On and Fatima. War Feathers sold for $50,000.

It was in 1928 that the "Solid South" was broken. Unable to persuade Calvin Coolidge to change his mind and seek reelection, the Republicans turned to Herbert C. Hoover, who had been secretary of commerce under Coolidge. Chosen as candidate for vice president was Senator Charles Curtis of Kansas.

Alfred E. Smith, governor of the state of New York, was the nominee of the Democratic party, despite warnings from the southern states that he would not be supported. Smith had previously been a strong contender for the nomination in the 1924 convention, and was one of the best-liked men in the nation.

Rhode Island and Massachusetts were the only northern states which Smith carried. Border states such as Maryland, Delaware, Kentucky, and Missouri went to the Hoover column, and from the "Solid South" the Republican won Florida, North Carolina, Tennessee, Texas, and Virginia. Hoover's electoral vote of 444 was the largest ever rolled up by any Presidential candidate. Following the election Hoover and a large party went on a good-will tour of Latin America.

This also was an important year in the motion-picture industry. On July 6, the first all-talking motion picture was shown. It was "The Lights of New York," produced by Warner Brothers. On July 6, at Rochester, New York, George Eastman held the first public demonstration of colored motion pictures.

The southern part of Florida was struck by a hurricane from the Windward Islands in the early part of 1928. More than 4,000 persons lost their lives.

Derby breakfast was served on the open veranda of the clubhouse, above, which is part of the main dining room. The photograph below was taken on the first turn.

CHURCHILL DOWNS
LOUISVILLE · KENTUCKY

54th Annual   Spring Meeting
1928

Pedigree

REIGH COUNT
(Chestnut colt)

- *Sunreigh
  - Sundridge
    - Amphion
    - Sierra
  - *Sweet Briar II
    - St. Frusquin
    - Presentation
- *Contessina
  - Count Schomberg
    - Aughrim
    - Clonavarn
  - Pitti
    - St. Frusquin
    - Florence

Tabulated Racing Record

Year	Age	Sts.	1st	2nd	3rd	Won
1927	2	14	4	3	0	$ 56,030
1928	3	8	7	0	0	112,640
1929	4	5	1	1	0	12,125†
		27	12	4	0	$180,795

†Includes winnings in England.

54th Kentucky Derby, May 19, 1928

Reigh Count

$50,000 added and $5,000 Gold Cup. 3-year-olds. Weight for age. Net value to winner $55,375; second $6,000; third $3,000; fourth 1,000. 196 nominations.

Horse	Eqt	Wt	PP	St	½	¾	1	Str	Fin	Jockey	Owner	Odds $1 Str't
Reigh Count	w	126	4	3	5ʰ	5ʰ	2¹½	1ʰ	1³	Lang	Mrs J Hertz	‡2.06
Misstep	w	126	1	1	1¹	1¹	1¹½	2⁴	2²	Garner	Le Mar Stock Farm	10.20
Toro	w	126	7	6	6ʰ	6ʰ	3½	3½	3⁴	Ambrose	E B McLean	4.75
Jack Higgins	w	126	8	7	8²	7²	4ʰ	4⁶	4¹½	Allen	W J Curran	†4.42
Reigh Olga	w	126	5	4	7½	8½	7¼	5⅜	5²	Pool	O Lehmann	‡2.06
Lawley	w	126	9	15	16¹	16½	9½	6⁵	6²	Thurber	Viking Stable	†4.42
Don Q	w	126	2	20	20¹	20¹	22	7¹	7²	Walls	Sagamore Stable	†4.42
Kobashela	w	126	20	11	11¹	11¹	5ʰ	11¹	8²	Fisher	Audley Farm	§12.08
Blackwood	wb	126	10	2	2¹½	2¹½	8½	8¹	9½	Chiavetta	Bloomfield Stable	†4.42
M'tie Flynn	wb	126	6	5	3¹	3¹½	6²	16¹	10ʰ	Fronk	S Peabody	14.18
Sun Beau	wb	126	18	16	18¹	18¹	14¹	10¹	11ʰ	Craigmyle	W S Kilmer	38.42
Sar None	wb	126	13	19	21¹	21¹	12¹	9²	12½	Kederis	Longridge Stable	†4.42
Distraction	wb	126	19	21	22	22	19¹	17½	13¹	McAuliffe	Wheatley Stable	11.51
Petee-Wr'k	wb	126	15	17	14¹	14¹	10¹	18¹	14³	Johnson	J R Macomber	†4.42
Typhoon	wb	126	17	22	19½	19²	18¹	12²	15¹	Barnes	Kenton Farm Stable	41.21
Replevin	wb	126	11	9	12ʰ	12ʰ	16¹	13¹	16¹	Peterson	F Johnson	†4.42
Cartago	wb	126	3	10	9¹	9¹	15¹	19²	17ʰ	Horvath	R E Leichleiter	†4.42
Sonivan		126	21	8	4ʰ	4ʰ	20⁴	15²	18²	Landolt	A A Kaiser	†4.42
Charmarten	wb	126	22	18	17½	17¹	13½	14½	19²	Butwell	Wild Rose Farm Stable	†4.42
Vito		126	12	13	10½	10½	11¹	20¹	20²	Kummer	A H Cosden	¶39.04
Sortie	wb	126	14	12	15¹	15¹	17½	21⁸	21¹²	Weiner	A C Schwartz	¶39.04
Strolling Player		126	16	14	12ʰ	13ʰ	21ʰ	22	22	Fields	Salubria Stable	§12.08

†Mutuel field. ‡Coupled in betting as Mrs. J. D. Hertz and O. Lehmann entry. §Coupled in betting as Audley Farm Stable and Salubria Stable entry. ¶Coupled in betting as A. H. Cosden and A. C. Schwartz entry.

Time, :24-1/5, :49-3/5, 1:15-4/5, 1:43-2/5, 2:10-2/5. Track Heavy.

$2 Mutuels Paid—Reigh Count (coupled with Reigh Olga as Mrs. J. D. Hertz and O. Lehmann entry), $6.12 straight, $5.78 place, $3.98 show; Misstep, $8.28 place, $5.90 show; Toro, $3.76 show.

Winner—Ch.c. by *Sunreigh—*Contessina, by Count Schomberg, trained by B. S. Michell; bred by Willis Sharpe Kilmer.

Went to Post—5:05. Off at 5:11.

Start good and slow. Won easily; second and third driving. Reigh Count was ridden vigorously in the early running and responded nobly, racing into a forward position in the first half-mile, then forced the pace and, under strong riding in the stretch, took the lead and drew away to win with speed in reserve. Misstep began fast next to the inner rail, showed fine speed and, setting a fast pace for the going, finished well, but was easily held safe. Toro suffered slightly from some interference, but when clear in the stretch came steadily and was running fast at the end.

Scratched—Colonel Shaw, 126; Mop Up, 126; Rumpelstiltskin, 126; Dowagiac, 126.

Reigh Count — Stakes Races

AT 2 YEARS
- WON — Walden Handicap, Kentucky Jockey Club Stakes.
- 2ND — Eastern Shore Handicap, Belmont Futurity.
- UNP — Pimlico Futurity.

AT 3 YEARS
- WON — Kentucky Derby, Miller Stakes, Huron Handicap, Saratoga Cup, Lawrence Realization, Jockey Club Gold Cup.
- UNP — Travers Mid-summer Derby.

AT 4 YEARS (In England)
- WON — Coronation Cup.
- 2ND — Ascot Gold Cup.
- UNP — Great Jubilee Handicap, Newbury Spring Cup Handicap, Lingfield Handicap.

The largest field ever to start in the Kentucky Derby came out for the fifty-fourth running in 1928. There were twenty-two horses in the parade which left the Churchill Downs paddock shortly before 5 o'clock. Four other horses that had been entered the preceding day were scratched before post time.

Few in the tremendous crowd believed there was little chance of beating the favored Reigh Count. Unable to pick one horse they believed could beat the son of *Sunreigh, the majority of those who did not bet on Reigh Count established the pari-mutuel field, which included twelve horses, as second choice. Apparently they believed their best chance lay in the greatest number.

Reigh Count's stablemate, Anita Peabody, had won the 1927 two-year-old championship, but there were few who thought Reigh Count could not have beaten the filly in the Futurity had the owner, Mrs. John D. Hertz, not wanted to win with Anita Peabody.

Jockey "Chick" Lang, who had attempted to steal an unsurmountable lead on Jock the preceding year, did not have to try the same riding tactics in the 1928 Derby. He was content to rate Reigh Count in fifth pace as Misstep set the pace for the first mile. As the field approached the stretch Jockey Lang moved Reigh Count to the front and won by three lengths, with Misstep holding the place safe from Toro's challenge.

The Derby was Reigh Count's first start at three, a season in which he was beaten only once. As a two-year-old, one of his two stakes triumphs was in the Kentucky Jockey Club Stakes, thus making him the first horse to win both this race and the Derby. Reigh Count was the best horse racing in 1928. At four he went to England where he made five starts.

As a sire he had brilliant success. He sired the 1943 Derby winner Count Fleet, and many other outstanding stakes horses, including Lady Reigh, Our Count, Count Arthur, Count Morse, and others. His daughter, Countess Time, produced the 1940 Derby winner Gallahadion.

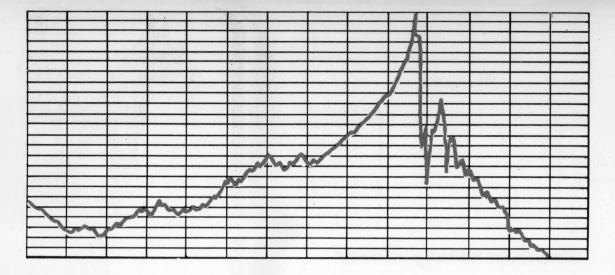

1929   When Herbert Clark Hoover, shown below, took office as the thirtieth President of the United States in March, 1929, there was much talk that the country was on the threshold of a long period of prosperity although we did admit Europe was in a very bad way economically.

During the first nine months of the year there were few unpleasant headlines in our daily newspapers as far as the national life was concerned. On July 24 President Hoover announced the Kellogg-Briand anti-war treaty was in effect. Sixty-two of the world's leading nations had renounced war as an instrument of national policy.

In Kentucky during the spring there were many protests voiced over a proposed plan to industrialize Cumberland Falls. The State Teachers Club was among the civic groups which demanded that Cumberland Falls should continue as a state park and tourist attraction.

On the west coast the longest tunnel in America was completed through the Cascade Mountains east of Seattle. The tunnel measured seven and eight-tenths miles in length. On September 24 James H. Doolittle gained the distinction of being the first pilot to fly "blind." He took a plane off from the ground and landed again by relying solely on the plane's instruments.

Early in October stocks began to sag. Then came "Black Friday," October 29. When that day was over an estimated $15,000,000,000 in stock values had been lost. The depression was here. The photograph, lower right, was taken outside the New York Stock Exchange building on October 29.

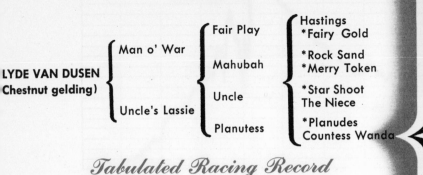

				Hastings
			Fair Play	*Fairy Gold
	Man o' War			*Rock Sand
LYDE VAN DUSEN		Mahubah		*Merry Token
Chestnut gelding)			Uncle	*Star Shoot
				The Niece
	Uncle's Lassie		Planutess	*Planudes
				Countess Wanda

Tabulated Racing Record

Year	Age	Sts.	1st	2nd	3rd	Won
1928	2	17	8	3	2	$ 55,768
1929	3	10	3	3	2	65,319
1930	4	5	1	0	1	1,025
1933	7	10	0	1	3	290
		42	12	6	8	$122,402

55th Kentucky Derby, May 18, 1929

Clyde Van Dusen

50,000 added and $5,000 Gold Cup. 3-year-olds. Weight for age. Net value to winner 53,950; second $6,000; third $3,000; fourth $1,000. 159 nominations.

orse	Eqt	Wt	PP	St	½	¾	1	Str	Fin	Jockey	Owner	Odds $1 Str't
V Dusen	wb	126	20	7	1½	1³	1²	1³	1²	McAtee	H P Gardner	3.00
Naishapur	wb	126	4	2	12ʰ	12²	8³	5½	2³	Allen	Wilshire Stable	5.57
anchio	wb	126	13	1	4²	3³	2ʰ	2½	3ⁿ	Coltiletti	Three D's Stock Farm	†§8.44
lue Larkspar	w	126	21	4	3ʰ	4½	5½	3ʰ	4¹½	M Garner	E R Bradley	‡1.71
Windy City	w	126	19	9	8ʰ	8¹	7³	8¹½	5ʰ	Pool	F M Grabner	22.84
Voltear	wb	126	1	8	5ʰ	5²	6ʰ	7ʰ	6ʰ	O'Donnell	Dixiana	18.42
he Nut	wb	126	18	3	17¹	10¹	4ʰ	6¹	7¹	Robertson	Warm Stable	40.62
olking	wb	126	14	18	2³	2¹½	3¹½	4³	8¹	Pascuma	H T Archibald	†8.44
arl Eitel	wb	126	10	16	7¹	7½	9ʰ	9ʰ	9⁴	Jones	J J Coughlin	28.80
pset Lad	w	126	5	13	10½	17¹	14¹	13¹	10⁶	Chiavetta	Belle Isle Stable	†8.44
alf Roper	wb	126	9	15	16¹	15¹	10³	10³	11ʰ	Hardy	Three D's Stock Farm	†§8.44
Minotaur	wb	126	7	14	10¹	9²	11²	11¹½	12ʰ	Halbert	J R Thompson	30.80
ay Beauty	wb	126	15	10	11¹	11½	12ʰ	17¹	13⁴	Horvath	E R Bradley	‡1.71
hicatie	wb	126	3	12	14¹	14ʰ	13¹	13¹	14½	W Garner	Fair Stable	87.09
aul Buny'n	wb	126	12	17	19²	19¹	18²	15¹	15½	Clelland	L M Severson	†8.44
ssare	wb	126	6	5	6½	6¹	15ʰ	14¹	16³	Connelly	Jacques Stable	†8.44
B'd'lbane	wb	126	8	11	13¹	13¹	16¹	16²	17²	Crump	D Breckinridge	†8.44
en M'hree	wb	126	16	21	20³	18ʰ	17¹	18¹	18¹	Abel	C C & G Y Hieatt	†8.44
hip	wb	126	11	20	21	20³	19³	19³	19⁶	Heupel	Mrs E L Swikard	†8.44
rince Pat	wb	126	17	19	18ʰ	21	21	20⁴	20⁴	Laidley	Three D's Stock Farm	†§8.44
araphrase	wb	126	2	6	9½	16ʰ	20¹	21	21	Fronk	H P Headley	†8.44

Mutuel field. ‡Coupled in betting as E. R. Bradley entry. §Coupled in betting as Three D's tock Farm entry.

ime, :24, :49, 1:15-2/5, 1:42-4/5, 2:10-4/5. Track muddy.

$2 Mutuels Paid—Clyde Van Dusen, $8.00 straight, $3.70 place, $3.06 show; Naishapur, 4.72 place, $3.26 show; Panchio (coupled with Calf Roper as Three D's Stock Farm entry and n the field), $3.50 show.

Winner—Ch.g. by Man o' War—Uncle's Lassie, by Uncle, trained by C. Van Dusen; bred by 1. P. Gardner.

Went to Post—4:58. Off at 5:11.

Start good and slow. Won easily; second and third driving. Clyde Van Dusen took the lead after the first quarter, saved ground while setting the pace and responded to light shaking up o the stretch to hold his opponents safe. Naishapur, slow to start and racing wide, began moving up after going five-eighths and, after being blocked in the stretch, where he swerved, finished with a rush when clear. Panchio was prominent for the entire race and, benefited by a strong ride, outfinished Blue Larkspur. The latter ran well to the stretch turn, where he dropped back, but came again gamely after going to the inside in the stretch and just failed to get up for third place. Windy City raced well and held on gamely. Voltear tired in the final drive. Ben Machree finished with a rush. Karl Eitel tired. Minotaur was always far back. Essare showed early speed. Folking was done after reaching the stretch.

Scratched—Ervast, 126; Boris, 126; The Choctaw, 126; St. Ignatius, 126; Hiram Kelly, 126.

Clyde Van Dusen — Stakes Races

AT 2 YEARS	WON	Kentucky Jockey Club Stakes, Orphanage Stakes, Valley Stakes, Idle Hour Stakes.
	2ND	American National Futurity.
	3RD	Breeders' Futurity.
	UNP	Fort Thomas Handicap, Hawthorne Juvenile Handicap, American National Juvenile Stakes, Bashford Manor Stakes.
AT 3 YEARS	WON	Kentucky Derby.
	2ND	Latonia Derby.
	3RD	Classic Stakes, Grainger Memorial Handicap.
	UNP	American Derby.
AT 4 YEARS	UNP	Clark Handicap.

Jockey Linus "Pony" McAtee, who had ridden Whiskery to victory in 1927, came back to Churchill Downs in 1929 to ride a Derby horse he had never seen. Trainer Clyde VanDusen, a former rider himself, met McAtee in the jockey quarters. Said VanDusen, "Now look here Mac, when you come to the paddock you're going to see a mighty little horse. Don't be surprised, and don't be discouraged. This horse, although he is little, can really run. He can win today if you ride him right."

McAtee countered with, "He can't be small enough to surprise me. I've ridden some mighty little horses." But Clyde VanDusen, the horse, was small enough to make McAtee's mouth drop open when he came to the paddock. However, Clyde VanDusen, the trainer, quickly reassured the jockey that the gelded son of Man o' War was a game race horse, and all he needed was a good ride.

The jockey who had never seen the horse before Derby Day gave him a masterful ride. From twentieth post position, McAtee broke Clyde Van-Dusen with the leaders and soon hustled him to the front. There the gelding stayed from the time the field went past the judges the first time until they got back to the wire.

Colonel E. R. Bradley's entry of Blue Larkspur and Bay Beauty was the favorite, with the former, one of the best horses ever to carry the familiar green and white silks in the Derby, finishing fourth. Many blamed Blue Larkspur's failure to win on the condition of the track. He had been shod for a fast track, but the downpour of rain just at posttime left the track muddy for the running of the Derby. In fact, the 1.19 inches of rain which fell May 18, 1929, gave Churchill Downs its dampest Derby Day.

The Derby was Clyde VanDusen's first race since he had won the Kentucky Jockey Club Stakes as a two-year-old the preceding fall. Thus, he was the second horse in succession to win both the spring and fall racing features at Churchill Downs. Following his racing career, Clyde Van-Dusen was retired as a pensioner.

1930

Although the national depression had moved right into the living room by 1930 and unemployment was steadily rising throughout the country there were some signs to the contrary.

For example, George Herman "Babe" Ruth, signed a two-year contract with the New York Yankees of the American League for $160,000. Another figure in the sports world also gained many of the year's biggest headlines.

He was Robert Tyre Jones, of Atlanta. This was the year that Jones scored his "grand slam" in golf. He won the American amateur and open championships and England's golf crowns. Andrew Mellon purchased $800,000 worth of Old Masters offered for sale by the Russians.

Mahatma Ghandi was still having his troubles in India. On May 5 he again was arrested by the authorities, while in Ethiopia Haile Selassie was crowned Emperor in a barbaric ceremony.

An indication that prohibition repeal was to come was given in the Wickersham report. This document declared there was a complete breakdown in enforcement of prohibition. Early in the year King George V opened a five-power naval parley in London which resulted in the signing of the London Naval Treaty.

Charles Evans Hughes was named to succeed William Howard Taft as chief justice of the Supreme Court when the latter resigned because of ill health. The

German liner Europa made a new trans-Atlantic record of four days, seventeen hours, and six minutes, and Charles A. Lindberg established a trans-continental flying record of fourteen hours and forty-five minutes.

Franklin D. Roosevelt, who had first sought the office in 1928 principally to aid the Presidential candidacy of Alfred E. Smith, was reelected governor of New York. In England Sir Arthur Conan Doyle, author of the Sherlock Holmes stories died. He promised to communicate from the spirit world. (To date he has not.)

The Earl of Derby, from whose family name the Kentucky Derby got its own, was in the United States in 1930 to witness the fifty-sixth running of the Churchill Downs race. He is shown upper right with Colonel Winn. The 1930 Derby was the first time a starting gate was used for starting the race. The first gate is shown below.

126

56th

Pedigree

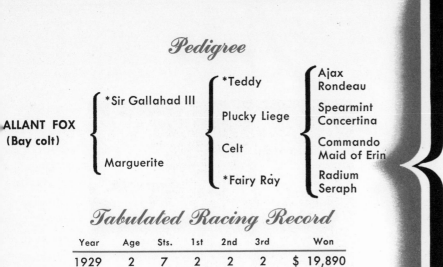

ALLANT FOX (Bay colt)	*Sir Gallahad III	*Teddy	Ajax
			Rondeau
		Plucky Liege	Spearmint
			Concertina
	Marguerite	Celt	Commando
			Maid of Erin
		*Fairy Ray	Radium
			Seraph

Tabulated Racing Record

Year	Age	Sts.	1st	2nd	3rd	Won
1929	2	7	2	2	2	$ 19,890
1930	3	10	9	1	0	308,275
		17	11	3	2	$328,165

56th Kentucky Derby, May 17, 1930

Gallant Fox

50,000 added and $5,000 Gold Cup. 3-year-olds. Weight for age. Net value to winner 50,725; second $6,000; third $3,000; fourth $1,000. 150 nominations.

orse	Eqt	Wt	PP	St	½	¾	1	Str	Fin	Jockey	Owner	Odds $1 Str't
allant Fox	wb	126	7	8	4^1	1^1	1^2	1^2	1^2	Sande	Belair Stud	1.19
al't Knight	wb	126	8	7	7^1	$6\frac{1}{2}$	3^3	$2\frac{1}{2}$	2^2	Schutte	Audley Farm	22.73
ed O	w	126	3	3	$12^1\frac{1}{2}$	13^h	$9\frac{1}{2}$	4^h	3^1	Mooney	G W Foreman	25.79
one Away	wb	126	10	14	$14\frac{1}{2}$	$11\frac{1}{2}$	$7\frac{1}{2}$	5^2	4^4	M Garner	W Ziegler Jr	52.92
'k Brigade	ws	126	6	13	6^1	4^{nk}	2^h	3^h	$5\frac{1}{2}$	Ellis	T M Cassidy	16.62
ongus	wb	126	1	15	15	14^4	10^h	7^1	6^2	O'Brien	R C Stable	†18.12
ncle Luther	w	126	2	12	$8\frac{1}{2}$	8^h	$6\frac{1}{2}$	6^1	7^2	Creese	L Stivers	†18.12
annery	w	126	12	2	3^1	3^1	5^h	$8\frac{1}{2}$	8^h	W Garner	E F Prichard	3.12
y Limited	wb	126	14	11	$10\frac{1}{2}$	$12^1\frac{1}{2}$	12^2	10^2	$9\frac{1}{2}$	Walls	Three D's Stock Farm	‡50.43
lcibiades	w	126	4	4	1^2	$2\frac{1}{2}$	4^h	9^h	10^h	Jones	H P Headley	†18.12
ilkerry	w	126	9	9	$11\frac{1}{2}$	10^h	$11\frac{1}{2}$	11^4	11^6	May	Three D's Stock Farm	‡50.43
r'z'g Thru	wb	126	13	6	13^1	9^2	14^h	13^1	12^5	Smith	E R Bradley	§8.75
keye Poet	wb	126	15	5	2^h	$5\frac{1}{2}$	$8\frac{1}{2}$	12^2	13^1	Legere	E R Bradley	§8.75
igh Foot	w	126	5	1	5^h	7^1	$13\frac{1}{2}$	14^8	14^8	Meyer	Valley Lake Stable	22.88
ick O'Hara	w	126	11	10	9^2	15	15	15	15	Barrett	P H Joyce	†18.12

*Mutuel field. ‡Coupled as Three D's Stock Farm Stable entry; §E. R. Bradley entry

ime, :23-3/5, :47-4/5, 1:14, 1:40-4/5, 2:07-3/5. Track good.

$2 Mutuels Paid—Gallant Fox, $4.38 straight, $3.76 place, $3.42 show; Gallant Knight, 14.60 place, $8.78 show; Ned O., $10.14 show.

Winner—B.c. by *Sir Gallahad III.—Marguerite, by Celt, trained by J. Fitzsimmons; bred by Belair Stud.

Went to Post—5:00. Off at 5:02½.

Start good out of machine. Won easily; second and third driving. Gallant Fox, in extremely close quarters for the first three-eighths, raced into the lead on the outside after straightening out in the backstretch, held command under restraint thereafter and won with something in reserve. Gallant Knight began slowly, worked his way up with a big loss of ground, offered a mild challenge entering the final eighth, but tired badly near the end. Ned O. began improving his position after five-eighths, lost ground on the last turn, but finished resolutely. Gone Away, on the extreme outside throughout, moved up fast on the stretch turn, but quit in the final eighth.

Scratched—Busy, 126.

Gallant Fox — Stakes Races

AT 2 YEARS	WON	Flash Stakes, Junior Champion Stakes.
	2ND	United States Hotel Stakes.
	3RD	Belmont Futurity.
	UNP	Tremont Stakes.

| AT 3 YEARS | WON | Kentucky Derby, Wood Memorial Stakes, Preakness Stakes, Belmont Stakes, Dwyer Stakes, Classic Stakes, Saratoga Cup, Lawrence Realization, Jockey Club Gold Cup. |
| | 2ND | Travers Stakes. |

Gallant Fox was the first of three Derby winners to date for James "Sunny Jim" Fitzsimmons, who started galloping horses for Brannon Brothers the day President Grover Cleveland was inaugurated. Equipoise was crowned the two-year-old champion of 1930. Jockey Clarence Kummer, who rode Man o' War in all but two of his three-year-old races, died during the year. Gifford A. Cochran, owner of the Derby winner Flying Ebony, died in early December

Only one horse among the fourteen that faced Gallant Fox in the 1930 Derby mustered any considerable support in the pari-mutuels from the crowd at Churchill Downs. Gallant Fox had won his first two starts at three, the Wood Memorial and Preakness, but E. F. Prichard's Tannery had trained marvelously at Lexington's track on which he was never beaten. Gallant Fox was held at $1.19-to-$1, while the odds on Tannery were $3.12.

The latter was a contender in the early stages, but finished eighth as Earl Sande piloted Gallant Fox to a two-lengths victory. Sande, who had announced his retirement in 1928, became the only jockey other than Negro Isaac Murphy to win the Kentucky Derby three times.

Following the Derby, the colt owned by Belair Stud went on to win the Belmont Stakes and become the second horse to win the Triple Crown. He had won the Preakness earlier. He was beaten only once at three, finishing second in the Travers Stakes to Jim Dandy, who won at odds of 100-to-1. In his three-year-old season Gallant Fox won $308,278, which was the greatest winnings of any horse in one year.

Gallant Fox's winnings projected his sire into first place among America's stallions. Gallant Fox also was the first of three Derby winners sired by *Sir Gallahad III, whose daughters produced the Derby winners Johnstown and Jet Pilot. Only two other horses have sired three Derby winners each.

The 1930 Derby winner retired to the stud at the end of his three-year-old campaign and in each of his first two crops was the three-year-old champion, including the Kentucky Derby winner of 1935, Omaha. He also sired numerous other good stakes winners.

Racing was saddened in 1930 by the death of H. P. Whitney, whose horses since 1905 had shattered all American and foreign records by winning $3,885,972. George J. Long, who, like Mr. Whitney, had won two runnings of the Derby, also died during 1930, as did the great rider "Snapper" Garrison.

At lower left is shown Knute Rockne, football coach at Notre Dame, who died March 31, 1931, in an airplane crash. During the 'twenties the Notre Dame team became the country's greatest and most colorful football eleven, and it was under Rockne's tutelage that such brilliant combinations as the "Four Horsemen" were developed.

Two weeks before the running of the Kentucky Derby, the world's tallest building was opened in New York City. The Empire State Building, upper right, was opened on May 1 of that year. The building of 102 stories is 1,100 feet tall.

On February 27, the same day that the famous New York World suspended publication and was sold to the Telegram, the United States passed the soldiers' bonus bill.

On June 6 it was announced that the Navy would abandon its base at Guam, declaring it was no longer of military value. A month later the fliers Post and

Gatty were back at Roosevelt Field, having completed their circuit of the globe in eight days, fifteen hours and fifty-one minutes. This broke the previous record of slightly more than twelve days, which was held by the Graf Zeppelin.

1931 was also the year of President Hoover's proposal for a debt moratorium of one year, which was ratified by the Senate on December 22. New York City opened its George Washington Bridge, 3,500-foot span, on October 24.

New York's Legislature ordered an investigation of New York City affairs, and on April 28 Governor Roosevelt cleared James J. Walker, mayor of the city, declaring the charges were too general.

Chic Sale made the headlines on Derby Day by suggesting that Spain's internal strife could be cured by sending the "Literary Digest over there and settle everything with a straw vote."

Pedigree

Twenty Grand

```
                              ┌ Swynford ──── ┌ John o' Gaunt
            ┌ *St. Germans ───┤               └ Canterbury Pilgrim
            │                 │
            │                 └ Hamoaze ───── ┌ Torpoint
TWENTY GRAND┤                                 └ Maid of the Mist
            │                 ┌ *All Gold ─── ┌ Persimmon
            └ Bonus ──────────┤               └ Dame d'Or
                              │
                              └ Remembrance ─ ┌ Hamburg
                                              └ Forget
```

Tabulated Racing Record

Year	Age	Sts.	1st	2nd	3rd	Won
1930	2	8	4	2	1	$ 41,380
1931	3	10	8	1	1	218,545
1932	4	2	1	1	0	915
1935	7	5	1	0	1	950
		25	14	4	3	$261,790

57th Kentucky Derby, May 16, 1931

$50,000 added and $5,000 Gold Cup. 3-year-olds. Weight for age. Net value to winner $52,350; second $6,000; third $3,000; fourth $1,000. 130 nominations.

Horse	Eqt	Wt	PP	St	½	¾	1	Str	Fin	Jockey	Owner	Odds $1 Str't
Tw'y Grand	wb	126	5	9	10¹½	6¹	2²	1¹	1⁴	Kurts'er	Greentree Stable	‡.88
Sweep All	wb	126	1	10	4¹	3¹½	1½	2³	2³	Coltiletti	Dixiana	26.96
Mate	w	126	10	11	7ʰ	4ʰ	3ʰ	3⁴	3⁴	Ellis	A C Bostwick	2.83
Spanish Play	w	126	6	4	8¹½	8¹	6¹½	5²	4¹½	Allen	Knebelkamp & Morris	45.09
Boys Howdy	w	126	7	3	2¹	5¹	5¹	4ʰ	5⁶	Riley	H C Hatch	23.26
nsco	wb	126	12	6	9ʰ	11¹	8³	6³	6¹	O'Donnell	G Watkins	†22.91
Pittsburgher	w	126	9	7	11³	10¹	9½	8ʰ	7ʰ	Corbett	Shady Brook Farm S'ble	8.49
The Mongol	w	126	3	1	5ʰ	9ʰ	11¹	9½	8¹	McCoy	Hamburg Place	†22.91
Ladder	wb	126	4	2	3½	1½	4³	7¹	9ʰ	Schaefer	W J Salmon	26.00
An's Aweigh	wb	126	2	12	12	12	10¹½	10⁶	10²	Steffen	Greentree Stable	‡.88
Surf Board	w	126	8	8	6ʰ	7¹	7½	11½	11⁸	Watters	Greentree Stable	‡.88
Pr D'Amour	wb	126	11	5	1ʰ	2½	12	12	12	James	J Leiter	76.23

†Mutuel field. ‡Coupled in betting as Greentree Stable entry.

Time, :23-1/5, :47-2/5, 1:12, 1:37-2/5, 2:01-4/5 (new track record). Track fast.

$2 Mutuels Paid—Twenty Grand (coupled with Anchors Aweigh and Surf Board as Greentree Stable entry), $3.76 straight, $3.00 place, $2.60 show; Sweep All, $15.58 place, $7.16 show; Mate, $3.62 show.

Winner—B.c. by *St. Germans—Bonus, by *All Gold, trained by J. Rowe, Jr.; bred by Greentree Stable.

Went to Post—5:02. Off at 5:03½.

Start good out of machine. Won easily; second and third driving. Twenty Grand, slow to begin, was sent up slowly after a half, raced strongly on the outside and, wearing down Sweep All, drew away fast and won with speed in reserve. Sweep All broke slowly, but saved ground, followed the leaders in the backstretch, raced into a good lead on the stretch turn, but could not withstand the winner's rush. Mate improved his position fast in the first quarter, saved ground on the second turn, but failed to rally under vigorous driving in the stretch. Spanish Play closed with good courage.

Scratched—Equipoise, Up, Don Leon.

Twenty Grand — Stakes Races

AT 2 YEARS
- WON — Kentucky Jockey Club Stakes, Junior Champion Stakes.
- 2ND — Pimlico Futurity.
- 3RD — Walden Handicap.
- UNP — Babylon Handicap.

AT 3 YEARS
- WON — Kentucky Derby, Wood Memorial Stakes, Belmont Stakes, Dwyer Stakes, Travers Mid-Summer Derby, Saratoga Cup, Lawrence Realization, Jockey Club Gold Cup.
- 2ND — Preakness Stakes.
- 3RD — Classic Stakes.

AT 7 YEARS
- UNP — Santa Anita Handicap (U.S.A.), Queen Anne Stakes (England).

"The horse that beats Sweep All in the Derby will break the track record," said Dixiana's Trainer Clyde VanDusen ten days before the race. He never made a truer prediction for Sweep All, four lengths behind Twenty Grand at the finish, himself ran the mile and a quarter faster than Old Rosebud's mark.

Broomstick and *McGee, each the sire of two Derby winners, died during the year. Sweep, a son of Ben Brush and sire of Sweep All, also died, as did Mahubah, dam of Man o' War. James Rowe, Jr., trainer of the 1931 Derby winner, Jefferson Livingston, and "Chicago" O'Brien were among the people prominent on the turf who died during the year.

Almost fifty years to the day from the afternoon that his father saddled his first Kentucky Derby winner when he sent the great Hindoo to the post on May 17, 1881, Trainer James Rowe, Jr., saddled Twenty Grand on May 16, 1931. Both horses were odds-on favorites and each won by four lengths.

The son of *St. Germans ran two of the greatest races ever watched at Churchill Downs. As a two-year-old in 1930 Twenty Grand had set a new American record of 1:36 for a mile for horses of that age, beating Equipoise a scant nose at the wire. Throughout most of the last eighth of the mile Twenty Grand and Equipoise raced "nose and nose." Those who watched the race still call it one of the greatest races ever run in America.

However, those who watched the 1931 Derby declare it was more thrilling than the two-year-old race. In the Derby race Twenty Grand, far back in the early stages, came roaring by horses as the field came off the back side, surged past the leaders to win going away in new record time of 2:01 4/5. A great disappointment of the day was the withdrawal of Equipoise from the Derby a few hours before the race because of an injury. The tremendous crowd of that afternoon had whetted its appetite for another brilliant duel.

In the presentation stand, Vice President Charles Curtis, himself a former jockey, presented the trophy to the owner, Mrs. Payne Whitney, and congratulated the Louisville jockey, Charles Kurtsinger. Twenty Grand's earnings of $218,545 placed him second among the year's leading money-winners. The leader was the great filly Top Flight, winner of $219,000.

When retired to the Whitney farm Twenty Grand proved impotent. He was brought back to racing again, both in this country and abroad but raced without any great success.

It was evident early on Derby Day that the Churchill Downs track was lightning fast. In the third race the two-year-old Adobe Post ran within one-fifth of a second of the track mark, while just before the Derby the four-year-old Gallant Knight, second in the 1930 Derby, set a world's record of 1:16 1/5 for six and one-half furlongs.

There were two firsts for women during 1932. On January 12, Hattie W. Caraway, of Arkansas, was elected to the United States Senate. She thus became the first woman to gain that distinction.

On May 20 Amelia Earhart Putnam, shown in the photograph below, became the first woman to fly across the Atlantic. She flew from Harbor Grave, Newfoundland, to Culmore, Ireland.

Early in his campaign, which resulted in his being named the Democratic Presidential candidate, Roosevelt made his "Forgotten Man" speech on April 7. In mid-June Hoover was named the Republican party's candidate, with Charles Curtis as the vice-presidential candidate.

The soldiers' bonus had been a touchy subject in the nation's capitol for a decade, and on June 2 Washington read that a "Bonus Army" of 3,500 veterans was marching toward the capital from the middlewest. It was on July 28 that the United States Army, under General Douglas MacArthur, drove the "Bonus Army" out of Washington with tanks and tear gas.

Also in Washington, President Hoover made his second appointment to the Supreme Court, naming Benjamin N. Cardozo as an associate justice to replace Oliver Wendell Holmes, who retired.

The entire nation was shocked over the kidnaping of the son of Charles A. Lindberg from the family home at Hopewell, New Jersey. In Chicago receivers were asked for the $1,300,000,000 utility empire of Samuel Insull. John D. Rockefeller, Jr., declared prohibition had been a failure, and asked the country to repeal the amendment.

During December, 1932, a large segment of the nation's adult population at least momentarily forgot the depression and all else. Their interest was in Sidney Lenz and the Culbertsons, who were engaged in a battle of contract bridge, each side out to prove its respective method of bidding.

On May 12 Masons from throughout the United States gathered at Alexandria, Virginia, for dedication of their granite temple in memory of George Washington. Twenty-two years earlier construction of the building had started. The temple is located on Shooters Hill, a location favored by Jefferson and Madison as the site for the national capitol building prior to the selection of Washington, D. C.

Mrs. Alice Liddell Hargreaves, 80, arrived in the United States from England. As a girl she had inspired the writing of "Alice In Wonderland." Convicts at the Joliet and Statesville prisons in Illinois contributed $800 to buy a gift for their warden, who was resigning his position. A $2,000,000 fire struck the Cunard Line pier in New York City.

Pedigree

Burgoo King

		*North Star III	Sunstar / Angelic
	Bubbling Over	Beaming Beauty	Sweep / Bellisario
BURGOO KING (Chestnut colt)		Lonawand	Cupbearer / St. Flora
	Minawand	*Mintless	Minting / Gorseberry

Tabulated Racing Record

Year	Age	Sts.	1st	2nd	3rd	Won
1931	2	12	4	0	1	$ 6,000
1932	3	4	2	1	0	102,825
1934	5	5	2	1	2	2,115
		21	8	2	3	$110,940

58th Kentucky Derby, May 7, 1932

50,000 added and $5,000 Gold Cup. 3-year-olds. Weight for age. Net value to winner 52,350; second $6,000; third $3,000; fourth $1,000. 115 nominations.

Horse	Eqt	Wt	PP	St	½	¾	1	Str	Fin	Jockey	Owner	Odds $1 Str't
Burgoo King	w	126	13	4	3¹	3²	2³	1⁴	1⁵	James	E R Bradley	‡5.62
Economic	wb	126	10	2	1²	1¹½	1ʰ	2¹½	2ʰ	Horn	J H Louchheim	16.92
Stepenf'chit	wb	126	4	12	9½	5¹	4¹½	4¹	3½	Ensor	Mrs J H Whitney	§3.23
r'don Mint	wb	126	11	3	2½	2ʰ	3¹	3ʰ	4ⁿ	Ellis	Brandon Stable	†6.68
Over Time	wb	126	5	13	13ʰ	8²	6³	5ʰ	5ⁿ	Sande	Mrs J H Whitney	§3.23
Tick On	wb	126	6	14	12¹	10²	5²	6⁶	6⁴	Wall	Loma Stable	1.84
Our Fancy	wb	126	3	1	4ʰ	7½	8²	7ʰ	7¹	Allen	J B Respess	†6.68
Gallant Sir	wb	126	19	18	11½	6ʰ	7³	8²	8²	Woolf	Northway Stable	†6.68
Hoops	wb	126	8	9	14²	11²	10⁴	9¹	9½	Fischer	W F Knebellkamp	28.62
Cold Check	wb	126	12	5	7½	4ʰ	9¹	10²	10¹½	Garner W	J W Parrish	45.88
Adobe Post	wb	126	7	20	16½	15ʰ	16ʰ	13¹	11³	Landolt	Knebelkamp & Morris	28.52
Crys'l Prince	w	126	1	8	20	14¹	12ʰ	12½	12³	Corbett	P C Thompson	†6.68
Oscillation	w	121	2	7	6¹	9ʰ	11¹	11ʰ	13²	Neal	Longridge Stable	†6.68
r Hotspur	wb	126	17	16	18¹	16¹	17²	16²	14¹½	And'son	J Leiter Estate	78.37
Tee Tee	wb	126	14	11	15¹	18²	15ʰ	15¹	15⁴	McCros'n	Dixiana	†6.68
Cathop	w	126	20	19	19¹	17¹½	18⁸	17²	16½	Pichon	R M Eastman	†6.68
Lucky Tom	wb	126	16	17	8ʰ	13²	14¹	14¹	17⁸	Pasc'ma	J J Robinson	10.64
Thistle Ace	wb	126	9	10	10½	19	19	19	18⁸	Elston	G Collins	†6.68
Brother Joe	w	126	18	6	5ʰ	12ʰ	13¹	18ʰ	19	Fator	E R Bradley	‡5.62
Lib Limited	wb	126	15	15	17ʰ	Broke down				Garner M	Three D's Stock Farm	†6.68

†Mutuel field. ‡Coupled in betting as E. R. Bradley entry. §Coupled in betting as Mrs. J. H. Whitney entry.

Time, :24-1/5, :48-1/5, 1:13, 1:38-4/5, 2:05-1/5. Track fast.

$2 Mutuels Paid—Burgoo King (coupled with Brother Joe as E. R. Bradley entry), $13.24 straight, $5.08 place, $4.00 show; Economic, $15.62 place, $8.54 show; Stepenfetchit (coupled with Over Time as Mrs J. H. Whitney entry), $3.52 show.

Winner—B.c. by Bubbling Over—Minawand, by Lonawand, trained by H. J. Thompson; bred by H. N. Davis and Idle Hour Stock Farm.

Went to Post—5:04. Off at 5:19½.

Start good out of machine. Won easily; second and third driving. Burgoo King, away fast and well rated, followed the pace closely until reaching the final three-eighths, where he easily wore down Economic and won easily. Economic set the pace under good rating, was no match for the winner, but outlasted Stepenfetchit. The latter saved ground in the early stages, was under restraint until reaching the closing half-mile and rallied mildly when taken to the outside in the stretch.

Burgoo King Stakes Races

AT 2 YEARS	3RD	Pimlico Futurity.
	UNP	Sanford Stakes, Hopeful Stakes, Champagne Stakes, Belmont Futurity, Richard Johnson Stakes, Spalding Lowe Jenkins Handicap.
AT 3 YEARS	WON	Kentucky Derby, Preakness Stakes.
	UNP	Withers Stakes.

Under 128 pounds on June 30, 1932, Equipoise set a world's record of 1:34 2/5 for one mile around turns. His owner, C. V. Whitney, was the leading money-winner. *Phar Lap, the great Australian champion, died. The daily double was introduced in this year on American race tracks. There were five deadheats in the country.

In Lexington, Kentucky, lives James T. Looney, who has travelled extensively throughout the United States preparing famous Kentucky burgoo for various large gatherings of persons. He is known as the "Burgoo King." It was for him that Colonel E. R. Bradley named the 1932 Kentucky Derby winner. Looney had prepared the burgoo for Colonel Bradley's one-day race meeting for orphans in 1930, and after tasting the food the Colonel told Looney he would name a horse in his honor.

Although Burgoo King did not win a stakes race as a two-year-old in 1931, his owner was not discouraged. In fact, he offered to bet $5,000 the son of Bubbling Over would beat any horse named by any taker the first time they met as three-year-olds. There were no takers, but Colonel Bradley did bet with P. A. Nash that Burgoo King would finish in front of Burning Blaze in the Derby. Burning Blaze, who had prepped exceptionally well for the big race, failed to get to the post as the result of being cut down in a preparatory race.

A crowd of 5,000 poured over the backside fence and into the centerfield on Derby Day while the police vainly attempted to halt the surge at its beginning, then stood helplessly by as the invaders rushed to points of vantage.

Favorite in the field of twenty was Loma Stable's Tick On. The Bradley pair of Burgoo King and Brother Joe was third choice. For fifteen and one-half minutes the large field milled about at the barrier, with Tick On creating most of the disturbance. It was J. H. Louchheim's Economic which set most of the early pace. Burgoo King, the colt which got cod liver oil and dried fish livers as part of his rations, did not get to the front until the field reached the stretch.

Following the Derby Burgoo King won the Preakness Stakes, which was his only other victory in four starts at three. He raced again at five. As a sire, he got Olney, Boy Angler, Doubt Not, Burgoo Miss, and other stakes winners. He died in 1946.

1933

The rolls of the unemployed were mounting as 1933 began. On January 4 Iowa farmers threatened to lynch an insurance-company representative when the company attempted to foreclose on a farm. By February the picture was worse; on February 14 Governor Comstock of Michigan declared a bank holiday and $50,000,000 was rushed to Detroit banks.

In Miami, Franklin Delano Roosevelt, lower left, who was inaugurated on March 4 as the thirty-first President of the United States, escaped death on February 15 when Mayor Cermak, of Chicago, was struck by the assassin's bullets. Giuseppe Zangara fired the shots.

The day after President Roosevelt took office he proclaimed a bank holiday, banned hoarding, and placed an embargo on gold. His first "fireside chat" came on March 12. Roosevelt's first year brought forth N. R. A. when he signed that bill on June 16, announcing his goal as 5,000,-000 jobs. Hugh A. Johnson was named N. R. A. administrator, and September 13 in New York 200,000 participated in a ten-hour N. R. A. parade up Fifth Avenue. One of the floats in that parade is shown at lower right.

At 5:22 P.M. on December 5 prohibition ended in the United States as Utah became the thirty-sixth State to ratify repeal. The striking out of this amendment was marked by celebrations such as the one shown below.

Other news highlights of 1933 included the Century of Progress Exposition which opened at Chicago on May 20. The exposition was visited in July by Italo Balbo who led a twenty-four plane armada to America from Italy. Wiley Post completed his solo flight around the world in seven days, eighteen hours, and forty-five minutes. Dr. Albert Einstein settled in Princeton, New Jersey. F. H. LaGuardia was elected mayor of New York City. Harry L. Hopkins joined the Roosevelt administration, and the airship Akron fell into the ocean off New Jersey, killing seventy-three men.

Pedigree

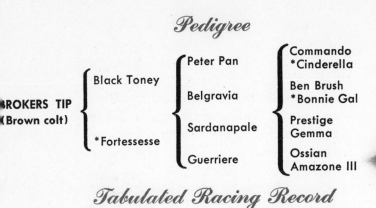

		Peter Pan	Commando *Cinderella
BROKERS TIP (Brown colt)	Black Toney		
		Belgravia	Ben Brush *Bonnie Gal
	*Fortessesse	Sardanapale	Prestige Gemma
		Guerriere	Ossian Amazone III

Brokers Tip

Tabulated Racing Record

Year	Age	Sts.	1st	2nd	3rd	Won
1932	2	4	0	1	1	$ 600
1933	3	5	1	1	0	49,000
1936	6	5	0	0	0	...
		14	1	2	1	$ 49,600

59th Kentucky Derby, May 6, 1933

$50,000 added and $5,000 Gold Cup. 3-year-olds. Weight for age. Net value to winner $48,925; second $6,000; third $3,000; fourth $1,000. 118 nominations.

Horse	Eqt	Wt	PP	St	½	¾	1	Str	Fin	Jockey	Owner	Odds $1 Str't
Brokers Tip	wb	126	11	11	11^1	$8\frac{1}{2}$	4^2	$2^1\frac{1}{2}$	1^n	Meade	E R Bradley	8.93
Head Play	w	126	7	5	$3\frac{1}{2}$	$1\frac{1}{2}$	1^1	1^h	2^4	Fisher	Mrs S B Mason	5.64
Charley O	wb	126	1	6	7^h	6^1	$2^1\frac{1}{2}$	3^4	$3^1\frac{1}{2}$	Corbett	R M Eastman Estate	6.02
Ladysman	wb	126	4	7	$5\frac{1}{2}$	7^3	$5^1\frac{1}{2}$	$5^1\frac{1}{2}$	4^n	Workm'n	W R Coe	‡1.43
Pomponious	w	126	12	12	$10\frac{1}{2}$	$9^1\frac{1}{2}$	$6\frac{1}{2}$	6^3	5^3	Bejshak	W R Coe	‡1.43
Spicson	wb	126	9	13	13	12^3	$10^1\frac{1}{2}$	7^1	$6^1\frac{1}{2}$	Fischer	L M Severson	†25.85
Kerry P'tch	wb	126	5	1	$6^1\frac{1}{2}$	$5\frac{1}{2}$	3^h	4^h	7^2	Schaefer	L Rosenberg	26.89
Mr. Khayyam	w	126	13	9	9^1	11^3	9^h	9^2	$8\frac{1}{2}$	Walls	Catawba Stable	§4.09
Inlander	wb	126	6	8	8^2	10^2	8^1	8^2	$9^1\frac{1}{2}$	Bellizzi	Brookmeade Stable	44.27
Strideaway	wb	126	8	4	$12\frac{1}{2}$	13	12^3	10^3	10^5	Beck	Three D's Stock Farm	†25.85
Dark Win'r	wb	126	3	10	4^2	4^h	7^2	11^8	11^{12}	Jones	W S Kilmer	†25.85
Isaiah	wb	126	10	2	$2^1\frac{1}{2}$	$3\frac{1}{2}$	11^2	12^8	12	McCros'n	J W Parrish	66.86
G'd Advice	wb	126	2	3	1^h	2^h	13	13	P. up.	Legere	Catawba Stable	§4.09

†Mutuel field. ‡Coupled in betting as W. R. Coe entry. §Coupled in betting as Catawba Stable entry.

Time, :23-1/5, :47-1/5, 1:12-4/5, 1:40-2/5, 2:06-4/5. Track good.

$2 Mutuels Paid—Brokers Tip, $19.86 straight, $6.28 place, $4.54 show; Head Play, $5.52 place, $4.08 show; Charley O., $3.84 show.

Winner—Br.c. by Black Toney—*Forteresse, by Sardanapale, trained by H. J. Thompson; bred by Idle Hour Stock Farm.

Went to Post—5:10. Off at 5:18.

Start good out of machine. Won driving; second and third same. Brokers Tip, much the best, began slowly, saved ground when leaving backstretch, but lost some on the stretch turn, then went to the inside and, overcoming interference, was up to win in the final strides after a long and tough drive. Head Play, rated close to the pace, went to front easily, bore out when increasing his lead on the stretch turn and bumped the winner. Charley O., in hand for three-quarters, challenged gamely, then tired, but held Ladysman safe. The latter raced wide most of the way and failed to rally when hard urged.

Scratched—Pompoleon, Sarada, Fingal, Warren Jr., Captain Red, Boilermaker, Silent Shot, At Top, Fair Rochester.

Brokers Tip — Stakes Races

AT 2 YEARS	3RD	Cincinnati Trophy.
AT 3 YEARS	WON	Kentucky Derby.
	UNP	Preakness Stakes, Maryland Handicap.

As Colonel Bradley became the first owner to win four renewals of the Kentucky Derby, his trainer H. A. "Derby Dick" Thompson became the first man to train four winners of the race, all for Bradley. That record for a trainer has since been equaled by Ben A. "Plain Ben" Jones. The Bradley stable was the second leading money-winner of the year and its trainer was second on the list of money-winning trainers.

Black Toney, sire of the winner, also was second among leading sires. Among the horses that died during the 1933 season was Black Toney's sire, Peter Pan, so prominent in many Derby winners' pedigrees. James Todhunter (Tod) Sloan, whose career as a jockey started at sixteen and made him famous in England and France as well as in America, died. He was born August 11, 1873.

Two other owners have since duplicated the feat, but when Colonel E. R. Bradley won the 1932 Kentucky Derby no other man had ever owned three winners of the racing classic. Now, after seventy-four runnings of the Kentucky Derby Colonel Bradley is the only man ever to own four winners.

His fourth winner was Brokers Tip, and the Derby was the only race won by the son of Black Toney, also sire of Black Gold, in three years of racing. Favorite in the race was W. R. Coe's entry of Ladysman, two-year-old champion of the preceding year, and Pomponious. Both Coe horses were sons of Pompey, who had faded before the charges of Bradley's Bubbling Over in 1926.

Second choice was Catawba Stable's Good Advice and Mr. Khayyam, the latter a son of the Derby winner *Omar Khayyam. Head Play was third choice. He had been purchased from Mrs. William Crump just a few hours prior to the Derby by Mrs. Silas B. Mason for $30,000. An earlier offer for the colt had been refused.

Brokers Tip, the maiden, and Head Play were easily the best of their Derby field. They finished four lengths in front of their rivals, while their jockeys rode with rodeo tactics through the last furlong. Both jockeys were suspended.

Brokers Tip broke down in the Preakness, won by Head Play. An effort was made to bring Brokers Tip back to racing as a six-year-old, but he was unable to place in any of his five starts. He was then retired to the stud. His best son was Market Wise, a top stakes winner and successful young sire.

More than one hundred newspapermen were in the Churchill Downs press box. It was the largest number of writers ever to cover the race. In the clubhouse were Mrs. Woodrow Wilson, Bernard Baruch, Joe E. Brown, James Roosevelt, and many other nationally known figures.

1934

During 1934 a new family became very important in the newspapers of North America. For the next few years hardly a week passed without news stories on the life of this family. The stories started on May 28 when the wire services flashed the news to all parts of the world that Mrs. Olivia Dionne had given birth to five daughters, shown below, at Corbeil, Ontario, Canada.

The newspaper stories on the development of the "quints" competed with such headlines as were given our depression worries, which included Harry Hopkins' announcement that there were 4,700,000 families on relief in the United States. Spring droughts in the midwest resulted in severe dust storms, and by mid-summer the country's "dust-bowl" had been created.

Air mail service in the United States was taken over by Army planes in February of 1934, but was returned to civilian air lines after twenty days of operation during which ten Army fliers had been killed. Earlier in the year a Navy plane had flown from California to Hawaii in twenty-four hours, forty-five minutes.

Congress gave President Roosevelt his first setback on March 28 when it overrode his veto of the Patman bonus bill. This came four days after the President had signed the Philippine Independence Bill. In New Orleans, Huey Long entered the city with troops to investigate his political enemies. During the summer food supplies became acute in San Francisco because of a strike in which all unions walked out in sympathy with longshoremen and marine workers.

In November of this year Japan denounced the 1922 naval treaty.

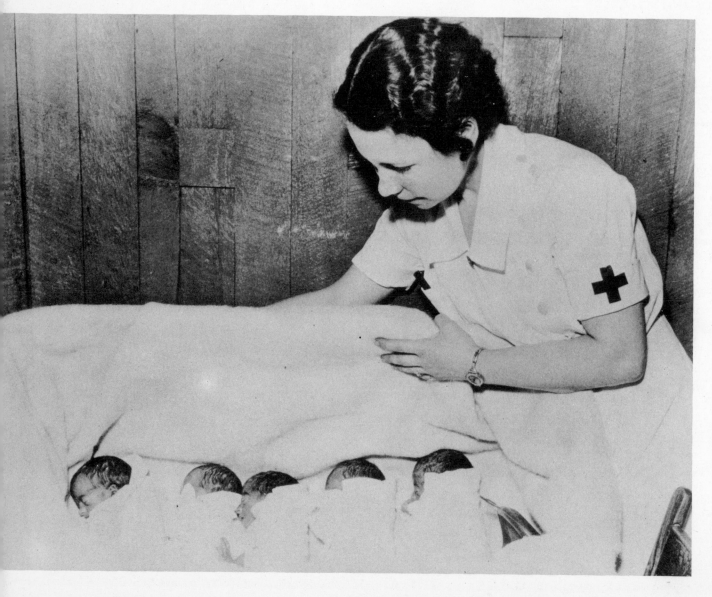

Pedigree

CAVALCADE (Brown colt)			
	*Lancegaye	Swynford	John o' Gaunt / Canterbury Pilgrim
		Flying Spear	Spearmint / Gallop-Along
	*Hastily	Hurry On	Marcovil / Tout Suite
		Henley	Junior / Helenora

Tabulated Racing Record

Year	Age	Sts.	1st	2nd	3rd	Won
1933	2	11	2	3	3	$ 15,730
1934	3	7	6	1	0	111,235
1935	4	2	0	1	0	200
1936	5	2	0	0	0	200
		22	8	5	3	$127,165

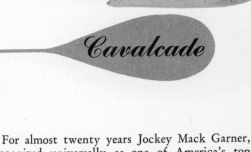

Cavalcade

60th Kentucky Derby, May 5, 1934

$30,000 added and $5,000 Gold Cup. 3-year-olds. Weight for age. Net value to winner $28,175; second $5,000; third $2,500; fourth $1,000. 124 nominations.

Horses	Eqt	Wt	PP	St	½	¾	1	Str	Fin	Jockey	Owner	Odds $1 Str't
Cavalcade	w	126	8	11	7^1	$5\frac{1}{2}$	3^1	2^3	$1^{2\frac{1}{2}}$	Garner	Brookmeade Stable	‡1.50
Discovery	wb	126	6	4	3^2	$3^{1\frac{1}{2}}$	1^2	1^{nk}	2^4	Bejshak	A G Vanderbilt	12.10
Agrarian	w	126	9	7	$10\frac{1}{2}$	$8\frac{1}{2}$	8^1	5^h	3^n	Kurts'g'r	Mrs F J Heller	14.90
Mata Hari	wb	121	3	1	1^h	1^h	2^h	3^4	4^n	Gilbert	Dixiana	6.30
Peace Ch'nce	w	126	2	12	$12\frac{1}{2}$	10^h	$9\frac{1}{2}$	6^1	$5\frac{1}{2}$	Wright	J E Widener	9.70
Spy Hill	w	126	11	10	9^1	$7\frac{1}{2}$	7^h	7^2	6^4	Coucci	Greentree Stable	33.30
Time Clock	wb	126	1	13	13	11^6	11^8	12^{10}	7^h	Bellizzi	Brookmeade Stable	‡1.50
Sing'g Wood	w	126	7	5	$4\frac{1}{2}$	$4\frac{1}{2}$	$4\frac{1}{2}$	$4\frac{1}{2}$	8^h	Jones	Mrs J H Whitney	24.10
Bazaar	w	121	12	9	6^1	$6^{1\frac{1}{2}}$	$6\frac{1}{2}$	8^2	9^6	Meade	E R Bradley	5.10
Speedmore	w	126	5	2	8^h	$9\frac{1}{2}$	$10\frac{1}{2}$	$10\frac{1}{2}$	$10\frac{1}{2}$	Horn	J H Louchheim	†10.40
Sgt. Byrne	wb	126	10	6	2^3	2^2	$5^{1\frac{1}{2}}$	9^4	11^3	Renick	J Simonetti	†10.40
Sir Thomas	wb	126	4	8	$11^{1\frac{1}{2}}$	13	12^4	11^2	12^{10}	Pascuma	A B Gordon	36.20
Quasimodo	wb	126	13	3	5^1	$12\frac{1}{2}$	13	13	13	Burke	Mrs B Franzheim	†10.40

†Mutuel field. ‡Coupled in betting as Brookmeade Stable entry.

Time, :23, :47-1/5, 1:12-1/5, 1:37-2/5, 2:04. Track fast.

$2 Mutuels Paid—Cavalcade (coupled with Time Clock as Brookmeade Stable entry), $5.00 straight, $4.00 place, $3.20 show; Discovery, $9.20 place, $5.80 show; Agrarian, $5.00 show.

Winner—Br.c. by *Lancegaye—*Hastily, by Hurry On, trained by R. A. Smith; bred by F. W. Armstrong.

Went to Post—5:13. Off at 5:21½.

Start good and slow. Won handily; second and third driving. Cavalcade, away slowly, was not permitted to make up much ground for a half-mile, then began moving up leaving the backstretch, where he came through between horses, wore down Discovery and drew out for a handy win. Discovery, away fast, drew into an easy lead approaching the stretch, and held on well, but was overmatched. Agrarian closed resolutely.

Scratched—Riskulus, Blue Again, Prince Pompey, Fogarty, Thomasville, Howard.

Cavalcade — Stakes Races

AT 2 YEARS	WON	Hyde Park Stakes.
	2ND	Spalding Lowe Jenkins Handicap, Eastern Shore Handicap, Sanford Stakes.
	3RD	Saratoga Sales Stakes, Walden Handicap.
	UNP	Richard Johnson Stakes, United States Hotel Stakes.
AT 3 YEARS	WON	Kentucky Derby, Chesapeake Stakes, American Derby, Detroit Derby, Classic Stakes.
	2ND	Preakness Stakes.

Two fillies were prominent in early speculation on the 1934 Derby. They were Dixiana's Mata Hari, 10-to-1 favorite in early winter-book odds, and Colonel Bradley's Bazaar, second choice at 15-to-1 along with two colts. Mata Hari ran fourth, Bazaar ninth. Both were outstanding as two-year-olds. Two other Derby fillies died during 1934. They were Regret, on April 14 at the age of 22, and Bronzewing, third to Old Rosebud the year before Regret's triumph. William Garth, who trained Paul Jones, also died.

For almost twenty years Jockey Mack Garner, recognized universally as one of America's top riders, had been attempting to win the Kentucky Derby. He had first tried in 1916, finishing sixth with A. K. Macomber's The Cock.

Even Lady Luck seemed to be against him. In 1928 when he got a fine mount in Misstep she sent along the top race horse Reigh Count to beat him. When he got the mount on the great Blue Larkspur in 1929, she flooded the track just before the race and left the course in a muddy condition which the eventual three-year-old champion could not handle.

In addition Garner had been third with Under Fire in 1919, sixteenth with Peace Pennant in 1920, sixth with Coyne in 1921, fourth with Nassau in 1923, eleventh with King Gorin II in 1924, ninth with Kentucky Cardinal in 1925, fourth with Rhinock in 1926, eleventh with Kiev in 1927, fourth with Gone Away in 1930, and his 1932 mount, Morpluck, broke down.

The veteran Garner's time as a jockey was running out in 1934 when he rode out of the Churchill Downs paddock on Derby Day astride Brookmeade Stable's Cavalcade. He carried with him the hopes of all his acquaintances that this was the day, and enough of the crowd's financial backing to make his horse favorite at $1.50-to-1. This time Jockey Garner wouldn't be denied his greatest of all triumphs. It had been a long trail for Garner who started riding in 1914.

Cavalcade's dam, *Hastily, was carrying him when she was imported by his breeder, who sold the colt as a yearling for $1,200 to Mrs. Dodge Sloane. She was the fifth woman to own a Derby winner. The colt was named for the successful English movie of the same name.

Trainer Bob Smith, who handled Cavalcade, had been in racing since 1883 when he went to work for David Pulsifer. He wanted a horse of his own so badly that in 1887 at Sheepshead Bay he paid $210 for a runt of a colt, which he proudly led back to the stable. Goaded by talk of high costs of feeding a horse and the size of his colt, he finally sold him. The colt was Tenny, Salvator's great rival.

1935

Two European dictators dominated the headlines in United States newspapers during 1935. They were Germany's Adolph Hitler and Italy's Mussolini. The former, on March 16, scrapped the Versailles treaty when he reestablished universal military training in his country.

Mussolini beat his chest and bellowed his ambitions to bring back to Italy the grandeur of the Roman Empire. In an effort to stop Mussolini, Ethiopia's Haile Selassi ceded oil rights in his country to American and British companies. Within a week, however, the State Department of this country forced American companies to cancel Ethiopia's concessions. Less than a month later Mussolini had rejected the League of Nations' peace proposal, and shortly invaded Ethiopia.

In America the Supreme Court unanimously voided the N.R.A. Other highlights in the Washington picture were the passage of the Wagner Labor Relations Act, Social Security Act, and A.A.A.

Dust storms which had caused great property damage the previous year were a great concern of the nation again in 1935. At the end of 1935 editors rated news of the dust storms high among the ten most important stories of the year. There were many pictures from the stricken area such as the one shown below. The dust storms continued in 1936.

At one time during this three-year pe-riod it was estimated that three-fourths of the population of one state in the affected area was on relief. As much as 300 million tons of top soil was lost in a single day by wind erosion, and the dust was blown as far east as the Atlantic Ocean.

In the sports field, Jim Braddock won the heavyweight boxing crown from Max Baer in fifteen rounds on June 14. The fight was held at Long Island City where the title changed hands each June, 1932 through 1935. Lawson Little won the amateur golf titles of the United States and England. Jesse Owens established three world's records and tied one other world mark in the Big Ten track meet. Sir Malcolm Campbell bettered an average of 300 miles per hour twice in his Bluebird Special automobile. An eleven-year-old girl won the women's diving title.

On August 15 the great American humorist Will Rogers was killed in a plane crash in Alaska. He was accompanying the noted flier, Wiley Post, who also was killed. Jane Addams, who had established the famous Hull House in Chicago, had died on May 21. Senator Huey Long was fatally shot early in September at Louisiana's state capitol building which he had built while governor.

The French liner Normandie made her maiden crossing of the Atlantic and established a new record of four days and eleven hours. Another liner, the Mohawk, sank off the coast of New Jersey. Forty-five persons lost their lives.

Pedigree

Omaha

OMAHA
(Chestnut colt)

- Gallant Fox
  - *Sir Gallahad III
    - *Teddy
    - Plucky Liege
  - Marguerite
    - Celt
    - *Fairy Ray
- Flambino
  - *Wrack
    - Robert le Diable
    - Samphire
  - *Flambette
    - *Durbar II
    - *La Flambee

Tabulated Racing Record

Year	Age	Sts.	1st	2nd	3rd	Won
1934	2	9	1	4	0	$ 3,850
1935	3	9	6	1	2	142,255
1936	4	4	2	2	0	‡8,650
		22	9	7	2	$154,755

‡Includes winnings in England.

61st Kentucky Derby, May 4, 1935

40,000 added and $5,000 Gold Cup. 3-year-olds. Weight for age. Net value to winner 39,525; second $6,000; third $3,000; fourth $1,000. 110 nominations.

orse	Eqt	Wt	PP	St	½	¾	1	Str	Fin	Jockey	Owner	Odds $1 Str't
Omaha	wb	126	10	12	9½	5¹	1²	1¹½	1¹½	Saunders	Belair Stud	4.00
o. Soldier	wb	126	3	10	11¹	8¹½	4ʰ	2²	2⁴	Balaski	Sachsenmaier & Reu'r	6.20
Whiskolo	w	126	8	15	12½	10¹½	2¹	3²	3¹½	Wright	Milky Way Farms	†8.40
Nellie Flag	w	121	9	1	8¹½	7½	5³	4³	4ʰ	Arcaro	Calumet Farm	3.80
Blackbirder	wb	126	13	14	14¹	11¹	11²	5¹	5²	Garner W	Mrs C Hainesworth	†8.40
Psychic Bid	wb	126	7	11	4ʰ	4¹	7¹	6³	6⁴	Jones	Brookmeade Stable	49.20
Morpluck	wsb	126	11	16	16¹	13²	12²	7ʰ	7ʰ	Garner M	J H Louchheim	†8.40
at Eye	w	126	15	4	1½	1½	3¹	8¹	8¹	Coucci	Greentree Stable	16.40
McCarthy	wb	126	4	18	18	15¹	14⁴	14¹	9³	Finnerty	Morrison & Keating	†8.40
om'nwealth	wb	126	17	17	17⁴	12¹	9ʰ	10²	10²	Woolf	Mrs W M Jeffords	9.50
un Fairplay	wb	126	5	3	10¹	9¹½	13³	11¹	11³	Renick	Fairfields Stable	52.30
oday	wb	126	16	6	6¹	6½	8¹	9²	12⁶	Work'an	C V Whitney	8.40
Whopper	wsb	126	2	9	5½	3½	6½	12¹	13¹½	Landolt	H P Headley	†8.40
Bluebeard	wb	126	6	2	7¹	14¹½	15¹	15¹	14¹½	Schutte	Mrs R B Fairbanks	†8.40
utticurio	wb	126	18	13	13ʰ	16⁴	16³	16⁴	15¹	Corbett	Brandon Stable	†8·40
oxthorn	wb	126	12	8	3¹½	2¹	10ʰ	13¹	16²	Meade	E R Bradley	5.00
t Bernard	w	126	1	5	2ʰ	18	18	18	17¹½	Keester	E G Shaffer	†8.40
Veston	wb	126	14	7	15ʰ	17¹	17¹	17¹	18	Young	Braedalbane Stable	†8.40

†Mutuel field.

ime, :23, :47-3/5, 1:13-2/5, 1:38-2/5, 2:05. Track good.

$2 Mutuels Paid—Omaha, $10.00 straight, $5.00 place, $3.80 show; Roman Soldier, $6.40 place, $4.20 show; Whiskolo (Field), $3.40 show.

Winner—Ch.c. by Gallant Fox—Flambino, by Wrack, trained by J. Fitzsimmons; bred by Belair Stud.

Went to Post—5:13. Off at 5:15½.

Start good and slow. Won easily; second and third driving. Omaha escaped interference in he early crowding, was taken to the outside after the first quarter, raced to the lead gradually fter reaching the half-mile post and held sway thereafter, winning easily. Roman Soldier worked his way to the outside after reaching the backstretch, responded well when called upon, ut could not menace the winner. Whiskolo raced to a contending position with a rush, lost round on the far turn and tired in the last three-sixteenths. Nellie Flag suffered interference oon after the start, was again impeded on the first turn and could not improve her position vhen clear in the last five-sixteenths.

Scratched—Color Bearer, Chanceview, Prince Splendor, Calumet Dick.

Omaha — Stakes Races

T 2 YEARS	2ND	Sanford Stakes.
	UNP	United States Hotel Stakes, Saratoga Special.
T 3 YEARS	WON	Kentucky Derby, Preakness Stakes, Belmont Stakes, Dwyer Stakes, Classic Stakes.
	2ND	Withers Stakes.
	3RD	Wood Memorial Stakes, Brooklyn Handicap.
T 4 YEARS (In England)	WON	Victor Wild Stakes, Queen's Plate.
	2ND	Ascot Gold Cup, Princess of Wales' Stakes.

The 1935 winner was not named for the Nebraska city of the same name. In explaining his naming, Owner Woodward said "My Thoroughbred stock comes down from the *Ormonde line. I was looking around for a good name starting with "O" and Omaha came to me first."

Kentucky's National Guardsmen made their first appearance at the 1935 Kentucky Derby. As a result, there was no deluge of people clambering over fences and into the centerfield.

Omaha was in the first crop of foals of his sire; the second Kentucky Derby winner owned by William Woodward and trained by James Fitzsimmons, but the third winner sired by a Derby winner, the third colt foal of his dam, and the third horse to win America's Triple Crown.

Two names which were destined to become important in Derby history appeared on the program for the first time that May 4, 1935, afternoon. They were Calumet Farm, which has since won three renewals of the classic, and Jockey Eddie Arcaro, who now has ridden more Derby winners than any other rider.

Strangely enough, Arcaro, who has ridden two of the winners owned by Calumet, was astride Calumet Farm's first Derby horse, Nellie Flag. The daughter of American Flag and Nellie Morse went to the post as favorite in the field of eighteen. She was the only filly other than Regret to be accorded such distinction. Who knows, perhaps the crowd sensed the terrific Derby combination that Calumet-Arcaro would become.

More likely, however, was the fact that it was raining that afternoon, and the crowd knew Nellie Flag could handle herself extremely well on the kind of track over which the race would be run. Omaha was second choice.

Jockey William (Smoky) Saunders, who had just celebrated his twentieth birthday less than a month earlier, was astride the Woodward colt. He kept the son of the 1930 Derby winner well up among the leaders. As he took the lead after the first mile Dave Newton, painter at Churchill Downs for twenty years, scurried off to his shop. He came out in a few minutes with a painted board freshly lettered "OMAHA," which he nailed alongside the name plaques of the previous sixty Derby winners.

The $142,255 won by Omaha as a three-year-old easily placed him at the top of the year's leading money-winners. In his four-year-old season Omaha was sent to England to race, as numerous other Derby winners had done. He later returned to this country where he entered the stud at Claiborne Farm.

1936

Two outstanding engineering accomplishments were completed in 1936. One was the world's largest dam; the other was the world's longest bridge.

In the photograph above is the Golden Gate Bridge between San Francisco and Oakland, California, which was opened November 12. However, it was not finally completed until the following year. This bridge, which has a channel span of 4,200 feet, is eight and one-quarter miles long.

The Hoover Dam, located in the Colorado River, was completed in 1936. This dam, which is 727 feet in height has a storage capacity of 9,938 billion gallons of water. It was originally named the Hoover Dam. The name was later changed to Boulder Dam, then back to Hoover Dam.

Also completed in 1936 was the world's largest ocean liner, England's Queen Mary. This liner established new Atlantic crossing records for both eastward and westward crossings in 1936 and lowered these records in 1938.

Early in the year the bonus bill, over which there had been wrangling for seventeen years, finally became law.

Another of the world's great dams is Norris Dam, shown in the photograph lower left, on Tennessee's Clinch River. This dam is part of the Tennessee Valley Authority, the power program of which was upheld by the Supreme Court in 1936.

Pedigree

OLD VENTURE
(Chestnut colt)

- *St. Germans
  - Swynford
    - John o' Gaunt
    - Canterbury Pilgrim
  - Hamoaze
    - Torpoint
    - Maid of the Mist
- Possible
  - Ultimus
    - Commando
    - *Running Stream
  - Lida Flush
    - *Royal Flush III
    - Lida H.

Tabulated Racing Record

Year	Age	Sts.	1st	2nd	3rd	Won
1935	2	8	3	2	0	$ 2,500
1936	3	3	3	0	0	65,800
		11	6	2	0	$ 68,300

Bold Venture

62nd Kentucky Derby, May 2, 1936

40,000 added and $5,000 Gold Cup. 3-year-olds. Weight for age. Net value to winner 37,725; second $6,000; third $3,000; fourth $1,000. 102 nominations.

Horse	Eqt	Wt	PP	St	½	¾	1	Str	Fin	Jockey	Owner	Odds $1 Str't
Bold Venture	w	126	5	13	$8\frac{1}{2}$	1^1	$1^{1\frac{1}{2}}$	1^1	1^h	Hanford	M L Schwartz	20.50
Brevity	wb	126	10	10	$9\frac{1}{2}$	$6\frac{1}{2}$	3^1	2^2	2^6	Wright	J E Widener	.80
Indian Br'm	wb	126	2	7	6^h	3^2	$2\frac{1}{2}$	3^5	3^3	Burns	A C T Stock Farm	5.10
Coldstream	w	126	13	6	2^h	4^1	5^3	5^3	4^5	Wall	Coldstream Stud	15.20
Bien Joli	wb	126	6	2	4^h	7^1	6^3	6^2	5^h	Balaski	E R Bradley	14.90
Moll Image	wb	126	14	12	12^1	11^1	$11^{1\frac{1}{2}}$	7^3	6^4	Fisher	Superior Stable	†43.40
He Did	wsb	126	3	1	1^2	$2\frac{1}{2}$	4^4	4^h	7^h	Kurts'g'r	Mrs S B Mason	33.80
Teufel	wb	126	8	9	$11\frac{1}{2}$	10^1	8^h	8^1	8^h	Lit'nb'ger	Wheatley Stable	‡10.60
Gold Seeker	wb	121	12	14	13	12^2	$10\frac{1}{2}$	10^4	9^4	Peters	Foxcatcher Farms	†43.40
Merry Pete	wb	126	1	8	$7\frac{1}{2}$	8^3	7^1	9^h	10^6	Malley	Belair Stud	‡10.60
The Fighter	w	126	7	3	5^h	9^h	12^6	11^4	11^5	Robertson	Milky Way Farms	§16.50
Grand Slam	wb	126	9	5	3^2	5^h	9^2	12^8	12^{10}	Workman	Bomar Stable	19.10
Sangreal	wb	126	11	11	10^2	13	13	13	13	Garner	Milky Way Farms	§16.50
Granville	wb	126	4	4	Lost rider.					Stout	Belair Stud	‡10.60

†Mutuel field. ‡Coupled in betting as Wheatley Stable and Belair Stud entry. §Coupled in betting as Milky Way Farms entry.

Time, :23-3/5, :47-4/5, 1:12-3/5, 1:37-4/5, 2:03-3/5. Track fast.

$2 Mutuels Paid—Bold Venture, $43.00 straight, $11.80 place, $6.60 show; Brevity, $5.00 place, $4.00 show; Indian Broom, $3.80 show.

Winner—Ch.c. by *St. Germans—Possible, by Ultimus, trained by M. Hirsch; bred by M. L. Schwartz.

Went to Post—4:41. Off at 4:45½.

Start good and slow. Won driving; second and third same. Bold Venture, in close quarters immediatey after the start, began to improve his position fast on the outside after about three-eighths, took an easy lead approaching the final half-mile and, holding on with fine courage under strong handling, withstood Brevity's bid. The latter, probably best and knocked to his knees within a few strides after the start, had to race wide thereafter, closed resolutely and was wearing down the winner. Indian Broom, blocked in the first quarter, raced to a contending position, made a bid entering the stretch, then weakened.

Scratched—Banister, Dnieper, Seventh Heaven, Forest Play, Silas.

Bold Venture   Stakes Races

AT 2 YEARS	UNP	Arlington Futurity, Hopeful Stakes.
AT 3 YEARS	WON	Kentucky Derby, Preakness Stakes.

When Trainer Max Hirsch left New York with Bold Venture for the Kentucky Derby, he left all his horses in charge of his daughter, Mary Hirsch. She was the first woman to be granted a trainer's license by The Jockey Club. While her father was at Louisville, she saddled the winners of both divisions of the Tester Purse.

"It has been the ambition of my life," said Owner Schwartz after the race. In 1935 Mr. Schwartz dispersed his Thoroughbred holdings. When Bold Venture was offered in the ring, only a few bids were made. "I won't let him go for that," declared his owner, "he's a $20,000 colt." He could not withdraw him from the sale, but had him bid in for $7,100.

Three sets of twin horses were foaled at Dixiana Farm in 1936, one set being foaled by Mata Hari, fourth in the 1934 Derby. The great jockey Laverne Fator, winner of 1,121 races, died during the year. His one great regret was that he never rode a winner of the Derby.

Charley Kurtsinger experienced one of the most unusual incidents to befall any jockey in the Kentucky Derby during the 1936 running of the race, in which he rode Mrs. Silas B. Mason's He Did. Kurtsinger broke his mount in front at the start and set the pace for better than the first half-mile.

As the field rounded the last turn for the stretch run to the wire, Kurtsinger had He Did in fourth position and on the rail. The jockey carried his whip in his left hand, ready to go to work on He Did in the final drive. However, standing atop the inner rail on the last turn was a long-armed spectator, who, according to Kurtsinger, reached out and grabbed the whip from the jockey's hand.

Bold Venture, the winner, had taken up the pace-making assignment when He Did gave it up after the first half mile. The son of *St. Germans, sire of the 1931 winner Twenty Grand, never relinquished the lead, winning by a head from the fast closing Brevity, owned by Joseph E. Widener.

The colt owned by Morton L. Schwartz started only once more. One week after the Derby he won the Preakness, becoming the fifth horse to win both races. He had started only once at three prior to the Derby, winning an allowance race at Jamaica by four lengths. In both the Derby and Preakness, Bold Venture withstood terrific stretch challenges, by Granville in the latter race.

Bold Venture's being forced out of racing was but a continuation of bad luck which dogged his path. He fell going to the post in one race at two, unseated his jockey in another, ran off and finished seventh in another race, was in trouble throughout in the Hopeful Stakes. While enroute to Saratoga as a two-year-old, a fire broke out in his horse car, caused the death of two horses while a groom held Bold Venture's head out an open door to keep him from suffocation.

The 1936 winner's odds were the longest on any Derby winner since Exterminator's triumph, fifth longest in the history of the race to that date.

1937

Louisville's Broadway during the 1937 flood is shown in the photograph above. The photograph was taken from Fourth and Broadway, looking west, during the height of the disaster, which was Louisville's worst since the tornado of 1890.

Thousands of residents of the city were moved to points of safety in surrounding Kentucky and Indiana towns, while a tremendous corps of volunteer workers in boats of all descriptions aided in removing residents from inundated areas.

In Washington, Franklin D. Roosevelt took office for his second term, the inauguration being held on January 20 instead of on the traditional March date. One of his first acts in the second term was a request to enlarge the Supreme Court to fifteen Justices. Elderly members of the Court had refused to approve part of his program. The plan was rejected by the Senate committee, 70-to-20, July 22.

John D. Rockefeller, who during his lifetime gave away $700,000,000, died on May 23. In the same month the dirigible Hindenberg exploded at its mooring mast at Lakehurst, New Jersey, killing thirty-six persons.

The world's heavyweight championship changed hands June 22 when Joe Louis defeated James J. Braddock. Louis was destined to hold the title longer than any champion since the bare-knuckle days.

On July 2 Amelia Earhart Putnam was reported missing in the Pacific on her round-the-world flight. Navy ships and planes joined in the search for her.

It was on December 13 that the United States gunboat Panay was sunk by Japanese planes.

Derby Day was a holiday for residents of Clifton, New Jersey. The occasion for the holiday there was in honor of the Kasper quadruplets. It was declared by city officials. Meanwhile the nation was celebrating National Baby Week.

Pedigree

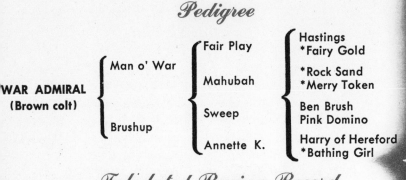

WAR ADMIRAL (Brown colt)			
	Man o' War	Fair Play	Hastings / *Fairy Gold
		Mahubah	*Rock Sand / *Merry Token
	Brushup	Sweep	Ben Brush / Pink Domino
		Annette K.	Harry of Hereford / *Bathing Girl

Tabulated Racing Record

Year	Age	Sts.	1st	2nd	3rd	Won
1936	2	6	3	2	1	$ 14,800
1937	3	8	8	0	0	166,500
1938	4	11	9	1	0	90,840
1939	5	1	1	0	0	1,100
		26	21	3	1	$273,240

63rd Kentucky Derby, May 8, 1937

War Admiral

$50,000 added and $5,000 Gold Cup. 3-year-olds. Weight for age. Net value to winner $52,050; second $6,000; third $3,000; fourth $1,000. 103 nominations.

Horse	Eqt	Wt	PP	St	½	¾	1	Str	Fin	Jockey	Owner	Odds $1 Str'
War Admiral	w	126	1	2	1¹½	1¹	1¹½	1³	1¹¾	Kurts'er	Glen Riddle Farms	1.60
Pompoon	w	126	14	6	5²	4¹	2²	2⁵	2⁸	Rich'rds	J H Louchheim	8.00
R'g Reward	wb	126	17	7	8½	6½	8³	5³	3³	Rob'tson	Milky Way Farms	‡4.60
Melodist	w	126	3	10	6ʰ	5¹	5ʰ	4ʰ	4¹	Longden	Wheatley Stable	15.10
Sceneshifter	wb	126	12	13	10½	12½	11ʰ	7¹½	5²	Stout	M Howard	§11.20
Heelfly	w	126	10	1	3¹½	2½	3³	3¹½	6ʰ	Wright	Three D's Stock Farm	16.20
Dellor	wb	126	2	4	7¹½	9½	6½	6½	7½	James	J W Parrish	13.70
Burn'g Star	wb	126	15	15	14¹	13¹	13¹	10¹	8ʰ	Parke	Shandon Farm	†9.30
C'rt Scandal	wb	126	6	11	12½	8ʰ	9³	12¹	9¹	Steffen	T B Martin	†9.30
Clodion	wb	126	13	14	13²	14½	12²	9ʰ	10¹	Anders'n	W A Carter	†9.30
Fairy Hill	wb	126	4	3	2¹½	3³	4½	8¹½	11¹½	Peters	Foxcatcher Farms	44.60
M'ry Maker	wb	126	7	19	17²	11¹	10½	11½	12½	Dabson	Miss E G Rand	†9.30
No Sir	wb	126	19	17	16ʰ	17¹	17½	13¹½	13ʰ	Le Blanc	Miss M Hirsch	†9.30
Grey Gold	wb	126	11	18	19²	19¹½	19¹	14½	14¹	Rosen	E W Duffy	†9.30
Military	wsb	126	5	9	15¹½	15¹	15¹	15¹	15½	Corbett	Milky Way Farms	‡4.60
S'set Trail II	wb	126	18	20	20	20	20	16¹½	16²	Dotter	R Walsh	†9.30
Fencing	wb	126	8	12	9½	10½	16ʰ	17²	17⁵	Westr'pe	M Howard	§11.20
Bernard F	w	126	16	16	18⁵	18³	19½	18³	18¹	Hardy	I J Collins	†9.30
Sir Damion	wb	126	20	8	11½	16ʰ	14³	19⁴	19¹²	Yager	Marshall Field	†9.30
Billionaire	wb	126	9	5	4ʰ	7½	7²	20	20	Woolf	E R Bradley	16.50

†Mutuel field. ‡Coupled in betting as Milky Way Farms entry. §Coupled in betting as M. Howard entry.

Time, :23-1/5, :46-4/5, 1:12-2/5, 1:37-2/5, 2:03-1/5. Track fast.

$2 Mutuels Paid—War Admiral, $5.20 straight, $4.20 place, $3.40 show; Pompoon, $9.40 place, $6.00 show; Reaping Reward (coupled with Military as Milky Way Farms entry), $3.80 show.

Winner—Br.c. by Man o' War—Brushup, by Sweep, trained by G. Conway; bred by S. D. Riddle. Went to Post—4:42. Off at 4:50½.

Start good and slow. Won easily; second and third driving. War Admiral, fractious at post, was away fast, was sent clear of his company, was taken under restraint after racing a quarter-mile, set the pace easily to the final half-mile, increased his advantage gradually on the stretch turn and won in hand. Pompoon, forced wide throughout, was reserved off the pace, offered good response when called upon, held on with fine courage, but did not seriously threaten the winner. Reaping Reward, in close quarters early, dropped back on the stretch turn, but came again, only to tire in the late stages. Melodist, a factor from the start, tired when the real test came. Sceneshifter lost much ground on the final turn, then closed well in a splendid effort. Heelfly, fractious at the post but away fast, tired in the stretch.

War Admiral Stakes Races

AT 2 YEARS	WON	Eastern Shore Handicap.
	2ND	Great American Stakes, Richard Johnson Stakes.
	3RD	National Stallion Stakes.
AT 3 YEARS	WON	Kentucky Derby, Chesapeake Stakes, Preakness Stakes, Belmont Stakes, Washington Handicap, Pimlico Special.
AT 4 YEARS	WON	Widener Handicap, Queens County Handicap, Wilson Stakes, Saratoga Cup, Whitney Stakes, Saratoga Cup, Jockey Club Gold Cup, Rhode Island Handicap.
	2ND	Pimlico Special.
	UNP	Massachusetts Handicap.

*Sun Briar was the leading two-year-old in 1917; his son, Pompey, was champion of that age in 1925, and 1935 found Pompoon, a son of the son, as the top two-year-old. The son, sire, and grandsire shared another distinction.

All three were ranked as favorites for the Derby in the early season speculation of their respective three-year-old seasons. But the similarity of the three, as far as the Derby is concerned, ended there. *Sun Briar failed to get to the post. Pompey finished fifth after being in the early contention. Pompoon, however, was a contender throughout the entire mile and one-quarter, finishing second by one and three-quarter lengths to War Admiral.

War Admiral was perhaps the best horse sired by the great Man o' War. He started in twenty-six races, winning twenty-one, was unplaced in only one start. War Admiral was the fourth horse to win the Triple Crown.

His time for the Kentucky Derby was the second fastest of any winner to that date. His rider was the same Charley Kurtsinger, who had ridden Twenty Grand when the Greentree Stable colt established a new record in 1931. The "Flying Dutchman," as Kurtsinger was called, was born only a short distance from Churchill Downs. He was the son of a less famous jockey.

During the year War Admiral won $166,500, which placed him at the top of the money-winning three-year-olds. Top money-winner of the season was Charles S. Howard's Seabiscuit, grandson of War Admiral's sire. It was the following year that Battleship, another son of Man o' War, won the England's Grand National at Aintree.

War Admiral raced again at four, made one start at five, then entered the stud in 1940 at his owner's Faraway Farm.

America's oldest living stallion at the time, Ballot, died at the age of thirty-three on May 15. He had been an outstanding racer both in this country and in England, and was a very successful sire. On his thirty-first birthday, he was guest of honor at a party given by Kentucky horsemen. Few Thoroughbred stallions had lived as long.

1938

The year 1938 was an outstanding one in the sport of harness horse racing. At Lexington, Kentucky, on September 28 Billy Direct established a new world's record for pacers when his driver sent him a mile in 1:55. The following afternoon, over the same track, Greyhound set a world's record of 1:55¼ for trotters. Greyhound, shown upper left, was driven by Sep Palin.

Greyhound's record-breaking effort had been planned for several days. Billy Direct, however, went for a new record against the watch after he failed to get away with his field in a race on the afternoon's racing program.

"Lazy, dishonest man, white, 24, will consider interview with a broadcasting station executive, or other high salaried technician who wishes to offer him a position. Must be good pay, short hours, not much work." The foregoing advertisement appeared in a Louisville newspaper in May.

For the second time in two years vandals painted historic Plymouth Rock at Plymouth, Massachusetts, with brilliant red paint. To attend a Pershing Rifles drill at Bowling Green, Kentucky, on Derby Day Gilbert Russell rode his bicycle from Dearborn, Michigan. The 500-mile trip required 147 hours of pedaling. Twenty-three persons sleeping in a Maryland house were aroused by a dog's bark, escaped the burning structure, forgot to take the dog out. He was burned to death.

On July 18, 1938, Douglas Corrigan set his monoplane down in Ireland and calmly told reporters no one was more surprised than himself. He declared that he had taken off from New York, planning to fly to California, but that somehow or other he had started in the wrong direction and wound up across the Atlantic Ocean. "Wrong Way" Corrigan is shown in the photograph at lower right.

Radio Actor Orson Welles was responsible for a widespread panic among American radio listeners on the evening of October 30, 1938. This was the date of his famous "Attack From Mars" radio sketch.

Actually, the worst catastrophe to hit the nation during 1938 was the New England hurricane, which was the worst ever recorded in the New England states and which killed 488 persons. In Washington the Wages and Hours bill was enacted into law, and the State Department protested Mexico's seizing of oil properties. Mexico rejected the protests, but later agreed to pay for the oil and land seizures.

Pedigree

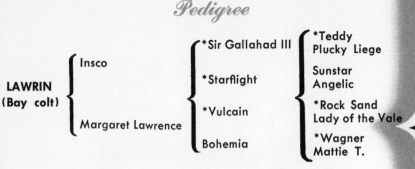

LAWRIN
(Bay colt)
- Insco
  - *Sir Gallahad III
    - *Teddy
    - Plucky Liege
  - *Starflight
    - Sunstar
    - Angelic
- Margaret Lawrence
  - *Vulcain
    - *Rock Sand
    - Lady of the Vale
  - Bohemia
    - *Wagner
    - Mattie T.

Tabulated Racing Record

Year	Age	Sts.	1st	2nd	3rd	Won
1937	2	15	3	6	0	$ 3,060
1938	3	11	6	2	2	123,215
		26	9	8	2	$126,275

64th Kentucky Derby, May 7, 1938

Lawrin

$50,000 added and $5,000 Gold Cup. 3-year-olds. Weight for age. Net value to winner $47,050; second $6,000; third $3,000; fourth $1,000. 103 nominations.

Horse	Eqt	Wt	PP	St	½	¾	1	Str	Fin	Jockey	Owner	Odds $1 Str't
Lawrin	w	126	1	5	5^h	$5\frac{1}{2}$	2^h	1^3	1^1	Arcaro	Woolford Farm	8.60
Dauber	wb	126	3	10	$9\frac{1}{2}$	$8\frac{1}{2}$	6^4	3^1	2^5	Peters	Foxcatcher Farms	9.70
Can't Wait	wb	126	7	4	4^1	$3^{1\frac{1}{2}}$	3^3	4^4	3^n	Balaski	M Selznick	24.20
Menow	wb	126	10	7	1^2	$1^{1\frac{1}{2}}$	$1^{1\frac{1}{2}}$	2^2	4^{nk}	Workm'n	H P Headley	8.50
The Chief	w	126	9	8	$6\frac{1}{2}$	6^1	5^h	5^4	5^6	Westrope	M Howard	12.00
Fighting Fox	w	126	5	6	2^3	2^h	$4\frac{1}{2}$	6^3	6^3	Stout	Belair Stud	1.40
Co-Sport	wb	126	2	9	$8^{1\frac{1}{2}}$	9^2	9^5	7^2	7^2	Woolf	B Friend	89.50
Bull Lea	wb	126	6	1	7^4	$7\frac{1}{2}$	8^3	8^1	8^h	Anderson	Calumet Farm	2.90
Elooto	wb	126	4	2	10	10	10	10	9^2	Faust	Blue Ridge Farm	122.30
Mou'n Ridge	w	126	8	3	$3^{1\frac{1}{2}}$	4^1	7^2	$9^{1\frac{1}{2}}$	10	Robertson	Milky Way Farms	105.20

Time, :23-1/5, :47-2/5, 1:12-2/5, 1:38-1/5, 2:04-4/5. Track fast.

$2 Mutuels Paid—Lawrin, $19.20 straight, $8.80 place, $4.80 show; Dauber, $12.00 place, $6.00 show; Can't Wait, $8.20 show.

Winner—Br.c. by Insco—Margaret Lawrence, by Vulcain, trained by B. A. Jones; bred by H. M. Woolf.

Went to Post—4:32. Off at 4:36½.

Start good and slow. Won driving; second and third same. Lawrin, saving much ground, responded willingly when called upon, came through on the inside when wearing down Menow, opened up a commanding advantage approaching the final eighth, then bore out through the last sixteenth, but held Dauber safe. The latter, badly outrun early, began to improve his position when racing wide on the stretch turn, continued near the middle of the track while closing with fine speed and was getting to the winner. Can't Wait, rated under steady reserve for about three-quarters, outfinished Menow in the last stride. The latter made a good pace under steady rating, swerved out on the stretch turn and tired under pressure thereafter. The Chief ran an even race. Fighting Fox did not respond when urged and gave way badly after a mile.

Lawrin — Stakes Races

AT 3 YEARS
- WON — Kentucky Derby, Hialeah Stakes, Flamingo Stakes, Hollywood Trial Stakes.
- 2ND — Derby Trial.
- UNP — Bahamas Handicap.

No mare ever produced two winners of the Kentucky Derby. Nevertheless the tremendous crowd which gathered at Churchill Downs for the 1938 Derby made Fighting Fox, full brother to Gallant Fox, the favorite at $1.40-to-1. They were more confident than ever as Fighting Fox went past the wire the first time close on the heels of the pacemaker. As the leader faltered on the backside Fighting Fox moved up, but gave way in the final quarter.

Three Derby winners, Behave Yourself, Bubbling Over, and *Omar Khayyam, died in 1938, as did Black Toney, sire of the winners Black Gold and Brokers Tip. Among the persons connected with the Turf who died were Mrs. R. M. Hoots, owner of Black Gold.

Although he was no newcomer to racing, having owned and trained a racing stable for many years, the name of Ben A. Jones, of Parnell, Missouri, was never as well known prior to the afternoon of Saturday, May 7, 1938, as it has been since that date on which he saddled the first of his four Kentucky Derby winners. His name now appears alongside that of H. A. "Derby Dick" Thompson. They have saddled four winners each.

Since winning his first Derby with Herbert M. Woolf's Lawrin, Jones has won other runnings of the race with Calumet Farm's Whirlaway, Pensive, and Citation. Three of the Jones-trained winners were ridden by Eddie Arcaro, only jockey to win four renewals of the race.

Earl Sande, who shared the jockey record first equaled then broken by Arcaro, was conceded to have one of the greatest winter racing stars that ever came to Churchill Downs in quest of the Derby. Sande's principal candidate was Colonel Maxwell Howard's Stagehand, who had won the Santa Anita Derby and Santa Anita Handicap during the California season.

Two days before the big race Colonel Howard's trainer announced Stagehand had a cold, was running a temperature, which would keep him from starting in the Churchill Downs race. The Howard stable, it was announced, would be represented only by The Chief, who on Tuesday of Derby week had won the first running of the Derby Trial Stakes, beating Lawrin, with Stagehand third. The Chief's time of 1:35 4/5 has not been bettered by any subsequent winner of the Derby Trial.

Lawrin had been winter-raced, winning the Hialeah Stakes and Flamingo Stakes before coming to Louisville. The second and third horses in the Derby also had been winter raced.

Lawrin's racing career prior to the Derby had been more extensive than any Derby winner in many years. He had started twenty-three times, at least twice a month every month from his first start on April 1, 1937, until February 26, 1938, when he was rested until the Churchill Downs meeting.

1939

War came to the world again in 1939. On January 4 President Roosevelt called upon the nation for an extensive defense program as the outbreak of war in Europe appeared to be a certainty.

Following the outbreak of World War II, the President asked Congress to repeal the arms embargo, adopt cash-and-carry sales for limited aid to the allies, ban credits to foreign nations, and curb the activity of United States ships. The United States closed its waters to belligerent submarines, forbade its own ships to enter North Sea, Baltic, and west European waters.

This latter order followed by two months the sinking of the Athenia off the coast of Scotland. Most of the 1,400 passengers aboard the liner were saved.

On the lighter side of the 1939 picture in the United States two expositions were opened. One was the Golden Gate Exposition which opened at San Francisco on February 18. The other was the New York World's Fair which opened April 30 with an attendance of 500,000. The photograph, upper right, is a view of the latter exposition. In New York on November 8 opened the stage play, "Life

With Father," which broke all records.

England's King George VI visited Canada and the United States. In the photograph below, the English monarch is shown with President Roosevelt in Washington where at a state dinner on June 8 the two pledged the friendship of their countries.

In January of 1939 Jacob Ruppert, owner of the New York Yankees, died. In June it became known that one of his greatest players, Lou Gehrig, suffered from a rare form of infantile paralysis, and could never play baseball again. The great Yankee first baseman died in 1940.

Other headlines of the year included the conviction of Tammany Leader James J. Hines, and indictment of Thomas J. Pendergast on charges of tax evasion.

Pedigree

JOHNSTOWN (Bay colt)	Jamestown { St. James	*Ambassador IV / *Bobolink II
	Mlle. Dazie	Fair Play / Toggery
	La France { *Sir Gallahad III	*Teddy / Plucky Liege
	*Flambette	*Durbar II / *La Flambee

Tabulated Racing Record

Year	Age	Sts.	1st	2nd	3rd	Won
1938	2	12	7	0	2	$ 31,420
1939	3	9	7	0	1	137,895
		21	14	0	3	$169,315

Johnstown

65th Kentucky Derby, May 6, 1939

50,000 added and $5,000 Gold Cup. 3-year-olds. Weight for age. Net value to winner 46,350; second $6,000; third $3,000; fourth $1,000. 115 nominations.

Horse	Eqt	Wt	PP	St	½	¾	1	Str	Fin	Jockey	Owner	Odds $1 Str't
Johnstown	wb	126	5	2	1²	1⁴	1⁴	1⁵	1⁸	Stout	Belair Stud	.60
Challedon	w	126	7	5	7⁵	5½	4⁶	3¹	2¹	Seabo	W L Brann	6.60
Heather Broom	w	126	2	6	4½	6¹	3ʰ	4⁶	3½	James	J H Whitney	12.00
Viscounty	wb	126	3	8	6¹	4¹	2¹	2ʰ	4⁶	Bierman	Valdina Farms	52.20
Technician	wb	126	6	4	5¹	7⁸	5½¹	5⁵	5⁸	Adams	Woolford Farm	5.80
El Chico	w	126	1	1	2½	2½	6⁴	6³	6³	Wall	W Ziegler Jr	8.20
T M Dors't	wb	126	8	3	3³	3¹	7¹²	7¹⁵	7	Haas	J W Brown	64.90
On Location	wb	126	4	7	8	8	8	8	P. up.	Robertson	Milky Way Farms	97.70

Time, :23-2/5, :47-2/5, 1:12-4/5, 1:38, 2:03-2/5. Track fast.

$2 Mutuels Paid—Johnstown, $3.20 straight, $3.00 place, $2.80 show; Challedon, $3.60 place, $3.20 show; Heather Broom, $3.00 show.

Winner—B.c. by Jamestown—La France, by *Sir Gallahad III., trained by J. Fitzsimmons; bred by A. B. Hancock.

Went to Post—4:29. Off at 4:29½.

Start bad and slow. Won easily; second and third driving. Johnstown swerved to the inside as he took command, made the pace for a mile, was lightly roused in the stretch and quickly increasing his advantage, won with speed in reserve. Challedon was between horses in the early running and began to move up after reaching the last five-eighths. Heather Broom dropped back when racing wide on the first turn, rallied after going seven-eighths and outfinished Viscounty.

Scratched—Challenge, Xalapa Clown.

Johnstown — Stakes Races

AT 2 YEARS	WON	Babylon Stakes, Richard Johnson Stakes, Remsen Handicap, Breeders' Futurity.
	3RD	Hopeful Stakes, Junior Champion Stakes.
	UNP	Flash Stakes, Belmont Futurity.
AT 3 YEARS	WON	Kentucky Derby, Wood Memorial, Paumonok Handicap, Withers Stakes, Belmont Stakes, Dwyer Stakes.
	3RD	Classic Stakes.
	UNP	Preakness Stakes.

*Sir Gallahad III, sire of Johnstown's dam, also sired the mare which produced Challedon, second horse in the Derby. Moreover, both Johnstown and the 1935 winner Omaha were grandsons of *Flambette, who had been imported by Owner Woodward in 1919. *Flambette won the Latonia Oaks in 1921, running the race in 2:03 2/5, which was Johnstown's time in the Derby. In that race she carried the same weight as did her grandson in the Derby. *Flambette, incidentally, is the only mare who is the grandam of two Derby winners.

Johnstown wasn't the leading money-winner of the year, but Belair Stud was the leading money-winning owner, Jockey Stout was leading money-winning jockey, Fitzsimmons was leading money-winning trainer, and Arthur B. Hancock, who bred the 1939 winner, was leading money-winning breeder.

Colonel E. R. Bradley had started twenty-two horses over a fourteen-year period before he won his third Kentucky Derby in 1933. William Woodward started his first horse in the race in 1930 and won, sent his second starter to the post in 1935 and won. In 1936 his entry of two finished unplaced, and Fighting Fox finished sixth in 1938.

The sixth Derby starter carrying the familiar white blouse and red dots of the Belair Stud stable was Johnstown, winner in 1939. It had taken Owner Woodward just ten years and six horses to win three runnings of the Churchill Downs race. As Johnstown galloped past the finish wire eight lengths in front, there were many who believed another four years would not pass before Bradley's record of four wins would be equaled.

Johnstown had gone to the post at the shortest odds since Agile had won thirty-four years earlier in 1905 at 1-to-3. Moreover, the field which opposed him was the smallest in twenty-one years; or since Exterminator had won in 1918.

El Chico, unbeaten in seven starts as a two-year-old during which season he won $84,100, was third choice in the Derby field and first out of the gate. However, by the time he raced past the finish wire the first time Johnstown was in front of El Chico. "I didn't want him to go to the front so early," said Jockey Stout, "but there was nothing I could do. He said he wanted to, so I just held on and let him go to the races." Stout had been unseated by Belair Stud's Granville at the start of the 1936 Derby.

Nick Wall, who rode El Chico, was quoted as saying, "All I'm thankful for is that Stout didn't whack Johnstown across the rear end once during the whole race, because, if he had'a, Johnstown would have won that race by a half-mile or so."

Johnstown did not race after his three-year-old season. He was retired to the stud at Claiborne Farm in 1940 and has sired numerous top stakes winners.

All other news in the United States during 1940 was overshadowed by President Roosevelt's decision to run for a third term. His nomination marked the first time any major political party of the United States had nominated the same man three times.

To oppose him the Republican party selected Wendell Willkie, lower right. Senator McNary was Willkie's running mate. Henry Wallace was selected as the Democratic vice presidential candidate. In accepting the nomination at Elwood, Indiana, Willkie challenged the President to a debate. A month later he launched one of the most gruelling campaigns ever conducted by a candidate. After two days his voice failed. In the election Roosevelt won thirty-eight of the states.

The election of Roosevelt resulted in John L. Lewis quitting as head of the C.I.O., something he had pledged to do if Roosevelt were reelected. Lewis, however, remained as head of the United Mine Workers.

During the year the country began its program of defense, and registered 16,-500,000 for selective service. Secretary of War Stimson is shown in the photograph above drawing the first names for the draft.

It was in 1940 that the following happened: Mashall Field founded the New York newspaper PM, which accepted no advertising; J. P. Morgan & Co., abandoned private banking and became a public corporation; Murder, Inc., was uncovered in Brooklyn; the world's third largest suspension bridge at Tacoma, Washington, collapsed in a high wind; $50,000,000 worth of plane construction at the Downey, California, Vultee plant was halted by a twelve-day strike; two policemen were killed by a time bomb in the British pavilion at New York's World's Fair; and we viewed an eclipse of the sun.

Pedigree

GALLAHADION
(Bay colt)

*Sir Gallahad III	*Teddy	Ajax / Rondeau
	Plucky Liege	Spearmint / Concertina
Countess Time	Reigh Count	*Sunreigh / *Contessina
	*Breathing Spell	Dark Ronald / *Romagne

Tabulated Racing Record

Year	Age	Sts.	1st	2nd	3rd	Won
1939	2	5	0	1	0	$ 180
1940	3	17	5	4	1	89,590
1941	4	14	1	1	3	2,850
		36	6	6	4	$ 92,620

Gallahadion

66th Kentucky Derby, May 4, 1940

$75,000 added and Gold Cup. 3-year-olds. Weight for age. Net value to winner $60,150; second $8,000; third $3,000; fourth $1,000. Trainer's awards: First $3,000; second $2,000; third $1,000. Breeders' awards: First $2,000; second $1,000; third $500.

Horse	Eqt	Wt	PP	St	½	¾	1	Str	Fin	Jockey	Owner	Odds $1 Str't
Gallahadion	wb	126	1	4	3h	2h	41	32	1½	Bierman	Milky Way Farms	35.20
Bimelech	w	126	2	1	2½	3h	1h	1½	2n	F A Smith	E R Bradley	.40
Dit	wb	126	6	5	41	41	33	2½	31	Haas	W A Hanger	6.70
Mioland	wb	126	3	3	52	5½	52	41	42	Balaski	C S Howard	6.40
Sirocco	wb	126	5	6	61	63	65	66	52	Longden	Dixiana	42.70
Roman	wb	126	4	2	1½	1½	2h	5h	66	McCombs	J E Widener	24.20
Royal Man	wb	126	7	7	72	7h	7½	73	73	Gilbert	Tower Stable	61.20
Pictor	w	126	8	8	8	8	8	8	8	Woolf	W L Brann	18.00

Photo for second.

Time, :11-3/5, :23-2/5, :35-3/5, :48, 1:02-3/5, 1:12-4/5, 1:25-1/5, 1:38-3/5, 1:51-3/5, 2:05. Track fast.

$2 Mutuels Paid—Gallahadion, $72.40 straight, $13.80 place, $4.80 show; Bimelech, $3.20 place; $2.40 show; Dit, $2.80 show.

Winner—B.c. by *Sir Gallahad III.—Countess Time, by Reigh Count, trained by R. Waldron; bred by R. A. Fairbairn.

Went to Post—4:48. Off at 4:50.

Start good and slow. Won driving; second and third same. Gallahadion, away well, moved forward with Bimelech, responded to strong urging when wearing down Bimelech, drew out, but won with little left. Bimelech, first in motion, went wide throughout, moved into command nearing the final quarter-mile, bore out on the stretch turn, held the lead approaching the final furlong, but was unable to hold the winner. Dit, steadied along early, was forced wide entering the stretch.

Scratched—True Star.

Gallahadion   Stakes Races

AT 3 YEARS	WON	Kentucky Derby, San Vicente Handicap.
	2ND	Derby Trial, Classic Stakes.
	3RD	Preakness Stakes.
	UNP	Santa Anita Derby, San Juan Capistrano Handicap, Belmont Stakes, Kent Handicap, American Derby, Lawrence Realization.
AT 4 YEARS	3RD	Clark Handicap, Stars and Stripes Handicap.
	UNP	Ben Ali Handicap, Churchill Downs Handicap, Dixie Handicap, Equipoise Mile

The Milky Way Farm Stable was established by Frank C. Mars in 1933 when he purchased twenty yearlings from Arthur B. Hancock. Before any of the horses had won, Mr. Mars died in 1934. During the next six years, Mrs. Mars purchased ninety-seven yearlings for $537,900. The Derby winner cost her $5,000.

Gallahadion was a maiden at two, winning his first race January 5, 1940. He also won his first stakes race, the San Vicente Handicap. His dam, Countess Time, was the first daughter of the Derby winner Reigh Count to produce a winner and his first daughter to produce a stakes winner, who was Gallahadion.

The racing world lost a number of prominent persons during 1940. Those who died included James Butler, William Butler, Maurice Galvin, and Willis Sharpe Kilmer, owner of Exterminator and breeder of Reigh Count.

Perhaps the greatest hush in all Kentucky Derby history fell over Churchill Downs as Gallahadion pulled away to his victory of almost two lengths in 1940. One hundred yards from the finish wire it was apparent to everyone that Bimelech was beaten.

The tremendous crowd was stunned to almost complete silence. They had sent Colonel Bradley's Bimelech to the post at 40 cents to $1, the shortest priced favorite since pari-mutuels had been used for Derby wagering, and one of the two shortest priced favorites in the history of the race to that time. The Bradley colt, last son of noble Black Toney, sire of two Derby winners, was unbeaten in eight races and had been one of the most impressive two-year-old champions in many years. He had won the Derby Trial Stakes just four days earlier, and the Blue Grass Stakes just nine days previously.

Not until the field came around the final turn for the run to the wire, however, did the tremendous crowd give out its first great cheer for Bimelech. It was on that turn that Bimelech first got to the front. The son of Black Toney held that lead for little more than an eighth of a mile as Gallahadion bore down on the rail to win.

Throughout the week Roy Waldron had told newspapermen he was going to win with Gallahadion. Bimelech had not impressed him in beating Gallahadion in the Derby Trial. Few heeded Waldron's statements. As a result Gallahadion's odds were the largest since Donerail won in 1913, and second largest in Derby history.

Neither Mrs. Ethel V. Mars, owner of Gallahadion, nor Colonel Bradley saw the 1940 Derby. The former was confined to her Chicago home by a severe cold, and the latter's doctors had advised him to remain at Idle Hour Farm. The winning owner heard an account of the running by radio, after which her daughter said, "I'm sure mother would have fainted had she not already been in bed."

The winning owner's trophy was accepted by Trainer Waldron, a native of Youngstown, Ohio, whose career in racing started as an exercise boy.

1941

At the beginning of 1941 there were comparatively few in the United States who did not believe this country would ultimately be drawn into World War II. The "Arsenal of Democracy" threw itself into high gear. From throughout the land to the industrial centers flowed a steady stream of workers to turn out the products needed for export under the Lend-Lease bill which was signed on March 11 by the President, Roosevelt, whose third term inauguration is shown in the photograph above.

Meanwhile, the first recruits under the Selective Service bill were going into training. Across the country military camps were mushrooming. There were labor troubles. A soft-coal strike started simultaneously with the calling of a strike at the Ford plant by the C.I.O. on April 1. The latter ended June 20 when the company signed with the union. On the West Coast strikes tied up $500,000,000 in ship contracts.

Although the country, generally, believed it impossible for the United States to escape the world conflict, it had not anticipated the event which precipitated our entry into the war. That came on Sunday morning, December 7, when Japan attacked Pearl Harbor and crippled our Pacific fleet, see picture below. The following day Congress voted for war by 470 to 1. On December 11 came Germany's declaration of war on the United States, which brought quick response from this country.

In the same year that the United States entered its second war against Germany, the head of that nation during the first war, Kaiser Wilhelm, died June 4. Ignace Jan Paderewski also died.

Pedigree

WHIRLAWAY (Chestnut colt)			
*Blenheim II	Blandford	Swynford	Blanche
	Malva	Charles O'Malley	Wild Arum
Dustwhirl	Sweep	Ben Brush	Pink Domino
	Ormonda	Superman	Princess Ormonda

Tabulated Racing Record

Year	Age	Sts.	1st	2nd	3rd	Won
1940	2	16	7	2	4	$ 77,275
1941	3	20	13	5	2	272,386
1942	4	22	12	8	2	211,250
1943	5	2	0	0	1	250
		60	32	15	9	$561,161

67th Kentucky Derby, May 3, 1941

Whirlaway

$75,000 added and Gold Cup. 3-year-olds. Weight for age. Net value to winner $61,275; second $8,000; third $3,000; fourth $1,000. Trainers' awards: First $3,000; second $2,000; third $1,000. Breeders' awards: First $2,000; second $1,000; third $500.

Horse	Eqt	Wt	PP	St	½	¾	1	Str	Fin	Jockey	Owner	Odds $1 Str't
Whirlaway	wb	126	4	6	8¹	6½	4¹	1³	1⁸	Arcaro	Calumet Farm	2.90
Staretor	w	126	2	1	7²	4½	5³	2½	2ⁿᵏ	Woolf	H S Nesbitt	36.00
M'rk't Wise	wb	126	7	5	6²	8⁴	6³	5³	3²	Anderson	L Tufano	19.10
Porter's Cap	wb	126	9	4	2ʰ	3⁵	2¹½	3ʰ	4¹	Haas	C S Howard	3.30
Little Beans	wb	126	5	10	10¹²	9⁵	8⁵	7²	5¹	Moore	Mrs L Palladino	12.10
Dispose	w	126	11	2	1²	1²	1ʰ	4ʰ	6¹½	Bierman	King Ranch	7.20
Blue Pair	wb	126	3	3	3⁵	2ʰ	3½	6½	7½	James	Mrs V S Bragg	20.60
Our Boots	w	126	10	9	4³	5½	7²	8⁵	8³	McCreary	Woodvale Farm	3.90
Rob't Morris	w	126	8	8	5½	7¹	9⁶	9⁸	9¹²	Richards	J F Byers	13.90
Valdina Paul	wb	126	6	7	9³	10¹⁵	10¹⁵	10¹⁵	10¹²	H Lem'ns	Valdina Farm	†24.30
Swain	wb	126	1	11	11	11	11	11	11	Adams	C Putnam	†24.30

†Mutuel field.

Time, :23-3/5, :46-3/5, 1:11-3/5, 1:37-2/5, 2:01-2/5 (new track record). Track fast.

$2 Mutuels Paid—Whirlaway, $7.80 straight, $5.00 place, $4.40 show; Staretor, $35.20 place, $17.00 show; Market Wise, $10.80 show.

Winner—Ch.c. by *Blenheim II.—Dustwhirl, by Sweep, trained by B. A. Jones; bred by Calumet Farm.

Went to Post—5:53. Off at 5:54½.

Start good and slow. Won easily; second and third driving. Whirlaway, eased back when blocked in the first eighth and taken to the inside approaching the first turn, started up after reaching the final half-mile, was taken between horses on the final turn, responded with much energy to take command with a rush and, continuing with much power, drew out fast in the final eighth. Staretor, away slowly, made his move gradually, drifted out slightly before straightening up in the stretch and held on well in the final drive. Market Wise, also well back early, rallied after reaching the last five-sixteenths and finished with courage. Porter's Cap, a strong factor from the start, tired after reaching the last three-sixteenths.

Whirlaway Stakes Races

AT 2 YEARS
- WON: Saratoga Special, Hopeful Stakes, Breeders' Futurity, Walden Stakes.
- 2ND: United States Hotel Stakes, Grand Union Hotel Stakes.
- 3RD: Arlington Futurity, Belmont Futurity, Pimlico Futurity.
- UNP: Hyde Park Stakes, Nedayr Stakes, Futurity Trial.

AT 3 YEARS
- WON: Kentucky Derby, Preakness Stakes, Belmont Stakes, Saranac Handicap, Travers Stakes, American Derby, Lawrence Realization, Dwyer Stakes.
- 2ND: Jockey Club Gold Cup, Blue Grass Stakes, Derby Trial, Classic Stakes, Narragansett Special.

AT 4 YEARS
- WON: Clark Handicap, Dixie Handicap, Brooklyn Handicap, Massachusetts Handicap, Trenton Handicap, Narragansett Special, Jockey Club Gold Cup, Washington Handicap, Pimlico Special, Governor Bowie Handicap, Louisiana Handicap.
- 2ND: Phoenix Handicap, Suburban Handicap, Butler Handicap, Arlington Handicap, match race with Alsab, Manhattan Handicap, Riggs Handicap.
- 3RD: Carter Handicap, New York Handicap.

AT 5 YEARS
- UNP: Equipoise Mile.

Whirlaway's Kentucky Derby was the biggest, richest, and fastest in the first sixty-seven runnings of the American racing classic. More than 100,000 persons entered the gates at Churchill Downs on Saturday afternoon, May 3, 1941, surpassing any previous attendance.

The added money had been increased to $75,000 in 1940, but the net in that year was $60,150 as compared to the $61,275 which Owner Warren Wright received through Whirlaway's victory. Two-fifths of a second were clipped off the time record of 2:01 4/5 which had been established by Twenty Grand in 1931.

Whirlaway was the favorite in the field of eleven which started in the 1941 Derby. The odds against him were $2.90-to-1. He might well have been the shortest priced favorite of all time had he accomplished in his two previous races what racing fans believed him capable of doing with ease.

However, ten days prior to the Derby he had been beaten six lengths by Our Boots, and in the Derby Trial, four days before the Derby, he had finished second to Blue Pair in the Derby Trial Stakes. Many experienced trainers declared after the latter race that no horse would be close to Whirlaway at the finish of the Derby. They based their belief on the way the Calumet colt came around the final turn into the stretch in the Trial. "Horses just can't run as fast as Whirlaway did around that turn," said one veteran. "He was going so fast I thought he was going right through the outside fence."

He ran much the same race in the Derby. At the mile he was fourth, more than two lengths behind the leader. In the next eighth of a mile, the spectators witnessed that same dazzling burst of speed as Whirlaway moved from fourth place to first, three lengths in front of the second horse.

Following his Derby triumph, Trainer Ben Jones declared, "Whirlaway is just getting good." The son of *Blenheim II went on to win the Triple Crown and $272,386 which made Calumet the leading owner. Before he retired from racing Whirlaway won a total of $561,161 to become the world's greatest money-winner.

History was written in 1942 which the United States will long remember. It was on January 2 that General Douglas MacArthur gave up Manila, but fought on for Bataan and Corregidor. On April 9 the U. S. forces on Bataan surrendered and Americans saw in their papers such pictures as the one below. On May 6 Corregidor surrendered after a heroic defense.

However, the year also was one of United States victories. The U. S. fleet weakened Japan's seapower in a three-day battle at Midway ending June 1; on August 8 Marines landed in the Solomons, seized Guadalcanal, the first stop on the road to Tokyo. On November 7 the United States and England successfully carried out the largest invasion in history with their landing of a great army in north Africa.

Early in the year the French liner Normandie capsized at its New York pier after a fire. In May nation-wide gasoline rationing was started in the United States.

On November 14 Captain Eddie Rickenbacker and his companions were rescued after being adrift for twenty-four days in the Pacific after their plane had crashed. Tragedy struck Boston when 433 persons died in the Cocoanut Grove night-club fire. Other highlights in the year's news included the completion of

Grand Coulee Dam, and the inauguration of Thomas E. Dewey as New York's governor.

Churchill Downs took on a military look with the establishment of Camp Matt Winn in the centerfield. A large display of military equipment was included, and at top Colonel Winn is shown beside one of the tanks.

Indian Lake, Ohio, was hit by a severe hail storm on Derby Day of this year. The hail stones which fell were so large that many pigs, chickens, and other small animals were killed. A forest fire in the Cumberland National Forest led revenue agents to the discovery and seizure of a 1,500-gallon moonshine still. Near Salt Lake City the same day an airliner crashed, killing seventeen persons.

Pedigree

Shut Out

SHUT OUT
(Chestnut colt)

- Equipoise
  - Pennant
    - Peter Pan
    - *Royal Rose
  - Swinging
    - Broomstick
    - *Balancoire II
- Goose Egg
  - *Chicle
    - Spearmint
    - Lady Hamburg II
  - Oval
    - Fair Play
    - Olympia

Tabulated Racing Record

Year	Age	Sts.	1st	2nd	3rd	Won
1941	2	9	3	2	1	$ 17,210
1942	3	12	8	2	0	238,972
1943	4	17	5	2	2	60,925
1944	5	2	0	0	1	400
		40	16	6	4	$317,507

68th Kentucky Derby, May 2, 1942

$75,000 added and Gold Cup. 3-year-olds. Weight for age. Net value to winner $64,225; second $8,000; third $3,000; fourth $1,000. Trainer awards: First $3,000; second $2,000; third $1,000. Breeder awards: first $2,000; second $1,000; third $500.

Horse	Eqt	Wt	PP	St	½	½	1	Str	Fin	Jockey	Owner	Odds $1 Str't
Shut Out	w	126	3	1	4²	3½	3ʰ	1½	1²¼	Wright	Greentree Stable	‡1.90
Alsab	wb	126	7	5	10¹	8¹	4½	4²	2ʰ	James	Mrs A Sabath	5.10
Val'a Orp'n	wb	126	14	10	2ʰ	2½	2²	2ʰ	3¹½	Bierman	Valdina Farm	§9.90
With Regards	w	126	15	4	1²	1¹	1½	3²	4½	Longden	Mr & Mrs T D Grimes	5.40
First Fiddle	wb	126	2	11	11½	10ʰ	9ʰ	6³	5³	McCreary	Mrs E Mulrenan	†9.20
Devil Diver	wb	126	5	2	5¹½	5½	5¹½	5²	6½	Arcaro	Greentree Stable	‡1.90
Fair Call	wb	126	1	7	6¹	6¹½	6¹	7¹	7ⁿᵏ	Lingberg	Mill River Stable	†9.20
Dogpatch	wb	126	10	3	3ʰ	4½	7ʰ	8½	8ʰ	Skelly	Milky Way Farm	59.70
Hollywood	w	126	6	14	14⁵	13¹	12²	10¹	9¹	Woolf	Valdina Farm	§9.90
Sw'p S'ger	wb	126	4	15	15	15⁵	13³	11²	10½	Shelhamer	T D Buhl	†9.20
Apache	wb	126	13	6	7¹	7½	8½	9¹	11¹	Stout	Belair Stud	16.90
Sir War	wb	126	8	8	9¹½	11½	11²	12⁴	12⁴	Adams	Circle M Ranch	†9.20
Fairy Man'h	wb	126	9	13	12¹	9ʰ	10¹	13²	13⁶	Gilbert	Foxcatcher Farm	39.90
Requested	w	126	12	9	8¹½	12½	14⁶	14⁵	14⁵	Haas	B F Whitaker	5.10
B't a. Spur	wb	126	11	12	13½	15	15	15	15	Craig	E C A Berger	†9.20

†Mutuel field. ‡Coupled as Greentree Stable entry. §Valdina Farm entry.

Time, :12-1/5, :35-2/5, :47-2/5, 1:00, 1:12-3/5, 1:25-4/5, 1:39, 1:50-4/5, 2:04-2/5. Track fast.

$2 Mutuels Paid—Greentree Entry (Shut Out and Devil Diver), $5.80 straight, $3.40 place, $3.00 show; Alsab, $6.20 place, $4.80 show; Valdina Farm Entry (Valdina Orphan and Hollywood), $5.20 show.

Winner—Ch.c. by Equipoise—Goose Egg, by *Chicle, trained by John M. Gaver; bred by Greentree Stable.

Went to Post—5:31. Off at 5:33.

Start good from stall gate. Won ridden out; second and third driving. Shut Out, taken in hand after being hustled along for three-eighths, went close to the pace under smooth rating, responded when called upon and, wearing down the leaders, continued strongly while drawing out through the last eighth. Alsab, taken to the outside after a half-mile, started up after three-quarters and closed resolutely to head Valdina Orphan in the final stride. Valdina Orphan forced a fast pace under clever rating, rallied when placed to strong pressure entering the stretch and held on gamely.

Scratched—First Prize, Sun Again.

Shut Out — Stakes Races

AT 2 YEARS
- WON — Grand Union Hotel Stakes.
- 2ND — Hopeful Stakes, Saratoga Special.
- 3RD — Ardsley Handicap.
- UNP — Pimlico Futurity, Belmont Futurity, Futurity Trial.

AT 3 YEARS
- WON — Kentucky Derby, Blue Grass Stakes, Belmont Stakes, Yankee Handicap, Classic Stakes, Travers Stakes.
- 2ND — Dwyer Stakes.
- UNP — Preakness Stakes, Gallant Fox Handicap.

AT 4 YEARS
- WON — Wilson Stakes, Laurel Stakes, Pimlico Special.
- 2ND — Edgemere Handicap, Riggs Handicap.
- 3RD — Washington Handicap, Saratoga Handicap.
- UNP — Whitney Stakes, Narragansett Special, Brooklyn Handicap, Suburban Handicap, Metropolitan Handicap, Toboggan Handicap.

Mrs. Payne Whitney, owner of Greentree Stable, already was the "First Lady of the Turf," and when her Shut Out won the 1942 running of the Kentucky Derby she became the first woman to win that race twice. Six times previously, starting with Mrs. C. E. Durnell's Elwood in 1904 and including Mrs. Whitney's triumph with Twenty Grand in 1931, the Derby had been won by a woman owner.

The other women owners and their horses had been: Mrs. R. M. Hoots with Black Gold in 1924, Mrs. John D. Hertz with Reigh Count in 1928, Mrs. Dodge Sloane with Cavalcade in 1934, and Mrs. Ethel V. Mars with Gallahadion in 1940. Six of the first seven horses to finish in the 1942 Derby were owned by women. Valdina Orphan, owned by Emerson F. Woodward's Valdina Farm, was third and the only one of the first seven not racing in a woman's name.

Although he had ridden Shut Out to victory in the Blue Grass Stakes ten days prior to the Derby after the Greentree Stable colt's stablemate, Devil Diver, had injured himself, Jockey Eddie Arcaro did not pick Shut Out as his Derby mount. The jockey had his choice and he selected Devil Diver, whom he and most of the others connected with the stable believed to be the better horse. Devil Diver finished sixth to the winner.

Undaunted, Arcaro again picked Devil Diver for his mount in the Preakness and again Devil Diver finished behind Shut Out who was fifth. However, by the time the Belmont Stakes was run, Arcaro was convinced and rode Shut Out to victory in that race. Arcaro has not been proved wrong many times, but how wrong he was early in the spring is emphasized by Shut Out's ending his three-year-old season as the leading money-winning horse of the year.

Shut Out continued racing through his five-year-old season after which he was retired as a stallion at Greentree Farm, near Lexington. His first foals came to the races in 1948.

 Restrictions at home became more stringent during 1943, but there was little complaining for certainly things were going much better as far as our war effort was concerned. Two important assignments were given General Dwight D. Eisenhower, lower right, during the year. On February 11 he was named to command the Allied armies in Europe, and on December 24 he was named to command the invasion of western Europe.

America's race tracks were among those seriously affected by the tightening of restrictions. Many closed because the only way they could be reached was by automobile or bus. Special trains to the Kentucky Derby were ruled out by the Office of Defense Transportation. This was the first "Street Car Derby," practically all of those who watched the 1943 running of the race coming to the track by street car, as shown in the photograph above.

Early in the year President Roosevelt asked Congress for $100 billion for our war effort, later met England's Prime Minister Winston Churchill at Casablanca where they agreed upon an unconditional surrender of the Axis nations. It was in December of this year that these two leaders, together with Stalin, held their Teheran Conference.

Highlights of the war news in this year included the breaking of the Germans' siege of Leningrad, completion of the African campaign, the first United States air raids over the Reich, landing of U. S. forces on Attu in the Aleutians, new landings in the Pacific, the invasion of Sicily and Salerno.

Count Fleet

Pedigree

COUNT FLEET
(Brown colt)

- Reigh Count
  - *Sunreigh
    - Sundridge
    - *Sweet Briar II
  - *Contessina
    - Count Schomberg
    - Pitti
- Quickly
  - Haste
    - *Maintenant
    - Miss Malaprop
  - Stephanie
    - *Stefan the Great
    - Malachite

Tabulated Racing Record

Year	Age	Sts.	1st	2nd	3rd	Won
1942	2	15	10	4	1	$ 76,245
1943	3	6	6	0	0	174,055
		21	16	4	1	$250,300

69th Kentucky Derby, May 1, 1943

$75,000 added and $5,000 Gold Cup. 3-year-olds. Weight for age. Net value to winner $60,725; second $8,000; third $3,000; fourth $1,000. Trainer awards: First $3,000; second $2,000; third $1,000. Breeder awards: First $2,000; second $1,000; third $500.

Horse	Eqt	Wt	PP	St	½	¾	1	Str	Fin	Jockey	Owner	Odds $1 Str't
Count Fleet	wb	126	5	1	1^h	1^2	1^2	1^2	1^3	Longden	Mrs J Hertz	.40
Blue Swords	wb	126	1	2	4½	4$^{1\frac{1}{2}}$	2$^{1\frac{1}{2}}$	2^2	2^6	Adams	A T Simmons	9.00
Slide Rule	wb	126	2	6	6½	3^h	4$^{1\frac{1}{2}}$	3^3	3^6	McCreary	W E Boeing	10.80
Amber Light	wb	126	7	5	5$^{1\frac{1}{3}}$	5^3	3½	4^2	4½	Robertson	Dixiana	17.50
Bankrupt	w	126	6	9	9^3	9^1	7½	6½	5$^{1\frac{1}{2}}$	Zufelt	T B Martin	†21.90
No Wrinkles	w	126	10	7	8^3	7½	6^1	7^h	6^h	Adair	Milky Way Farm	34.60
Dove Pie	wb	126	4	10	10	10	8^2	8^1	7^3	Eads	J W Rodgers	86.50
Gold Shower	w	126	9	4	2^4	2^1	5^3	5½	8^{10}	Atkinson	V S Bragg	12.10
Modest Lad	wb	126	3	8	7^h	6^h	9^4	9^4	9^8	Swain	Mrs H Finch	71.20
Burnt Cork	wb	126	8	3	3^1	8$^{1\frac{1}{2}}$	10	10	10	Gonzalez	E Anderson	†21.90

†Mutuel field.

Time, :12-2/5, :23-1/5, :34-2/5, :48-3/5, :59-2/5, 1:12-3/5, 1:25, 1:37-3/5, 1:50-2/5, 2:04-2/5. Track fast.

$2 Mutuels Paid—Count Fleet, $2.80 straight, $2.40 place, $2.20 show; Blue Swords, $3.40 place, $3.00 show; Slide Rule, $3.20 show.

Winner—Br.c. by Reigh Count—Quickly, by Haste, trained by G. D. Cameron; bred by Mrs. J. Hertz.

Went to Post—5:30½. Off at 5:31½.

Start good from stall gate. Won handily; second and third driving. Count Fleet began fast, was hustled along, shook off the bid of Gold Shower and won handily. Blue Swords was in hand until reaching the last half-mile, came determinedly, but was not good enough. Slide Rule was blocked when approaching the final turn and, taken out for the drive, could not reach the leaders. Amber Light made a game bid entering the stretch but tired.

Scratched—Twoses, Ocean Wave.

Count Fleet   Stakes Races

AT 2 YEARS
- WON — Champagne Stakes, Pimlico Futurity, Walden Stakes, Wakefield Stakes.
- 2ND — East View Stakes, Washington Park Futurity.
- 3RD — Belmont Futurity.

AT 3 YEARS
- WON — Kentucky Derby, Wood Memorial, Preakness Stakes, Withers Stakes, Belmont Stakes.

Owners who have won the only Derby in which they have had a starter have been: William Astor (1876), T. J. Nichols (1878), J. S. Shawhan (1880), James B. Haggin (1886), Labold Brothers (1887), Chicago Stable (1888), Jacobin Stable (1891), Cushing and Orth (1893), Leigh and Rose (1894), Byron McClellan (1895), M. F. Dwyer (1896), A. H. & D. H. Morris (1899), F. B. Van Meter (1901), Mrs. C. F. Durnell (1904), J. Hal Woodford (1907), C. E. Hamilton (1908), H. C. Hallenbeck (1912), H. C. Applegate (1914), John Sanford (1916), Billings and Johnson (1917), Major Ral Parr (1920), Mrs. R. M. Hoots (1924), H. P. Gardner (1929), Morton L. Schwartz (1936), Glen Riddle Farms (1937), and Fred W. Hooper (1945).

Twenty-six owners have seen their racing colors carried to victory in the only Kentucky Derby in which they were represented. Twenty-five of the twenty-six started only one horse. The other owner, Major Ral Parr, started an entry of Paul Jones and Blazes in the 1920 renewal. Paul Jones won and Blazes was sixth.

Mrs. John D. Hertz has started horses in the Kentucky Derby twice and has won each time. Her first Derby horse was Reigh Count, winner in 1928 over the largest field that ever went to the post in this racing classic.

On March 24, 1940, the best son of the 1928 Derby winner was foaled at Mrs. Hertz's Stoner Creek Farm in Bourbon County, Kentucky. He was the second foal of Quickly, by Haste. The brown colt came to the races as Count Fleet in 1942. During his two-year-old season Count Fleet won ten of his fifteen starts and $76,245. Occupation was named the two-year-old champion of the year because of his greater money-winnings, but practically all horsemen believed the son of Reigh Count to be the better horse.

In his first season of racing Count Fleet had established a new record for two-year-olds at one mile. He ran that distance in 1:34 4/5. It was no surprise that he was quoted at odds of 5-to-2 in the winter books, dropping to 1-to-2 Derby week.

Like his sire Count Fleet was sent to the post as favorite, but at a much shorter price. He was held at 40 cents to $1, the shortest price on any Derby horse since Bimelech. To ride Count Fleet the owner picked English-born Jockey Johnny Longden, who had been unplaced in his two previous efforts in the Derby.

The winner led from start to finish, winning by three lengths, which was about as close as any horse got to him in his six starts at three. Count Fleet was retired following his victory in the Belmont Stakes, which made him the sixth Triple Crown winner in America. Count Fleet also was the fourth Derby winner sired by a Derby winner.

153

1944

Throughout the spring of 1944 America and the rest of the world were tense, alert, and waiting. Men, equipment, and supplies overran England as the Allies prepared for D-Day.

Finally, it came on June 6 as the American, British, and Canadian forces poured across the English channel into France. The drive toward Berlin from the west had started. The Americans entered Germany September 12. By October 4 the American forces had broken through the Germans' west wall. Each day Americans grabbed their newspapers to see how much farther General George Patton's men of the Third Army had driven.

Then came December 16 and the Germans' counter-offensive in Belgium, and the Battle of the Bulge in which the Germans were finally halted after nine days with the help of a 7,000-plane raid. In the Pacific, American forces landed on the Admiralty Islands, then Guam, then Palau, the Philippines, and on the day the Germans began their counter-offensive the Americans were on Mindoro, 150 miles from Manila.

At home it was another election year. In April, Wendell Willkie, who had opposed Roosevelt in 1940, withdrew from the race. On June 28 the Republican party named Thomas E. Dewey, Governor of New York, as its candidate. A month later Roosevelt and Senator Harry S. Truman were selected as the Democratic ticket.

Hartford, Connecticut, was the scene of a horrible tragedy on July 6 when 152 persons died and 250 others were injured in a circus fire. This also was the year that the federal government seized the Montgomery Ward and Company in Chicago as the result of a strike.

It was in 1944 that the Kentucky Dam, another unit in TVA, was completed on the Tennessee River in Kentucky, creating a fisherman's paradise. A view of the dam, one of the country's largest, is shown below.

Pedigree

PENSIVE
(Chestnut colt)

- Hyperion
  - Gainsborough
    - Bayardo
    - *Rosedrop
  - Selene
    - Chaucer
    - Serenissima
- *Penicuik II
  - Buchan
    - Sunstar
    - Hamoaze
  - Pennycomequick
    - Hurry On
    - Plymstock

Pensive

Tabulated Racing Record

Year	Age	Sts.	1st	2nd	3rd	Won
1943	2	5	2	0	2	$ 5,490
1944	3	17	5	5	2	162,225
		22	7	5	4	$167,715

70th Kentucky Derby, May 6, 1944

$75,000 added and $5,000 Gold Cup. 3-year-olds. Weight for age. Net value to winner $64,675; second $8,000; third $3,000; fourth $1,000. Trainer awards: First $3,000; second $2,000; third $1,000. Breeder awards: First $2,000; second $1,000; third $500.

Horse	Eqt	Wt	PP	St	½	¾	1	Str	Fin	Jockey	Owner	Odds $1 Str't
Pensive	w	126	4	4	13¹	10ʰ	5½	3½	1⁴½	McCreary	Calumet Farm	7.10
Broadcloth	wb	126	9	7	3½	3²	1½	1ʰ	2¹	Woolf	Mrs G Poulsen	7.40
Stir Up	wb	126	5	5	4¹½	4¹	2²	2ʰ	3ʰ	Arcaro	Greentree Stable	1.40
Shut Up	wb	126	10	12	14³	13¹½	7½	5²	4ʰ	Eccard	Erlanger Stable	†7.70
Brief Sigh	wb	126	13	3	9½	8½	3½	4¹½	5¾	Nodarse	River Divide Farm	†7.70
Gay Bit	w	126	7	16	16	16	16	6¹½	6¹	Westrope	Bobanet Stable	25.80
Bell Buzzer	wb	126	3	15	15¹	15³	13²	9²	7¹½	Thompson	D Ferguson	†7.70
Gr'ps Image	wb	126	14	10	11¹	12½	9²	8ʰ	8⁴	Grohs	Mrs A J Abe	20.00
Skytracer	wb	126	2	1	7½	6ʰ	6½	7½	9²	Caffarella	M B Goff	8.40
Chal'nge Me	wb	126	1	2	6¹½	7½	10³	10⁵	10½	W Garner	Brolite Farm	8.90
Alorter	wb	126	6	6	5ʰ	5ʰ	11²	11⁴	11⁵	Adams	A C Ernst	19.50
Comenow	wb	126	16	11	2¹	2¹½	4½	12¹¹½	12²	Layton	Philip Godfrey	†7.70
Val'y Flares	wb	126	11	14	8½	11¹½	12¹	13²	13²	Burns	B R Patno	†7.70
Diavolaw	wb	126	12	9	1¹	1½	8½	14½	14¹	Molbert	W C Hobson	†7.70
Rock'd Boy	wb	126	8	8	10¹	9ʰ	14¹½	15¹½	15⁵	Bailey	W C Davis	†7.70
Amer. Eagle	wb	126	15	13	12²	14²	15⁴	16	16	Higley	J V Maggio	†7.70

†Mutuel field.

Time, :12, :23-3/5, :35, :47-1/5, 1:12-2/5 1:25, 1:38-1/5, 1:51-2/5, 2:04-1/5. Track good.

$2 Mutuels Paid—Pensive, $16.20 straight, $7.20 place, $4.60 show; Broadcloth, $6.80 place, $4.60 show; Stir Up, $3.00 show.

Winner—Ch.c. by Hyperion—*Penicuik II, by Buchan, trained by B. A. Jones; bred by Calumet Farm.

Went to Post—5:17. Off at 5:19½. Central War Time.

Start good from stall gate. Won ridden out; second and third driving. Pensive worked his way forward on the outside, was sent to the inside when the leaders swung wide approaching the stretch, came willingly when put to strong pressure, wore down the leaders swiftly and won drawing away. Broadcloth took command after three-quarters, was unable to draw clear and failed to withstand the winner. Stir Up moved forward with Broadcloth, was forced to lose some ground when challenging for the lead. Shut Up worked his way forward through the field and closed with a rush. Brief Sigh tired in the drive.

Scratched—Peace Bells, 121; Autocrat, 126; Comanche Peak, 126.

Pensive   Stakes Races

AT 2 YEARS
- **3RD** Champagne Stakes, Oden Bowie Stakes.
- **UNP** Belmont Futurity.

AT 3 YEARS
- **WON** Kentucky Derby, Rowe Memorial Handicap, Preakness Stakes.
- **2ND** Bowie Handicap, Chesapeake Stakes, Belmont Stakes.
- **3RD** Classic Stakes.
- **UNP** Stars and Stripes Handicap, Skokie Handicap, Dick Welles Handicap, American Derby, Washington Park Handicap.

The American Turf lost its "First Lady" in the death of Mrs. Helen Hay Whitney on September 24, 1944. Between 1922 and 1944 her Greentree Stable horses had started in eight runnings of the Derby, had won two.

The history of the 1944 Kentucky Derby winner was something of a parallel to that of the 1934 winner. *Hastily had been bred to *Lancegaye in England, imported to this country while she was carrying the 1934 winner who was foaled in New Jersey.

In 1940 Arthur B. Hancock, owner of Claiborne Farm in Kentucky, received a cablegram from England's Lord Astor, who offered three mares for sale. One of the mares was *Penicuik II, by Buchan. Part of the Englishman's offer was that one of the mares could be bred to the English Derby winner Hyperion.

Breeder Hancock bought the mares, directed that *Penicuik II be bred to Hyperion. After the mares arrived at Claiborne Farm, Owner Warren Wright became interested in *Penicuik II, whom he purchased from Hancock late in 1940. The following February at Calumet Farm *Penicuik II foaled a chestnut colt.

The colt was Pensive, who became the second Derby winner in the Calumet silks and the second winner of that race bred by Wright. It was from Hancock that Wright had purchased the mare that produced his first Derby winner, Whirlaway. The latter, like Pensive, was a son of a winner of the English Derby.

For Trainer Ben A. Jones, Pensive was his third winner of the Kentucky Derby and placed him within striking distance of the record of H. J. "Derby Dick" Thompson, who had saddled four winners of the race. Calumet Farm possessed such an outstanding collection of fine Thoroughbred stock that horsemen believed it only a matter of a few years before Jones would equal Thompson's mark.

The 1944 Derby marked the first time that Jones had won a Derby without the help of Jockey Eddie Arcaro. The rider, was under contract to Greentree Stable which started Stir Up. When the stable of Colonel E. R. Bradley was at its peak, the Derby axiom was, "When in doubt, bet on Bradley." Racing fans felt the same way about Arcaro and in the 1944 Derby they made Greentree's Stir Up favorite. He was a contender throughout, but finished third.

1945

The date, May 7; the time 2:41 A.M., French time. Although war still existed with Japan, American cities celebrated Germany's surrender with demonstrations such as the one shown below.

Americans felt that the conflict with Japan could not last much longer, but they were not aware that the United States had such a weapon as the atomic bomb, left above, which was dropped on Hiroshima on August 5. A trial bomb had been tested in New Mexico on July 16.

Four days later another atom bomb was dropped, on Nagasaki, and on August 14 Japan accepted America's surrender terms. World War II was over.

It was also in 1945 that an Army bomber crashed into the Empire State Building.

Franklin Delano Roosevelt, the only man ever to be elected President of the United States four times, died suddenly at Warm Springs, Georgia, on April 12. The tremendous problems of a nation in depression, then in war, had taken their toll. At 3:35 that afternoon Harry S. Truman, upper right, was inaugurated as the thirty-second President.

Less than a month after President Roosevelt's death Germany surrendered.

Pedigree

HOOP JR.
(Bay colt)

- *Sir Gallahad III
  - *Teddy
    - Ajax
    - Rondeau
  - Plucky Liege
    - Spearmint
    - Concertina
- One Hour
  - *Snob II
    - Prestige
    - May Dora
  - Daylight Saving
    - *Star Shoot
    - Tea Enough

Tabulated Racing Record

Year	Age	Sts.	1st	2nd	3rd	Won
1944	2	5	2	3	0	$ 5,300
1945	3	4	2	1	0	93,990
		9	4	4	0	$ 99,290

71st Kentucky Derby, June 9, 1945

Hoop Jr.

$75,000 added and $5,000 Gold Cup. 3-year-olds. Weight for age. Net value to winner $64,850; second $8,000; third $3,000; fourth $1,000. Trainers awards: First $3,000; second $2,000; third $1,000. Breeders' awards: First $2,000; second $1,000; third $500.

Horse	Eqt	Wt	PP	St	¼	½	¾	Str	Fin	Jockey	Owner	Odds $1 Str't
Hoop Jr	w	126	12	2	1¹	1¹	1¹	1⁶	1⁶	Arcaro	F W Hooper	3.70
Pot O'Luck	w	126	7	15	14½	10½	8²	5²	2¾	Dodson	Calumet Farm	3.30
D'by Dieppe	w	126	9	16	12ʰᵈ	9¹	6½	3½	3ⁿᵏ	Calvert	Mrs W G Lewis	5.60
Air Sailor	w	126	5	5	5½	5²	3⁴	4²	4⁴	Haas	T D Buhl	20.90
Jeep	wb	126	3	6	7½	7½	5ʰ	6⁴	5³	Kirkland	C V Whitney	6.80†
Bymeabond	wb	126	10	1	2½	2³	2½	2ʰ	6³	F A Smith	J K Houssels	†6.80
Sea Swallow	wb	126	2	3	6½	8½	10³	7½	7½	Woolf	Mrs C S Howard	†6.80
Fighting Step	w	126	13	11	4²	4¹	4¹	8¹	8½	South	Murlogg Farm	19.80
Burn'g Dream	w	126	6	7	10½	11½	11⁴	9⁴	9²	Snider	E R Bradley	15.80
Alexis	w	126	11	4	3½	3½	7½	11⁶	10½	Scawth'n	Christiana Stables	12.20
Foreign Ag't	wb	126	4	9	9¹	6ʰᵈ	9½	10½	11⁵	Knott	Lookout Stock Farm	25.90
Misweet	w	121	1	8	8ʰ	13¹	13¹	13⁴	12⁵	Craig	A Rose	†6.80
Tiger Rebel	w	126	8	10	11¹	12⁴	12⁵	12ʰᵈ	13½	Layton	Brent & Talbot	†6.80
Bert G	wb	126	14	14	15⁴	15¹⁵	15²⁰	14¹	14¹⁰	Summers	T L Graham	‡†6.80
Jacobe	wb	126	15	12	13½	14⁴	14⁴	15²⁰	15⁸	Lindberg	A R Wright	†6.80
Kenilw'th L'd	wb	126	16	13	16	16	16	16	16	Weid'm'n	T L Graham	‡†6.80

†Mutuel field. ‡Coupled, Bert G. and Kenilworth Lad.

Time, :23-1/5, :48, 1:14, 1:41, 2:07. Track muddy.

$2 Mutuels Paid—Hoop Jr., $9.40 straight, $5.20 place, $4.00 show; Pot O' Luck, $4.80 place, $3.60 show; Darby Dieppe, $4.00 show.

Winner—B.c. by *Sir Gallahad III.—One Hour, by *Snob II, trained by I. H. Parke; bred by R. A. Fairbairn.

Went to Post—6:17. Off at 6:22.

Start good from stall gate. Won easily; second and third driving. Hoop Jr., away well, opened up a clear advantage in the first three-sixteenths-mile, was taken in hand to make the pace under a steadying hold to the stretch, responded with much energy when called upon and won with something left. Pot O' Luck, away slowly, started up after reaching the final five furlongs, lost ground on the final turn but cut to the inside while closing fast and overtook Air Sailor and Darby Dieppe in swift succession near the end. Darby Dieppe bettered his position gradually from a sluggish start but weakened suddenly near the end. Air Sailor went forwardly placed on the outside from the start, rallied only mildly and also faltered in the late stages. Jeep, always clear as he raced wide, did not respond when called upon. Bymeabond, taken to the inside early, forced the early pace in hand, made a bold bid on the stretch turn but gave way steadily in the last quarter-mile. Sea Swallow had no mishap. Fighting Step weakened after racing well to the final quarter-mile and swerved in the last furlong. Burning Dream raced wide and never threatened. Alexis, kept up under pressure, flattened out badly before going a mile. Foreign Agent dropped out of contention on the second turn.

Hoop Jr.

Stakes Races

AT 2 YEARS — **2ND** — Bowie Kindergarten Stakes, Aberdeen Stakes, Pimlico Nursery Stakes.

AT 3 YEARS
- **WON** — Kentucky Derby, Wood Memorial Stakes.
- **2ND** — Preakness Stakes.

Hoop Jr.'s racing career was halted after the Preakness. He came out of that race, after finishing second, with a bowed tendon and was retired to the stud. At two, he had not been too sound, which accounted for his starting in only five races. From his nine starts he was unplaced in only one race.

157

Practically all the great race riders of America had ridden in the Kentucky Derby since its first running in 1875. Many of them retired from the saddle without having won the Kentucky Derby—the goal of all.

When the Negro Isaac Murphy won the Derby for the third time in 1891, Turfmen acknowledged that was a feat which would become increasingly difficult to duplicate. By 1929 six riders had won the race twice. Each had tried desperately to win the third time and at least equal Murphy's record.

It was thirty-nine years after Murphy had won his third Derby that Sande, who believed he had retired permanently a few years earlier, came back to the races and won his third Derby with Gallant Fox. Murphy's feat had been equaled at last, but horsemen believed it would be even more than thirty-nine years before it would be done again.

Eddie Arcaro and Ben A. Jones had combined as a jockey-trainer combination to score their first two Derby victories. But in 1944 Jones pulled ahead with his third win when Conn McCreary rode Pensive to victory, beating Arcaro on Stir Up.

Arcaro, not to be outdone, turned the tables on Jones in the 1945 Kentucky Derby in which he rode Fred W. Hooper's Hoop Jr., to victory, beating Calumet Farms' Pot o' Luck, trained by Jones. The score was again even. Arcaro had ridden his third winner, eleven years after he rode in his first Derby.

Owner Hooper had purchased Hoop Jr., for $10,200 when he was a yearling. He was the first yearling ever purchased by the owner, who commented after the Derby, "I never thought that I'd make it so quick." Hoop Jr., was the second Derby winner bred by R. A. Fairbairn, who had sold Gallahadion for $5,000 as a yearling. Both were sons of Sir Gallahad III.

Trainer of the 1945 winner was Ivan Parke, who came out of Idaho as a rider in 1922 and the following year was the leading jockey of the country, his accomplishments of that year including five winners at Latonia on October 16.

 It was in late 1946 that the United Nations accepted the Rockefeller gift of a permanent headquarters site in New York City. Above, Secretary of State James F. Byrnes is shown addressing the U. N. Security Council at Hunter College.

The world was at peace, but labor and capital in this country were not. Something like four and one-half million people were involved in strikes, and on May 15 President Truman seized the nation's railroads.

John L. Lewis led his United Mine Workers back to the American Federation of Labor. Lewis figured in the news again later in the year when Judge Goldsborough put him on trial for contempt of court for refusing to call off the coal strike. The "Humming Bird", lower right, made its first run into Louisville.

The Philippines were granted independence on July 4. Two months later the President fired Henry Wallace from his cabinet. Later Wallace headed the Progressive Party as its presidential candidate in 1948.

Many national and world-wide figures died during the year. They included the writers Damon Runyon and Booth Tark-

ington, the former heavyweight champion Jack Johnson, Roosevelt's aide Harry Hopkins, the actor George Arliss, the jurist Harlan Fiske Stone, the financier Henry Morganthau, the great baseball pitcher Walter Johnson, Barney Oldfield, James J. Walker, William S. Hart, and others.

In the 1946 elections a Republican victory gave the party control of the Senate and House.

A technical legal question arose during the year when a seventeen-year-old boy, sentenced to die, survived the throwing of the switch when he was strapped in the electric chair. The question arose as to whether the state had the right to attempt another electrocution.

Three inmates and two guards were killed in a rebellion at Alcatraz prison.

Pedigree

ASSAULT (Chestnut colt)	Bold Venture	*St. Germans	Swynford
			Hamoaze
		Possible	Ultimus
			Lida Flush
	Igual	Equipoise	Pennant
			Swinging
		Incandescent	*Chicle
			Masda

Tabulated Racing Record

Year	Age	Sts.	1st	2nd	3rd	Won
1945	2	9	2	2	1	$ 17,250
1946	3	15	8	2	3	424,195
1947	4	7	5	1	1	181,925
1948	5	2	1	0	0	3,250
		33	16	5	5	$626,620

72nd Kentucky Derby, May 4, 1946

Assault

100,000 added and $5,000 Gold Cup. 3-year-olds. Weight for age. Net value to winner 96,400; second $10,000; third $5,000; fourth $2,500. Trainers' awards: First $3,000; second 2,000; third $1,000. Breeders' awards: First $2,000; second $1,000; third $500.

orse	Eqt	Wt	PP	St	½	¾	1	Str	Fin	Jockey	Owner	Odds $1 Str't
ssault	wb	126	2	3	$5\frac{1}{2}$	4^{hd}	$3\frac{1}{2}$	$1^{2\frac{1}{2}}$	1^{8}	Mehrtens	King Ranch	8.20
py Song	w	126	6	2	1^{2}	$1\frac{1}{2}$	$1\frac{1}{2}$	2^{2}	2^{hd}	Longden	Dixiana	7.80
ampden	wb	126	17	14	6^{1}	5^{hd}	$4^{2\frac{1}{2}}$	5^{2}	3^{1}	Jessop	Foxcatcher Farm	5.80
ord Boswell	w	126	3	1	$9\frac{1}{2}$	$7\frac{1}{2}$	$9^{1\frac{1}{2}}$	$3\frac{1}{2}$	$4^{1\frac{1}{2}}$	Arcaro	Maine Chance Farm	‡1.10
nockdown	w	126	11	4	$2\frac{1}{2}$	$2\frac{1}{2}$	$2^{1\frac{1}{2}}$	$4\frac{1}{2}$	5^{4}	Permane	Maine Chance Farm	‡1.10
lamond	wb	126	7	8	$11\frac{1}{2}$	$8\frac{1}{2}$	11^{2}	6^{1}	6^{1}	Kirkland	A C Ernst	65.30
ob Murphy	wb	126	13	16	$13\frac{1}{2}$	$11\frac{1}{2}$	6^{2}	$7\frac{1}{2}$	$7\frac{1}{2}$	Bodiou	D Ferguson	†31.80
ellicle	wb	126	8	11	12^{2}	$9\frac{1}{2}$	8^{hd}	8^{hd}	$8^{1\frac{1}{2}}$	Hettinger	H P Headley	16.10
erf't Bahram	w	126	5	12	15^{3}	13^{2}	$10\frac{1}{2}$	$11\frac{1}{2}$	$9\frac{1}{2}$	Atkinson	Maine Chance Farm	‡1.10
ippey	w	126	14	7	4^{hd}	6^{1}	5^{hd}	9^{1}	10^{1}	Zufelt	W Helis	10.20
obar	w	126	16	17	17	17	16^{4}	16^{4}	$11^{1\frac{1}{2}}$	Layton	H W Fielding	†31.80
ark Jungle	wb	126	12	6	$3^{1\frac{1}{2}}$	3^{hd}	$7\frac{1}{2}$	$10\frac{1}{2}$	12^{2}	LoTurco	Lucas B Combs	60.70
lworth	wb	126	4	10	10^{1}	12^{1}	13^{hd}	13^{3}	$13\frac{1}{2}$	Scurlock	Mrs R D Patterson	†31.80
Vith Pl'sure	wb	126	10	9	$7\frac{1}{2}$	10^{1}	14^{2}	14^{2}	$14^{1\frac{1}{2}}$	Wahler	Brolite Farm	48.30
'rine V't'ry	wb	126	15	15	14^{1}	14^{3}	15^{3}	$15\frac{1}{2}$	15^{1}	Padgett	Bobanet Stable	45.00
Vee Admir'l	wb	126	9	5	$8^{1\frac{1}{2}}$	16^{1}	$12\frac{1}{2}$	12^{2}	16^{3}	Watson	R S McLaughlin	59.40
endor	wb	126	1	13	16^{6}	15^{1}	17	17	17	Johnson	Mrs D Hollingsworth	†31.80

Coupled, Lord Boswell, Knockdown and Perfect Bahram. †Mutuel field.

ime, :12, :23-2/5, :35-2/5, :48, 1:01-1/5, 1:14-1/5, 1:27-2/5, 1:40-4/5, 1:53-3/5, :06-3/5. Track slow.

$2 Mutuels Paid—Assault, $18.40 straight, $9.60 place, $6.80 show; Spy Song, $9.00 place, 6.60 show; Hampden, $5.20 show.

Vinner—Ch.c. by Bold Venture—Igual, by Equipoise, trained by M. Hirsch; bred by King Ranch. Vent to Post—5:17. Off at 5:20 Central Daylight Time.

Start good from stall gate. Won driving; second and third the same. Assault, forwardly placed nd saving ground from the beginning, came through on the inside entering the stretch, quickly lisposed of Spy Song and drew out to win with little left. Spy Song assumed command early, nade the pace until reaching the stretch, then gave way to the winner, but continued resolutely o hold Hampden. The latter, on the extreme outside at the beginning, raced in the middle of he track the entire trip, was pulled up sharply when his rider misjudged the finish, then came gain when roused, but could not better his position. Lord Boswell, in hand for six furlongs, vas blocked near the upper turn, came again when clear, but could not overhaul the leaders vhen hard ridden through the stretch. Knockdown forced the pace to the mile, then gave way.

Assault Stakes Races

AT 2 YEARS	WON	Flash Stakes.
	3RD	Babylon Handicap.
	UNP	East View Stakes, Cowdin Stakes.
AT 3 YEARS	WON	Kentucky Derby, Experimental Free Handicap, Wood Memorial Stakes, Preakness Stakes, Belmont Stakes, Dwyer Stakes, Pimlico Special, Westchester Handicap.
	2ND	Jersey Handicap, Roamer Handicap.
	3RD	Discovery Handicap, Manhattan Handicap, Gallant Fox Handicap.
	UNP	Derby Trial, Arlington Classic.
AT 4 YEARS	WON	Grey Lag Handicap, Dixie Handicap, Suburban Handicap, Brooklyn Handicap, Butler Handicap.
	2ND	Belmont Special.
	3RD	Belmont Gold Cup.
AT 5 YEARS	UNP	Widener Handicap.

Assault is the only winner of the Kentucky Derby that was foaled in the biggest state of the Union. He came from the largest ranch in that state, the 970,000-acre King Ranch at Kingsville, Texas.

In 1939 Robert J. Kleberg had purchased the 1936 Derby winner Bold Venture from Morton L. Schwartz for $40,000 and moved him to King Ranch. The sire made his first season at the Texas ranch in 1940. Among broodmares bred to him in 1942 was Igual, a daughter of Equipoise.

Igual had never been off the King Ranch. She was a sickly foal and for a while her owners considered destroying her. However, the ranch veterinarian brought her around, but she was not trained for racing. Instead, she was bred as a two-year-old. Assault was her third foal and inherited some of her misfortune. As a yearling he stepped on a nail, which resulted in his having a malformed frog in one of his front feet.

Assault was trained by another native Texan. Max Hirsch's career with racing had started in that state as a jockey in quarter horse racing. His career as a trainer began in 1897. Assault was the fifth Derby winner by a Derby winner and Trainer Hirsch became the third trainer to win with a father and son. H. J. Thompson had been the first, saddling both Bubbling Over and Burgoo King. James Fitzsimmons was the second, winning with Gallant Fox and Omaha.

A confident Dixiana trainer, Jack Hodgins, had told newspapermen on the morning of the Derby, "They're going to have to catch my horse this afternoon." When the numbers had been hung up for the finish, he declared, "Well, he caught me." It had been Dixiana's Spy Song that went to the front almost immediately after the start and held his lead until the stretch where he gave way to the winner.

Assault's money-winnings as a three-year-old surpassed any amount that had ever been won by any horse in a single season. The previous record had been set by Gallant Fox the year he won the Kentucky Derby.

Colonel E. R. Bradley, the only man to win the Kentucky Derby four times, died August 15.

"Is this call an emergency?" was one of the most frequently asked questions of 1947. It started April 7 when 300,000 telephone workers, including operators, went out on strike in forty-two states. A coal miners' walkout was averted during the year, first when John L. Lewis called off the strike set for April 1, and again on July 7 when his United Mine Workers gained a pay boost of forty-four and one-half cents per hour. It was that union's biggest pay boost in history.

In Buffalo, New York, 2,400 school teachers went out on strike. This was the largest of this kind ever experienced. Eighty schools were closed.

Biggest tragedy of the year was the Texas City, Texas, disaster. On April 16 the nitrate ship Grandcamp blew up in the Texas City harbor, killing 468 persons and causing more than $50,000,000 in property damage. Below is a picture showing a portion of the devastated city. The burning of the Ohio River steamer Island Queen at Pittsburgh struck a deep note of sorrow throughout the Ohio valley. This famous river steamer, shown

upper right, had long been the Queen of the Ohio.

Andrew J. Volstead, author of the bill which brought prohibition to the United States, and Al Capone, who rose to power and wealth as a direct result of it, both died during 1947. Man o' War also died during the year

Georgia started the year with two Governors. That office was claimed by Herman Talmadge, elected by the General Assembly. The election was called illegal by Retiring Governor Arnall, who refused to yield the office. On March 19 the State's Supreme Court ruled against Talmadge.

Pedigree

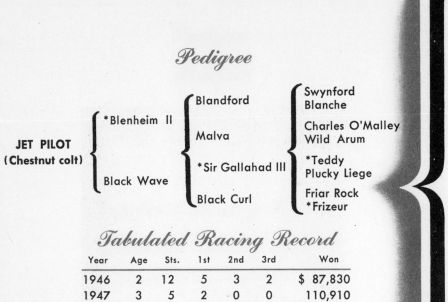

			Swynford
		Blandford	Blanche
	*Blenheim II		
JET PILOT		Malva	Charles O'Malley
(Chestnut colt)			Wild Arum
		*Sir Gallahad III	*Teddy
	Black Wave		Plucky Liege
		Black Curl	Friar Rock
			*Frizeur

Tabulated Racing Record

Year	Age	Sts.	1st	2nd	3rd	Won
1946	2	12	5	3	2	$ 87,830
1947	3	5	2	0	0	110,910
		17	7	3	2	$198,740

Jet Pilot

73rd Kentucky Derby, May 3, 1947

$100,460 added and $5,000 Gold Cup. 3-year-olds. Weight for age. Net value to winner $92,160; second $10,000; third $5,000; fourth $2,500. Trainers' awards: First $3,000; second $2,000; third $1,000. Breeders' awards: First $2,000; second $1,000; third $500.

Horse	Eqt	Wt	PP	St	½	¾	1	Str	Fin	Jockey	Owner	Odds $1 Str't
Jet Pilot	w	126	13	1	1¹⁄₂	1¹	1¹⁄₂	1¹⁄₂	1ʰ	Guerin	Maine Chance Farm	5.40
Phalanx	wb	126	8	13	13	10²	5¹⁄₂	5¹⁄₂	2ʰ	Arcaro	C V Whitney	2.00
Faultless	w	126	3	2	6²¹⁄₂	6¹¹⁄₂	4¹⁄₂	3ʰ	3¹	Dodson	Calumet Farm	6.30
On Trust	wb	126	9	5	2ʰ	2¹	3¹	2ʰ	4²¹⁄₄	Longden	E O Stice & Sons	6.70
Cosmic B'mb	wb	126	1	4	3¹⁄₂	3¹¹⁄₂	6²¹⁄₂	6¹⁄₂	5²	Clark	W Helis	31.90
Star Reward	w	126	5	3	5¹	4ʰ	2ʰ	4¹	6¹	Brooks	Dixiana	11.20
Bullet Proof	w	126	4	6	9ʰ	7¹⁄₂	7³	7⁵	7⁵	Wright	Mrs M E Whitney	13.10
W L Sickle	wb	126	7	11	8²	8¹⁄₂	8ʰ	8¹⁄₂	8ʰ	Campbell	W-L Ranch	‡16.50
Stepfather	wb	126	6	9	12¹	9¹	9³	9²	9⁶	Westrope	W-L Ranch	‡16.50
Liberty Road	wb	126	12	10	10¹	11¹	11⁵	10¹	10¹⁄₂	Jessop	Brookmeade Stable	45.20
Riskolater	wb	126	10	12	11¹	12¹⁄₂	10⁵	11⁶	11⁶	Balz'etti	Circle M Farm	15.00
Double Jay	wb	126	2	7	4³	5¹⁄₂	12⁶	12⁶	12¹⁵	Gilbert	Ridgewood Stable	47.30
Jett-Jett	w	126	11	8	7ʰ	13	13	13	13	Hanka	W M Peavey	†99.40

‡Coupled, W. L. Sickle and Stepfather. †Mutuel field.

Time, :12-1/5, :24, :36, :49, 1:01-2/5, 1:14-2/5, 1:27-1/5, 1:40-2/5, 1:53, 2:06-4/5. Track slow.

$2 Mutuels Paid—Jet Pilot, $12.80 straight, $5.20 place, $4.00 show; Phalanx, $4.00 place, $3.00 show; Faultless $4.60 show.

Winner—Ch.c. by *Blenheim II—Black Wave, by *Sir Gallahad III., trained by Tom Smith; bred by A. B. Hancock & Mrs. R. A. Van Clief.

Went to Post—4:47½. Off at 4:50½. Central Standard Time.

Start good from stall gate. Won driving; second and third the same. Jet Pilot, alertly handled, assumed command at once, made the pace to the stretch under good rating and, responding readily when hard ridden in the drive, lasted to withstand Phalanx. The latter, away very sluggishly and outrun during the first half mile, worked his way forward steadily thereafter and, taken out for the stretch run, finished fast and was getting to the winner at the end. Faultless, never far back and steadied along to the stretch, responded readily when set down in the drive, then closed strongly in a sharp effort. On Trust, forwardly placed from the beginning and in a good effort, failed to rally when roused for the drive and faltered near the finish. Cosmic Bomb a sharp factor early, engaged Jet Pilot for five furlongs, then weakened. Star Reward made a good bid approaching the stretch, then gave way. Bullet Proof went evenly and had no mishap. W L Sickle was never prominent. Stepfather, away slowly, was never a serious factor. Liberty Road was far back the entire trip. Riskolater was off sluggishly and was never a serious factor. Double Jay had brief speed and pulled up sore. Jett-Jett unseated his rider at the post, ran off a quarter and showed nothing in the running.

Scratched—(22173) Balheim, 126.

Jet Pilot — Stakes Races

AT 2 YEARS	WON	Pimlico Nursery Stakes, National Stallion Stakes, Tremont Stakes, Pimlico Futurity.
	2ND	Arlington Futurity, Commonwealth Stakes.
	3RD	Futurity Stakes, Champagne Stakes.
	UNP	Hyde Park Stakes, Sagamore Stakes.
AT 3 YEARS	WON	Kentucky Derby, Jamaica Handicap.
	UNP	Withers Stakes, Preakness Stakes, San Felipe Stakes.

Two days prior to the running of the 1946 Kentucky Derby one of the worst fires in racing's history destroyed twenty-two two-year-olds owned by Maine Chance Farm at a Chicago track. The youngsters had cost their owner $282,700 as yearlings the preceding summer.

Newspaper stories said the only two-year-olds of Maine Chance Farm that were not lost were War Fan and "Jet Plane." These two had been shipped to Churchill Downs along with Lord Boswell, Perfect Bahram, and Knockdown who made up the Maine Chance Farm entry in the 1946 Derby.

Actually, it was War Fan and Jet Pilot that had been sent along with the Derby candidates. The latter was started at Churchill Downs on Derby Day and galloped home an easy winner in the first race of his career.

The son of *Blenheim II and Black Wave started eleven more times in his two-year-old season, winning four more races and $87,830 which was more than double the $41,000 he had cost his owner as a yearling. Jet Pilot made another trip to Churchill Downs.

He came back in the spring of 1947 to start in the Kentucky Derby, meeting C. V. Whitney's Phalanx, Calumet Farm's Faultless and ten others in the mile and one-quarter classic. Winner in California and New York before he came to Kentucky, Jet Pilot was second choice to Phalanx in the mutuels.

The finish of that Derby was one of the most thrilling in the long history of the race.

Jockey Eric Guerin hand rode the winner to the wire to stave off the rush of Phalanx on the outside and Faultless in the middle. It was the first time in Derby history that the placing judges had ever found it necessary to look at a photograph of the finish before naming the winner.

Co-breeder of Jet Pilot was Arthur B. Hancock who also was closely identified with the second and third horses. Phalanx was out of Jacola, a daughter of La France that had produced the Derby winner Johnstown at Hancock's farm. Faultless was a son of Unerring by Insco, who was a son of *Sir Gallahad III of the Hancock Nursery.

1948

No year in America's political history was quite equal in surprise to 1948. Not even 1916 and its Wilson-Hughes political race compares with what happened in 1948.

The Republicans went into convention with Senator Taft of Ohio, Governor Thomas E. Dewey of New York, former Governor Harold Stassen of Minnesota, and Senator Arthur Vandenberg of Michigan all considered potential nominees for the Presidency. It was Dewey who was chosen early with Governor Earl Warren of California as his running mate. The Republicans left Philadelphia confident of victory.

A powerful portion of the Democratic party was attempting to draft General Ike Eisenhower, who had already been selected to head Columbia University. From the start Truman had chosen to fight, and predicted he would be the party's candidate.

He was, with Kentucky's distinguished Senator Alben W. Barkley as his running mate. The Dixiecrats walked out of the Democratic convention, and later held their own.

President Truman came away from Philadelphia, confident he would be returned to the White House. Many of his own party didn't think he would. The polls showed he wouldn't. But the one man who was right was Harry S. Truman, who will be President of United States in his own right when the Diamond Jubilee Kentucky Derby is run.

American flyers recorded an outstanding accomplishment in the successful operation of the Berlin air lift. The Olympic Games were resumed when England was host to the event. The United States mourned the passing of its greatest baseball figure, Babe Ruth.

Louisville, the business section of which is shown below, was a much greater city in the year of the Diamond Jubilee Derby, than it was the afternoon in 1875 when Aristides won.

Pedigree

CITATION
(Bay colt)

- Bull Lea
  - *Bull Dog
    - *Teddy
    - Plucky Liege
  - Rose Leaves
    - Ballot
    - *Colonial
- *Hydroplane II
  - Hyperion
    - Gainsborough
    - Selene
  - Toboggan
    - Hurry On
    - Glacier

Tabulated Racing Record

Year	Age	Sts.	1st	2nd	3rd	Won
1947	2	9	8	1	0	$155,680
1948	3	20	19	1	0	709,470
		29	27	2	0	$865,150

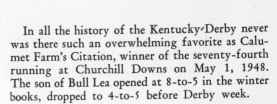

74th Kentucky Derby, May 1, 1948

Citation

$100,000 added and $5,000 Gold Cup. 3-year-olds. Weight-for-age. Net value to winner $83,400; second $10,000; third $5,000; fourth $2,500. Trainer awards: First $3,000; second $2,000; third $1,000. Breeder awards: First $2,000; second $1,000; third $500.

Horse	Eqt	Wt	PP	St	½	¾	1	Str	Fin	Jockey	Owner	Odds $1 Str't
Citation	w	126	1	2	2^h	2^3	2^5	1^2	$1^{3\frac{1}{2}}$	E Arcaro	Calumet Farm	a-.40
Coaltown	wb	126	2	1	1^6	$1^{3\frac{1}{2}}$	$1^{\frac{1}{2}}$	2^4	2^3	N L Pierson	Calumet Farm	a-.40
My Request	w	126	6	3	4^h	4^3	$3^{1\frac{1}{2}}$	3^1	$3^{1\frac{1}{2}}$	D Dodson	B F Whitaker	3.80
Billings	w	126	5	6	$5^{\frac{1}{2}}$	$3^{\frac{1}{2}}$	4^8	4^{15}	4^{20}	M Peterson	Walmac Stable	14.70
Grandpere	w	126	4	4	3^2	6	6	$5^{\frac{1}{2}}$	5^{nk}	J Gilbert	Mrs J P Adams	17.80
Escadru	wb	126	3	5	6	5^6	$5^{1\frac{1}{2}}$	6	6	A Kirkland	W L Brann	7.10

a-Citation and Coaltown coupled as Calumet Farm entry.
Time, :12-1/5, :23-2/5, :34-3/5, :46-3/5, :59-1/5, 1:11-2/5, 1:24-3/5, 1:38, 1:51-2/5, 2:05-2/5. Track sloppy.

$2 Mutuels Paid—Calumet Farm entry (Citation and Coaltown), $2.80 straight. No place or show betting.
Winner—B.c. by Bull Lea—*Hydroplane II, by Hyperion, trained by B. A. Jones; bred by Calumet Farm.
Went to Post—4:32. Off at 4:32-1/2.

Start good from stall gate. Won handily; second and third driving. Citation, away forwardly, and losing ground while racing back of Coaltown to the stretch, responded readily to a steady hand ride after disposing of the latter and drew clear. Coaltown began fast, established a clear lead before going a quarter and, making the pace on the inside in the stretch, continued willingly, but was not good enough for Citation, although easily the best of the others. My Request, bothered slightly after the start, was in hand while improving his position to the stretch, then failed to rally when set down for the drive. Billings suffered interference after the break when Grandpere bore to the outside, was in close quarters on the first turn when caught between Escadru and Citation, then could not better his position when clear. Grandpere broke into Billings at the start, displayed speed for a half mile, then gave way. Escadru, forced to take up when in close quarters entering the backstretch, could not reach serious contention thereafter and tired badly after going three-quarters of a mile.

Scratched—Galedo.

Citation   Stakes Races

AT 2 YEARS

WON — Elementary Stakes, Futurity Stakes, Pimlico Futurity.

2ND — Washington Park Futurity.

AT 3 YEARS

WON — Kentucky Derby, Derby Trial, Seminole Handicap, Everglades Handicap, Flamingo Stakes, Chesapeake Stakes, Preakness Stakes, Jersey Stakes, Belmont Stakes, Stars and Bars Handicap, American Derby, Sysonby Mile, Jockey Club Gold Cup, Pimlico Special, Tanforan Handicap.

2ND — Chesapeake Stakes.

Citation, 1948 Derby winner, was foaled at Calumet Farm on April 11, 1945. His dam, *Hydroplane, had been imported from England during the war. She was shipped to the United States by way of Australia to avoid the Nazi submarines. Citation's sire, Bull Lea, was eighth in the 1938 Kentucky Derby. In 1947 he became the first American horse to sire the winners of more than $1,000,000. In addition to Citation his outstanding racers of that season included Bewitch, champion two-year-old filly, and Armed, champion of the handicap division.

In all the history of the Kentucky Derby never was there such an overwhelming favorite as Calumet Farm's Citation, winner of the seventy-fourth running at Churchill Downs on May 1, 1948. The son of Bull Lea opened at 8-to-5 in the winter books, dropped to 4-to-5 before Derby week.

Early in the 1948 season Citation was being hailed as an even greater race horse than Man o' War. From Florida's racing scene came stories that E. O. Stice, of California, had offered Owner Warren Wright $250,000 for the colt. The offer failed to arouse any interest. There were numerous horsemen who thought the son of Bull Lea a bargain at twice that amout. Before the colt had finished his two-year-old season breeders had approached Wright seeking to breed mares to Citation when his racing days were over.

Citation's greatness had been established during the summer of his two-year-old season when he and his stablemates, including Bewitch and Free America, made a show of all other horses of that age. On one occasion in Chicago a trainer was reported to have remarked to Trainer Jones about the short odds on a Calumet entry including Citation. The price was 4-to-5.

"Short odds? Why, Citation ought to be 8-to-5 right now to win the Kentucky Derby next year," was the reply attributed to the trainer of the Calumet horses.

Jones and Eddie Arcaro, who had won their first Derby with Woolford Farm's Lawrin ten years earlier, each won his fourth Derby with Citation. To Arcaro it gave the distinction of having ridden more winners of the race than any other jockey. To Jones it gave the honor of equalling the record of H. J. Thompson, and to Owner Wright went the record of having bred and owned three winners. Only Colonel E. R. Bradley had bred and owned more winners, and the Turf wondered how much time the Wright-Jones combination would require to surpass the record established by the Bradley-Thompson team.

Horsemen agreed Arcaro might easily ride another winner before he retires.

DATA SECTION

WINNING HORSES

Agile	1905	Johnstown	1939
Alan-A-Dale	1902	Judge Himes	1903
Apollo	1882	Kingman	1891
Aristides	1875	Lawrin	1938
Assault	1946	Leonatus	1883
Azra	1892	Lieut. Gibson	1900
Baden-Baden	1877	Lookout	1893
Behave Yourself	1921	Lord Murphy	1879
Ben Ali	1886	Macbeth II	1888
Ben Brush	1896	Manuel	1899
Black Gold	1924	Meridian	1911
Bold Venture	1936	Montrose	1887
Brokers Tip	1933	Morvich	1922
Bubbling Over	1926	Old Rosebud	1914
Buchanan	1884	Omaha	1935
Burgoo King	1932	*Omar Khayyam	1917
Cavalcade	1934	Paul Jones	1920
Chant	1894	Pensive	1944
Citation	1948	Pink Star	1907
Clyde Van Dusen	1929	Plaudit	1898
Count Fleet	1943	Regret	1915
Day Star	1878	Reigh Count	1928
Donau	1910	Riley	1890
Donerail	1913	Shut Out	1942
Elwood	1904	Sir Barton	1919
Exterminator	1918	Sir Huon	1906
Flying Ebony	1925	Spokane	1889
Fonso	1880	Stone Street	1908
Gallahadion	1940	Twenty Grand	1931
Gallant Fox	1930	Typhoon II	1897
George Smith	1916	Vagrant	1876
Halma	1895	War Admiral	1937
Hindoo	1881	Whirlaway	1941
His Eminence	1901	Whiskery	1927
Hoop Jr.	1945	Wintergreen	1909
Jet Pilot	1947	Worth	1912
Joe Cotton	1885	Zev	1923

OWNERS OF WINNERS

H. C. Applegate 1914
Noah Armstrong 1889
Wm. Astor 1876
Bashford Manor 1892
   (G. J. Long)
Belair Stud 1930-1935-1939
   (Wm. Woodward)
Billings & Johnson 1917
Ben Block 1922
E. R. Bradley 1921-1932-1933
   (See Idle Hour Stock Farm)
Brookmeade Stable 1934
   (Mrs. Isabel Dodge Sloane)
S. S. Brown 1905
J. C. Cahn 1897
Calumet Farm 1941-1944-1948
   (Warren Wright)
R. F. Carman 1911
Chicago Stable 1888
   (Hankins & Johnson)
Chinn & Morgan 1883
G. A. Cochran 1925
Edward Corrigan 1890
W. Cottrill 1884
Cushing & Orth 1893
Geo. W. Darden & Co. 1879
Mrs. C. E. Durnell 1904
Dwyer Bros. (M.F. & P.J.) 1881
M. F. ("Mike") Dwyer 1896
C. R. Ellison 1903
H. P. Gardner 1929
Wm. Gerst 1910
Glen Riddle Farm Stable 1937
   (Samuel D. Riddle)
Greentree Stable 1931-1942
   (Mrs. Payne Whitney)
Jas. B. Haggin 1886
H. C. Hallenbeck 1912
C. E. Hamilton 1908
T. P. Hayes 1913

Mrs. John D. Hertz 1928-1943
Fred W. Hooper 1945
Mrs. R. M. Hoots 1924
Idle Hour Farm 1926
   (E. R. Bradley)
Jacobin Stable 1891
W. S. Kilmer 1918
King Ranch 1946
   (Robert J. Kleberg)
Labold Bros. 1887
Leigh & Rose 1894
George J. Long 1906
   (See Bashford Manor)
John E. Madden 1898
Maine Chance Farm 1947
   (Mrs. Elizabeth Graham)
Milky Way Farm 1940
   (Mrs. Ethel V. Mars)
Byron McClelland 1895
T. C. McDowell 1902
H. P. McGrath 1875
A. H. & D. H. Morris 1899
Morris & Patton 1882
T. J. Nichols 1878
Ral Parr 1920
Rancocas Stable 1923
   (H. F. Sinclair)
J. B. Respess 1909
J. K. L. Ross 1919
John Sanford 1916
M. L. Schwartz 1936
J. S. Shawhan 1880
Chas. H. Smith 1900
Daniel Swigert 1877
F. B. VanMeter 1901
H. P. Whitney 1915-1927
J. T. Williams 1885
J. Hal Woodford 1907
Woolford Farm 1938
   (Herbert J. Woolf)

COLONEL E. R. BRADLEY, left, owner of four winners is shown with COLONEL WINN.

BREEDERS OF WINNERS

A. J. Alexander
.......1877-1880-1885-1894-1901
F. W. Armstrong 1934
Noah Armstrong 1899
Baker & Gentry 1900
Belair Stud 1930-1935
  (William Woodward)
E. R. Bradley (Idle Hour
  Stock Farm) 1921
E. R. Bradley & H. N. Davis........1932
Calumet Farm 1941-1944-1948
  (Warren Wright)
J. N. Camden 1903
J. T. Carter 1879
Chinn & Forsythe 1916
Clay & Woodford 1896
E. F. Clay 1905
J. M. Clay 1878
Cottrill & Guest 1884
C. H. Durkee 1890
Eastin & Larrabie 1895
John B. Ewing 1897
R. A. Fairbairn 1940-1945
A. C. Franklin 1891
H. P. Gardner 1929
Greentree Stable 1931-1942
  (Mrs. Payne Whitney)
J. B. Haggin 1908
A. B. Hancock 1939
A. B. Hancock and
  Mrs. R. A. Van Clief 1947
C. L. Harrison 1911

T. P. Hayes 1913
Mrs. John D. Hertz 1943
Mrs. R. M. Hoots 1924
Idle Hour Stock Farm 1926-1933
  (E. R. Bradley)
Willis Sharpe Kilmer 1928
King Ranch 1946
  (R. J. Kleberg)
F. D. Knight 1918
Rufus Lisle 1888
George J. Long 1892-1899-1906
Madden & Gooch 1919
John E. Madden...1914-1920-1923-1925
T. C. McDowell 1902
H. P. McGrath 1875
John Henry Miller 1883
Dr. J. D. Neet 1898
R. H. McC. Potter 1912
Mrs. J. B. Prather 1904
J. B. Respess 1909
Samuel D. Riddle (Glen
  Riddle Farm Stable) 1937
Sir John Robinson (of England)....1917
M. H. Sanford 1876
M. L. Schwartz 1936
Scoggan Bros. 1893
A. B. Spreckels 1922
Daniel Swigert 1881-1882-1886
H. P. Whitney 1915-1927
J. Hal Woodford 1907
Herbert Woolf 1938
Milton Young 1887-1910

JOHN E. MADDEN

A. J. ALEXANDER

WINNING JOCKEYS

E. Arcaro	1938-1941-1945-1948	J. Loftus	1916-1919
G. Archibald	1911	J. Longden	1943
C. Bierman	1940	J. Martin	1905
J. Boland	1900	L. McAtee	1927-1929
H. Booker	1903	J. McCabe	1914
C. Borel	1917	C. McCreary	1944
J. Carter	1878	J. McLaughlin	1881
A. Clayton	1892	D. Meade	1933
G. Covington	1888	W. Mehrtens	1946
W. Donohue	1883	A. Minder	1907
P. Duffy	1886	J. D. Mooney	1924
F. Garner	1897	I. Murphy	1884-1890-1891
M. Garner	1934	J. Notter	1915
F. Goodale	1894	J. ("Soup") Perkins	1895
R. Goose	1913	A. Pickens	1908
E. Guerin	1947	V. Powers	1909
I. Hanford	1936	F. Prior	1904
E. Henderson	1885	T. Rice	1920
F. Herbert	1910	E. Sande	1923-1925-1930
Babe Hurd	1882	W. Saunders	1935
E. James	1932	C. Shauer	1879
A. Johnson	1922-1926	C. H. Shilling	1912
T. Kiley	1889	Willie Simms	1896-1898
W. Knapp	1918	J. Stout	1939
E. Kunze	1893	R. Swim	1876
C. Kurtsinger	1931-1937	Fred Taral	1899
C. Lang	1928	C. Thompson	1921
G. Lewis	1880	R. Troxler	1906
I. Lewis	1887	W. Walker	1877
O. Lewis	1875	J. Winkfield	1901-1902
		W. D. Wright	1942

EARL SANDE

EDDIE ARCARO

ISAAC MURPHY

TRAINERS OF WINNERS

Dud Allen	1891	C. Mack	1909
A. Anderson	1875	John E. Madden	1898
H. G. Bedwell	1919	J. P. Mayberry	1903
Wm. Bird	1884	Byron McClelland	1895
Ed. Brown	1877	Henry McDaniel	1918
Fred Burlew	1922	Wm. McDaniel	1893
J. C. Cahn	1897	T. C. McDowell	1902
G. D. ("Don") Cameron	1943	John McGinty	1887
John Campbell	1888	B. S. Michell	1928
Hardy Campbell	1896	Green B. Morris	1882
R. Colston	1883	John H. Morris	1892
George Conway	1937	Jim Murphy	1886
Edward Corrigan	1890	C. T. Patterson	1917
Peter Coyne	1906	Lee Paul	1878
W. B. Duke	1925	Ivan H. Parke	1945
C. E. Durnell	1904	Alex Perry	1885
A. Ewing	1911	Geo. Rice	1879
Jas. Fitzsimmons	1930-1935-1939	John Rodegap	1889
W. H. Fizer	1907	James Rowe, Jr.	1931
Wm. Garth	1920	James Rowe, Sr.	1881-1915
John M. Gaver	1942	Robt. A. Smith	1934
J. Hall	1908	Tom Smith	1947
Geo. Ham	1910	Frank M. Taylor	1912
T. P. Hayes	1913	H. J. Thompson	1921-1926-1932-1933
Max Hirsch	1936-1946	Robt. Tucker	1905
Fred Hopkins	1927	Clyde Van Dusen	1929
Chas. H. Hughes	1900	F. B. VanMeter	1901
Hollie Hughes	1916	Robt. J. Walden	1899
Tice Hutsell	1880	Roy Waldron	1940
Ben A. Jones	1938-1941-1944-1948	Hanly Webb	1924
D. J. Leary	1923	F. D. Weir	1914
Eugene Leigh	1894	Jas. Williams	1876

BEN A. JONES   H. J. THOMPSON

SIRES OF WINNERS

°Australian 1877
Black Toney 1924-1933
°Blenheim II 1941-1947
Bob Miles 1899
Bold Venture 1946
Bramble 1896
Broomstick 1911-1915
Bubbling Over 1932
°Buckden 1884
Bull Lea 1948
Dick Welles 1909
Duke of Montrose 1887
Equipoise 1942
°Esher 1903
Falsetto 1894-1901-1906
Free Knight 1904
Gallant Fox 1935
°Glengary 1891
G. W. Johnson 1900
Halma 1902
Hanover 1895
Himyar 1898
Hyder Ali 1889
Hyperion (England) 1944
Insco 1938
Jamestown 1939
King Alfonso 1880-1885
°Knight of the Thistle 1912
°Lancegaye 1934
°Leamington 1875
Lever 1882
Longfellow 1883-1890
Longstreet 1908
Macduff 1888
Man o' War 1929-1937
Marathon 1921
Marco (England) 1917
°McGee 1913-1918
°North Star III 1926
°Out of Reach 1916
Pat Malloy 1879
Pink Coat 1907
Reform 1892
Reigh Count 1943
Runnymede 1922
°Sea King 1920
Sir Dixon 1905
°Sir Gallahad III....1930-1940-1945
°St. Germans 1931-1936
Star Davis 1878
°Star Shoot 1919
°Sunreigh 1928
The Finn 1923-1925
°Top Gallant 1897
Troubadour 1893
Uncle 1914
Virgil 1876-1881-1886
Whisk Broom II 1927
°Woolsthorpe 1910

NOTE:—Runnymede, sire of Morvich, is
not the horse of same name which ran in
1882 Derby.

FALSETTO

*SIR GALLAHAD III

KENTUCKY DERBY STARTERS

HORSE	FINISHED	YEAR	HORSE	FINISHED	YEAR	HORSE	FINISHED	YEAR
Abe Frank	4th	1902	Ben Machree	18th	1929	Brokers Tip	1st	1933
Acabado	15th	1917	Berlin	14th	1917	Bronzewing	3rd	1914
Ada Glenn	unp	1879	Bernard F.	18th	1937	Brother Joe	19th	1932
Admiral	unp	1884	Bersagliere	9th	1920	Bubbling Over	1st	1926
Adobe Post	11th	1932	Bersan	2nd	1885	Buchanan	1st	1884
Agile	1st	1905	Bert G.	14th	1945	Buckeye Poet	13th	1930
Agrarian	3rd	1934	Bet Mosie	2nd	1922	Buck McCann	unp	1893
Air Sailor	4th	1945	Better Luck	13th	1923	Buckner	unp	1879
Alamond	6th	1946	Bewithus	14th	1927	Buddy Bauer	6th	1927
Alan-a-Dale	1st	1902	Bien Joli	5th	1936	Bullet Proof	7th	1947
Alard Scheck	unp	1901	Bill Bruce	7th	1875	Bullion	unp	1876
Al Boyer	unp	1894	Bill Herron	7th	1908	Bull Lea	8th	1938
Alcibiades	10th	1930	Billings	4th	1948	Burgundy	unp	1878
Alexandria	unp	1888	Billionaire	20th	1937	Burning Dream	9th	1945
Alexis	10th	1945	Bill Letcher	2nd	1890	Burning Star	8th	1937
Alfambra	3rd	1881	Billy Kelly	2nd	1919	Burnt Cork	10th	1943
Almadel	13th	1925	Bimelech	2nd	1940	Burgoo King	1st	1932
Alorter	11th	1944	Blackbirder	5th	1935	†Busy American		1922
Alsab	2nd	1942	Black Gold	1st	1924	By Golly	7th	1920
Altawood	4th	1924	Black Panther	10th	1927	By Gosh	9th	1922
Alworth	13th	1946	Black Servant	2nd	1921	Bymeabond	6th	1945
Amber Light	4th	1943	Blackwood	9th	1928	Calcutta	17th	1923
American Eagle	8th	1918	Blazes	6th	1920	Calf Roper	11th	1929
American Eagle	16th	1944	Blondin	9th	1926	Calycanthus	unp	1881
Amur	unp	1901	Bluebeard	14th	1935	Campeon	9th	1909
Anchors Aweigh	10th	1931	Blue Larkspur	4th	1929	Cannon Shot	12th	1924
Apache	11th	1942	Blue Pair	7th	1941	Canter	8th	1926
Apollo	1st	1882	Blue Swords	2nd	1943	Can't Wait	3rd	1938
Aristides	1st	1875	Blue Wing	2nd	1886	Captain Hal	2nd	1925
Ascender	unp	1883	Bobashela	8th	1928	Careful	5th	1921
Ascension	10th	1875	Bob Cook	unp	1884	Cartago	17th	1928
Aspiration	8th	1923	Bob Miles	unp	1884	Cathop	16th	1932
Assault	1st	1946	Bob Murphy	7th	1946	Cassius	unp	1889
Audrain	3rd	1884	Bobtail	19th	1924	Cavalcade	1st	1934
Autocrat	unp	1888	Bob Wooley	4th	1875	Cee Tee	15th	1932
Azra	1st	1892	Bold Venture	1st	1936	Challedon	2nd	1939
Babcock	unp	1882	Bombay	unp	1876	Challenge Me	10th	1944
Backbone	14th	1925	Bo McMillan	12th	1923	Champ De Mars	12th	1926
Baden-Baden	1st	1877	Bon Homme	9th	1921	Chant	1st	1894
Bad News	4th	1903	Bonivan	18th	1928	Charley O.	3rd	1933
Baffling	17th	1924	Booker Bill	16th	1915	Charlie Bush	unp	1878
Bagenbaggage	2nd	1926	Boola Boola	4th	1910	Charmarten	19th	1928
Balgowan	2nd	1891	Boon Companion	10th	1925	Chatter	unp	1883
Banridge	5th	1908	Bootmaker	unp	1889	Cherry Pie	20th	1923
Banburg	unp	1887	Boot and Spur	15th	1942	Chesapeake	8th	1875
Bancroft	3rd	1880	Boreas	unp	1884	Chicatie	14th	1929
Bankrupt	5th	1943	Bostonian	5th	1927	Chief Uncas	20th	1925
Ban Yan	unp	1887	Boulevard	unp	1880	Chilhowee	2nd	1924
Bar None	12th	1928	Boundless	3rd	1893	Chip	19th	1929
Basso	2nd	1895	Bourbon	3rd	1903	Chittagong	5th	1923
Bay Beauty	13th	1929	Boxthorn	16th	1935	Citation	1st	1948
**Baywood Colt	6th	1875	Boys Howdy	5th	1931	Clarion	unp	1887
Bazaar	9th	1934	Bracadale	5th	1924	Clay Pate	unp	1885
Beau Butler	3rd	1924	Brancas	3rd	1904	Cleopatra	15th	1920
Be Frank	6th	1919	Brandon Mint	4th	1932	Clodion	10th	1937
Behave Yourself	1st	1921	Breezing Thru	12th	1930	Clyde Van Dusen	1st	1929
Bell Buzzer	7th	1944	Brevity	2nd	1936	Coaltown	2nd	1948
Ben Ali	1st	1886	Brief Sigh	5th	1944	Cold Check	10th	1932
Ben Brown	unp	1897	Bright Tomorrow	10th	1923	Coldstream	4th	1936
Ben Brush	1st	1896	Broadcloth	2nd	1944	Col. Hogan	7th	1911
Ben Eder	2nd	1896	Broadway Jones	11th	1925	Colston	3rd	1911
Bengal	3rd	1882	Broadway Limited	9th	1930	Col. Zeb Ward	unp	1888

HORSE	FINISHED	YEAR	HORSE	FINISHED	YEAR	HORSE	FINISHED	YEAR
Come Now	12th	1944	Escoba	2nd	1918	Han d'Or	4th	1898
Commonwealth	10th	1935	Espino	6th	1926	Harrodsburg	unp	1886
Corsini	2nd	1899	Essare	16th	1929	Harry Gilmore	unp	1882
Cosmic Bomb	5th	1947	Eternal	10th	1919	Harry Hill	3rd	1876
Co-Sport	7th	1938	Exploit	unp	1884	Hart Wallace	4th	1891
Count Fleet	1st	1943	Exterminator	1st	1918	Headlight	unp	1877
Court Scandal	9th	1937	Fair Call	7th	1942	Head Play	2nd	1933
Coyne	6th	1921	Fairy Hill	11th	1937	Heather Broom	3rd	1939
Crack Brigade	5th	1930	Fairy Manah	13th	1942	He Did	7th	1936
Creedmoor	2nd	1876	Falsetto	2nd	1879	Heelfly	6th	1937
Crystal Prince	12th	1932	Faultless	3rd	1947	Herron	11th	1920
Cudgel	11th	1917	Favor	unp	1885	High Foot	14th	1930
Curator	4th	1895	Fencing	17th	1937	Highflyer	unp	1882
Damask	4th	1920	Fighting Bob	3rd	1910	Highland Lad	unp	1900
Dan K.	unp	1877	Fighting Fox	6th	1938	High Tariff	3rd	1891
Darby Dieppe	3rd	1945	Fighting Step	8th	1945	Himyar	2nd	1878
Dark Jungle	12th	1946	First Fiddle	5th	1942	Hindoo	1st	1881
Dark Winter	11th	1933	First Mate	unp	1896	Hindoocraft	unp	1889
Dauber	2nd	1938	Flamma	3rd	1912	Hindus	unp	1900
David Harum	4th	1920	Florizar	2nd	1900	His Eminence	1st	1901
Day Star	1st	1878	Flying Ebony	1st	1925	His Excellency	unp	1900
Deadlock	4th	1922	Folking	8th	1929	His Lordship	unp	1899
Debar	5th	1906	Fonso	1st	1880	Hodge	2nd	1914
Dellor	7th	1937	Foreign Agent	11th	1945	Holl Image	6th	1936
Devil Diver	6th	1942	For Fair	9th	1915	Hollywood	9th	1942
Diavolaw	14th	1944	Foundation	4th	1913	Hoop Jr.	1st	1945
Dick O'Hara	15th	1930	Fountainebleu	unp	1899	Hoops	9th	1932
Diogenes	14th	1924	Frank Bird	8th	1908	Huron	2nd	1892
Direct	6th	1909	Franklin	3rd	1916	Hydromel	4th	1927
Discovery	2nd	1934	Fred, Jr.	8th	1927	Hyperion II	4th	1906
Display	10th	1926	Free Knight	3rd	1886	Indian Broom	3rd	1936
Dispose	6th	1941	Free Lance	4th	1912	Inlander	9th	1933
Distraction	13th	1928	Friend Harry	5th	1909	In Memoriam	11th	1923
Dit	3rd	1940	Frogtown	11th	1919	Insco	6th	1931
Dodge	4th	1916	Gallahadion	1st	1940	Inventor	2nd	1902
Dogpatch	8th	1942	Gallant Fox	1st	1930	Irish Pat	unp	1885
Dominant	7th	1916	Gallant Knight	2nd	1930	Isabey	3rd	1898
Donau	1st	1910	Gallant Pirate	7th	1910	Isaiah	12th	1933
Donerail	1st	1913	Gallant Sir	8th	1932	Jack Denman	5th	1911
Donnacona	5th	1920	Gallifet	2nd	1888	Jack Higgins	4th	1928
Don Q.	7th	1928	Gay Bit	6th	1944	Jacobe	15th	1945
Dortch	8th	1915	General Pike	unp	1879	Jacobin	3rd	1887
Double Eagle	7th	1915	Gen'l Thatcher	16th	1923	James Reddick	3rd	1906
Double Joy	12th	1947	George Smith	1st	1916	James T. Clark	6th	1918
Dove Pie	7th	1943	Germantown	unp	1876	Jeep	5th	1945
Drake Carter	2nd	1883	Getaway	unp	1881	Jet Pilot	1st	1947
Dr. Barkley	3rd	1909	Gold Mine	15th	1875	Jett-Jett	13th	1947
Dr. Catlett	3rd	1897	Gold Seeker	9th	1936	Jim Gore	2nd	1887
Driscoll	3rd	1901	Gold Shower	8th	1943	Jim Gray	unp	1886
Dr. Shepard	unp	1897	Goldcrest Boy	12th	1915	Jimmie Gill	7th	1913
Dunvegan	3rd	1908	Golden Rule	19th	1923	Jobar	11th	1946
Duval	2nd	1912	Gone Away	4th	1930	Jock	3rd	1927
Earl of Beaconsfield	unp	1878	†Good Advice		1933	Joe Cotton	1st	1885
Early	2nd	1903	Goshen	unp	1897	Joe Morris	2nd	1910
Early Light	unp	1877	Governor Gray	2nd	1911	John Finn	3rd	1922
Economic	2nd	1932	Gowell	3rd	1913	John Furlong	6th	1910
Ed Crump	10th	1915	Gramps Image	8th	1944	John Gund	4th	1914
Ed Tierney	2nd	1904	Grandpere	5th	1948	Johnstown	1st	1939
El Chico	6th	1939	Grand Slam	12th	1936	Karl Eitel	9th	1929
Elector	16th	1925	†Granville		1936	Kendor	17th	1946
Elooto	9th	1938	Green Jones	12th	1917	Kenilworth Lad	16th	1945
Elwood	1st	1904	Grey Gold	14th	1937	Kentucky Cardinal	9th	1925
Emerson Cochran	5th	1915	Grimaldi	unp	1886	Kentucky Farmer	unp	1900
††Enquirer's Colt	10th	1875	Guaranola	5th	1912	Keokuk	unp	1885
Enchantment	6th	1923	Guy Fortune	8th	1917	Kerry Patch	7th	1933
Enlister	11th	1875	Halma	1st	1895	Kiev	11th	1927
Escadru	6th	1948	Hampden	3rd	1946	Kilkerry	11th	1930

HORSE	FINISHED	YEAR	HORSE	FINISHED	YEAR	HORSE	FINISHED	YEAR
Kimball	2nd	1880	Melodist	4th	1937	Paul Jones	1st	1920
King Gorin II	11th	1924	Menow	4th	1938	Peace Chance	5th	1934
Kingman	1st	1891	Meridian	1st	1911	Peace Pennant	16th	1920
King William	3rd	1877	Merry Maker	12th	1937	Pearl Song	2nd	1894
Kinney	8th	1916	Merry Pete	10th	1936	Pebbles	2nd	1915
Klondyke	9th	1924	Miami	2nd	1909	Pellicle	8th	1946
Knockdown	5th	1946	Michael Angelo	7th	1909	Pendennis	unp	1887
Ladder	9th	1931	Midway	3rd	1917	Pensive	1st	1944
Lady Navarre	2nd	1906	Milford	6th	1908	Perfect Bahram	9th	1946
Ladysman	4th	1933	Military	15th	1937	Petee-Wrack	14th	1928
Lafitte	unp	1886	Minotaur	12th	1929	Phalanx	2nd	1947
Laureate	3rd	1895	Mioland	4th	1940	Phil Dwyer	3rd	1892
Lawley	6th	1928	Mistral	unp	1882	Picketer	15th	1923
Lawrin	1st	1938	Mirage	unp	1893	Pictor	8th	1940
Layson	3rd	1905	Misstep	2nd	1928	Pike's Pride	unp	1883
Leamingtonian	unp	1876	Misweet	12th	1945	Pink Star	1st	1907
Lee O. Cotner	18th	1925	Modest	13th	1924	Pittsburgher	7th	1931
Lelex	2nd	1881	Modest Lad	9th	1943	Planet	10th	1921
Lena Misha	9th	1916	Monogram	unp	1882	Plat Eye	8th	1935
Leochares	8th	1913	Montrose	1st	1887	Plaudit	1st	1898
Leonard	2nd	1877	Morpluck	7th	1935	Playfair	unp	1885
Leonardo II	7th	1921	Morvich	1st	1922	Plutus	2nd	1893
Leo Ray	6th	1915	Mountain Ridge	10th	1938	Pompey	5th	1926
Leonatus	1st	1883	Mr. Khayyam	8th	1933	Pomponius	5th	1933
Letterman	6th	1922	Mr. Mutt	16th	1924	Pompoon	2nd	1937
Leveler	3rd	1878	Mud Sill	4th	1911	Porter's Cap	4th	1941
†Liberty Limited		1932	Muskallonge	12th	1921	Pot o'Luck	2nd	1945
Liberty Road	10th	1947	My Play	5th	1922	Powhattan III	unp	1884
Lieber Karl	2nd	1898	My Request	3rd	1948	Pravus	21st	1923
Lieut. Gibson	1st	1900	Naishapur	2nd	1929	Prince d'Amour	12th	1931
Light Carbine	7th	1926	Nassau	4th	1923	Prince Fonso	unp	1890
Lijero	unp	1886	Nautical	15th	1924	Prince Hotspur	14th	1932
Linger	unp	1893	Ned O.	3rd	1930	Prince K	9th	1923
Lisbon	unp	1877	Needle Gun	8th	1925	Prince of Bourbon	5th	1925
Little Beans	5th	1941	Nellie Flag	4th	1935	Prince Pal	13th	1920
Little String	11th	1915	Newsboy	unp	1882	Prince Pat	20th	1929
Loftin	2nd	1884	Norse King	15th	1915	Prince Silverwings	4th	1904
Longus	6th	1930	No Sir	13th	1937	Proctor Knott	2nd	1889
Lookout	1st	1893	No Wrinkles	6th	1943	Proceeds	5th	1904
Lord Boswell	4th	1946	Odd Fellow	unp	1877	Prudery	3rd	1921
Lord Braedalbane	17th	1929	Old Ben	5th	1914	Psychic Bid	6th	1935
Lord Coleridge	unp	1885	Old Rosebud	1st	1914	Quasimodo	13th	1934
Lord Marshall	6th	1913	Omaha	1st	1935	Quito	unp	1880
Lord Murphy	1st	1879	Omar Khayyam	1st	1917	Quatrain	12th	1925
Lord Raglan	3rd	1883	Once Again	3rd	1889	Ram's Horn	2nd	1905
Lost Cause	unp	1882	One Dime	unp	1879	Reaping Reward	3rd	1937
Lucky B	5th	1918	†On Location		1939	Recollection	11th	1926
Lucky Tom	17th	1932	On Trust	4th	1947	Redcoat	unp	1876
McCarthy	9th	1935	On Watch	3rd	1920	Red Gauntlet	4th	1907
McCreery	12th	1875	Orlandwick	6th	1907	Regalo	9th	1919
McHenry	unp	1878	Ornament	2nd	1897	Regret	1st	1915
McWhirter	unp	1877	Oscillation	13th	1932	Reigh Count	1st	1928
Mad Play	10th	1924	Osmand	2nd	1927	Reigh Olga	5th	1928
Macbeth II	1st	1888	Our Boots	8th	1941	Revenue Agent	7th	1924
Malvern	unp	1877	Our Fancy	7th	1932	Replevin	16th	1928
Manister Toi	6th	1917	Outbound	unp	1889	Requested	14th	1942
Manuel	1st	1899	Outlook	unp	1890	Respard	unp	1878
Marie Michon	unp	1876	Ovelando	3rd	1907	Rhinock	4th	1926
Marine Victory	15th	1946	Overtime	5th	1932	Rialto	7th	1923
Market Wise	3rd	1941	Palisade	unp	1890	Rickety	4th	1917
Martie Flynn	10th	1928	Panchio	3rd	1929	Riley	1st	1890
Martingale	2nd	1923	Paraphrase	21st	1929	Rippey	10th	1946
Mate	3rd	1931	Parole	unp	1876	Rip Rap	13th	1927
Mata Hari	4th	1934	Parson	unp	1896	Riskolater	11th	1945
Match Me	10th	1909	Patches	10th	1920	Robert Bruce	unp	1882
Masterpiece	unp	1886	††Pat Malloy's Colt	unp	1882	Robert Morris	9th	1941
Mazo	3rd	1899	Paul Bunyan	15th	1929	Robespierre	3rd	1890

HORSE	FINISHED	YEAR	HORSE	FINISHED	YEAR	HORSE	FINISHED	YEAR
Rock Man	3rd	1926	Star Voter	11th	1921	Tutticurio	15th	1935
Rockwood Boy	15th	1944	St. Bernard	8th	1919	Twenty Grand	1st	1931
Rolled Stocking	12th	1927	St. Bernard	17th	1935	Typhoon	15th	1928
Roman	6th	1940	Sterling	17th	1920	Typhoon II	1st	1897
Roman Soldier	2nd	1935	Step Along	5th	1925	Ulysses	unp	1896
Round the World	6th	1911	Stepenfetchit	3rd	1932	Uncle Bryn	13th	1915
Royal II	4th	1915	Stepfather	9th	1947	Uncle Luther	7th	1930
Royal Julian	7th	1927	Stir Up	3rd	1944	Uncle Velo	8th	1921
Royal Man	7th	1940	Stone Street	1st	1908	Under Fire	3rd	1919
Roycrofter	13th	1926	Strathmore	3rd	1879	Upset	2nd	1920
Runnymede	2nd	1882	Strideaway	10th	1933	Upset Lad	10th	1929
Sailor	7th	1919	Strolling Player	22nd	1928	Vagabond	14th	1875
Sandy Beal	12th	1920	Sun Beau	11th	1928	Vagrant	1st	1876
Sangreal	13th	1936	Sun Fairplay	11th	1935	Valdina Orphan	3rd	1942
Sannazarro	2nd	1901	Sunset Trail II	16th	1937	Valdina Paul	10th	1941
Scapa Flow	9th	1927	Surf Board	11th	1931	Valley Flares	13th	1944
Sceneshifter	5th	1937	Surf Rider	7th	1922	Velours	6th	1906
Searcher	9th	1875	Surprising	6th	1914	Vera Cruz	unp	1877
Sea Swallow	7th	1945	Swain	11th	1941	Verdigris	3rd	1875
Semper Ego	3rd	1896	Sweep All	2nd	1931	Vigil	3rd	1923
Sennings Park	5th	1919	Sweeping Away	15th	1925	Vindex	12th	1919
Sewell Combs	7th	1918	Sweep Swinger	10th	1942	Viscounty	4th	1939
Sgt. Byrne	11th	1934	Swope	6th	1925	Vito	20th	1928
Sharpshooter	4th	1915	Synchronized	4th	1908	Viva America	3rd	1918
Shut Out	1st	1942	Tannery	8th	1930	Volcano	2nd	1875
Shut Up	4th	1944	Technician	5th	1939	Voltaic	19th	1925
Sigurd	3rd	1894	Ten Booker	3rd	1885	Voltear	6th	1929
Singing Wood	8th	1934	Ten Broeck	5th	1875	Vulcanite	4th	1919
Single Foot	4th	1925	Ten Point	2nd	1913	Wallansee	unp	1882
Sir Barton	1st	1919	Tetan	14th	1915	War Admiral	1st	1937
Sir Catesby	4th	1909	Teufel	8th	1936	War Cloud	4th	1918
Sir Cleges	2nd	1908	The Bat	17th	1925	War Eagle	15th	1927
Sir Damion	19th	1937	The Chevalier	unp	1888	Warfield	8th	1909
Sir Huon	1st	1906	The Chief	5th	1938	Warsaw	13th	1875
Sir Joseph	unp	1886	The Clown	18th	1923	War Star	5th	1917
Sirocco	5th	1940	The Cock	6th	1916	Watermelon	7th	1914
Sir Thomas	12th	1934	The Dragon	unp	1896	Wee Admiral	16th	1946
Sir War	12th	1942	The Fighter	11th	1936	Wendover	unp	1882
Skeptic	7th	1917	The Mongol	8th	1931	Weston	18th	1935
Skytracer	9th	1944	The Nut	7th	1929	Wheelwright	7th	1912
Slide Rule	3rd	1943	The Rival	3rd	1902	Whirlaway	1st	1941
Sligo	unp	1881	The Winner	unp	1896	Whiskery	1st	1927
Solicitor	unp	1878	Thistle	unp	1885	Whiskolo	3rd	1935
Sonada	6th	1912	Thistle Ace	18th	1932	White	3rd	1888
Son of John	3rd	1925	Thorndale	8th	1924	Whopper	13th	1935
Sortie	21st	1928	Thrive	3rd	1900	Wida	14th	1923
Spanish Play	4th	1931	Thunderer	5th	1916	Wildair	8th	1920
Speedmore	10th	1934	Ticket	2nd	1917	Wild Aster	18th	1924
Spicson	6th	1933	Tick On	6th	1932	Windy City	5th	1929
Spokane	1st	1889	Tiger Rebel	13th	1945	Wintergreen	1st	1909
Sportsman	unp	1889	Time Clock	7th	1934	Wissahicken	unp	1879
Spy Hill	6th	1934	T. M. Dorsett	7th	1939	With Pleasure	14th	1946
Spy Song	2nd	1946	Today	12th	1935	With Regards	4th	1942
Standiford Keller	unp	1883	Tom Elmore	unp	1894	W. L. Sickle	8th	1947
Staretor	2nd	1941	Topland	5th	1910	Woodlake	5th	1903
Star Hawk	2nd	1916	Top O' The Wave	13th	1917	Wool Sandals	5th	1907
Star Gazer	10th	1917	Toro	3rd	1928	Worth	1st	1912
Star Master	9th	1917	Transmute	6th	1924	Yankee Notions	5th	1913
Star Reward	6th	1947	Treacy	6th	1903	Zal	2nd	1907
Startle	8th	1922	Trinidad	unp	1879	Zev	1st	1923
			Tryster	4th	1921			

†Busy American broke down in 10-horse field (1922).
†Good Advice pulled up in 13-horse field (1933).
†On Location pulled up in 8-horse field (1939).

†Liberty Limited broke down in 20-horse field (1932).
†Granville lost rider in 14-horse field (1936).
†Lord Murphy previously ran as Patmos.

††The above list includes the names of all but three starters in the Kentucky Derby; the other three were without name when they went to the post in their Derby years. One was mentioned in the 1875 summaries only as "Gen. A. Buford's br. c. by Baywood, out of Lute;" another, in the 1876 summaries, appeared only as "F. B. Harper's blk. c. by Enquirer, out of dam by Imp. Albion," and the third, racing in 1882, is mentioned in the summaries as "P. C. Fox's ch. c. by Pat Malloy, dam Canary Bird;" later named Bassett.

OWNERS OF STARTERS IN KENTUCKY DERBY

Two owners of Thoroughbreds saw their colors go to the post in the Kentucky Derby for the first time in 1948. That brought the total number of owners who have had Derby starters to 448.

Harry Payne Whitney, with nineteen starters in his name, had the greatest number of representatives in the American racing classic. However, twenty-eight starters wore the famous green and white silks of Colonel E. R. Bradley, but only sixteen started in his own name, the others racing in the name of Idle Hour Stock Farm.

Mrs. Payne Whitney, who died in 1944, and Mrs. Ethel V. Mars, who died in 1946, were next to the two leaders both in the number of horses sent to the post and the number of attempts made to win the Derby. Greentree Stable, owned by Mrs. Whitney until her death, started twelve horses in eight Derbies, winning with Twenty Grand in 1930 and with Shut Out in 1942. She was third with Stir Up in 1944. Mrs. Mars, owner of the Milky Way Farm racing stable sent ten horses to the post in eight Derbies, saw her Whiskolo and Reaping Reward finish third in 1935 and 1937, respectively, and her Gallahadion win in 1940.

Mrs. C. E. Durnell was the first woman to own a starter in and winner of the Kentucky Derby. Elwood carried her silks to victory in the 1904 running of the turf classic. Since then four other women, in addition to Mrs. Whitney and Mrs. Mars have won the Derby. The other four were Mrs. Dodge Sloane, whose Cavalcade won in 1934: Mrs. John D. Hertz, winner in 1928 with Reigh Count and in 1943 with Count Fleet; Mrs. R. M. Hoots, whose Black Gold defeated the 1924 Kentucky Derby Field, and Mrs. Elizabeth Graham, winner in 1947 with Jet Pilot.

Three owners watched their horses run one-two in the Churchill Downs race. Commander J. K. L. Ross was the first when his Sir Barton and Billy Kelly finished in that order in 1919. Colonel Bradley accomplished the same thing twice, in 1921 and 1926. Citation and Coaltown, owned by Calumet, were one-two in 1948. In 1893 Lookout and Boundless, owned by Cushing and Orth, ran first and third, which was duplicated by the T. C. McDowell entry of Alan-A-Dale and The Rival in 1902. Ed Corrigan's entry of Huron and Phil Dwyer ran second and third in 1892. This also was duplicated only once when the C. R. Ellison entry of Lady Navarre and James Reddick ran two-three in 1906.

Below are listed the names in which Derby horses have been started, together with the horses started under each name and the year in which each raced in the Kentucky Derby. Where only the year appears, it indicates that the horse or horses, finished unplaced.

—A—

ABEL, MRS. A. J.: Gramp's Image (1944)
A. C. T. STOCK FARM: Indiana Broom (1936, third)
ADAMS, MRS. JOHN PAYSON; Grandpere (1948)
ALEXANDER, K. S.: Escoba (1918, second)
ALLEN, G. R.: Calcutta (1923)
ALVAREZ, E.: Herron (1920)
ALVEY, E.: Friend Harry (1909)
ANDERSON, E.: Burnt Cork (1943)
ANDERSON & GOODING: Al Boyer (1894)
ANDERSON, R. H.: Joe Morris (1910, second)
APPLEGATE, H. C.: Old Rosebud (1914, won)
APPLEGATE, W. E.: Wool Sandals (1907)
ARCHIBALD, H. T. Folking (1929)
ARMSTRONG, D.: Synchronized (1908)
ARMSTRONG, N.: Lord Raglan (1883, third), Spokane (1889, won)
ASTE, A. L.: Ten Point (1913, second)
ASTOR, WILLIAM: Vagrant (1876, won)
AUDLEY FARM: The Clown (1923), Bobashela (1928), Gallant Knight (1930, second)

—B—

BAIN, F. C.: Patches (1920)
BAKER, A.: John Gund (1914)
BAKER, G. F.: Uncle Velo (1921), John Finn (1922, third)
BAKER, R. L.: Emerson Cochran (1915)
BAKER, W. H.: Green Jones (1917)
BALDWIN, E. J.: Lijero (1886)
BASHFORD MANOR STABLE; (see Geo. J. Long also): Hart Wallace (1891), Azra (1892, won), Plutus (1893, second), Sigurd (1894, third), Curator (1895)

BELAIR STUD (William Woodward): Gallant Fox (1930, won), Omaha (1935, won), Merry Pete and Granville (1936), Fighting Fox (1938), Johnstown (1939, won), Apache (1942)
BELLE ISLE STABLE: Upset Lad (1929)
BENNETT, G. C. & CO.: Abe Frank (1902)
BERGER, E. C. A.: Boot and Spur (1942)
BEVERWYCKE STABLE: Cassius (1889), Lena Misha (1916), Top O The Wave (1917)
BIANCHI, O. A.: Lucky B(1918), Sennings Park(1919)
BILLINGS & JOHNSON: Omar Khayyam (1917, won)
BLOCK, BENJAMIN: Morvich (1922, won), Aspiration and Better Luck (1923), Thorndale (1924)
BLOOMFIELD STABLE: Blackwood (1928)
BLUE RIDGE FARM: Elooto (1938)
BOBANET STABLE: Gay Bit (1944), Marine Victory (1946)
BOEING, W. E.: Slide Rule (1943, third)
BOMAR STABLE: Grand Slam (1936)
BOSTWICK, A. C.: Mate (1931, third)
BOWEN, G. W. & CO.: One Dime (1879), Alframbra (1881, third), Bengal (1882, third)
BRADLEY, E. R. (see Idle Hour Stock Farm also): By Golly (1920), Behave Yourself and Black Servant (1921, won and second), Blue Larkspur and Bay Beauty (1929), Breezing Thru and Buckeye Poet (1930), Burgoo King and Brother Joe (1932, won), Brokers Tip (1933, won), Bazaar (1934), Boxthorn (1935), Bien Joli (1936), Billionaire (1937), Bimelech (1940, second), Burning Dream (1945)
BRAEDALBANE STABLE: Weston (1935)
BRAGG, MRS. VERA S.: Blue Pair (1941), Cold Shower (1943)
BRANDON STABLE: Brandon Mint (1932), Tutti-curio (1935)

BRANN, W. L.: Challedon (1939, second), Pictor 1940), Escadru (1948)
BRANNON, B. J.: St. Bernard (1919)
BRECKINRIDGE, D.: Lord Braedalbane (1929)
BRENT & TALBOT: Tiger Rebel (1945)
BROLITE FARM: Challenge Me (1944), With Pleasure (1946)
BROOKMEADE FARM: Inlander (1933), Cavalcade and Time Clock (1934, won and seventh), Psychic Bid (1935), Liberty Road (1947)
BROWN, ED: Ulysses (1896)
BROWN, J. W.: T. M. Dorsett (1939)
BROWN, S. S.: Masterpiece (1886), Proceeds (1904), Agile (1905, won)
BUFORD, GEN. ABE: McCreery and Brown Colt by Baywood (1875), McWhirter (1877), McHenry (1878), General Pike (1879)
BUHL, T. D.: Sweep Swinger (1942), Air Sailor (1945)
BUSCH, A. A.: Chief Uncas (1925)
BUTLER, J.: Pebbles (1915, second)
BYERS, J. F.: Robert Morris (1941)

—C—

CADWILLADER, GEORGE: Strathmore (1879, third)
CAHN, J. C.: Typhoon II (1897, won), Thrive (1900, third)
CALUMET FARM (Warren Wright): Nellie Flag (1935), Bull Lea (1938), Whirlaway (1941, won), Pensive (1944, won), Pot o' Luck (1945, second), Faultless (1947, third), Citation and Coaltown (1948, won and second)
CAMDEN, J. N.: Dunvegan (1908, third), Miami (1909, second), Boola Boola (1910), Wheelwright (1912), Hydromel (1927)
CARMEN, R. F.: Meridian (1911, won), Surprising (1914)
CARTER, W. A.: Clodian (1937)
CASSIDY, T. M.: Crack Brigade (1930)
CATAWBA STABLE: Mr. Khayyam and Good Advice (1933)
CHICAGO STABLE: (Hankins & Johnson): Macbeth II (1888, won)
CHINN & MORGAN: Leonatus (1883, won), Harrodsburg (1886)
CHRISTIANA STABLE: Alexis (1945)
CIRCLE M. FARM (Edward S. Moore): Sir War (1942), Riskolater (1947)
CLAY, GREEN: Red Coat (1876)
CLAY, T. J.: The Chevalier (1888), Balgowan (1897, second)
CLAY, WOODFORD: Driscoll (1901, third)
CLAY & WOODFORD: Admiral (1884)
COCHRAN, G. A.: Bersagliere (1920), Revenue Agent (1924), Flying Ebony (1925, won)
COE, W. R.: David Harem and Cleopatra (1920), Pompey (1926), Ladysman and Pomponious (1933)
COLDSTREAM STUD: Coldstream (1936)
COLLINS, G.: Thistle Ace (1932)
COLLINS, I. J.: Bernard F. (1937)
COLLINS, R. W.: Lee O. Cotner (1925)
COLSTON, R.: Colston (1911, third)
COMBS, LUCAS B.: Dark Jungle (1946)
CONDRAN, G. F.: Flamma (1912, third)
CORRIGAN, E.: Irish Pat (1885), Riley (1890, won), Huron and Phil Dwyer (1892, second and third), Corsini (1899, second)
CORRIGAN, P.: Free Knight (1886, third)
COSDEN, A. H.: Vito (1928)
COSDEN, J. S.: Martingale and Golden Rule (1923, second and nineteenth), Nautical (1924)
COTTRILL, W.: Kimball (1880, second), Harry Gilmore (1882), Buchana (1884, won), Lord Coleridge (1885)
COUGHLIN, J. J.: Karl Eitel (1929)
COWAN, S. A.: Boon Companion (1925)
COYNE, PETE: King Gorin II (1924)
CROISSANT, G. F.: Ky Cardinal (1925), Roycrofter (1926)

CURRAN, W. J.: Jack Higgins (1928)
CUSHING & ORTH: Lookout and Boundless (1893, first and third)

—D—

DARDEN, GEO. W. & CO.: Lord Murphy (1879, won), Playfair (1885)
DARDEN, W. W.: Dortch (1915)
DAVIS, W. C.: Rockwood Boy (1944)
DIXIANA (Charles T. Fisher): Voltear (1929) Sweep All (1931, second), Cee Tee (1932), Mata Hari (1934), Sirocco (1940), Amber Light (1943), Spy Song (1946, second), Star Reward (1947)
DOERHOEFER & WEST: Jimmie Gill (1913)
DOYLE, M.: Ovelando (1907)
DUFFY, E. W.: Grey Gold (1937)
DUNNE, P.: Under Fire (1919, third)
DURNELL, MRS. C. E.: Elwood (1904, won)
DWYER, M. F.: Ben Brush (1896, won)
DWYER BROTHERS: Quito (1880), Hindoo (1881, won), Runnymede (1882, second)

—E—

EASTIN & LARABIE: High Tariff (1891, third), First Mate (1896)
EASTMAN, R. M.: Cathop (1932)
EASTMAN, R. M. ESTATE: Charley O. (1933, third)
ELLISON, C. R.: Judge Himes (1903, won), Lady Navarre and James Reddick (1906, second and third)
ERLANGER STABLE: Shut Up (1944)
ERNST A. C.: Alorter (1944), Alamond (1946)
EVANS, GEORGE: Pike's Pride (1883)

—F—

FAIR STABLE (Mrs. Graham Fair Vanderbilt): Chicatie (1929)
FAIRBANKS, MRS. R. B.: Bluebeard (1935)
FAIRFIELDS STABLE: Sun Fairplay (1935)
FARRIS, W. H.: Buckner (1879)
FAY & WEHMHOFF: Ed Tierney (1904, second)
FERGUSON, D.: Bell Buzzer (1944), Bob Murphy 1946)
FIELD, L. B.: Headlight (1877)
FIELD, MARSHALL: Sir Damion (1937)
FIELDING, H. W.: Jobar (1946)
FINCH, MRS. H.: Modest Lad (1943)
FISHER, H. C.: Muskallonge (1921), Mr. Mutt (1924), Swope (1925)
FIZER, W. H.: Milford (1908)
FLEETWOOD STABLE: Clarion (1887), Outbound (1889)
FLEISCHMANN, C.: Ben Brown (1897)
FOREMAN, G. W.: Ned O. (1930, third)
FORSYTHE, J. M.: Fontainbleu (1899)
FOSTER BROTHERS: Dr. Shepherd (1897)
FOX, P. C.: Chestnut Colt by Pat Malloy (1882)
FOXCATCHER FARMS (William du Pont, Jr.): Gold Seeker (1936), Fairy Hill (1937), Dauber (1928, second), Fairy Manah (1942), Hampden (1946, third)
FRANKLIN, H.: Velours (1906)
FRANZHEIM, MRS. B.: Quasimodo (1934)
FRIEND, B.: Co-Sport (1938)
FUNK, JOHN: Harry Hill (1876, third)

—G—

GALLAHER BROTHERS: Duvall (1912, second), Sewell Combs (1918), Regalo (1919), Chilhowee (1924, second)
GARDNER, H. P.: Clyde Van Dusen (1929, won)
GARRISON, C. M.: Be Frank (1919)
GERRY, R. L.: Voltaic (1925)
GERST, W.: Brancas (1904, third), Zal (1907, second), Donau (1910, won)
GIBSON, D.: Autocrat (1888)

GLEN RIDDLE FARM (S. D. Riddle): War Admiral (1937, won)
GODFREY, PHILIP: Comenow (1944)
GOFF, M. B.: Skytracer (1944)
GORDON, A. B.: Sir Thomas (1934)
GOREY, A. J.: Match Me (1909)
GRABNER, F. M.: Step Along (1925), Windy City (1929)
GRAHAM, TOM L.: Bert G. and Kenilworth Lad (1945)
GRANT, S. W.: Fred Jr. (1927)
GRAY & CO.: Jim Gray (1886)
GREENER, J. G. & CO.: Lafitte (1886)
GREENTREE STABLE: Letterman (1922), Rialto and Cherry Pie (1923), Wild Aster (1924), Twenty Grand, Anchors Aweigh, and Surf Board (1931, won, tenth, eleventh), Spy Hill (1934), Plat Eye (1935), Shut Out and Devil Diver (1942, won, sixth), Stir Up (1944, third)
GRIFFITH, J. E.: Single Foot (1925), Canter (1926)
GRIMES, MR. & MRS. T. D.: With Regards (1942)
GRINSTEAD, JAMES A.: Gold Mine (1875), Marie Michon (1876)
GRUBER, M. B.: Little Strings (1915)

—H—

HAGGIN, J. B.: Ben Ali (1886, won)
HAINSWORTH, MRS. C.: Blackbirder (1934)
HALLENBACH, H. C.: Worth (1912, won)
HAMBURG PLACE: The Mongol (1931)
HAMILTON, C. E.: Stone Street (1908, won)
HANGER, W. ARNOLD: Dit (1940, third)
HANKINS, G. V.: Robespierre (1890, third)
HARNED BROTHERS: Coyne (1921)
HARPER, F. R.: Ten Broeck (1875), Germantown and black colt by Enquirer (1876), Early Light (1877)
HARTWELL, C. A.: Cannon Shot (1924)
HATCH, H. C.: Boys Howdy (1931)
HAWKS, J. S. & CO.: Hyperion II (1906)
HAYES, T. P.: Layson (1905, third), Red Gauntlet (1907), Sir Catesby (1909), Donerail (1913, won), Kinney (1916)
HAYES, WILLIAM: Sannazarro (1901, second)
HEAD, C. BRUCE: Altawood (1924)
HEADLEY, HAL PRICE: Planet (1921), Almadel (1925), Paraphrase (1929), Alcibiades (1930), Whopper (1935), Menow (1938), Pellicle (1946)
HELIS, WILLIAM: Rippey (1946), Cosmic Bomb (1947)
HELLER, MRS. F. J.: Agrarian (1934, third)
HENDERSON & HOGAN: Col. Hogan (1911), Guaranola (1912)
HENDRIE, G.: Michael Angelo (1909)
HERTZ, JOHN D.: Chittagong (1923)
HERTZ, MRS. JOHN D.: Reigh Count (1928, won), Count Fleet (1943, won)
HERZ, E.: Mainster Toi (1917)
HEWITT, H. H.: Skeptic (1917), Startle (1922)
HIEATT, C. C. & G. Y.: Ben Machree (1929)
HIMYAR-STABLE: Parson (1896)
HIRSCH, MARY: No Sir (1937)
HOBSON, W. C.: Diavolaw (1944)
HOLLINGSWORTH, MRS. D. M.: Kondar (1946)
HOOPER, FRED W.: Hoop Jr. (1945, won)
HOOTS, MRS. R. M.: Black Gold (1924, won)
HOT SPRINGS STABLE: Ben Eder (1896, second)
HOUSSELLS, J. K.: Bymeabond (1945)
HOWARD, C. S.: Mioland (1940), Porter's Cap (1941)
HOWARD, MRS. C. S.: Sea Swallow (1945)
HOWARD, MAXWELL: Sceneshifter and Fencing 1937), The Chief (1938)
HUGHES, S. K. & CO.: Tom Elmore (1894)
HUGHES, W. A.: Frank Bird (1908)
HULL, W. C.: Ascension (1875)
HUMPHREY, A. P., JR.: Bronzewing (1914, third)
HUMPHREYS, I. B.: Light Carbine (1926)
HUNT, W. P.: Keokuk (1885)

—I—

IDLE HOUR STOCK FARM (see E. R. Bradley also): Bet Mosie, By Gosh, and Busy American (1922, second, ninth and broke down), Bright Tomorrow (1923), Beau Butler, Baffling, Bob Tail (1924, third, seventeenth, nineteenth), Broadway Jones (1925), Bubbling Over and Bagenbaggage (1926, won and second), Buddy Bauer and Bewithus (1927).

—J—

JACKSON, A.: Robert Bruce (1882)
JACOBIN STABLE: Kingman (1891, won)
JACQUES STABLE: Essare (1929)
JEFFORDS, W. M.: Scapa Flow (1927)
JEFFORDS, MRS. W. M.: Diogenes (1924), Commonwealth (1935)
JENNINGS & HUNT: Charlie Bush (1878)
JOHNSON, F.: Nassau (1923), Quatrain (1925), Replevin (1928)
JOHNSON, J. F.: Double Eagle (1915)
JOHNSON, R. A. & CO.: Loftin and Powhattan III (1884, second and unplaced)
JOHNSON & CROSSTHWAITE: Tetan (1915)
JOHNSON & MILLS: Dan K. (1877)
JONES, MONTFORT: Surf Rider (1922)
JOYCE, P. H.: Dick O'Hara (1930)

—K—

KAISER, A. A.: Captain Hal (1925, second), Bonivan (1928)
KEENE, J. O. & G. H.: Lord Marshall (1913)
KEENELAND STUD FARM (J. O. Keene): Champ De Mars (1926)
KENTON FARM STABLE: Typhoon (1928)
KILMER, W. S.: Exterminator (1918, won) Frogtown (1919), Sun Beau (1928), Dark Winter (1933)
KING RANCH (Robert J. Kleberg): Dispose (1941), Assault (1946, won)
KNAPP, H. K.: Yankee Notions (1913)
KNEBELKAMP, W. F.: Hoops (1932)
KNEBELKAMP & MORRIS: Spanish Play (1931), Adobe Post (1932)
KOHN & THEISEN: Recollection (1926)
KUHNS, G. & CO.: Highflyer (1882)

—L—

LABOLD BROTHERS: Montrose (1887, won)
LA BRAE STABLE: Elector (1925)
LAKELAND, W.: Babcock (1882)
LEHMAN, O.: Reigh Olga (1928)
LEICHLEITER, R. E.: Cartago (1928)
LEITER, J. ESTATE: Prince D'Armour (1931), Prince Hotspur (1932)
LEIGH & ROSE: Chant (1894, won)
LE MAIRE, F. B.: Norse King (1915)
LE MAR STOCK FARM (Leo J. Marks): Misstep (1928, second)
LESH, J. H.: Warfield (1909)
LETCHER, W. R.: Bill Letcher (1890, second)
LEWIS, A. B. & CO.: Vagabond (1875)
LEWIS, C. A.: Verdigris (1875, second)
LEWIS, MRS. W. G.: Darby Dieppe (1945, third)
LEXINGTON STABLE: My Play (1922), Prince of Bourbon (1925)
LISLE, R.: Jacobin (1887, third)
LIVINGSTON, J.: Royal II (1915)
LOFT, G. W.: On Watch and Donnacona (1920, third and fifth)
LOMA STABLE: Tick On (1932)
LONG, GEORGE J. (see Bashford Manor also): Hindus (1900), Amur (1901), Sir Huron (1906, won) Sir Cleges (1908, second), Campeon (1909), Free Lance (1912)
LONGRIDGE STABLE (W. V. Thraves): Bar None (1928), Oscillation (1932)
LOOKOUT STOCK FARM (J. Brink): Foreign Agent (1945)

LOONEY, J. T.: Leo Ray (1915)
LORILLARD, P.: Parole (1876)
LOUCHHEIM, J.: Economic (1932, second), Speedmore (1934), Morpluck (1935), Pompoon (1937, second)

—M—

McCAMPBELL, A. G.: Jim Gore (1887, second)
McCLELLAND, B.: Halma (1895, won)
McCLELLAND, J. W.: Sailor and Eternal (1919)
McCLELLAND, R. M.: Boreas and Bob Cook (1884)
McCURDY, W. C.: Chatter (1883)
McDOWELL, T. C.: His Excellency (1900), Alan-A-Dale and The Rival (1902, won and third), Bourbon and Woodlake (1903, third and fifth), American Eagle (1918)
McGAVOCK, W. C. & CO.: Boulevard (1880)
McGRATH, H. P.: Aristides and Chesapeake (1875, won and unplaced), Leonard (1877, second), Wissahicken (1879), Sligo and Calycanthus (1881)
McKENNA, C. W.: Foundation (1913)
McLAUGHLIN, R. S.: Wee Admiral (1946)
McLEAN, E. B.: Modest (1924), Jock and War Eagle (1927, third and fifteenth), Toro (1928, third)
MACKENZIE, R. J.: Direct (1909)
MACOMBER, A. K.: Star Hawk and The Cock (1916, second and sixth), War Star, Star Master, Star Gazer (1917), War Cloud (1918)
MACOMBER, J. R.: Petee-Wrack (1928)
MADDEN, J. E.: Plaudit (1898, won), Mazo (1899, third), Watermelon (1914)
MAGGIO, J. V.: American Eagle (1944)
MAINE CHANCE FARM (Mrs. Elizabeth Graham): Lord Boswell, Knockdown, and Perfect Bahram (1946), Jet Pilot (1947, won)
MARSHALL BROTHERS: Prince K. (1923)
MARTIN, T. B.: Court Scandal (1937), Bankrupt (1943)
MASON, MRS. SILAS B.: Head Play (1933, second), He Did (1937)
MEGIBBEN, J. K. & CO.: Sportsman (1889)
MEGIBBEN, T. J.: Newsboy (1882), Audrain (1884, third)
MELBOURNE STABLE (W. S. Barnes): Blue Wing (1886, second), Callifet and Alexandria (1888, second and unplaced)
MERRILL, J. J.: Odd Fellow (1877)
MILKY WAY FARM: Whiskolo (1935, third), The Fighter and Sangreal (1936), Reaping Reward and Military (1937, third and fifteenth), Mountain Ridge (1938), On Location (1939), Gallahadion (1940, won), Dogpatch (1942), No Wrinkles (1943)
MILL RIVER STABLE (Mrs. Barclay Douglas): Fair Call (1942)
MILLER, A.: Ticket (1917, second)
MILLER, G. M.: For Fair (1915)
MOORE, M. C.: Booker Bill (1915)
MOORE, T. W.: Inventor (1902, second)
MORRIS, A. H. & D. H.: Manuel (1899, won)
MORRIS AND PATTON: Apollo (1882, won), Drake Carter (1882, second), Bersan and Favor (1885, second and unplaced)
MORRISEY, J. D.: Banburg (1887)
MORRISON & KEATING: McCarthy (1935)
MUELLER, T. E.: Wida (1923)
MULRENAN, MRS. E.: First Fiddle (1942)
MURLOGG FARM: Fighting Step (1945)
MURRAY, W. S.: Sandy Beal (1920)

—N—

NESBITT, H. S.: Staretor (1941, second)
NEVADA STOCK FARM: General Thatcher (1923)
NICHOLS, T. J.: Day Star (1878, won)
NORTHWAY STABLE: Gallant Sir (1932)

—O—

OWENS, R. H.: Leveler (1878, third)

—P—

PALLADINO, MRS. L.: Little Beans (1941)
PARKVIEW STABLE: Rhinock (1926)
PARR, RAL: Paul Jones and Blazes (1920, won and sixth)
PARRISH, J. W.: Midway (1917, third), Rolled Stocking (1927), Cold Check (1932), Isaiah (1932), Dellor (1937)
PARSONS, S. L.: Sharpshooter (1915, third)
PASTIME STABLE: Laureate (1895, third), Guy Fortune (1917)
PATE, R. C.: Ascender (1883), Clay Pete (1885)
PATNO, B. R.: Valley Flares (1944)
PATTERSON, C. T. & CO.: Ornament (1897, second)
PATTERSON, MRS. R. D.: Alworth (1946)
PEABODY, S.: Martie Flynn (1928)
PEAVEY, W. M.: Jett Jett (1947)
PENDERGRAST, T. J.: Bo McMillan (1923)
PEPPER, JAMES E.: Mirage (1893), The Dragon (1896)
POLSON, W. F.: Vulcanite (1919), Peace Pennant (1920)
PONS, F. J.: Jack Denman (1911)
POULSEN, MRS. G.: Broadcloth (1944, second)
PRITCHARD, E. F.: Tannery (1930)
PUTNAM, C.: Swain (1941)

—R—

R. C. STABLE: Longus (1930)
RAILEY, C. E.: Linger (1893)
RANCOCAS STABLE (Harry F. Sinclair): Zev (1923, won), Brocadale and Mad Play (1924)
RAND, MISS E. G.: Merry Maker (1937)
REIF, G.: Fighting Bob (1910, third)
RESPESS, J. B.: Wintergreen (1909, won), Our Fancy (1932)
REYNOLDS, J. W. H.: Falsetto (1879, second)
RICE, GEORGE H.: Volcano (1875, second), Malvern (1877)
RICHARDS, A. KEENE: Bullion (1876)
RIDGEWOOD STABLE (Boines & Tigani): Double Jay (1947)
RINGGOLD, L. B.: Semper Ego (1896, third)
RIVER DIVIDE FARM: Brief Sigh (1944)
ROBINSON, J. J.: Lucky Tom (1932)
ROBINSON, MORGAN & CO.: Bob Wooley (1875)
RODE, J. B.: Searcher (1875)
RODEGAP, J.: Goshen (1897)
RODES & CARR: Respond (1878), Wallensee (1882)
RODGERS, J. W.: Dove Pie (1943)
ROGERS, J. C.: John Furlong (1910)
ROSE, ARTHUR: Misweet (1945)
ROSENBERG, L.: Kerry Patch (1933)
ROSS, J. K. L.: Sir Barton and Billy Kelly (1919, won and second), Star Voter (1921)
RYE, G. M.: Col. Zeb Ward (1888)

—S—

SABATH, MRS. A.: Alsab (1942, second)
SACHSENMAIER & REUTER: Roman Soldier (1935, second)
SAGAMORE STABLE: Rock Man (1926, third), Don Q (1928)
SAGE STABLE: Rip Rap (1927)
SALMON, WALTER J.: Careful (1921), Vigil (1923, third), Display (1926), Black Panther (1927), Ladder (1931)
SALUBRIA STABLE: Strolling Player (1928)
SALYERS, S. J.: Bill Bruce (1875)
SANFORD, J.: George Smith (1916, won)
SANTA ANITA STABLE: Pendennis (1887)
SCHORR, J. W.: Lieber Karl (1898, second), Alard Scheck (1901), Leochares (1913), Ed Crump and Goldcrest Boy (1915), Cudgel (1917), J. T. Clark (1918)

SCHRIEBER, B.: Banridge (1908)
SCHWARTZ, A. C.: Sortie (1928)
SCHWARTZ, M. L.: Bold Venture (1936, won)
SCOGGAN, H. J.: Florizar and Highland Lad (1900, second and unplaced)
SCOGGAN & BRYANT: Proctor Knott (1889, second)
SCOGGAN BROTHERS: Hindoocraft (1889), Buck McCann (1893)
SCOTT, D. W.: Son of John (1925, third)
SCULLY, W. O.: Ban Yan (187), White (1888, third)
SELLERS, J. B. & CO.: Wendover (1882)
SELZNICK, MYRON: Can't Wait (1938, third)
SEVERSON, L. M.: Paul Bunyon (1929), Spicson (1933)
SHADY BROOK FARM STABLE: Pittsburgher (1931)
SHAFFER, E. G.: St. Bernard (1935)
SHANDON FARM: Burning Star (1937)
SHANNON, H. & CO.: De Bar (1906)
SHANNON, R. H.: Deadlock (1922)
SHAWHAN, J. S.: Fonso (1880, won)
SIMMONS, A. T.: Blue Swords (1943, second)
SIMMS & OLIVER: Prince Pal (1920)
SIMONETTI, J.: Sgt. Byrne (1934)
SINGERLY, G. A.: Han d'Or (1898)
SMALLWOOD & CO.: King William (1877, third)
SMITH, C. H.: Pearl Song (1894, second), Basso (1895, second), Lieut. Gibson (1900, won)
SMITH, J. D.: His Lordship (1899)
SMITH, R. N.: Governor Gray (1911, second)
SMITHA, L.: Dr. Barkley (1909, third)
SPENCE, K.: Hodge (1914, second)
SPETH, P. G.: Thistle (1885)
SPRINGFIELD & CLAY: Enlister & Warsaw (1875)
STANTON & TUCKER: Isabey (1898, third)
STEELE, A. S.: Orlandwick (1907)
STEVENS, T .H.: Treacy (1903)
STICE, E. O. & SON: On Trust (1947)
STIVERS. L.: Uncle Luther (1930)
STRAUS, A. & CO.: Earl of Beaconfield (1878)
SUPERIOR STABLE: Holl Image (1936)
SWIGERT, D.: Bombay (1876), Baden-Baden and Lisbon (1877, won and unplaced), Trinidad (1879)
SWIGERT, J. & J.: Grimaldi (1886)
SWIGERT, R. A.: Sir Joseph (1886)
SWIKARD, MRS. E. L.: Chip (1929)

—T—

TALBOT BROTHERS: Prince Silverwings. (1904)
TARLTON, L. P., JR.: Solicitor (1878), Mistral (1882)
THOMAS, BARAK G.: Himyar (1878, second), Lelex (1881, second)
THOMPSON, J. R.: Minotaur (1929)
THOMPSON, P. C.: Crystal Prince (1932)
THREE D'S STOCK FARM: Panchio, Calf Roper, Prince Pat (1929, third, eleventh, twentieth), Broadway Limited and Kilkerry (1930, ninth and eleventh), Liberty Limited (1932), Strideaway (1933), Heelfly (1937)
TICHENO, M. H. & CO.: Early (1903, second)
TOWER STABLE: Royal Man (1940)
TREACY, B. J.: Outlook (1890)
TUFANO, L.: Market Wise (1941, third)
TURNEY BROTHERS: Dr. Catlett (1897, third)
TWYMANN, J. C. & CO.: Prince Fonso (1890)

—V—

VALDINA FARMS (Emerson F. Woodward): Viscounty (1939), Valdina Paul (1941), Valdina Orphan and Hollywood (1942, third and ninth)
VALLEY LAKE STABLE: High Foot (1930)
VANDERBILT, A. G.: Discovery (1934, second)
VAN METER, C. C.: Topland (1910), Sterling (1920)
VAN METER, F. B.: His Eminence (1901, won)
VIKING STABLE :Lawley (1928)
VISSMAN, H. F.: Leamingtonian (1876)

—W—

WAINWRIGHT, J. R.: Gallant Pirate (1910)
WALDEN, R. W.: Uncle Bryn (1915)
WALLACE, WILLIAM: The Winner (1896)
WALMAC FARM (R. W. McElwain): Billings (1948)
WALSH, R.: Sunset Trail II (1937)
WARD, J. S.: Berlin (1917)
WARM STABLE (Silas B. Mason): The Nut (1929)
WATKINS, G.: Insco (1931)
WATTS, J. R.: Standiford Keller (1883)
WEAVER, J. T.: Gowell (1913, third)
WEBER & WARD: Franklin and Dodge (1916, third and fourth)
WEIDEMANN, C.: In Memoriam (1923)
WHEATLEY STABLE: Distraction (1928), Teufel (1936), Melodist (1937)
WHITAKER, B. F.: Requested (1942), My Request (1948, third)
WHITEHOUSE, W. H.: Royal Julian (1927)
WHITENY, C. V.: Today (1935), Jeep (1945), Phalanx (1947, second)
WHITNEY, H. P.: Regret (1915, won), Thunderer and Dominant (1916), Rickety (1917), Vindex (1919), Upset, Damask, Wildair (1920, second, fourth, eighth), Prudery and Tryster (1921, third and fourth), Enchantment and Picketer (1923), Transmute and Klondyke (1924), Backbone and The Bat (1925), Bendin (1926), Whiskery and Bostonian (1927, won and fifth)
WHITNEY, JOHN HAY: Heather Broom (1939, third)
WHITNEY, MRS. M. E.: Stepenfetchit and Over Time (1932, third and fifth), Singing Wood (1934), Bullet Proof (1947)
WICKLIFFE STABLE: Acabado (1917)
WIDENER, J. E.: Osmand and Kiev (1927, second and twelfth), Peace Chance (1934), Brevity (1936, second), Roman (1940)
WIELAND, F.: Pravus (1923)
WILD ROSE FARM: Charmarten (1928)
WILLIAMS, J. T.: Vera Cruz (1877), Bob Miles (1884), Joe Cotton (1885, won)
WILLIAMS, S.: Palisade (1890)
WILLIAMS, W. S. & CO.: Ram's Horn (1905, second)
WILLIAMS & OWINGS: Creedmoore (1876, second)
WILSHIRE STABLE: Naishapur (1929, second)
WILSON, G. D.: Ada Glen (1879)
WILSON & YOUNG: Bootmaker (1889)
W-L RANCH: W. L. Sickle, Stepfather (1947)
WOODFORD, S.: Sonada (1912)
WOODFORD, J. HAL: Pink Star (1907, won)
WOODFORD & BUCKNER: Kentucky Farmer (1900), Bad News (1903), Mud Sill (1911)
WOODING, J. M.: Burgundy (1878)
WOODING AND PURYEAR: Exploit (1884)
WOODVALE FARM: Our Boots (1941)
WOOLFORD FARM (Herbet J. Woolf: Lawrin (1938, won), Technician (1939)
WORTHINGTON, C. T.: Viva America (1918, third)
WRIGHT, A. R.: Jacobe (1945)

—X—

XALAPA FARM STABLE (E. Simms): Leonardo II and Bon Homme (1921), Sweeping Away (1925)

—Y—

YANKE, W. G.: Round the World (1911), Old Ben (1914)
YOUNG, M.: Bancroft (1880, third), Getaway (1881), Lost Cause (1882), Ten Booker (1885, third), Once Again (1889, third)
YOUNG, W. J.: Bill Herron (1908)

—Z—

ZIEGLER, JR., WILLIAM: Needle Gun (1925), Espino (1926), Gone Away (1930), El Chico (1939)

DERBY DAY WEATHER

Louisville Weather Bureau records show the following for Derby Days since 1927.

DERBY DATE	RAINFALL (INCHES)	HIGH TEMP.	DERBY DATE	RAINFALL (INCHES)	HIGH TEMP.
May 14, 1927	.35	64	May 7, 1938	—	80
May 19, 1928	.62	75	May 6, 1939	—	83
May 18, 1929	1.19	77	May 4, 1940	—	62
May 17, 1930	.11	69	May 3, 1941	—	76
May 16, 1931	—	84	May 2, 1942	—	87
May 7, 1932	—	83	May 1, 1943	—	54
May 6, 1933	.09	59	May 7, 1944	—	54
May 5, 1934	.04	76	June 9, 1945	.50	77
May 4, 1935	.14	47	May 4, 1946	.01	68
May 2, 1936	.34	78	May 3, 1947	.02	57
May 8, 1937	—	71	May 1, 1948	.08	72

POST-TIME FAVORITES

Thirty-six post-time favorites in the Kentucky Derby won their races, an average of a trifle under 50 per cent; of the others, 17 ran second, four were third, and 17 unplaced.

The shortest priced favorite during the 74 years was Himyar, held at 1 to 4 odds-on, and which finished second to Day Star, in 1878. The shortest priced favorites since installation of pari-mutuel machines in 1908 have been Bimelech in 1940, Count Fleet in 1943, and Citation in 1948 at 40c to $1. Bimelech finished second, but Count Fleet and Citation won.

The longest priced winners were in this order: 1913, 1940, 1918, 1908, 1936, 1923 and 1920. Donerail, the 1913 winner, paid $91.45 to $1.

Here is a list showing the Derby post-time favorites since 1875, what happened to them, and what was the pay-off on the winner:

YEAR	FAVORITE	PRICE	FINISHED	WINNER AND PRICE
1875	H. P. McGrath Entry (Aristides-Chesapeake)	2-1	Aristides—1st Chesapeake—8th	Same
1876	Vagrant	9-5	First	Same
1877	Leonard	7-5	Second	Baden-Baden, 8-1
1878	Himyar	1-4	Second	Day Star, 3-1
1879	Lord Murphy	11-10	First	Same
1880	Kimball	3-5	Second	Fonso, 7-1
1881	Hindoo	1-3	First	Same
1882	Runnymede	4-5	Second	Apollo, 10-1
1883	Leonatus	9-5	First	Same
1884	Audrain	2-1	Third	Buchanan, 3-1
1885	Joe Cotton	1-1	First	Same
1886	Ben Ali	1.72-1	First	Same
1887	Banburg	7-5	Fourth	Montrose, 10-1

YEAR	FAVORITE	PRICE	FINISHED	WINNER AND PRICE
1888	Gallifet (Gallifet coupled with Alexandria as Melbourne Stable entry)	1-1	Second	Macbeth II, 6-1
1889	Proctor Knott	1-2	Second	Spokane, 10-1
1890	Robespierre	1-1	Third	Riley, 4-1
1891	Kingman	1-2	First	Same
1892	Azra	3-2	First	Same
1893	Cushing-Orth Entry (Lookout-Boundless)	7-10	Lookout—1st Boundless—3rd	Same
1894	Chant	1-2	First	Same
1895	Halma	1-3	First	Same
1896	Ben Brush	1-2	First	Same
1897	Ornament	1-1	Second	Typhoon II, 3-1
1898	Lieber Karl	1-3	Second	Plaudit, 3-1
1899	Manuel	11-20	First	Same
1900	Lieut. Gibson	7-10	First	Same
1901	Alard Scheck	7-10	Fifth	His Eminence, 3-1
1902	Abe Frank	3-5	Fourth	Alan-a-Dale, 3-2
1903	Early	3-5	Second	Judge Himes, 15-1
1904	Proceeds	1-1	Third	Elwood, 15-1
1905	Agile	1-3	First	Same
1906	Sir Huon	11-10	First	Same
1907	Red Gauntlet	3-2	Fourth	Pink Star, 15-1
1908	Sir Cleges	9-5	Second	Stone Street, 23.72-1
1909	Wintergreen	1.96-1	First	Same
1910	Donau	1.65-1	First	Same
1911	Governor Gray	1-1	Second	Meridian, 2.90-1
1912	Worth	4-5	First	Same
1913	Ten Point	1.20-1	Second	Donerail, 91.45-1
1914	Old Rosebud	85c to 1	First	Same
1915	Regret	2.65-1	First	Same
1916	H. P. Whitney Entry (Thunderer-Dominant)	1.05-1	Thunderer—5th Dominant—7th	Geo. Smith, 4.15-1
1917	Ticket	1.45-1	Second	*Omar Khayyam, 12.80-1
1918	War Cloud	1.45-1	Fourth	Exterminator, 29.60-1
1919	J. W. McClelland Entry (Sailor-Eternal)	2.10-1	Sailor—7th Eternal—10th	J. K. L. Ross Entry (Sir Barton) 2.60-1
1920	H. P. Whitney Entry (Upset-Damask-Wildair)	1.65-1	Upset—2nd Damask—4th Wildair—8th	Ral Parr Entry (Paul Jones) 16.20-1
1921	H. P. Whitney Entry (Prudery-Tryster)	1.10-1	Prudery—3rd Tryster—4th	E. R. Bradley Entry (Behave Yourself), 8.65-1

YEAR	FAVORITE	PRICE	FINISHED	WINNER AND PRICE
1922	Morvich	1.20-1	First	Same
1923	H. P. Whitney and Greentree Entry (Enchantment-Whitney) (Picketer-Whitney) (Rialto-Greentree) (Cherry Pie-Greentree)	2.30-1	Enchantment—6th Rialto—7th Picketer—15th Cherry Pie—20th	Zev, 19.20-1
1924	Black Gold	1.75-1	First	Same
1925	Quatrain	1.95-1	Twelfth	Flying Ebony (in field), 3.15-1
1926	E. R. Bradley Entry (Bubbling Over-Bagenbaggage)	1.90-1	Bubbling Over—1st Bagenbaggage—2nd	Same
1927	H. P. Whitney Entry (Whiskery-Bostonian)	2.40-1	Whiskery—1st Bostonian—5th	Same
1928	Reigh Count (Mrs. John Hertz) Reigh Olga (O. Lehmann) (Both trained by B. S. Michell, ran as entry)	2.06-1	Reigh Count—1st Reigh Olga—5th	Same
1929	E. R. Bradley Entry (Blue Larkspur-Bay Beauty)	1.71-1	Blue Larkspur—4th Bay Beauty—13th	Clyde Van Dusen, 3-1
1930	Gallant Fox	1.19-1	First	Same
1931	Greentree Stable (Twenty Grand-Anchors Aweigh-Surf Board)	88c to 1	Twenty Grand—1st Anchors Aweigh—10th Surf Board—11th	Same
1932	Tick On	1.84-1	Sixth	E. R. Bradley Entry (Burgoo King), 5.61-1
1933	W. R. Coe Entry (Ladysman-Pomponius)	1.43-1	Ladysman—4th Pomponius—5th	Brokers Tip, 8.93-1
1934	Brookmeade Stable (Cavalcade-Time Clock)	1.50-1	Cavalcade—1st Time Clock—7th	Same
1935	Nellie Flag	3.80-1	Fourth	Omaha, 4-1
1936	Brevity	80c to 1	Second	Bold Venture, 20.50-1
1937	War Admiral	1.60-1	First	Same
1938	Fighting Fox	1.40-1	Sixth	Lawrin, 8.60-1
1939	Johnstown	60c to 1	First	Same
1940	Bimelech	40c to 1	Second	Gallahadion, 35.20-1
1941	Whirlaway	2.90-1	First	Same
1942	Greentree Entry (Shut Out-Devil Diver)	1.90-1	Shut Out—1st Devil Diver—6th	Same
1943	Count Fleet	40c to 1	First	Same
1944	Stir Up	1.40-1	Third	Pensive, 7.10-1
1945	Pot o'Luck	3.30-1	Second	Hoop Jr., 3.70-1
1946	Maine Chance Farm Entry (Lord Boswell-Knockdown-Perfect Bahram)	1.10-1	Lord Boswell—4th Knockdown—5th Perfect Bahram—9th	Assault, 8.20-1
1947	Phalanx	2.00-1	Second	Jet Pilot, 5.40-1
1948	Calumet Farm Entry (Citation-Coaltown)	40c to 1	Citation—1st Coaltown—2nd	Same

DERBY DAY WAGERING

Auction pools from start, in 1875, until after 1888 Derby. Revived for 1908 Derby; discarded after 1911. Pari-mutuels from 1878 Derby until after 1889 Derby. Revived in 1908 and that is only form of wagering that has been permitted since then. In 1878 only $5 win tickets were sold. In 1885 $5 place tickets sold for the first time. In 1889 show betting was introduced. In 1911 tickets reduced to minimum of $2. In 1939 tickets sold in the "bleachers" were at a minimum of $1; discontinued after 1943 Derby.

Bookmaking was first introduced in 1882. With exception of Derby days in 1884 and 1886, bookmaking continued until after 1907 Derby, when it was abandoned.

YEAR	TOTAL	ON DERBY	YEAR	TOTAL	ON DERBY
1908	$ 67,570	$ 18,300	1929	1,790,670	675,106
1909	†103,694	31,710	1930	1,664,409	584,894
1910	†146,520	43,465	1931	1,374,822	495,886
1911	†170,834	†49,380	1932	850,809	277,105
1912	†208,640	†54,945	1933	745,603	229,312
1913	232,771	64,680	1934	999,140	382,584
1914	259,561	80,248	1935	1,031,072	412,846
1915	303,675	†88,755	1936	1,269,188	472,750
1916	356,674	†99,468	1937	1,535,604	585,606
1917	409,509	109,395	1938	1,511,689	528,742
1918	525,648	161,565	1939	1,674,599	584,977
1919	833,643	292,244	1940	1,593,983	465,149
1920	1,055,191	375,249	1941	1,935,651	654,353
1921	1,202,342	391,604	1942	1,983,011	631,198
1922	1,195,147	397,848	1943	1,801,899	537,392
1923	1,424,288	408,262	1944	2,139,982	651,444
1924	1,898,566	618,536	1945	2,380,796	776,408
1925	1,871,614	661,857	1946	3,608,208	1,202,474
1926	2,096,613	694,870	1947	3,636,403	1,253,042
1927	1,934,232	676,443	‡1948	3,051,779	670,833
1928	1,890,050	620,643			

†Indicates these totals were estimated from incomplete figures that are available. All other totals are official. ‡Straight betting only.

RACE	1940	1941	1942	1943	1944	1945	1946	1947	1948
1	$ 66,442	$ 86,825	$ 91,221	$ 72,779	$ 91,461	$ 69,722	$ 126,611	$ 131,395	$ 125,939
2	95,789	128,469	123,630	114,534	118,923	115,828	209,662	202,569	183,548
3	130,867	147,606	160,357	157,700	164,846	221,652	281,088	296,987	247,503
4	145,737	192,025	203,471	161,097	198,057	220,266	355,851	344,206	314,911
5	188,629	201,121	208,283	204,464	235,734	261,354	381,200	379,807	409,122
6	186,311	212,613	221,847	223,101	264,461	283,969	415,464	417,717	457,749
Derby	465,149	654,353	631,198	537,392	651,444	776,408	1,202,474	1,253,042	670,833
8	158,711	150,914	163,211	177,627	202,730	197,341	310,372	296,920	329,158
9	156,348	161,725	179,793	153,205	212,326	234,256	325,486	313,760	313,016
	$1,593,983	$1,935,651	$1,983,011	$1,801,899	$2,139,982	$2,380,796	$3,608,208	$3,636,403	$3,051,779

WINNING DERBY POST POSITIONS

YEAR	NAME	BOX NO.	YEAR	NAME	BOX NO.	YEAR	NAME	BOX NO.
1900	Lieut. Gibson	3	1916	George Smith	8	1933	Brokers Tip	11
1901	His Eminence	3	1917	Omar Khayyam	8	1934	Cavalcade	8
1902	Alan-a-Dale	4	1918	Exterminator	5	1935	Omaha	10
1903	Judge Himes	4	1919	Sir Barton	1	1936	Bold Venture	5
1904	Elwood	3	1920	Paul Jones	2	1937	War Admiral	1
1905	Agile	1	1921	Behave Yourself	1	1938	Lawrin	1
1906	Sir Huon	4	1922	Morvich	4	1939	Johnstown	5
1907	Pink Star	6	1923	Zev	10	1940	Gallahadion	1
1908	Stone Street	4	1924	Black Gold	1	1941	Whirlaway	4
1909	Wintergreen	6	1925	Flying Ebony	6	1942	Shut Out	3
1910	Donau	7	1926	Bubbling Over	11	1943	Count Fleet	5
1911	Meridian	5	1927	Whiskery	7	1944	Pensive	5
1912	Worth	5	1928	Reigh Count	4	1945	Hoop Jr.	12
1913	Donerail	5	1929	Clyde Van Dusen	20	1946	Assault	2
1914	Old Rosebud	6	1930	Gallant Fox	7	1947	Jet Pilot	13
1915	Regret	2	1931	Twenty Grand	5	1948	Citation	1
			1932	Burgoo King	13			

Johnstown (1939) wore saddle-cloth No. 6, but moved into starting box No. 5 by withdrawal of No. 1 horse after programs were printed.

CONDENSED HISTORY—KENTUCKY DERBY

Date	Winner	Won by	Jockey	Wt.	Second	Third	Sub-scribers	Starters	Net to Winner	Time	Track
May 17, 1875	Aristides	1 lgth.	O. Lewis	100	Volcano	Verdigris	42	15	$2,850	2:37¾	Fast
May 15, 1876	Vagrant	2 lgths.	R. Swim	97	Creedmoor	Harry Hill	34	11	2,950	2:38¼	Fast
May 22, 1877	Baden-Baden	2 lgths.	W. Walker	100	Leonard	King William	41	11	3,300	2:38	Fast
May 21, 1878	Day Star	2 lgths.	J. Carter	100	Himyar	Leveler	56	9	4,050	2:37¼	Good
May 20, 1879	Lord Murphy	1 lgth.	C. Shauer	100	Falsetto	Strathmore	46	9	3,550	2:37	Fast
May 18, 1880	Fonso	1 lgth.	G. Lewis	105	Kimball	Bancroft	47	5	3,800	2:37½	Fast
May 17, 1881	Hindoo	4 lgths.	J. McLaughlin	105	Lelex	Alfambra	62	6	4,410	2:40	Fast
May 16, 1882	Apollo	½ lgth.	B. Hurd	102	Runnymede	Bengal	64	14	4,560	2:40¼	Good
May 23, 1883	Leonatus	3 lgths.	W. Donohue	105	Drake Carter	Lord Raglan	50	7	3,760	2:43	Heavy
May 16, 1884	Buchanan	2 lgths.	I. Murphy	110	Loftin	Audrain	51	9	3,990	2:40¼	Good
May 14, 1885	Joe Cotton	Neck.	E. Henderson	110	Bersan	Ten Booker	69	10	4,630	2:37¼	Good
May 14, 1886	Ben Ali	½ lgth.	P. Duffy	118	Blue Wing	Free Knight	107	10	4,890	2:36½	Fast
May 11, 1887	Montrose	2 lgths.	I. Lewis	118	Jim Gore	Jacobin	119	7	4,200	2:39¼	Fast
May 14, 1888	Macbeth II	1 lgth.	G. Covington	115	Gallifet	White	95	7	4,740	2:38¼	Fast
May 9, 1889	Spokane	Nose	T. Kiley	118	Proctor Knott	Once Again	94	8	4,880	2:34½	Fast
May 14, 1890	Riley	2 lgths.	I. Murphy	118	Bill Letcher	Robespierre	115	6	5,460	2:45	Heavy
May 13, 1891	Kingman	1 lgth.	I. Murphy	122	Balgowan	High Tariff	83	4	4,550	2:52¼	Good
May 11, 1892	Azra	Nose	A. Clayton	122	Huron	Phil Dwyer	68	3	4,230	2:41½	Heavy
May 10, 1893	Lookout	5 lgths.	E. Kunze	122	Plutus	Boundless	60	6	3,840	2:39¼	Fast
May 15, 1894	Chant	2 lghts.	F. Goodale	122	Pearl Song	Sigurd	55	5	4,020	2:41	Fast
May 6, 1895	Halma	3 lgths.	J. Perkins	122	Basso	Laureate	57	4	2,970	2:37½	Fast
May 6, 1896	Ben Brush	Nose	W. Simms	117	Ben Eder	Semper Ego	171	8	4,850	2:07¾	Slow
May 12, 1897	Typhoon II	Head	F. Garner	117	Ornament	Dr. Catlett	159	6	4,850	2:12½	Heavy
May 4, 1898	Plaudit	Neck	W. Simms	117	Lieber Karl	Isabey	179	4	4,850	2:09	Slow
May 4, 1899	Manuel	2 lgths.	F. Taral	117	Corsini	Mazo	151	5	4,850	2:12	Fast
May 3, 1900	Lieut. Gibson	4 lgths.	J. Boland	117	Florizar	Thrive	131	7	4,850	2:06¼	Fast
Apr. 29, 1901	His Eminence	2 lgths.	J. Winkfield	117	Sannazarro	Driscoll	113	5	4,850	2:07¾	Fast
May 3, 1902	Alan-a-Dale	Nose	J. Winkfield	117	Inventor	The Rival	112	4	4,850	2:08¾	Fast
May 2, 1903	Judge Himes	¾ lgth.	H. Booker	117	Early	Bourbon	140	6	4,850	2:09	Fast
May 2, 1904	Elwood	½ lgth.	F. Pryor	117	Ed. Tierney	Brancas	140	5	4,850	2:08½	Fast
May 10, 1905	Agile	3 lgths.	J. Martin	122	Ram's Horn	Layson	145	3	4,850	2:10¾	Heavy
May 2, 1906	Sir Huon	2 lgths.	R. Troxler	117	Lady Navarre	James Reddick	110	6	4,850	2:08⅕	Fast
May 6, 1907	Pink Star	2 lgths.	A. Minder	117	Zal	Ovelando	128	6	4,850	2:12⅗	Heavy
May 5, 1908	Stone Street	1 lgth.	A. Pickens	117	Sir cleges	Dunvegan	114	8	4,850	2:15⅕	Heavy
May 3, 1909	Wintergreen	4 lgths.	V. Powers	117	Miami	Dr. Barkley	117	10	4,850	2:08⅕	Slow
May 10, 1910	Donau	½ lgth.	F. Herbert	117	Joe Morris	Fighting Bob	117	7	$4,840	2:06⅖	Fast
May 13, 1911	Meridian	¾ lgth.	G. Archibald	117	Governor Gray	Colston	117	7	4,850	2:05	Fast
May 11, 1912	Worth	Neck	C. H. Schilling	117	Duval	Flamma	131	8	4,850	2:09⅖	Muddy
May 10, 1913	Donerail	½ lgth.	R. Goose	117	Ten Point	Gowell	32	8	5,475	2:04⅘	Fast
May 9, 1914	Old Rosebud	8 lgths.	J. McCabe	114	Hodge	Bronzewing	47	7	9,125	2:03⅖	Fast
May 8, 1915	Regret	2 lgths.	J. Notter	112	Pebbles	Sharpshooter	68	16	11,450	2:05⅖	Fast
May 13, 1916	George Smith	Neck	J. Loftus	117	Star Hawk	Franklin	56	9	9,750	2:04	Fast
May 12, 1917	*Omar Khayyam	2 lgths.	C. Borel	117	Ticket	Midway	76	15	16,600	2:04⅗	Fast
May 11, 1918	Exterminator	1 lgth.	W. Knapp	114	Escoba	Viva America	70	8	14,700	2:10⅘	Muddy
May 10, 1919	Sir Barton	5 lgths.	J. Loftus	112	Billy Kelly	Under Fire	75	12	20,825	2:09⅘	Heavy
May 8, 1920	Paul Jones	Head	T. Rice	126	Upset	On Watch	107	17	30,375	2:09	Slow
May 7, 1921	Behave Yourself	Head	C. Thompson	126	Black Servant	Prudery	109	12	38,450	2:04⅕	Fast
May 13, 1922	Morvich	1½ lgths.	A. Johnson	126	Bet Mosie	John Finn	92	10	46,775	2:04⅗	Fast
May 19, 1923	Zev	1½ lgths.	E. Sande	126	Martingale	Vigil	145	21	53,600	2:05⅖	Fast
May 17, 1924	Black Gold	½ lgth.	J. D. Mooney	126	Chilhowee	Beau Butler	152	19	52,775	2:05⅕	Fast
May 16, 1925	Flying Ebony	1½ lgths.	E. Sande	126	Captain Hal	Son of John	139	20	52,950	2:07⅗	Sloppy
May 15, 1926	Bubbling Over	5 lgths.	A. Johnson	126	Bagenbaggage	Rock Man	164	13	50,075	2:03⅘	Fast
May 14, 1927	Whiskery	Head	L. McAtee	126	Osmond	Jock	162	15	51,000	2:06	Slow
May 19, 1928	Reigh Count	3 lgths.	C. Lang	126	Misstep	Toro	196	22	55,375	2:10⅖	Heavy
May 18, 1929	Clyde Van Dusen	2 lgths.	L. McAtee	126	Naishapur	Panchio	159	21	53,950	2:10⅘	Muddy
May 17, 1930	Gallant Fox	2 lgths.	E. Sande	126	Gallant Knight	Ned O.	150	15	50,725	2:07⅗	Good
May 16, 1931	Twenty Grand	4 lgths.	C. Kurtsinger	126	Sweep All	Mate	130	12	48,725	2:01⅘	Fast
May 7, 1932	Burgoo King	5 lgths.	E. James	126	Economic	Stepenfetchit	115	20	52,350	2:05⅕	Fast
May 6, 1933	Brokers Tip	Nose	D. Meade	126	Head Play	Charley O.	118	13	48,925	2:06⅘	Good
May 5, 1934	Cavalcade	2½ lgths.	M. Garner	126	Discovery	Agrarian	124	13	28,175	2:04	Fast
May 4, 1935	Omaha	1½ lgths.	W. Saunders	126	Roman Soldier	Whiskolo	110	18	39,525	2:05	Good
May 2, 1936	Bold Venture	Head	I. Hanford	126	Brevity	Indian Broom	102	14	37,725	2:03⅗	Fast
May 8, 1937	War Admiral	1¾ lgths.	C. Kurtsinger	126	Pompoon	Reaping Reward	103	20	52,050	2:03⅕	Fast
May 7, 1938	Lawrin	1 lgth.	E. Arcaro	126	Dauber	Can't Wait	103	10	47,050	2:04⅘	Fast
May 6, 1939	Johnstown	8 lgths.	J. Stout	126	Challedon	Heather Broom	115	8	46,350	2:03⅖	Fast
May 4, 1940	Gallahadion	1½ lgths.	C. Bierman	126	Bimelech	Dit	127	8	60,150	2:05	Fast
May 3, 1941	Whirlaway	8 lgths.	E. Arcaro	126	Staretor	Market Wise	112	11	61,275	2:01⅖	Fast
May 2, 1942	Shut Out	2½ lgths.	W. D. Wright	126	Alsab	Valdina Orphan	150	15	64,225	2:04⅖	Fast
May 1, 1943	Count Fleet	3 lgths.	J. Longden	126	Blue Swords	Slide Rule	110	10	60,725	2:04	Fast
May 6, 1944	Pensive	4½ lgths.	C.M.McCreary	126	Broadcloth	Stir Up	148	16	64,675	2:04⅕	Fast
June 9, 1945	Hoop Jr.	6 lgths.	E. Arcaro	126	Pot o'Luck	Darby Dieppe	155	16	64,850	2:07	Muddy
May 4, 1946	Assault	8 lgths.	W. Mehrtens	126	Spy Song	Hampden	149	17	96,400	2:06⅗	Slow
May 3, 1947	Jet Pilot	Head	E. Guerin	126	Phalanx	Faultless	135	13	92,160	2:06⅘	Slow
May 1, 1948	Citation	3½ lgths.	E. Arcaro	126	Coaltown	My Request	109	6	83,400	2:05⅖	Sloppy

*Indicates imported horse.

Total starters, 74 years, 771, annual average, 11.

Total nominations, 74 years, 7,904, annual average, 106.

Distance—from 1875 to 1895 inclusive, the distance was one mile and a half; in 1896 it was reduced to one mile and a quarter.

Spokane's mark (1889) is record for mile and a half; Whirlaway's (1941) is record for a mile and a quarter.

No.	Year	WINNER	SIRE	BREEDER	OWNER	TRAINER	FAVORITE	Odds on Winner
1	1875	Aristides, ch. c.	*Leamington	H. P. McGrath	H. P. McGrath	A. Anderson	Winner (Entry)	2-1
2	1876	Vagrant, br. g.	Virgil	M. H. Sanford	William Astor	James Williams	Winner	9-5
3	1877	Baden-Baden, ch. c.	*Australian	A. J. Alexander	Daniel Swigert	Ed Brown	Leonard (7-5)	8-1
4	1878	Day Star, ch. c.	Star Davis	J. M. Clay	T. J. Nichols	Lee Paul	Himyar (1-4)	3-1
5	1879	Lord Murphy, b. c.	Pat Malloy	J. T. Carter	Geo. W. Darden & Co.	George Rice	Winner	11-10
6	1880	Fonso, ch. c.	King Alfonso	A. J. Alexander	J. S. Shawhan	Tice Hutsell	Kimball (3-5)	7-1
7	1881	Hindoo, b. c.	Virgil	Daniel Swigert	Dwyer Bros.	Jas. Rowe, Sr.	Winner	1-3
8	1882	Apollo, ch. g.	Lever	Daniel Swigert	Morris & Patton	Green B. Morris	Runnymede (4-5)	10-1
9	1883	Leonatus, b. c.	Longfellow	J. Henry Miller	Chinn & Morgan	R. Colston	Winner	9-5
10	1884	Buchanan, ch. c.	*Buckden	Cottrill & Guest	W. Cottrill	Wm. Bird	Audrain (2-1)	3-1
11	1885	Joe Cotton, ch. c.	King Alfonso	A. J. Alexander	J. T. Williams	Alex Perry	Winner	1-1
12	1886	Ben Ali, br. c.	Virgil	Daniel Swigert	J. B. Haggin	Jim Murphy	Winner	1.72-1
13	1887	Montrose, b. c.	Duke of Montrose	Milton Young	Labold Bros.	John McGinty	Banburg (7-5)	10-1
14	1888	Macbeth II, b. g.	Macduff	Rufus Lisle	Chicago Stable	John Campbell	Melbourne Stable Ent.(1-1)	8-1
15	1889	Spokane, ch. c.	Hyder Ali	Noah Armstrong	Noah Armstrong	John Rodegap	Proctor Knott (1-2)	10-1
16	1890	Riley, b. c.	Longfellow	C. H. Durkee	Edward Corrigan	Edward Corrigan	Robespierre (1-1)	4-1
17	1891	Kingman, b. c.	*Glengarry	A. C. Franklin	Jacobin Stable	Dud Allen	Winner	1-2
18	1892	Azra, b. c.	Reform	Geo. J. Long	Bashford Manor	John H. Morris	Winner	3-2
19	1893	Lookout, ch. c.	Troubadour	Scoggan Bros.	Cushing & Orth	Will McDaniel	Winner (Entry)	7-10
20	1894	Chant, b. c.	Falsetto	A. J. Alexander	Leigh & Rose	Eugene Leigh	Winner	1-2
21	1895	Halma, blk. c.	Hanover	Easton & Larrabie	Byron McClelland	Byron McClelland	Winner	1-3
22	1896	Ben Brush, b. c.	Bramble	Clay & Woodford	M. F. Dwyer	Hardy Campbell	Winner	1-2
23	1897	Typhoon II, ch. c.	*Top Gallant	John E. Ewing	J. C. Cahn	J. C. Cahn	Ornament (1-1)	3-1
24	1898	Plaudit, b. c.	Himyar	Dr. J. D. Neet	J. E. Madden	J. E. Madden	Lieber Karl (1-3)	3-1
25	1899	Manuel, b. c.	Bob Miles	George J. Long	A. H. & D. H. Morris	Robert J. Walden	Winner	11-20
26	1900	Lieut. Gibson, b. c	G. W. Johnson	Baker & Gentry	Charles H. Smith	Chas. H. Hughes	Winner	7-10
27	1901	His Eminence, b. c.	Falsetto	A. J. Alexander	F. B. VanMeter	F. B. VanMeter	Alard Scheck (7-10)	3-1
28	1902	Alan-a-Dale, ch. c.	Halma	T. C. McDowell	T. C. McDowell	T. C. McDowell	Abe Frank (3-5)	3-2
29	1903	Judge Himes, b. c.	*Esher	J. N. Camden	C. R. Ellison	J. P. Mayberry	Early (3-5)	10-1
30	1904	Elwood, b. c.	Free Knight	Mrs. J. B. Prather	Mrs. C. E. Durnell	C. E. Durnell	Proceeds (1-1)	15-1
31	1905	Agile. b. c.	Sir Dixon	E. F. Clay	S. S. Brown	Robert Tucker	Winner	1-3
32	1906	Sir Huon, b. c.	Falsetto	George J. Long	George J. Long	Peter Coyne	Winner	11-10
33	1907	Pink Star, b. c.	Pink Coat	J. Hal Woodford	J. Hal Woodford	W. H. Fizer	Red Gauntlet (3-2)	15-1
34	1908	Stone Street, b. c.	Longstreet	J. B. Haggin	C. E. Hamilton	J. Hall	Sir Cleges (9-5)	23.72-1
35	1909	Wintergreen, b. c.	Dick Welles	J. B. Respess	J. B. Respess	C. Mack	Winner	1.96-1
36	1910	Donau, b. c.	*Woolsthorpe	Milton Young	William Gerst	George Ham	Winner	1.65-1
37	1911	Meridian, b. c.	Broomstick	C. L. Harrison	R. F. Carman	A. Ewing	Governor Gray (1-1)	2.90-1
38	1912	Worth, br. c.	*Knight of Thistle	R. H. McC. Potter	H. C. Hallenbeck	Frank M. Taylor	Winner	4-5
39	1913	Donerail, b. c.	*McGee	T. P. Hayes	T. P. Hayes	T. P. Hayes	Ten Point (1.20-1)	91.45-1
40	1914	Old Rosebud, b. g.	Uncle	J. E. Madden	H. C. Applegate	F. D. Weir	Winner	85c to 1
41	1915	Regret, ch. f.	Broomstick	H. P. Whitney	H. P. Whitney	Jas. Rowe, Sr.	Winner	2.65-1
42	1916	George Smith, blk. c.	*Out of Reach	Chinn & Forsythe	John Sanford	Hollie Hughes	Whitney Entry (1.05-1)	4.15-1
43	1917	*Omar Khayyam, ch. c.	Marco	Sir John Robinson	Billings & Johnson	C. T. Patterson	Ticket (1.45-1)	12.80-1
44	1918	Exterminator, ch. g.	*McGee	F. D. Knight	W. S. Kilmer	Henry McDaniel	*War Cloud (1.45-1)	29.60-1
45	1919	Sir Barton, ch. c.	*Star Shoot	Madden & Gooch	J. K. L. Ross	H. G. Bedwell	McClelland Entry (2.10-1)	2.60-1
46	1920	Paul Jones, br. g.	*Sea King	J. E. Madden	Ral Parr	Wm. Garth	Whitney Entry (1.65-1)	16.20-1
47	1921	Behave Yourself, b. c.	Marathon	E. R. Bradley	E. R. Bradley	H. J. Thompson	Whitney Entry (1.10-1)	8.65-1
48	1922	Morvich, br. c.	Runnymede	A. B. Spreckles	B. Block	Fred Burlew	Winner	1.20-1
49	1923	Zev. br. c.	The Finn	J. E. Madden	Rancocas Stable	D. J. Leary	Whitney-G'treeEnt(2.30-1)	19.20-1
50	1924	Black Gold, blk. c.	Black Toney	Mrs. R. M. Hoots	Mrs. R. M. Hoots	Hanly Webb	Winner	1.70-1
51	1925	Flying Ebony, blk. c.	The Finn	J. E. Madden	G. A. Cochran	W. B. Duke	Quatrain (1.95-1) (Field)	3.15-1
52	1926	Bubbling Over, ch. c.	*North Star III	Idle Hour Stock Farm	Idle Hour Stock Farm	H. J. Thompson	Winner (Entry)	1.90-1
53	1927	Whiskery, b. c.	Whisk Broom II	H. P. Whitney	H. P. Whitney	Fred Hopkins	Winner (Entry)	2.40-1
54	1928	Reigh Count, ch. c.	*Sunreigh	Willis Shape Kilmer	Mrs. J. D. Hertz	B. S. Michell	Winner (Entry)	2.05-1
55	1929	Clyde Van Dusen, ch. g.	Man o'War	H. P. Gardner	H. P. Gardner	C. Van Dusen	E. R. Bradley Entry (1.71-1)	3-1
56	1930	Gallant Fox, b. c.	*Sir Gallahad III	Belair Stud	Belair Stud	James Fitzsimmons	Winner	1.19-1
57	1931	Twenty Grand, b. c.	*St. Germans	Greentree Stable	Greentree Stable	Jas. Rowe, Jr.	Winner	88c toc1
58	1932	Burgoo King, ch. c.	Bubbling Over	E. R. Bradley and H. N. Davis	E. R. Bradley	H. J. Thompson	Tick On (1.84-1)	5.62-1
59	1933	Brokers Tip, br. c.	Black Toney	Idle Hour Stock Farm	E. R. Bradley	H. J. Thompson	W. R. Coe Entry (1.43-1)	8.93-1
60	1934	Cavalcade, br. c.	*Lancegaye	F. W. Armstrong	Mrs. Dodge Sloane	R. A. Smith	Winner (Entry)	1.50-1
61	1935	Omaha, ch. c.	Gallant Fox	Belair Stud	Belair Stud	James Fitzsimmons	Nellie Flag (3.80-1)	4-1
62	1936	Bold Venture, ch. c.	*St. Germans	M. L. Schwartz	M. L. Schwartz	Max Hirsch	Brevity (4-5)	20.50-1
63	1937	War Admiral, br. c.	Man o'War	Samuel D. Riddle	Glen Riddle Farm	George Conway	Winner	1.60-1
64	1938	Lawrin, b. c.	Insco	Herbert Woolf	Woolford Farm	B. A. Jones	Fighting Fox (1.40-1)	8.60-1
65	1939	Johnstown, b. c.	Jamestown	A. B. Hancock	Belair Stud	James Fitzsimmons	Winner	60c to 1
66	1940	Gallahadion, b. c.	*Sir Gallahad III	R. A. Fairbairn	Milky Way Farm	Roy Waldron	Bimelech (40c-1)	35.20-1
67	1941	Whirlaway, ch. c.	*Blenheim II	Calumet Farm	Warren Wright	Ben A. Jones	Winner	2.90-1
68	1942	Shut Out, ch. c.	Equipoise	Greentree Stable	Greentree Farm	John M. Gaver	Winner (Entry)	1.90-1
69	1943	Count Fleet, br. c.	Reigh Count	Mrs. John D. Hertz.	Mrs. John D. Hertz.	G. D. Cameron	Winner	40c-1
70	1944	Pensive, ch. c.	Hyperion	Calumet Farm	Calumet Farm	Ben A. Jones	Stir Up	7.10-1
71	1945	Hoop Jr., b. c.	*Sir Gallahad III	R. A. Fairbairn	F. W. Hooper	I. H. Parke	Pot o'Luck (3.30-1)	3.70-1
72	1946	Assault, ch. c.	Bold Venture	King Ranch	King Ranch	Max Hirsch	Maine Chance Ent.(1.10-1)	8.20-1
73	1947	Jet Pilot, ch. c.	*Blenheim II	A. B. Hancock and Mrs. R. A. Van Clief	Maine Chance Farm	Tom Smith	Phalanx (2-1)	5.40-1
74	1948	Citation, ch. c.	Bull Lea	Calumet Farm	Calumet Farm	B. A. Jones	Winner (Entry)	40c-1

*Imported horse

Key to owners of stable and farm names above: Chicago Stable (Hankins & Johnson) Bashford Manor (George J. Long), Idle Hour Stock Darm (E. R. Bradley), Rancocas Stable (H. F. Sinclair), Belair Stud (William Woodward). Greentree Stable (Mrs. Payne Whitney), Glen Riddle Farm (Samuel D. Riddle), Woolford Farm (Herbert M. Woolf), Milky Way Farms (Mrs. Ethel V. Mars), Calumet Farm (Warren Wright) King Ranch (Robert J. Kleberg), Maine Chance Farm (Mrs. Elizabeth Graham).

Year	Nominations	Nominating Fee	Starters	Starting Fee	Total Stakes	Churchill Downs Added	Gross Value	Winner's Net Share	2nd Horse	3rd Horse	4th Horse
1875	42	$50	15	....	$2,100	$1,000	$3,100	$2,850	$200	....	....
1876	34	50	11	....	1,700	1,500	3,200	2,950	200	....	....
1877	41	50	11	....	2,050	1,500	3,300	3,300	200	....	....
1878	56	50	9	....	2,800	1,500	4,300	4,050	200	....	....
1879	46	50	9	....	2,300	1,500	3,800	3,550	200	....	....
1880	47	50	5	See Note	See Note	1,500	See Note	3,800	200	....	....
1881	62	50	6	"	"	1,500	"	4,410	200	....	....
1882	64	50	14	"	"	1,500	"	4,560	200	....	....
1883	50	50	7	"	"	1,500	"	3,760	200	....	....
1884	51	50	9	"	"	1,500	"	3,990	200	....	....
1885	69	50	10	See Note	See Note	1,500	See Note	4,630	200	....	....
1886	107	50	10	"	"	1,500	"	4,890	300	150	....
1887	119	50	7	"	"	1,500	"	4,200	300	150	....
1888	95	50	7	"	"	2,500	"	4,740	500	200	....
1889	94	50	8	"	"	2,500	"	4,880	300	150	....
1890	115	50	6	"	"	2,500	"	5,460	300	150	....
1891	83	50	4	"	"	2,500	"	4,550	300	150	....
1892	68	50	3	"	"	2,500	"	4,230	300	150	....
1893	60	50	6	"	"	3,000	"	3,840	400	150	$100**
1894	55	50	5	"	"	2,500	"	4,020	300	150	100**
1895	57	50	4	"	"	2,500	"	2,970	300	150	100**
1896	171	50	8	"	"	See Note	*6,000	4,850	700	300	....
1897	159	50	6	"	"	"	*6,000	4,850	700	300	....
1898	179	50	4	"	"	"	*6,000	4,850	700	300	....
1899	151	50	5	"	"	"	*6,000	4,850	700	300	....
1900	131	50	7	"	"	"	*6,000	4,850	700	300	....
1901	113	50	5	"	"	"	*6,000	4,850	700	300	....
1902	112	50	4	"	"	"	*6,000	4,850	700	300	....
1903	140	See Note	6	"	"	"	*6,000	4,850	700	300	....
1904	140	"	5	"	"	"	*6,000	4,850	700	300	....
1905	145	"	3	"	"	"	*6,000	4,850	700	300	....
1906	110	"	6	"	"	"	*6,000	4,850	700	300	....
1907	128	"	6	"	"	"	*6,000	4,850	700	300	....
1908	114	"	8	"	"	"	*6,000	4,850	700	300	....
1909	117	"	10	"	"	"	*6,000	4,850	700	300	....
1910	117	"	7	"	"	"	*6,000	4,850	700	300	....
1911	117	"	7	"	"	"	*6,000	4,850	700	300	....
1912	131	"	8	"	"	"	*6,000	4,850	700	300	....
1913	32	25	8	$100	$1,600	5,000	6,600	5,475	700	300	225**
1914	47	25	7	200	2,575	10,000	12,575	9,125	2,000	1,000	225**
1915	68	25	16	200	4,900	10,000	14,900	11,450	2,000	1,000	225**
1916	56	25	9	200	3,200	10,000	13,200	9,750	2,000	1,000	225**
1917	76	25	15	250	5,650	15,000	20,650	16,600	2,500	1,000	275**
1918	70	25	8	250	3,750	15,000	18,750	14,700	2,500	1,000	275**
1919	75	25	12	250	4,875	20,000	24,875	20,825	2,500	1,000	275**
1920	107	25	17	250	5,925	30,000	35,925	30,375	4,000	1,000	275**
1921	109	25	12	250	5,725	50,000	55,725	38,450	10,000	5,000	2,000
1922	92	25	10	500	7,300	50,000	57,300	46,775	6,000	3,000	1,000
1923	145	25	21	500	14,125	50,000	64,125	53,600	6,000	3,000	1,000
1924	152	25	19	500	13,300	50,000	63,300	52,775	6,000	3,000	1,000
1925	139	25	20	500	13,475	50,000	63,475	52,950	6,000	3,000	1,000
1926	164	25	13	500	10,600	50,000	60,600	50,075	6,000	3,000	1,000
1927	162	25	15	500	11,525	50,000	61,525	51,000	6,000	3,000	1.000
1928	196	25	22	500	15,900	50,000	65,900	55,375	6,000	3,000	1,000
1929	159	25	21	500	14,475	50,000	64,475	53,950	6.000	3,000	1,000
1930	150	25	15	500	11,250	50,000	61,250	50,725	6,000	3,000	1,000
1931	130	25	12	500	9,250	50,000	59,250	48,725	6,000	3,000	1,000
1932	115	25	20	500	12,875	50,000	62,875	52,350	6,000	3,000	1,000
1933	118	25	13	500	9,450	50,000	59,450	48,925	6,000	3,000	1,000
1934	124	25	13	300	7,000	30,000	37,000	28,175	5,000	2,500	1,000
1935	110	25	18	400	9,950	40,000	49,950	39,525	6,000	3,000	1,000
1936	102	25	14	400	8,150	40,000	48,150	37,725	6,000	3,000	1,000
1937	103	25	20	500	12,575	50,000	62,575	52,050	6,000	3,000	1,000
1938	103	25	10	500	7,575	50,000	57,575	47,050	5,000	3,000	1,000
1939	115	25	8	500	6,875	50,000	56,875	46,350	6,000	3,000	1,000
1940	127	25	8	500	7,175	75,000 (note)	82,175 (note)	60,150	8,000	3,000	1,000
1941	112	25	11	500	8,300	75,000 (note)	83,300 (note)	61,275	8,000	3,000	1,000
1942	150	25	15	500	11,250	75,000 (note)	86,250 (note)	64,225	8,000	3,000	1,000
1943	110	25	10	500	7,750	75,000 (note)	82,750 (note)	60,725	8,000	3,000	1,000
1944	148	25	16	500	11,700	75,000 (note)	86,700 (note)	64,675	8,000	3,000	1,000
1945	155	25	16	500	11,875	75,000 (note)	86,875 (note)	64,850	8,000	3,000	1,000
1946	149	50	17	1000	24,450	100,000 (note)	124,450 (note)	96,400	10,000	5,000	2,500
1947	135	50	13	1000	19,750	100,460 (note)	120,210	92,160	10,000	5,000	2,500
1948	109	50	6	1000	11,450	100,000	111,450	83,400	10,000	5,000	2,500
TOTALS	7,904	—	771	—	—	—	—	1,845,640	231,000	105,750	38,675

*Churchill Downs guaranteed gross value of Stakes at $6,000.

**Fourth horses saved stake money.

Note: 1880 Conditions provided $100 nominating fee, half to be forfeited if horse did not go to post.

1881—$100 half forfeit nominating fee; if horse declared out May 1 before his Derby year, owner forfeited only $20; if not declared out until May 1 of his Derby year, forfeit was $40; if not declared out until after May 1, forfeit was $50.

1882-1885, inclusive—Conditions same as in 1881.

1886-1895, inclusive—Conditions same as 1881, except that early declaration forfeits reduced from $20—$40 to $10—$20.

1896—Conditions required nominations of horse as yearling, when $5 had to accompany nominations. $51 to be paid on May 1st, of horse's 2-year-old form; $30 on May 1st of his Derby year; $100 additional to start, Jockey Club guaranteed value of stake to be $6,000, of which $700 to second, and $300 to third.

1897—Conditions same, except that $30 payment date was advanced from May 1st to March 1st. 1898-1912, inclusive—Conditions same as 1897.

Note: 1940—Downs stipulated $8,000 go to owner of second horse. $3,000 third horse, $1,000, fourth horse; that $6,000 be divided among trainers of first, second and third horses ($3,000, $2,000, $1,000); that $3,500 be divided among breeders of first, second and third horses ($2,000, $1,000, $500). 1941, 1942, 1943, 1944, 1945—Same conditions as 1940.

1946-1947-1948—$10,000 to second; $5,000 to third; $2,500 to fourth. Trainers and breeders received same awards as in 1940-45.

FILLIES IN THE DERBY

Twenty-eight fillies have been starters in the Kentucky Derby. Only one, Harry Payne Whitney's Regret in 1915, has won, and six others have finished second or third.

Two fillies were post-time favorites. They were Regret and Calumet Farm's Nellie Flag, which finished fourth in the 1935 Derby. The H. P. Whitney entry of the filly Prudery and the colt Tryster was the favorite in the 1921 Derby. Prudery was third. The twenty-eight fillies which have started in the Kentucky Derby and where they finished follow:

YEAR	FILLY	FINISH	YEAR	FILLY	FINISH
1875	Gold Mine	(15th)	1918	Viva America	(3rd)
1875	Ascension	(10th)	1919	Regalo	(9th)
1876	Marie Michon	(unp)	1920	Cleopatra	(15th)
1877	Early Light	(unp)	1921	Prudery	(3rd)
1879	Ada Glen	(unp)	1921	Careful	(5th)
1879	Wissahicken	(unp)	1922	Startle	(8th)
1883	Pike's Pride	(unp)	1929	Ben Machree	(18th)
1906	Lady Navarre	(2nd)	1930	Alcibiades	(13th)
1911	Round the World	(6th)	1932	Oscillation	(10th)
1912	Flamma	(3rd)	1934	Mata Hari	(4th)
1913	Gowell	(3rd)	1934	Bazaar	(9th)
1914	Bronzewing	(3rd)	1935	Nellie Flag	(4th)
1914	Watermelon	(7th)	1936	Gold Seeker	(9th)
1915	Regret	(1st)	1945	Misweet	(12th)

FATE OF WINTER-BOOK FAVORITES

The records reveal that only 5 of the 29 different winter-book favorites, from 1919 to 1948 (1945 excluded because there was no winter-book because of the racing ban) lived up to earliest hopes and raced home in front on Derby Day indicating odds of 6 to 1 against any winter-book favorite.

Here is the story of the winter-book favorites since 1919:

YEAR	OPENING FAVORITE	ODDS	FINISHED
1919	ETERNAL	4-1	10th

Sir Barton, opening in winter books at 30 to 1, was winner; $2 win tickets paid $7.60; was coupled with Billy Kelly.

1920	DAMASK	4-1	4th

Paul Jones, opening at 50 to 1, was winner; $2 win tickets paid $34.40.

1921	TRYSTER	5-1	4th

Behave Yourself, opening at 40 to 1, was winner; $2 win tickets paid $19.30; was coupled with Black Servant.

1922	MORVICH	5-1	1st

$2 win tickets paid $4.40, or odds of $1.20 to 1.

1923	ENCHANTMENT	8-1	6th

Zev, opening at 12-1, was winner; $2 win tickets paid $40.40.

1924	SARAZEN / WISE COUNSELLOR ⎰ Joint favorites ⎱	6-1	Did not start

Black Gold, opening at 25 to 1, was winner; $2 win tickets paid $5.50.

1925   QUATRAIN 6-1   12th
Flying Ebony, opening at 40 to 1, was winner; $2 win tickets paid only $8.30, due to fact Flying Ebony was coupled in the field with six other horses.

1926   POMPEY 6-1   5th
Bubbling Over, opening at 10 to 1, was winner; $2 win tickets paid $5.80; was coupled with Bagenbaggage.

1927   OSMAND 6-1   2nd
Whiskery, opening at 20 to 1, was winner; $2 win tickets paid $6.80; was coupled with Bostonian.

1928   REIGH COUNT 4-1   1st
$2 win tickets paid $6.12, or odds of $2.06 to 1.

1929   BLUE LARKSPUR 7-1   4th
Clyde Van Dusen, opening at 10 to 1, was winner; $2 win tickets paid $8.

1930   GALLANT FOX 10-1   1st
$2 win tickets paid $4.38, or odds of $1.19 to 1. Equal opening favorites at 10 to 1 were High Foot, which finished 14th; Flying Heels, Desert Light and Dedicate, which did not start.

1931   EQUIPOISE 4-1   Did not start
Twenty Grand, opening at 6 to 1, was winner; $2 win tickets paid $3.76.

1932   TOP FLIGHT 8-1   Did not start
Burgoo King, opening at 30 to 1, was winner; $2 win tickets paid $13.24; was coupled with Brother Joe.

1933   LADYSMAN 8-1   4th
Brokers Tip, opening at 40 to 1, was winner; $2 win tickets paid $19.86.

1934   MATA HARI 10-1   4th
Cavalcade, opening at 20 to 1, was winner; $2 win tickets paid $5; was coupled with Time Clock.

1935   CHANCE SUN 6-1   Did not start
Omaha, opening at 8 to 1, won; $2 win tickets paid $10.

1936   HOLLYROOD 6-1   Did not start
Bold Venture, opening at 40 to 1, was winner; $2 win tickets paid $43.

1937   POMPOON 8-1   2nd
War Admiral, opening at 12 to 1, was winner; $2 win tickets paid $5.20.

1938   STAGEHAND 6-1   Did not start
Lawrin, opening at 20 to 1, won; $2 win tickets paid $19.20.

1939   EL CHICO 4-1   6th
Johnstown, opening at 10 to 1 in the winter books, was winner. Mutuel payoff on Johnstown $3.20, $3.00, $2.80.

1940   BIMELECH 3-1   2nd
Bimelech closed at 7 to 10 in winter books during Derby week. Gallahadion opened at 80 to 1, closed at 40 to 1. The payoff, across the board on Gallahadion was $72.40, $13.80 and $4.80.

1941   OUR BOOTS 3-1   8th
Whirlaway, opening at 8 to 1, was winner. The mutuel payoff across the boards was $7.80, $5.00, $4.40.

1942   ALSAB 5-1   2nd
Shut Out, opening at 30 to 1, won. Closed at 7 to 1. Mutuel payoff on Shut Out, coupled with Devil Diver as Greentree entry, $5.80, $3.40, $3.00 on $2 tickets.

1943   COUNT FLEET 2½   1st
Closed at 1 to 2 during Derby Week. Pari-Mutuel payoff on Count Fleet was $2.80, $2.40, $2.20 for $2 tickets across the board.

1944   PUKKA GIN 6-1   Did not start
Platter opened as second choice, at 8 to 1, and did not start. Pensive, the winner, opened at 20 to 1, and closed at 15 during Derby week.

1946   KNOCKDOWN 6-1   5th
Knockdown dropped to 4 to 1 after winning the Santa Anita Derby, and was one of three horses in the Maine Chance Farm entry, which was the favorite at post time.

1947   PHALANX 8-1   2nd
Phalanx opened as first choice and dropped to 2-1 before Derby Day.

1948   CITATION 8-5   1st
Citation opened at 8 to 5, closed at 4 to 5, and was held at 40c to $1 as part of Calumet Farm entry.

KENTUCKY OAKS

Originated 1875, for three-year-old fillies . . . Distance one and a half miles, 1875-1891, inclusive . . . one and a quarter, 1892-1895, inclusive . . . one and a sixteenth, 1896-1919, inclusive . . . and one and an eighth since 1920.

Year	Winner	Owner	Jockey	Wt.	Second	Wt.	Third	Wt.	Value	Time
1875	Vinaigrette	A. B. Lewis & Co.	J. Houston	97	Gyptis	97	Elemi	97	$1,175	1:29¾
1876	Necy Hale	F. B. Harper	James	97	Plenty	97	Lady Clipper	97	1,900	2:42½
1877	Felicia	J. W. H. Reynolds	James	97	Bradamante	97	Aunt Betsy	97	2,550	2:39
1878	Belle of Nelson	Mattingly & Co.	Booth	97	Buena Vista	97	Fortuna	97	2,650	2:39
1879	Liahtunah	J. A. Grinstead	Hightower	97	Ada Glenn	97	Buckden Lass	97	3,350	2:40½
1880	Longtitude	J. G. Malone	J. McLaughlin	102	Bye and Bye	102	Ersilia	102	3,250	2:41¾
1881	Lucy May	R. F. Johnson	Wolre	102	Belle of the Highlands	102	Mrs. Chubbs	102	3,000	2:41
1882	Katie Creel	Johnson & Co.	J. Stoval	102	Pinafore	102	Issie	102	3,240	2:39
1883	Vera	R. C. Pate	J. Stoval	102	Orange Blossom	102	Billetta	102	3,220	2:39¾
1884	Modesty	E. Corrigan	I. Murphy	105	Highflight	105	Bluette	105	3,030	2:48¼
1885	Lizzie Dwyer	E. Corrigan	Fuller	105	Constellation	105	Exile	105	3,800	2:40¾
1886	Pure Rye	Melbourne Stable	E. Garrison	113	Red Girl	113	Ada D.	113	4,170	2:41
1887	Florimore	T. H. Stevens	Johnston	113	Wary	113	Bannail	113	3,330	2:40¾
1888	Ten Penny	M. Welsh	A. McCarthy, Jr	113	Los Angeles	114	Quindara Belle	113½	3,770	2:42
1889	Jewel Ban	J. T. Clay	J. Stobal	113	Brandolette	113	Retrieve	113	3,850	2:41
1890	English Lady	Scoggan Bros.	Hollis	113	Marie K.	113			3,610	2:42½
1891	Miss Hawkins	Talbott Bros.	T. Britton	117	Ethel	117	Joanna	117	2,780	2:16
1892	Miss Dixie	J. E. Pepper	H. Ray	117	Unadilla	117	Scuttle	117	2,600	2:15
1893	Monrovia	E. Brown	J. Reagan	117	Elizabeth L.	117	Bonnie Bird	117	3,860	2:18¼
1894	Selika	Bashford Manor	A. Clayton	117	Charity	117	Greenwich	117	3,470	2:14¼
1895	Voladora	Pastime Stable	A. Clayton	117	Alabama	117	Kathryn	117	1,830	2:16¾
1896	Souffle	J. M. Murphy	C. Thorpe	112	Myrtle Harkness	112	La Gascoyne	112	2,860	1:54½
1897	White Frost	E. S. Gardner & Son	T. Burns	112	Rosinante	112	Taluca	112	2,410	1:49
1898	Crocket	J. C. Cahn	J. Hill	112	Lannep	112	Alleviate	112	2,860	1:51½
1899	Rush	T. C. McDowell	J. Hill	112	May Hempstead	117	The Lady in Blue	112	2,410	1:52½
1900	Etta	E. Brown & Co.	M. Overton	112	Scarlet Lily	112	Cleora	112	2,410	1:48
1901	Lady Schorr	J. W. Schorr	J. Woods	117	Isobel	112	Edith Q.	112	2,410	1:53
1902	Wain-a-Moimen	Talbott Bros.	M. Coburn	112	Marque	112	Autumn Leaves	112	2,410	1:51¼
1903	Lemco	E. Corrigan	J. Reiff	112	Mary Lavana	112	The Crisis	112	2,410	1:49¾
1904	Audience	S. S. Brown	Helgesen	117	Outcome	112	White Plume	112	2,410	1:51
1905	Janeta	Casson & Rogers	D. Austin	112	Mum	112	Sis Lee	112	2,410	1:49¾
1906	King's Daughter	T. C. McDowell	E. Robinson	112	Lady Navarre	117	Lady Anne	112	2,410	1:47⅘
1907	Wing Ting	J. S. Hawkins	J. Lee	112	Altuda	112	Lillie Turner	112	2,410	1:40⅕
1908	Ellen-a-Dale	T. C. McDowell	V. Powers	105	Boema	112	Estradia	105	2,410	1:46⅗
1909	Floreal	W. H. Fizer & Co.	Heidel	112	Pink Wings	105	Cordova	112	2,410	1:49⅕
1910	Samaria	J. P. Ross & Co.	R. Scoville	112	Foxy Mary	112	My Gal	112	$1,910	1:50⅕
1911	Bettie Sue	A. Brown	T. Rice	112	Princess Callaway	112	Ilma	112	1,910	1:48
1912	Flamma	El F. Condran	J. Butwell	112	Floral Day	112	Beautiful	105	1,910	1:51⅕
1913	Cream	C. C. Van Meter	C. Ganz	112	Floral Park	112	Gowell	117	1,950	1:47⅗
1914	Bronzewing	A. P. Humphrey, Jr.	W. Obert	117	Casuarina	112	Brackt'n Bell	112	2,320	1:45⅗
1915	Waterblossom	T. C. McDowell	E. Martin	117	One Step	112	Lady Rotha	112	2,530	1:46⅗
1916	Kathleen	Geo. J. Long	R. Goose	112	Mandy Hamilton	117	Lady Always	112	2,410	1:47⅖
1917	Sunbonnet	A. K. Macomber	J. Loftus	112	Diamond	112	Battle	112	3,035	1:46⅘
1918	Viva America	C. T. Worthington	W. Warrington	112	Fern Handley	112	Mistress Polly	112	2,580	1:46⅘
1919	Lillian Shaw	J. Livingston	T. Murray	117	Milkmaid	117	Dancing Spray	112	4,190	1:45
1920	Lorraine	J. N. Camden	D. Connelly	116	Truly Rural	116	Dresden	116	5,470	1:58⅖
1921	Nancy Lee	P. A. Clark	L. McAtee	116	Prudery	116	Lady Madcap	116	8,980	1:50⅖
1922	Startle	H. H. Hewitt	D. Connelly	116	Martah Fallon	116	Precious Lula	116	9,920	1:52⅗
1923	Untidy	Mrs. Payne Whitney	J. Corcoran	116	Sweetheart	116	Gadfly	121	10,060	1:53
1924	{ Princess Doreen	Audley Farm Stable	H. Stutts	116	Nellie Morse	121	Befuddle	116	10,160	1:51⅘
	{ Glade finished first; was disqualified.									
1925	Deeming	C. B. Dailey	J. McCoy	116	Buckwheat Cake	116	Little Visitor	121	10,280	1:54
1926	Black Maria	W. R. Coe	A. Mortensen	121	Dark Phantom	116	Helen's Babe	116	10,960	1:55⅖
1927	Mary Jane	Gallaher & Combs	D. Connelly	121	Handy Mandy	111	Fresco	116	10,900	1:53⅖
1928	Easter Stockings	B. B. Jones	W. Crump	116	Pink Lily	116	Reveries' Gal	121	9,140	1:51⅗
1929	Rose of Sharon	J. N. Camden	W. Crump	121	Lady Broadcast	116	Current	116	10,080	1:51
1930	Alcibiades	Hal Price Headley	R. Finnerty	116	Rich Widow	116	Galady	116	9,760	1:52⅗
1931	Cousin Jo	Charles Nuckols	E. James	116	Sunny Lassie	116	Town Limit	116	9,610	1:53
1932	Suntica	W. S. Kilmer	A. Pascuma	116	I Say	116	Depression	116	4,590	1:52⅕
1933	Barn Swallow	E. R. Bradley	D. Meade	116	At Top	116	Bright Bubble	116	4,280	1:51⅕
1934	Fiji	Young Bros.	G. Elston	116	Far Star	116	Penncote	116	2,230	1:51⅗
1935	Paradisical	I. J. Collins	G. Fowler	116	Mid Victorian	116	Spanish Babe	116	2,310	1:51⅕
1936	Two Bob	C. V. Whitney	R. Workman	116	Threadneedle	116	Seventh Heaven	116	4,625	1:52⅖
1937	Mars Shield	Mrs. E. V. Mars	A. Robertson	116	Shatterproof	116	Alkit	116	4,590	1:53⅖
1938	Flying Lee	Hal Price Headley	L. Haas	116	Janice	116	Fantine	116	4,720	1:52⅘
1939	Flying Lil	Mrs. C. H. Cleary	C. Bierman	116	Bala Ormont	116	Rude Awakening	110½	4,820	1:51
1940	Inscolassie	Woolford Farm	R. L. Vedder	116	June Bee	116	Shine O'Night	116	6,120	1:54⅖
1941	Valdina Myth	Valdina Farm	G. King	116	Silvestra	116	Mystery Marvel	116	4,240	1:52⅗
1942	Miss Dogwood	Brownell Combs	J. Adams	116	Questvive	116	Miss Glamour	116	4,810	1:47
1943	Nellie L.	Calumet Farm	W. Eads	116	Valdina Mari	116	Edie Jane	116	4,160	1:48⅗
1944	Canina	A. Hirschberg	J. Adams	116	Harriet Sue	121	Paddie	110	4,200	1:48⅗
1945	Come and Go	Thos. Piatt	C. L. Martin	121	On Your Toes	116	Miss Blindfold	116	3,840	1:49⅘
1946	First Page	H. G. Jones	J. R. Layton	116	Athenia	116	Buzzaround	116	9,175	1:51⅖
1947	Blue Grass	A. B. Hancock, Jr.	J. Longden	116	Cosmic Missile	121	Mother	116	21,680	1:51⅗
1948	Challe Anne	F. L. Flanders	W. Garner	116	Reigh Belle	116	Back Talk	116	19,800	1:48⅗

CLARK HANDICAP

Originated in 1875, as Clark Stakes, exclusively for three-year-olds . . . changed to Clark Handicap after 1901 running . . . since 1902 has been handicap for three-year-olds and upward . . . distance, two miles, 1875-1880 . . . reduced to one and a quarter, 1881-1895, inclusive . . . one and an eighth 1896-1901 . . . also in 1922, 1923 and 1924 . . . distance one and a sixteenth, 1902-1921, inclusive, and since 1925. Figures in parentheses indicate age of horse.

Year	Winner	Owner	Jockey	Wt.	Second	Wt.	Third	Wt.	Value	Time
1875	Voltigeur	W. G. Harding	McGrath	100	Calvin	100	Millionaire	100	$1,425	3:50¾
1876	Creedmoor	Williams & Co.	W. Williams	100	Vagrant	97	Henry Owings	100	2,150	3:34¾
1877	McWhirter	A. Buford	C. Miller	100	Vera Cruz	97	Hyena	97	2,000	3:30½
1878	{ Leveler	R. H. Owens	R. Swim	100	{ Day Star (dead	100	....		2,150	3:37
	{	....	....		{ Solicitor heat)	100	....		.....	.....
1879	Falsetto	J. W. H. Reynolds	I. Murphy	100	Bucktie	100	Trindidad	100	2,100	3:40½
1880	Kinkead	R. H. Owens	J. McLaughlin	105	Aurora's Baby	105	Bye and Bye	102	2,350	3:37¾
1881	Hindoo	Dwyer Bros.	J. McLaughlin	105	Alfambra	105	Bootjack	105	3,500	2:10¼
1882	Runnymede	Dwyer Bros.	J. McLaughlin	105	Babcock	105	Apollo	102	3,180	2:15½
1883	Ascender	R. C. Pate	J. Stoval	102	Cardinal McCloskey	102	Markland	103	3,270	2:18
1884	Buchanan	W. Cottrill	I. Murphy	110	Loftin	110	Audrain	110	3,230	2:12
1885	Bersan	G. B. Morris	I. Murphy	110	Troubadour	110	Joe Cotton	110	3,420	2:09¼
1886	Blue Wing	Melbourne Stable	E. Garrison	118	Free Knight	118	Endurer	118	4,190	2:10
1887	Jim Gore	A. G. McCampbell	L. Jones	118	Libretto	118	Ban Clocke	118	3,630	2:11¼
1888	Gallifet	Melbourne Stable	McCarthy	118	White	118	Long Roll	118	3,510	2:15¼
1889	Spokane	Montana Stable	E. Kiley	118	Proctor Knott	118	Once Again	118	3,510	2:12½
1890	Riley	E. Corrigan	I. Murphy	118	Robespierre	118	Bill Letcher	118	4,140	2:16¼
1891	High Tariff	Eastin & Larrabie	J. Overton	122	Dickerson	122	Milt Young	118	3,370	2:12
1892	Azra	Bashford Manor	A. Clayton	122	Phil Dwyer	122	....		3,040	2:20
1893	Boundless	Cushing & Orth	E. Kunze	122	Buck McCann	122	Decapod	122	2,300	2:12
1894	Chant	Leigh & Rose	W. Martin	122	Pearl Song	122	Buckrene	122	2,730	2:19½
1895	Halma	B. McClelland	J. Perkins	122	Curator	122	....		1,720	2:15½
1896	Ben Eder	M. F. Dwyer	W. Simms	117	Semper Ego	117	Parson	109	3,350	1:56½
1897	Ornament	C. T. Patterson	A. Clayton	117	Dr. Catlett	117	Panmure	117	3,350	1:55
1898	Plaudit	J. E. Madden	R. Williams	127	Lieber Karl	122	....		3,350	1:56½
1899	Corsini	E. Corrigan	N. Turner	122	Hapsburg	117	His Lordship	110	3,350	2:01¾
1900	Lieut. Gibson	C. H. Smith	J. Boland	127	Flaunt	117	Dieudonne	107	3,350	1:54
1901	His Eminence	F. B. Van Meter	J. Winkfield	127	The Puritan	117	Driscoll	110	3,350	1:55
1902	Death (7)	H. Robinson	J. Slack	116	Jim Clark	101	L. Strathmore	108	1,900	1:47
1903	Love's Labor (6)	C. E. Rowe	L. Scully	100	Harry New	111	Airlight	92	2,150	1:48
1904	Colonial Girl (5)	C. E. Rowe	R. Lyne	109	Monsr. Beaucraire	116	Reservation	116	2,170	1:48¾
1905	Batts (4)	W. F. Schulte	D. Nicol	104	Early Boy	98	Brancas	109	2,070	1:53¾
1906	Hyperion II (3)	J. S. Hawkins	W. McIntyre	103	Envoy	104	Kercheval	108	2,100	1:49
1907	The Minks (4)	D. N. Prewitt	D. Nicol•	110	Brancas	110	Harry Scott	102	1,820	1:50⅘
1908	Polly Prim (5)	J. R. Wainwright	V. Powers	117	The Minks	107	Pinkola	105	1,670	1:53⅘
1909	Miami (3)	J. N. Camden	M. McGee	103	Arcite	112	Huck	105	1,820	1:45⅕
1910	King's Daughter (7)	T. C. McDowell	T. Koerner	124	T. M. Green	109	Crystal Maid	114	1,600	1:45⅗
1911	Star Charter (3)	J. W. Schorr	J. Wilson	105	Countless	132	Joe Morris	108	1,900	1:47⅘
1912	Adams Express (4)	H. C. Hallenbeck	C. H. Schilling	122	Mary Davis	100	Cherryola	106	1,620	1:45⅕
1913	Buckhorn (4)	R. J. Mackenzie	R. Goose	122	Flora Fina	106	Any Port	102	2,080	1:48⅕
1914	Belloc (3)	J. MacManus	A. Mott	95	Cream	108	Old Ben	91½	2,510	1:45
1915	Hodge (4)	W. J. Weber	C. Borel	108	Short Grass	124	B's Choice	112	2,380	1:44⅗
1916	Hodge (5)	W. J. Weber	C. Hunt	120	Ed Crump	120	Dr. Carmen	107	2,520	1:45⅖
1917	Old Rosebud (6)	H. C. Applegate & Co.	D. Connelly	117	Roamer	128	Embroaidery	106	2,230	1:45⅕
1918	Beaverkill (4)	S. M. Henderson	O. Willis	104	Fruit Cake	110	Midway	119	2,380	1:48⅕
1919	Midway (5)	J. W. Parrish	H. Thurber	117	Beaverkill	109	Hodge	109	4,360	1:46⅗
1920	Boniface (5)	J. K. L. Ross	E. Sande	121	Ginger	108	King Gorin	121	10,360	1:45⅘
1921	Ginger (5)	W. E. Applegate	T. Murray	112	Upset	122	Dan Spray	96½	9,495	1:45
1922	Exterminator (7)	W. S. Kilmer	A. Johnson	133	Lady Madcap	111	Rouleau	107	11,375	1:50
1923	Audacious (7)	Mrs. L. Viau	B. Kennedy	120	Anna M. Humphrey	99	Bon Homme	108	11,200	1:54⅗
1924	Chilhowee (3)	Gallaher Bros.	B. Harvey	100	Chacolet	124	Hopeless	111	11,200	1:54⅖
1925	Spic and Span (4)	J. C. McGill	G. Fields	103	Son of John	102½	Little Celt	117	12,000	1:47⅗
1926	San-Utar (5)	E. W. Corrigan	M. Garner	114	Moonraker	107	Roycrofter	104	13,750	1:46⅖
1927	Helen's Babe (4)	H. P. Headley	W. Lilley	113	Old Slip	114	Percentage	108	12,325	1:46
1928	Jock (4)	E. B. McLean	E. Ambrose	122	Cartago	105½	Flat Iron	124	10,925	1:45
1929	Martie Flynn (4)	Stuyvesant Peabody	C. Meyer	113	Easter Stockings	111	Cartago	111	10,975	1:46⅗
1930	Stars and Bars (4)	Mrs. Payne Whitney	L. Jones	108	Easter Stockings	113	Pigeon Hole	106	10,900	1:47⅖
1931	Bargelio (5)	C. V. Whitney	K. Russell	110	Royal Julian	105	Playtime	108½	10,325	1:44⅘
1932	Pittsburgher (4)	T. E. Mueller	C. Corbett	112	Spanish Play	115	Canfli	106	4,310	1:50⅕
1933	Osculator (4)	W. R. Coe	S. Coucci	112	The Nut	109	Waylayer	111	4,840	1:45⅖
1934	Esseff (4)	Chas. T. Fisher	L. Humphries	115	Barn Swallow	112	Tick On	114	2,170	1:44
1935	Beaver Dam (3)	T. S. & J. S. Mulvihill	R. Montgomery	102	Blackbirder	108½	Bring Back	108	2,270	1:47⅖
1936	Corinto (4)	Mrs. E. Denemark	C. Kurtsinger	114	Ariel Cross	116	Coldstream	109	4,510	1:44⅘
1937	Count Morse	Warren Wright	I. Anderson	119	Sir Jim James	110	Giant Killer	112	9,200	1:45⅕
1938	Main Man (4)	J. B. Respess	W. F. Ward	124	Teddy Haslam	109	Old Nassau	112	4,530	1:46⅘
1939	Arab's Arrow (5)	L. J. Hickman	C. Bierman	116	Torchy	115	Sortie Star	110	2,130	1:45⅕
1940	Up The Creek (4)	Mrs. Ethel V. Mars	G. Wallace	110	Arabs Arrow	120	Shot Put	107½	3,050	1:46
1941	Haltal (4)	Woodvale Farm	C. McCreary	115	Viscounty	115	Gallahadion	115	2,110	1:44⅘
1942	Whirlaway (4)	Warren Wright	W. Eads	127	Aonbarr	115	Fairmond	110	2,150	1:44⅘
1943	Anticlimax (4)	Hal Price Headley	C. Bierman	112	Corydon	110	Shot Put	109	2,135	1:47⅖
1944	Alquest (4)	A. C. Ernst	J. Adams	116	Anticlimax	114	Parasang	108	4,050	1:45⅕
1945	Sentiment Sake (4)	W. R. Knebelkamp	F. Wirth	102	Old Kentuck	110	Black Pepper	107	3,910	1:47⅕
1946	Hail Victory (4)	Calumet Farm	D. Dodson	118	Too Reward	111	Bull Play	110	7,775	1:47⅘
1947	Jack S. L. (7)	Mrs. J. S. Letellier	S. Brooks	116	Pellicle	118	Letmenow	110	7,825	1:49⅗
1948	Star Reward (4)	Dixiana	S. Brooks	117	Jack S. L.	111	Sun Herod	109	11,800	1:46⅗

PHOTOGRAPHIC CREDITS

All pictures of the Kentucky Derby winners are from Caufield and Shook, with the exception of the pictures of Alan-a-Dale, Behave Yourself, Morvich, Whiskery, Clyde VanDusen, Gallant Fox, Burgoo King, Cavalcade, War Admiral, and Lawrin. To obtain these the files of The Courier-Journal, Ashby Collection, McClure Collection, and The Blood-Horse were used.

The aerial views used for the end sheets were taken by Billy Davis, head of the Courier-Journal photographic department. Other credits are:

PAGE
11 Churchill Downs collection.
16 *top*, R. G. Potter collection; *bottom*, Brown Brothers.
18 *top*, Caufield & Shook; *bottom*, Brown Brothers.
20 Brown Brothers.
22 Brown Brothers.
24 Brown Brothers.
26 L. & N. Railroad Magazine.
28 Brown Brothers.
30 Brown Brothers.
32 *top*, Brown Brothers; *bottom*, McClure collection.
34 Brown Brothers.
36 *lower*, Brown Brothers.
38 *center*, Caufield & Shook; *bottom*, Brown Brothers.
40 Caufield & Shook.
42 Brown Brothers.
44 *lower right*, Caufield & Shook; *others*, Brown Brothers.
46 *bottom*, Brown Brothers; *right center*, R. G. Potter collection.
48 *lower left*, R. G. Potter collection; *upper right*, Widener collection.
50 Brown Brothers.
52 Brown Brothers.
54 *upper right*, Caufield & Shook; *others*, Brown Brothers.
56 *upper right*, Brown Brothers; *lower right*, Ed Perkins.
58 *top*, R. G. Potter collection; *lower bottom*, Brown Brothers.
60 Brown Brothers.
62 Brown Brothers.
64 Brown Brothers.
66 Brown Brothers.
68 Brown Brothers.
70 *top*, Brown Brothers; *bottom*, The Courier-Journal.
72 *top*, Churchill Downs collection; *bottom*, Brown Brothers.
74 Brown Brothers.
76 Brown Brothers.
78 *top*, Brown Brothers; *bottom*, Churchill Downs collection.
80 *top*, The Courier-Journal; *bottom*, Brown Brothers.
82 *top*, Brown Brothers; *bottom*, The Courier-Journal.
84 Brown Brothers.
86 Churchill Downs collection.
88 *top*, Brown Brothers; *bottom*, Churchill Downs collection.

PAGE
90 *top*, R. G. Potter collection; *others*, Brown Brothers.
92 Brown Brothers.
94 *bottom*, Churchill Downs collection; *others*, Brown Brothers.
96 *top*, Caufield & Shook; *bottom*, Brown Brothers.
98 *top*, Brown Brothers; *bottom*, Churchill Downs collection.
100 Brown Brothers.
102 The Courier-Journal.
104 Caufield & Shook.
106 Brown Brothers.
108 Brown Brothers.
110 The Associated Press.
112 *top*, Caufield & Shook; *bottom*, Brown Brothers.
114 *top*, Brown Brothers; *bottom*, Churchill Downs collection.
116 *top*, Caufield & Shook; *bottom*, J. C. Meadors.
118 *top*, Brown Brothers; *bottom*, Caufield & Shook.
120 Brown Brothers.
122 Caufield & Shook.
124 Brown Brothers.
126 Churchill Downs collection.
128 Brown Brothers.
130 Brown Brothers.
132 Brown Brothers.
134 Brown Brothers.
136 The Associated Press.
138 Brown Brothers.
140 Caufield & Shook.
142 *upper*, Billy Davis; *lower*, The Courier-Journal.
144 The Associated Press.
146 The Associated Press.
148 The Associated Press.
150 *top*, Caufield & Shook; *bottom*, Brown Brothers.
152 *top*, Caufield & Shook; *bottom*, The Associated Press.
154 The Courier-Journal.
156 Brown Brothers.
158 *top*, Brown Brothers; *bottom*, L. & N. Railroad Magazine.
160 The Associated Press.
162 Billy Davis.
167 Ashby collection.
168 *James E. Madden*, Hass; *A. J. Alexander*, from oil painting.
169 *Arcaro*, The Blood-Horse; *Sande*, Ashby collection; *Murphy*, Widener collection.
170 *Thompson*, Ashby collection; *Jones*, The Blood-Horse.
171 *Falsetto*, McClure collection; °*Sir Gallahad III*, J. A. Estes.

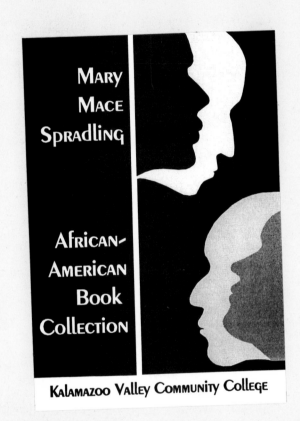

MARY
MACE
Spradling

African-
American
Book
Collection

Kalamazoo Valley Community College

1. Mile chute
2. Clubhouse parking
3. Ground level boxes
4. Section L boxes
5. Clubhouse entrance
6. Third floor boxes
7. Roof boxes
8. Derby Day dining room
9. Press box C
10. Radio and press boxes A & B
11. Finish pole
12. Centerfield pari-mutuels
13. Stable area
14. Main dining room
15. Presentation stand
16. Room 21 boxes
17. Gardens
18. Steward stand
19. Ground level boxes
20. Totalizator odds board
21. Lane to paddock